CONGRESS AND THE AMERICAN TRADITION

CONGRESS AND THE AMERICAN TRADITION

BY JAMES BURNHAM

Gateway Editions
REGNERY PUBLISHING, INC.
WASHINGTON, D.C.

Library of Congress Cataloging-in-Publication Data

Burnham, James, 1905–1987.
    Congress and the American tradition/James Burnham ; with a new
introduction by Newt Gingrich.
        p.   cm.
    Includes index.
    ISBN 0-89526-717-9 (acid-free paper)
    1. United States. Congress.   2. United States.
Congress—Powers and duties.   I. Title.
JK1021.B87   1996   96-20943
328.73—dc20   CIP

Published in the United States by
Regnery Publishing, Inc.
An Eagle Publishing Company
422 First Street, SE
Washington, DC 20003

Distributed to the trade by
National Book Network
4720-A Boston Way
Lanham, MD 20706

Printed on acid-free paper.
Manufactured in the United States of America
1996 Printing

Books are available in quantity for promotional or premium use. Write to
Director of Special Sales, Regnery Publishing, Inc., 422 First Street, SE,
Suite 300, Washington, DC 20003, for information on discounts and terms
or call (202) 546-5005.

To Marcia
who, somewhat to her surprise, caused this book

I speak now of mixed bodies, as commonwealths and sects, and I say that those alterations are salutiferous which reduce them toward their first principles; and therefore the best ordered and longest lived are they who (by their own order) may be often renewed, or by some accident (without the help of the said orders) may tend to renovation: 'tis as clear as the day, that no bodies of men are of long duration, unless they be renewed; and the way to renew them is to reduce them to their principles. For the fundamentals of all sects, commonwealths and kingdoms have always something of good in them, by means of which they recover their first reputation and grandeur. And because in process of time that goodness corrupts, the body must of necessity die, unless something intervenes that reduces it to its first principles.

NICCOLO MACHIAVELLI,
Discourses on Livy

CONTENTS

PART THREE • *The Future of Congress*

INTRODUCTION
BY NEWT GINGRICH

*C*ongress and the American Tradition should be read by all conservatives who insist that a major reduction in the role of government is essential to the commonweal. It is one of the classics of American political philosophy.

Henry Regnery, the founder of this publishing house, had originally asked Burnham, who ranks as one of the founding fathers of modern conservative philosophy, to produce a book on the sources of legitimacy of the congressional investigatory power, which includes the prerogative to compel testimony even when the executive branch is involved, a power then under attack. Instead, the book Burnham wrote is nothing less than the definitive study of the proper place of Congress in the American system of government.

Burnham was an unabashed fan of Congress. He saluted it as the most populist branch of government because it responds most directly to the concerns of the voter. Burnham argued that the "legislative supremacy" implicit in the Constitution and the debates at the Philadelphia convention had been eroded by two quasi-structural changes to our system of government: the consolidation of power by a managerial executive branch and the rise of an independent bureaucracy that pursues its own agenda at the expense of a heavily taxed citizenry.

Burnham regarded the bureaucracy as a new, fourth branch of government, and understood just how powerful it had become. When Burnham was writing, the bureaucracy was embryonic but its essential character was already established: the bureaucracy, by its

very nature, Burnham argued, is statist. Any measure designed to reduce federal spending or power is a direct threat to the bureaucracy.
"For a bureaucrat to advocate anti-statism," he shows us, "is the
equivalent of asking to have his economic throat cut."

Always able to provide apt historical comparison, Burnham compared the bureaucracy, which operates largely behind the scenes and
the scrutiny of the press, to the Carolingian Mayors of Palace, who
ruled France for generations before the extent of their power was
widely recognized. Bureaucrats are scornful of the democratic process. Because of their unique form of job security, they are often
people who are, as Burnham so astutely put it, "more suited by nature to passing examination and manipulating files than to the
rougher, man-to-man battles of elections and the spoils system."

A series of interviews with people who worked in the bureaucracy, "leaked" to Burnham by an inside source, shows this innate
hostility to the democratic process. A bureaucrat believes so firmly
in the rightness of his cause, according to one of the interviews
quoted, that "the question of whether or not Congress has authorized it is not so important to him. He figures that if Congress really
had the facts and knew what was right, it would agree with him. So
he goes ahead, getting away with as much as he can." "Congress,"
sneered another anonymous bureaucrat, "represents the selfish
wishes of the people; it is concerned with getting votes, whereas the
bureaucracy isn't...."

Ever the disciple of the Founding Fathers, whose writings and
debates he knew with a remarkable intimacy, Burnham also
lamented what he had already come to recognize as an abrogation of
power by the executive branch and the judiciary. Legislative dominance was the norm during the early days of the republic. Burnham's examination of the process by which Franklin D. Roosevelt
began the aggrandizement of the executive branch is both brilliant
and fresh. What would the Founding Fathers think of present developments? Read Burnham.

One of the ironies of our current situation is that those among the

Founding Fathers who feared the rise of an imperial presidency were concerned that the executive branch would become monarchical. To the contrary, Burnham argues, in one of those passages that will delight all who rejoice in the play of ideas, the executive branch regards itself as the embodiment of "the masses." Congress, on the other hand, regards itself as the representatives of "the people."

While "the masses" are "anonymous and undifferentiated by definition," Burnham notes, "the people" cannot be seen in the abstract. They are "real human beings in their existential setting." Unlike the masses, the people "are not statistical abstractions, not political common denominators. [T]hey make a living by this or that kind of work, occupy house or palace or apartment or shanty... belong to this Church or that, like change or stability, seek glory or wealth or peace or pleasure."

When Congress tries to lift some of the heavy burden of taxes on these very real human beings who toil in very real jobs, the elitists decry this as (to borrow as word from the anonymous bureaucrat of thirty-five years ago) "selfish." Burnham not only shows us how this elitist perspective developed but also drives home the absolute necessity of change, if people are to enjoy the liberty envisioned by the Founding Fathers and be allowed to keep more of the money they earn. Burnham arms us with the philosophical background for the conservative transformation—which, of course, is nothing more than a return to our first principles. Burnham longed for those halcyon days in the nineteenth century when the great issues were settled not in the courts or by executive fiat but "in the halls of Congress."

So do we all.

While I don't agree with everything Burnham wrote in this marvelous book, I am delighted that it is once again available. To get at the roots of the important issues that now confront us, you can do no better than to read Burnham. I urge you to do so.

ACKNOWLEDGMENTS

HENRY REGNERY first had the idea that I should write this book of what I suppose would once have been called "political philosophy." His continuing enthusiasm and advice have been above and beyond the normal duty of a publisher. A grant from the Foundation for Foreign Affairs made the undertaking practicable. My obligations to those who have written on these matters are too many for listing, and are only in part suggested by the footnotes. I must particularly thank, for having made me acquainted with information peculiarly their own, Henry F. Ashurst, Anne Brunsdale, Arthur Krock and Lucius Wilmerding, Jr.

I wish to thank the following for permission to quote from books that they have published: Appleton-Century-Crofts, Inc. (*Documents of American History,* edited by Henry Steele Commager); Ballantine Books (*The Space Merchants,* by Frederick Pohl and C. R. Kornbluth); University of Chicago Press (*The Genius of American Politics,* by Daniel J. Boorstin); Columbia University Press (*Congressional Politics in the Second World War,* by Roland Young); Coward-McCann, Inc. (*The Coming Caesars,* by Amaury de Riencourt); Thomas Y. Crowell Co. (*The Legislative Process in Congress,* by George B. Galloway); Crown Publishers, Inc. (*Best Plays of the Modern American Theater,* edited by John Gassner); John Day Company (*The Managerial Revolution* and *The Machiavellians,* by James Burnham); Harcourt, Brace & Co. (*The American Presidency,* by Clinton Rossiter); Harper & Bros. (*The American Presidency,* by Harold J. Laski); Little, Brown & Co. and Atlantic Monthly Press (*The Public Philosophy,* by Walter

Lippmann); The Macmillan Company (*The Federalists* and *The Jeffer-sonians*, by Leonard D. White); McGraw-Hill Publishing Co. (*The Ruling Class*, by Gaetano Mosca); National Bureau of Economic Research (*A Century and a Half of Federal Expenditures*, by M. Slade Kendrick); New York University Press (*The President: Office and Powers*, by Edward S. Corwin; *Congress, Its Contemporary Role*, by Ernest S. Griffith); W. W. Norton & Co. (*The American Constitution*, by Alfred H. Kelly and Winfred A. Harbison; *Stanton*, by Fletcher Pratt); G. P. Putnam's Sons (*The American Plan of Government*, by Charles W. Bacon); Rinehart & Co. (*Congress, Corruption and Compromise*, by H. H. Wilson); Simon & Schuster, Inc. (*Grand Inquest*, by Telford Taylor); Time, Inc. (*Memoirs*, by Harry S. Truman, published by Doubleday & Co.); Yale University Press (*The Spending Power*, by Lucius Wilmerding, Jr.). Also Garson Kanin (*Born Yesterday*, published by the Viking Press) and Arnaud d'Usseau (*Deep Are the Roots*, by Arnaud d'Usseau and James Gow, published by Charles Scribner's Sons).

PART ONE

The American System of Government

When the mariner has been tossed for many days in thick weather and on an unknown sea, he naturally avails himself of the first pause in the storm, the earliest glance of the sun, to take his latitude and ascertain how far the elements have driven him from his true course. Let us imitate this prudence; and before we float farther on the waves of this debate, refer to the point from which we departed, that we may, at least, conjecture where we now are.

DANIEL WEBSTER, *Reply to Hayne*

I

THE MIRACLE OF GOVERNMENT

I N ANCIENT TIMES, before the illusions of science had corrupted traditional wisdom, the founders of Cities were known to be gods or demigods. Minos, author of the Cretan constitution and of the navy through which Crete ruled the Aegean world, was the son of Zeus and Europa, and husband of the moon goddess, Pasiphaë. On his death he was made one of the three judges of the underworld, at the entrance to which—in Dante's description—he sits "horrific, and grins; examines the crimes upon the entrance; judges, and sends" each soul to its due punishment.

The half human, half dragon Cecrops, first king of Athens, who numbered its tribes, established its laws of marriage, property and worship, and taught it writing, was reputed to be the secret husband of Athena, whom he chose as guardian of his City. Minos, doubting whether Theseus, who was later to bring the rest of Attica under Athenian command, was indeed the son of Poseidon, flung a ring into the sea, and was answered when Theseus, plunging into his father's realm, brought back not only the ring but the golden crown of Amphitrite.

It was the pious Aeneas, son of Venus, who led to Italy those Trojans whose descendants were to transform a village into a world empire. The local king, Evander, told him of the old days:

> These woods were first the seat of sylvan pow'rs,
> Of Nymphs and Fauns, and savage men, who took
> Their birth from trunks of trees and stubborn oak.

Nor laws they knew, nor manners, nor the care
Of lab'ring oxen, or the shining share,
Nor arts of gain, nor what they gain'd to spare.
Their exercise the chase; the running flood
Supplied their thirst, the trees supplied their food.
Then Saturn came, who fled the pow'r of Jove,
Robb'd of his realms, and banish'd from above.
The men, dispers'd on hills, to towns he brought,
And laws ordain'd, and civil customs taught,
And Latium call'd the land where safe he lay
From his unduteous son, and his usurping sway.[1]

The seven hills were linked as one city through the exploits of the child of Mars, Romulus, suckled by a wolf and fed by a woodpecker, metamorphosed after death into the god, Quirinus.

Our own John Adams, in spite of his distaste for such modes of explanation, recognized that "it was the general opinion of ancient nations that the Divinity alone was adequate to the important office of giving laws to men. . . . The laws of Lacedaemon were communicated by Apollo to Lycurgus; and, lest the meaning of the deity should not have been perfectly comprehended or correctly expressed, they were afterwards confirmed by his oracle at Delphos. Among the Romans Numa was indebted for those laws which procured the prosperity of his country to his conversations with [the fountain nymph] Egeria. . . . Woden and Thor were divinities too; and their posterity ruled a thousand years in the north. . . . Manco Capac was the child of the sun, the visible deity of the Peruvians, and transmitted his divinity, as well as his earthly dignity and authority, through a line of Incas. . . . There is nothing in which mankind have been more unanimous."[2]

1. *Aeneid,* Book VIII (Dryden translation).
2. John Adams, *A Defence of the Constitutions of Government of the United States.*

The great principles upon which our own civilization is founded are traced to the commands issued on a mountain top by God Himself to the man who was at once His prophet and His people's chief, to be confirmed and amplified by His Son.

John Adams—though destined to become himself almost a demigod—was inclined to our modern agreement that these old tales are "prejudice," "popular delusion" and "superstitious chimeras." He suggested also one of the favored scientific explanations of their persistent recurrence:

> Is it that obedience to the laws can be obtained from mankind in no other manner? Are the jealousy of power and the envy of superiority so strong in all men that no considerations of public or private utility are sufficient to engage their submission to rules for their own happiness? Or is the disposition to imposture so prevalent in men of experience that their private views of ambition and avarice can be accomplished only by artifice?[3]

Or, rephrased as statement instead of question: A superstitious belief in the superhuman origin of government is foisted by rulers on their subjects as one of the devices by which the subjects are kept in line.

A rival and also widespread scientific account stresses a kind of imaginative play rather than political deceit as source of the superstitions. As example, the *Encyclopaedia Britannica* in comment on the story of Romulus:

> The whole story [of Romulus and Remus] . . . is artificial and shows strong Greek influence. The birth, exposure, rescue, and subsequent adventures of the twins are a Greek tale of

3. *Ibid.,* p. 116.

familiar type. Mars and his sacred beast, the wolf, are introduced on account of the great importance of this cult. The localities described are ancient sacred places; the Lupercal, near
the *ficus ruminalis,* was naturally explained as the she-wolf's
den. . . . Another Greek touch is the deification of an epony-
mous [name-giving] hero. The rape of the Sabine women is
clearly aetiological, invented to account for the custom of
simulated capture in marriage; these women and also Titus
Tatius represent the Sabine element in the Roman population.
The name Romulus (=*Romanus*) means simply "Roman."[4]

In short: the story of the founding of the City is a set of poetic
variations on the City's name.

2

There is no need to reject such explanations by modern science,
viewed in their own frame, in order to suggest from another perspective that the ancient peoples, who were not notably more foolish than we, were perhaps also communicating truths by their
accounts of the origin of Cities, though admittedly they used a
rhetorical system quite other than that of the *Encyclopaedia Britannica.*

The central truth is the insight that there is no adequate rational
explanation for the existence and effective working of government,
much less for good or fairly good government. (I rule out of the
definition of "government" a dominion exercised directly and exclusively by physical strength—a social form which by the nature of
the case cannot exist in a group that contains more than three or
four human beings.) The universality of this insight is really attested
by the scientific writers on society as much as by the ancients. Without exception they too introduce a myth in order to explain the

4. *Encyclopaedia Britannica,* 1945 edition, Vol. XIX, p. 522.

origin of the City. The only difference is that post-Renaissance scientists use a less picturesque language. Instead of Cecrops or Minos or Romulus, they write of a "state of nature" (benign or horrific), an isolated Island with first one and then more than one resident, "primitive communism," the Dialectic, "challenge and response," the Zeitgeist, and a host of other mythic entities that have no substantial reality outside of the scientists' own lively but shamefaced imaginations.

Moreover, apart from a few gross and almost self-evident cases, no one has found a purely rational theory to explain why some governments, though very different from each other, do well, whereas others, though closely similar, do badly. When you drop scientist ideology, it becomes clear that you cannot explain the success of some and the failure of other governments without including a non-rational factor that we call, according to our metaphysical habits, chance, luck, accident, magic, or Providence.

Government is then in part, though only in part, non-rational. Neither the source nor the justification of government can be put in wholly rational terms. This is and must be so because the problem of government is, strictly speaking, insoluble; and yet it is solved. The double fact, though real and part of historical life, is a paradox.

Consider the problem of government from the point of view of the reflective individual. I, as an individual, do in fact submit myself (at least within certain limits) to the rule of another—to government. But suppose that I ask myself: *why* should I do so? why should I submit to the rule of another? *what* justifies his rule? To these questions there are no objectively convincing answers in rational terms alone.

Is he physically stronger than I? Granted that his strength might enable him actually to rule me (though I might of course outsmart him), does it give him the *right* to do so? Is he taller, fairer, swifter than I? Is one or the other of these a political credential? He is more intelligent? Very well; but in government may not character or experience or faith be more relevant than brains? And who decides the

degree of his possession of any of these fluid qualities? He is rich?
But do not riches corrupt? He is poor, then. If so, will he not be
tempted the more?

> Nature hath made men so equal in the faculties of the body,
> and mind; as that though there be found one man sometimes
> manifestly stronger in body, or of quicker mind than another;
> yet when all is reckoned together, the difference between
> man, and man, is not so considerable, as that one man can
> thereupon claim to himself any benefit, to which another may
> not pretend, as well as he. For as to the strength of body, the
> weakest has strength enough to kill the strongest, either by se-
> cret machinations, or by confederacy with others. . . . And as
> to the faculties of the mind . . . , prudence is but experience;
> which equal time equally bestows on all men, in those things
> they equally apply themselves unto. That which may perhaps
> make such equality incredible, is but a vain conceit of one's
> own wisdom, which almost all men think they have in a
> greater degree, than the vulgar; that is, than all men but them-
> selves, and a few others, whom by fame, or for concurring
> with themselves, they approve.[5]

Is there a sign that the gods have chosen this man as ruler? Is he
the first-born of a certain father? or *named* ruler by the voice of one-
half plus one of the adults, or a designated class of the adults, of the
City? We begin to reach, it will seem, arguments of more weight.
"Arguments?" Axioms or sentiments, rather, which can indeed settle the problem of rule, if by an act of prior faith we share them: one
of them, that is, and reject the others, because believing simultaneously in more than one might plunge us into contradiction. These
are what Gugliemo Ferrero called "principles of legitimacy," belief
in which can "legitimize" rule or government: the theocratic prin-

5. Thomas Hobbes, *Leviathan.*

ciple, the hereditary principle, and the democratic principle are respectively implicit in the three questions at the start of this paragraph. These principles are the Guardians of the City, which make it possible, when one of them is accepted by the community, for government to be something other than mere brute force.

But why should I accept the hereditary or democratic or any other principle of legitimacy? Why should such a principle justify the rule of that man over me? Does it prove him better than I because he had his father instead of my father, his color skin in place of mine, because his arts can win more votes than mine? I accept the principle, well . . . because I do, because that is the way it is and has been. This may be a sufficient and proper argument, but it is certainly not a rational one.

Ferrero's countryman, Gaetano Mosca, used the term "political formula" for "principle of legitimacy," and explained in this way:

> According to the level of civilization in the peoples among whom they are current, the various political formulas may be based either upon supernatural beliefs or upon concepts which, if they do not correspond to positive realities, at least appear to be rational. We shall not say that they correspond in either case to scientific truths. A conscientious observer would be obliged to confess that, if no one has ever seen the authentic document by which the Lord empowered certain privileged persons or families to rule his people on his behalf, neither can it be maintained that a popular election, however liberal the suffrage may be, is ordinarily the expression of the will of a people, or even of the will of the majority of a people.
>
> And yet that does not mean that political formulas are mere quackeries aptly invented to trick the masses into obedience. Anyone who viewed them in that light would fall into grave error. The truth is that they answer a real need in man's social nature; and this need, so universally felt, of governing and knowing that one is governed not on the basis of mere mate-

rial or intellectual force, but on the basis of moral principle, has beyond any doubt a practical and real importance.[6]

A familiar sophistry is often brought up to close the logical breach. By rational argument I can prove it desirable that there should be government in human society. I can in fact prove that government is essential for the satisfying of human interests and values that are all but universal. And if government is necessary, then there must be someone, or some group, to govern. Therefore. . . . Well, therefore just what? My rational argument is non-specific, and thus non-historical. I establish the rational necessity of government in general, in the abstract; I prove that there must be governors, rulers. But I have proved nothing whatever about this particular government here and now, nor that this particular man—myself or another—should be the one who rules.

This impasse is not mere theory. In historical fact we find that groups which do not accept a principle of legitimacy derived from tradition, custom or faith always undergo a crisis in trying to solve the problem of succession, no matter how rational their pretensions. When the leader of such a group dies (normally by assassination), either the group disintegrates or a new leader must establish his position by unadorned force.

The death of Stalin provoked a grandiose recent test of this general law. The Soviet Empire is a revolutionary and nihilist society, which in establishing its own existence abandoned all the principles that had formerly legitimized the governments of Russia and the ancillary nations. The new regime has not, however, replaced these principles with any other. First the Bolshevik Party and then Stalin gained de facto rule simply by force, direct and roundabout; nor, with power consolidated, did they succeed—or even seriously at-

6. Gaetano Mosca, *The Ruling Class,* edited and revised, with an Introduction by Arthur Livingston, translated by Hannah D. Kahn (New York: McGraw-Hill, 1939), p. 71.

tempt—to construct a new political formula. At Stalin's death in 1953, which was probably hastened by his colleagues, the Soviet regime faced the logical impasse sketched above.

The members of the Soviet elite have studied the problems of power more seriously than any other men have ever done. Each communist in the leading stratum understood that the Soviet governmental structure was built as a pyramid with a single leader at the apex, and that its stability depended on installing an accepted replacement for the dead chief. Delay in finding a successor was bound to lead—and in the event did lead—to mounting conflicts and a weakening of the entire Soviet system.

The need for a successor and the damaging consequences of the failure to name one were rationally demonstrable. None of the principal communists (the members of the Presidium, for example) doubted the demonstration. But this did not at all solve the specific historical problem. Granted that there must be an accepted successor, a new No. 1, who is it to be, who is the man? Do not I (Beria, Malenkov, Khrushchev, . . . Suslov) have as good a claim as any other? To the specific question there was no rational answer; and there was no shared faith in a non-rational principle (inheritance, election under prescribed rules, drawing lots or whatever) that would have jumped the logical gap. Therefore the answer, if they were ever to find it, could only be obtained from the ultimate non-rational test of force.

Let me restate the argument of this section, so that it will not seem to say more than I intend.

Both the theory and the practice of government are incomplete without the introduction of a non-rational element. Without some allowance for magic, luck or divine favor, we cannot give convincing explanations why this government does so much better than that, why this one succeeds and endures, and that one fails. Without acceptance by habit, tradition or faith of a principle which completes the justification for government, government dissolves, or falls back wholly on force—which is itself, of course, non-rational.

3

I have been referring without definition to "good," "worse," and "better" governments, to governments that "work" or "fail." What, then, is a "good government"? How do we recognize that a government is functioning properly? What is badness or evil in government?

Americans are fortunate in knowing the purposes of government, from which knowledge we may judge the quality of a particular government's performance. We know these purposes because they are stated as the preamble to the charter through which our government came into formal existence: ". . . to form a more perfect Union, establish Justice, insure domestic Tranquility, provide for the common defence, promote the general Welfare, and secure the Blessings of Liberty to ourselves and our Posterity . . ."[7]

The wording of this preamble is not so casual as might seem from the fact that it was prepared at the last moment, without instruction or explanation, by the committee on style and arrangement of the Philadelphia Convention, and adopted without debate as part of the final (September 14) draft of the Constitution. The absence of discussion meant that the Fathers were unanimously agreed to what the preamble said, and took also for granted that there would be no significant disagreement outside the Convention. The same doctrine had been often repeated in their previous writings, and in con-

7. It replaced an earlier wording, adopted on August 7, which did not designate the purposes of government, but stated merely that "We the people of the States of New Hampshire, Massachusetts . . . [which the final version changed to "We, the people of the United States . . ."] do ordain, declare, and establish the following Constitution for the government of ourselves and our posterity."

stitutions of the several States. The Massachusetts Constitution and Bill of Rights, for example, adopted in 1780 in a text largely by John Adams, affirmed:

> The end of the institution, maintenance, and administration of government, is to secure the existence of the body-politic, to protect it, and to furnish the individuals who compose it with the power of enjoying in safety and tranquillity their natural rights, and the blessings of life. . . .

At Philadelphia James Madison asserted even more summarily (on May 31) that "he should shrink from nothing which should be found essential to such a form of government as would provide for the safety, liberty and happiness of the community."

In order to fulfill these purposes, a government must be possessed of two distinguishable qualities. If it is to "provide for the common defence" and "insure domestic Tranquility," then a government must be *strong*. If it is to "establish Justice, . . . promote the general Welfare, and secure the Blessings of Liberty," then a government must be *just*. In briefest definition, then, a "good" government is a strong and just government.[8]

What is the relation between these two qualities, strength and justice? Does one have priority over the other in defining the "goodness" of a government? To avoid confusion in the answer, one more distinction must be carefully made.

In their relation to goodness or excellence in government, strength has a causal priority; justice, an ethical priority. Unless it is

8. According to Plato's classic formulation in the *Republic,* the virtues of a government are wisdom, temperance, courage and justice. Other writers (and Plato in other dialogues) have varied and expanded the list. However, for my purpose here it is not necessary to enter into an intricate analysis. A rough discrimination between government as an organization of power (strength) and government as a means for the realization of human rights and values other than power (justice) is sufficient.

sufficiently strong, a government cannot exist at all, and therefore cannot be good. It must be strong enough to defend the organized society (the nation) which it directs from enemies both external and domestic. Otherwise the nation will be destroyed or dissolved. In the causal order, therefore, a government must first be strong, must be strong in order to be. From this there follow consequences that are not always accepted by those who do not like to check ideas by fact.

We might set up the following ratio: strength is to a government as food is to an individual human organism. Causally, food has a priority over intelligence and beauty, say, in a human being, because without food a human being cannot exist at all. And as a human organism can have too much food (too much for its own goodness, that is), so can a government have too much power.

Strength is causally prior to justice in constituting the goodness of a government, but few persons assign much positive value to strength, or power, in and of itself. Ethically, justice takes hardly questioned priority over strength. To exist, a government must be strong (strong enough to survive); to be good, it must be just.

But the relationship between strength and justice in government is more subtle, as we may see if we ask, not what is good or the best government, but what government is worst? Now the worst government is the one that in relation to its own citizens is absolutely weak *or* absolutely strong, no-government or all-government: that is, an anarchic or a totalitarian society. The well-being of the organism is destroyed by either starvation or gluttony.

The evil of total government has been thoroughly annotated in our day, when the theoretic limit of totalitarianism has been closely approached by Nazism and communism. There is still some dispute as to whether the same effects must follow from the same causes: whether the indefinite extension of the internal power of government will invariably bring elsewhere the same kind of evil human consequences that came in Germany and the Soviet Empire. But even socialists have tempered their orthodox call for the governmental absorption of political, economic and social activities.

There is no longer much dispute outside communist circles about the evil of all-government, but there are still many, of otherwise diverse views, who cling to an ideal of no-government, who believe that anarchy is the best form of society. In principle, this is the doctrine of communists, in spite of their contradictory current practice. Communists contend that the dictatorship of the proletariat, which they advocate and exercise, is only a transitional social form that will evolve into a classless, non-violent society in which the state will have withered entirely away. This ultimate communist society is the same in descriptive outline as the society proposed by the anarchists proper. Right wing and conservative "libertarians," moreover, like the late Albert Jay Nock and his *laisser faire* successor, Frank Chodorov, project from a very different starting point an ironically similar vision.

In the abstract—divorced, that is, from an existential context in history—the anarchist ideal of no-government has always been attractive. Human beings voluntarily associated together, freely cooperating in the accomplishment of shared goals, uncoerced by law, police or army . . . The picture is so idyllic as to seem almost inevitably the goal of mankind. If we inspect the canvas more carefully, we may still feel the picture to be charming, but we will see that it has nothing to do with men.

Anarchism's departure from the real world is symbolized by the myths in which the anarchic ideal is usually expressed. Rousseau's serene anarchic savages, on whom the chains of society have not yet been fastened, live in a Golden Age that Rousseau well knew to be outside of history. The anarchic Paradise of Adam and Eve was also, and markedly, before true history, which could not begin until sin had come to the world. Both Marxism's prehistoric "primitive communism" and his post-historic "ideal communism" are products of sociological fantasy unhampered by fact. The anarchic world of the avowed anarchists like Prince Kropotkin, wherein each, shorn of selfishness, envy and the will to power, willingly finds his own happiness in loving cooperation with all, becomes moderately credible only because angels instead of men are tacitly assumed to be its inhabitants. "If men were angels," wrote James Madison, "no government would be necessary"; and only, he made clear, in that event.

Remote from our world as is this ideal image, we have had practical experience of anarchy—of absence of government; and frequently enough to learn what in fact it is like. Anarchy is found under two fairly common circumstances: in remote, scantly populated frontiers; and in the catastrophic stages of massive military defeat, revolution and inflation.

The remote frontier is beyond the reach of government. There are no officials, courts, police, army or jails. Instead there are gunmen, lynch gangs, brigands, the noose, knives and assassins. The picturesque anarchy of the frontier is first-rate material for movies and romances of adventure. One may even add that for certain sorts of men—physically strong, egocentric, emotionally self-sufficient— it offers a good, even the best life. But the joys of the frontier are limited to trappers, explorers, prospectors, hunters and gatherers, bandits. For most men and all women the cost in narrowness and insecurity is too high. The frontier, by its definition, excludes civilization and all of the cultivated arts.

> Every man is enemy to every man. . . . There is no place to industry; because the fruit thereof is uncertain: and consequently no culture of the earth; no navigation, nor use of the commodities that may be imported by sea; no commodious building; no instruments of moving, and removing, such things as require much force; no knowledge of the face of the earth; no account of time; no arts; no letters, no society; and which is worst of all, continual fear, and danger of violent death; and the life of man, solitary, poor, nasty, brutish, and short.[9]

9. Thomas Hobbes, *Leviathan*.

Hobbes wrote this famous passage as a deduction from his principles rather than as a generalization from empirical data, but it is accurate enough as a description of the anarchic society of the remote
frontier, and its grim tone is appropriate to the anarchic plunge into
which society is often pushed by military defeat, revolution, or un-
bridled inflation. Family, home, Church, possessions, art, morality
are consumed in the wild flames of shifting mass passions. With the
inevitability of a physical law, the disintegration of government coincides with the spread of insecurity, immorality and terror.

> *The specialty of rule hath been neglected: . . .*
> *The unworthiest shows fairly in the mask . . .*
> *What plagues, and what portents, what mutiny,*
> *What raging of the sea, shaking of the earth,*
> *Commotion in the winds, frights, changes, horrors,*
> *Divert and crack, rend and deracinate*
> *The unity and married calm of states . . .*
> *And, hark! what discord follows: each thing meets*
> *In mere oppugnancy: the bounded waters*
> *Should lift their bosoms higher than the shores,*
> *And make a sop of all this solid globe:*
> *Strength should be lord of imbecility,*
> *And the rude son should strike his father dead:*
> *Force should be right; or rather, right and wrong—*
> *Between whose endless jar justice resides—*
> *Should lose their names, and so should justice too.*
> *Then every thing includes itself in power,*
> *Power into will, will into appetite;*
> *And appetite, a universal wolf,*
> *So doubly seconded with will and power,*
> *Must make perforce a universal prey,*
> *And last eat up himself.*[10]

10. *Troilus and Cressida*, I, iii.

Anarchy's charm and romance are located in literature only, not in history. Perhaps there are times when the correction of abuses grown intolerable under established government justifies the period of anarchy that is normally part of a mass revolution. A moral man, to choose so black a means, will make very sure of the excellence—and the possibility—of his end, and of the exclusion of every other road.

II

IDEOLOGY AND TRADITION

TOTAL GOVERNMENT and no-government—totalitarianism and anarchy—define the bad. A good government, fulfilling the purposes of government, is a *via media* between these two illicit extremes—not a "compromise" somehow combining the two, but a path of right reason in the Aristotelian and medieval sense, avoiding both the excess and the defect that are both damned. Strength and justice are the special virtues of good government.

Just here lies the second paradox before which the abstractly rational approach to government falters.

We have considered the first paradox from the point of view of the individual. Rationally I can demonstrate the necessity of government, the truth that some one must rule. But I cannot demonstrate merely by reason that it should be this man rather than that, another rather than I.

The second paradox may be seen from a social rather than an individual perspective. It may be stated this way: a good government must be both strong and just; but both it cannot be. Cannot, that is to say, when analyzed from a purely rational standpoint. In historic actuality, though there are no ideal governments, there have been a number of good ones that have in fact been both fairly strong and fairly just. This is exactly the paradox, that though good governments have existed (and do indeed exist), their existence is counter to reason.

For a government to be strong enough to survive, it must be too strong to be just. That is the insoluble rational problem. To survive, the government (and thus the governors who compose the government) must be strong enough to defend the nation against its external enemies, and strong enough to preserve domestic tranquillity against an effort at its disruption by any person or combination of persons within. But to be just means to temper strength to the claims of moral desert and social utility. And who or what—in the natural order—is strong enough to tame the stronger?

It was the insight of the Greek sophists—like Thrasymachus of Plato's *Republic*—that brought this paradox pitilessly to light; and the sophists had the intellectual courage to face it bare instead of smearing it with sentiment.

> Have you a nurse? [Thrasymachus asked Socrates, and to the demand that he explain why he asked, he replied:] Because she leaves you to drivel, and omits to wipe your nose when you require it, so that in consequence of her neglect you cannot even distinguish between sheep and shepherd. . . . You think that shepherds and herdsmen regard the good of their sheep and of their oxen, and fatten them and take care of them with other views than to benefit their masters and themselves; and you actually imagine that the rulers in states, those I mean who are really rulers, are otherwise minded towards their subjects than as one would feel towards sheep, or that they think of anything else by night and by day than how they may secure their own advantage.

The sophists did not solve the paradox. How could they have done so, rationalists as they were in their own "realist" manner? By intellectual decree, they liquidated it. In the case of government, they said in effect, there is no distinction between "strength" and "justice." *Justice is the interest of the stronger,* nothing more. Whoever rules is right, so long as he rules, and his successor, even his assassin, is also right. There is no special problem of "good government." There are only the history and morphology of power.

The Fathers of our own government were aware that this second paradox was central in the destiny of the nation that they were founding. "Among the difficulties encountered by the convention," Alexander Hamilton commented in *Federalist* No. 37, "a very important one must have lain in combining the requisite stability and energy in government, with the inviolable attention due to liberty and to the republican form. Energy in government is essential to that security against external and internal danger, and to that prompt and salutary execution of the laws which enter into the very definition of good government. Stability in government is essential to national character. . . . On comparing, however, these valuable ingredients with the vital principles of liberty, we must perceive at once the difficulty of mingling them together in their due proportions." In the previous paper he had written: "It was a thing hardly to be expected that in a popular revolution the minds of men should stop at that happy mean which marks the salutary boundary between POWER and PRIVILEGE, and combines the energy of government with the security of private rights."

Madison, in *Federalist* No. 51, stated plainly: "In framing a government which is to be administered by men over men, the great difficulty lies in this: you must first enable the government to control the governed; and in the next place oblige it to control itself."

The Continental Congress had confronted the paradox with little expectation of solving it, in practice or in theory. The reply made to Rhode Island's objection to an import duty (April, 1783) relates the *via media* of good government to the opposing extremes, but does not boast that the *via media* has been found:

There is a happy mean between too much confidence and excessive jealousy, in which the health and prosperity of a state consist. Either extreme is a dangerous vice; the first is a temptation to men in power to arrogate more than they have a right to; the latter enervates government, prevents system in the administration, defeats the most salutary measures, breeds confusion in the state, and disgusts and discontents among the people; and may eventually prove as fatal to liberty as the opposite temper.

President Lincoln, as on so many other matters, put the issue most starkly of all: "Must a government, of necessity, be too strong for the liberties of its people, or too weak to maintain its own existence?" It is not certain that he had an answer that convinced him wholly.

The paradox can be expressed as a dilemma. A good government must be both strong and just. But any government must be either too strong for justice to be preserved, or not strong enough to survive. Therefore it is impossible that a good government should exist. (The paradox results from the existential fact that nevertheless good governments, both strong and just, do exist.) For the Fathers, this dilemma drew its force and historical relevance from the nature of man, from the fact that men are limited creatures moved by passion or interest more often than by reason.

If men were rational and good, or if their weakness and corruption were due only to social institutions that could be changed, then the dilemma would collapse. The governors might be possessed of any amount of strength, unlimited strength, so that the common defense and domestic tranquillity would be unshakably guaranteed; but, being rational and good, they would not turn their strength against the welfare and liberties of the governed.

But the Fathers did not believe that men were continuously both rational and good. They believed, rather, like John Adams, that "human passions are insatiable" and that "reason, justice and equity never had weight enough on the face of the earth to govern the councils of men." With Hamilton they knew that "men will pursue their interests," and they objected only to the absoluteness with which Gouverneur Morris harped on the "political depravity" of men. Because their view of human nature was based on their own experience, if clothed in the common rhetoric of the 18th century, they rejected, as Hamilton explained in the *Federalist,* the "supposition of universal venality in human nature" as well as the contrary supposition "of universal rectitude." But, though they were willing to "allow benevolence and generous affections to exist in the human breast, yet every moral theorist will admit the selfish passions in the generality of men to be the strongest. There are few who love the public better than themselves, though all may have some affection for the public. We are not, indeed, commanded to love our neighbor better than ourselves. Self-interest, private avidity, ambition, and avarice will exist in every state of society and under every form of government."[1]

Because they believed that human nature is limited and imperfect, the Fathers did not suppose that all social and political problems can be fully solved. They did not expect to be able to institute an ideal government,[2] but were ready to settle for a good government—a government strong enough to have a fair chance of survival against inevitable perils domestic and external, and sufficiently just to enable the citizens to pursue their well-being exempt from despotic oppression. "The plan now to be formed," George Mason told the Convention on June 11, "will certainly be defective, as the Confederation has been found on trial to be. Amendments, therefore, will be necessary; and it will be better to

---

1. John Adams, *A Defence of the Constitutions.*
2. They would, in fact, have agreed with Gaetano Mosca (*The Ruling Class,* p. 288): "Human sentiments being what they are, to set out to erect a type of political organization that will correspond in all respects to the ideal of justice, which a man can conceive but can never attain, is a utopia, and the utopia becomes frankly dangerous when it succeeds in bringing a large mass of intellectual and moral energies to bear upon the achievement of an end that will never be achieved and that, on the day of its purported achievement, can mean nothing more than triumph for the worst people and distress and disappointment for the good. Burke remarked more than a century ago that any political system that assumes the existence of superhuman or heroic virtues can result only in vice and corruption."

provide for them in an easy, regular and constitutional way, than to trust to chance and violence." In the papers of the *Federalist*, Hamilton, Madison and Jay did not recommend the new Constitution to "the People of the State of New York" as a perfect document, or as a sure chart to a perfect society. In their eyes, unglazed by utopian distortion, the incompleteness was rather a promise than a defect. Granted the real circumstances and the real play of force and interest, this Constitution was the best that the best qualified men of the society could produce. With good fortune the government that was to issue from it would be strong, just and great; with God's help it might become—not ideal—but the best that men had yet achieved.

But whatever may be the judgment on the competency of the architects of the Constitution, or whatever may be the destiny of the edifice prepared by them, I feel it a duty to express my profound and solemn conviction, derived from my intimate opportunity of observing and appreciating the views of the Convention, collectively and individually, that there never was an assembly of men, charged with a great and arduous trust, who were more pure in their motives, or more exclusively or anxiously devoted to the object committed to them, than were the members of the Federal Convention of 1787, to the object of devising and proposing a constitutional system which should best supply the defects of that which it was to replace, and best secure the permanent liberty and happiness of their country.[3]

---

3. This is the last paragraph of Madison's introduction to his journals of the 1787 Convention. My quotations from these journals, and from Madison's journals of the Congress of the Confederacy, are from the original 3 volume edition of *The Papers of James Madison*, published by order of Congress, by Langtree & O'Sullivan (Washington: 1840).

2

I do not wish to be understood to say too much. Government, in theory and in practice, involves a non-rational element, a factor that is apart from, beyond or above reason. But this is an element only: perhaps decisive for a government's success or failure, but quantitatively minor. Luck or Grace, though needed, do not spring from deliberate effort. Good government is the consequence also and obviously of wise laws, viable institutions and able governors. To gain and secure these is the political task of reasonable men, even when they know that these gained are not enough.

Although the Fathers recognized the partly non-rational basis of both the origin and task of government, most of them would have resented any comparison between their own role and that of Lycurgus, Cecrops, or Romulus. Most of them were, in their own eyes, matter-of-fact men of affairs, trained to see and meet the common difficulties that arise in the everyday life of war and peace, and tested successfully in the crucial challenge of a war of independence prepared, fought and won by young, scattered communities against the established might of one of the world's great powers.

Many of them boasted, like pious John Adams, of their purely secular common sense:

> The United States of America have exhibited, perhaps, the first example of governments erected on the simple principles of nature; and if men are now sufficiently enlightened to disabuse themselves of artifice, imposture, hypocrisy, and superstition, they will consider this event as an era in their history. Although the detail of the formation of the American governments is at present little known or regarded either in Europe or in America, it may hereafter become an object of curiosity. It will never be pretended that any persons employed in that service had interviews with the gods or were in

any degree under the inspiration of Heaven, more than those at work upon ships or houses, or laboring in merchandise or agriculture; it will forever be acknowledged that these governments were contrived merely by the use of reason and the senses. . . . Neither the people nor their conventions, committees, or subcommittees considered legislation in any other light than as ordinary arts and sciences, only more important.[4]

Adams, writing this in 1786, was referring to the constitutions of the several states, not to the Federal Constitution. Even he, with all his scorn of "superstition," knew that the rising nation was lucky in the occasion of its constitutional formation. "Governments in general," said James Wilson at Philadelphia the year following, "have been the result of force, of fraud, and of accident. After a period of six thousand years have elapsed since the creation, the United States exhibit to the world the first instance, as far as we can learn, of a nation, unattacked by external force, unconvulsed by domestic insurrections, assembling voluntarily, deliberating fully, and deciding calmly, concerning that system of government under which they would wish that they and their posterity should live."

Delegate Benjamin Franklin—in one of the few vocal interventions that he found strength to make—reminded the Convention on June 28 that more than luck was needed for the successful completion of their more than human task:

Mr. President, the small progress we have made after four or five weeks close attendance and continual reasonings with each other . . . is, me-thinks, a melancholy proof of the imperfection of the human understanding. . . .

In this situation of this Assembly, groping as it were in the dark to find political truth, and scarce able to distinguish it when presented to us, how has it happened, Sir, that we have

4. John Adams, *op. cit.*

not hitherto once thought of humbly applying to the Father of lights, to illuminate our understanding? In the beginning of the contest with Great Britain, when we were sensible of danger, we had daily prayer in this room for the divine protection. Our prayers, Sir, were heard, and they must have observed frequent instances of a superintending Providence in our favor. To that kind Providence we owe this happy opportunity of consulting in peace on the means of establishing our future national felicity. And have we now forgotten that powerful friend? Or do we imagine that we no longer need his assistance? I have lived, Sir, a long time, and the longer I live, the more convincing proofs I see of this truth—*that God governs in the affairs of men*. And if a sparrow cannot fall to the ground without his notice, is it probable that an empire can rise without his aid? We have been assured, Sir, in the sacred writings, that "except the Lord build the house they labor in vain that build it." I firmly believe this; and I also believe that without his concurring aid we shall succeed in this political building no better than the builders of Babel.

Though the impatient Hamilton rather shied away from these reflections on that day, he made the same acknowledgment a few months later in the *Federalist* (No. 37):

Would it be wonderful if, under the pressure of all these difficulties, the convention should have been forced into some deviations from that artificial structure and regular symmetry which an abstract view of the subject might lead an ingenious theorist to bestow on a Constitution planned in his closet or in his imagination? The real wonder is that so many difficulties should have been surmounted, and surmounted with a unanimity almost as unprecedented as it must have been unexpected. It is impossible for any man of candor to reflect on this circumstance without partaking of the astonishment. It is impossible for the man of pious reflection not to perceive in it a finger of that Almighty hand which has been so frequently and signally extended to our relief in the critical stages of the revolution.

This last sentence echoed in the words with which the first of the Fathers inaugurated so solemnly his duties as the new nation's chief magistrate:

No people can be bound to acknowledge and adore the invisible hand which conducts the affairs of men, more than the people of the United States. Every step by which they have advanced to the character of an independent nation, seems to have been distinguished by some token of providential agency; and in the important revolution just accomplished in the system of their united government, the tranquil deliberations, and voluntary consent of so many distinct communities, from which the event has resulted, cannot be compared with the means by which most governments have been established, without some return of pious gratitude, along with an humble anticipation of the future blessings which the past seem to presage.

In their handling of the problem and problems of government, the Fathers were indeed reasonable, and precisely therefore they—in such notable contrast to their French contemporaries—admitted the limits of reason. They were fecund in ideas, but were not ideologues. The grim cult of the goddess, Reason, bathed in the blood flowing from the guillotine, did not flourish in New York or Boston or Philadelphia.

Hamilton was making the all-important distinction when in the quotation just cited he contrasted with our plan of government an "artificial structure and regular symmetry which an abstract view of the subject might lead an ingenious theorist to bestow on a Con-

stitution planned in his closet or in his imagination." It is the *ideologue* who so plans, who compels all reality to squeeze into the strait
bed of his monolithic system of deductively chained ideas, into the
rigid frame of his *ideology.* The Fathers had anticipated Mosca's
conclusion:

> The absolute preponderance of a single political force, the
> predominance of any over-simplified concept in the organi-
> zation of the state, the strictly logical application of any sin-
> gle principle in all public law are the essential elements in
> any type of despotism, whether it be a despotism based upon
> divine right or a despotism based ostensibly on popular
> sovereignty.[5]

The scholars have traced the ideas of the Fathers back to a numerous intellectual ancestry—not only Locke and Montesquieu,
but Aristotle and Cicero and Plutarch, Hobbes, Burlamaqui, Mil-
ton, Hooker, Bolingbroke, Blackstone, Burke, Shaftesbury and a
score of collateral branches. But the Fathers were the masters, not
the victims, of these inherited ideas, and sometimes it is the rhetoric
more than the ideas that is taken over. The Fathers were protected
from ideology not only by piety and a native skepticism toward abstract reason, but by their persistent sense of fact, of the specific. The
phrases of Locke, Montesquieu, Cicero and the others often figured
in the Philadelphia debates, but they were never divorced from the
specific problems that had brought the delegates together.

Professor Daniel J. Boorstin, in his book, *The Genius of American
Politics,* has stressed this sense of fact and the specific, contrasting it
particularly with the impulse toward universalization displayed
throughout the French Revolution and its European successors to
and through the Russian Revolution of our own time ("the French
Revolution rewritten on the Gargantuan scale and acting with the

5. Gaetano Mosca, *op. cit.,* p. 134.

terrifying efficiency of the twentieth century"). The French Declaration of the Rights of Man and the Citizen dealt, in De Tocqueville's words, with "the citizen in the abstract, independent of particular social organizations," with "the general rights and duties of mankind," divested "of all that was peculiar to one race or time." Our Declaration of Independence "is essentially a list of specific historical instances. . . . It is closely tied to time and place."[6]

The Constitution, also, was firmly grounded in the specific. The Articles of Confederation having failed to provide a government sufficiently strong and just, the delegates met at Philadelphia to remedy its defects, with which they were intimately familiar in their own conduct and business. When, exceeding their formal instructions, they offered a new Constitution to the Congress and their countrymen, they motivated their presumption in a Letter to Congress that appealed not to the imperatives of an abstract reason, but to problems and needs of which everyone was aware:

> The friends of our country have long seen and desired, that the power of making war, peace, and treaties; that of levying money, and regulating commerce, and the correspondent executive and judicial authorities, should be fully and effectually vested in the general government of the Union. . . .
>
> That [the Constitution] is liable to as few exceptions as could reasonably have been expected, we hope and believe; that it may promote the lasting welfare of that country so dear to us all; and secure her freedom and happiness, is our most ardent wish.

The specific, the now, the individuated fact, like the magical and the divine, though in another mode, exceed the attainment of a merely abstract reason. But government is bound irretrievably to the fact, the this and the here and the now.

6. Daniel J. Boorstin, *The Genius of American Politics* (Chicago: Univ. of Chicago Press, 1953; copyright 1953 by the University of Chicago) pp. 7, 82–3.

3

The miracle of government, like other miracles, occurs in time. In and through time, the paradox is resolved, reason merges with what is beyond or outside of reason, the word is made flesh. If we translate into political and historical terms: the problem of government, insoluble by abstract reason alone, by ideology, becomes solved by social experience acting through time—that is, by *tradition*.

John Dickinson of Delaware, arguing in the Convention for the provision that limited to the House of Representatives the right of originating money bills, declared: "Experience must be our only guide. Reason may mislead us. It was not reason that discovered the singular and admirable mechanism of the English constitution. It was not reason that discovered, or ever could have discovered, the odd, and, in the eyes of those who are governed by reason, the absurd mode of trial by jury. Accidents probably produced these discoveries, and experience has given a sanction to them."

Under the stress of debate he was putting his point rather too extremely, but in its gist his fellow delegates—except, perhaps, James Wilson, who sometimes allowed himself to be victimized by democratist ideology—would have concurred. And this attitude was curious in these men, who were leaders of a new nation in a new land, only a few years out of a successful war against their traditional sovereign ties, and now gathered together to set up by explicit compact a new government, in some at least of its features unlike any that had previously existed.

The Fathers were bold innovators where they had to be in dealing with novel problems brought by independence or in adapting the political structure to the requirements of "a people, spread and spreading over a vast territory, stretching and to stretch almost from the rising to the setting sun,"[7] sole "lords and proprietors of a vast

---

7. From Senator Asher Robbins' speech in Congress advocating passage of a resolution to acquire the Madison papers.

tract of continent, comprehending all the various soils and climates of the world, and abounding in all the necessaries and conveniences of life."[8] But they did not think of themselves as "revolutionists" in the sense of the Jacobins or of the Bolsheviks of our century. They did not aim to remake society from its foundations according to a rationally certified general plan.

> The most obvious peculiarity of our American Revolution [Dr. Boorstin comments], is that, in the modern European sense, it was hardly a revolution at all. The Daughters of the American Revolution . . . have always insisted in their literature that the American Revolution was no revolution but merely a colonial rebellion. The more I have looked into the subject, the more convinced I am of the wisdom of their naiveté. . . .
>
> The American Revolution seemed in the minds of most of its leaders an affirmation of the tradition of British institutions. The argument . . . was not, on the whole, that America had institutions or a culture superior to that of the British. Rather their position, often misrepresented and sometimes simply forgotten, was that the British by their treatment of the American colonies were being untrue to the ancient spirit of their own institutions.[9]

In the debates of the Convention there were more frequent references to the constitutional practices and common law of England than to Montesquieu or Bolingbroke or Locke. In reaching their decisions, moreover, the Fathers had even more closely before them the experience and tradition of the several colonies, evolved without sharp leap into sovereign states, eight of which had lately crystallized their political ways into constitutions. In one or another of

8. George Washington, Letter to the Governors on disbanding the army, June, 1783.
9. Boorstin, *op. cit.,* pp. 68, 69, 71.

these early state charters may be found many of the seemingly most novel features of the Federal Constitution.

Surely it must have been their faith in tradition as a living and continuous force that reconciled the Fathers to a document that, as the lawyers that many of them were, they would never have accepted as a valid contract: internally contradictory, with its assertions of dual and divided sovereignty; ambiguous as well as unfinished in its definition and assignment of rights, duties and power. Pure reason could not guarantee a good government, strong, just and free. But reasonable men, drawing on the wisdom of the past shaped into institutions as well as principles, and relying on the future interplay between individuals and their inheritance of tradition, might devise an orienting directive which would itself become an essential, even critical, part of the living tradition.

So, of course, has the Constitution become, so that it seems the précis, the distillation of the entire American political tradition. Our governmental structure, whether good or not as conceived rational system, *becomes, is made,* good and even the best through time and history. The Constitution is like a man's wife who, though to tell the truth that would be revealed by an objective scale, she is not the most beautiful and talented creature in the world, nevertheless through twenty or thirty or fifty years of successful marriage *becomes,* as a living and therefore historical being, a good and indeed the best of all possible wives. Let not a rational Satan explain to him that this other woman is richer, that one more gently tongued, the one yonder a better cook, and he will therefore do better to change to X or Y or Z. For him there can be no better; his reality and hers have been fused by time, and to deny her is to deny himself.

The new nation, with its Constitution and its responsible leaders channeling new traditions out of the inherited traditions of the past, creates and confirms its own traditions. Its own way of living as a nation becomes established; through the mysteries of time and existence, the paradoxes are overcome, the rational gulf is bridged. I accept it as right that Congress, the President and the courts shall govern me because they have been chosen by prescribed forms (however strange in themselves, and very strange they are) that have been honored by observance and prior acceptance. The governors do not use their strength to destroy justice, because not only the stated rules but firm institutions, long usage and seasoned attitudes put bounds to the exercise of any single mode of power.

It is, then, only a seeming and not an existential paradox that the commander of the rebellion should have made the problem of tradition the most solemn topic of his official farewell to his countrymen:

> Towards the preservation of your Government, and the permanency of your present happy state, it is requisite, not only that you steadily discountenance irregular oppositions to its acknowledged authority, but also that you resist with care the spirit of innovation upon its principles, however specious the pretexts. . . . In all the changes to which you may be invited, remember that time and habit are at least as necessary to fix the true character of governments as of other human institutions; that experience is the surest standard by which to test the real tendency of the existing constitution of a country; that facility in changes, upon the credit of mere hypothesis and opinion, exposes to perpetual change, from the endless variety of hypothesis and opinion.[10]

4

It is observable that the attitudes which men hold toward the problems of government tend to fall into typical clusters or patterns. With respect to issues that have been under discussion in these two

10. George Washington, *The Farewell Address.*

chapters, we will find that one group, in which George Washington is to be numbered, exhibits:

(a) a conviction that there is a non-rational factor involved in government, together with a correlative distrust in abstract political ideology and in the rigid, unilateral application to political life of any single rational principle or formula;

(b) a belief that men, not by accident or merely by social environment but by ineradicable nature, are partially corrupt (evil) and limited in their potential, together with a correlative distrust in utopias and "ultimate solutions" of major social problems;

(c) a respect for tradition, for established institutions and traditional modes of conduct, together with a consequent reluctance to initiate quick and deep alterations in traditional forms, and an effort to restrict the extent or slow the pace of changes that have become unavoidable or morally imperative.

A second group is in each respect the contrary of the first, though in practice the distinctions blur at the edges. Roughly, however, individuals belonging to the second group:

(a′) have a general confidence in the ability of the human mind to comprehend through rational science all problems of government and society, and often a specific trust in some particular ideology as the sufficient key to the knowledge and successful practice of government;

(b′) believe that most human weakness and error are the result of incorrect social structure or inadequate education, that human potentialities, even if not infinite, have no discernible a priori limitations, and that therefore it is not unrealistic for human beings to set themselves the goal of an ideal society in which such major problems as war, poverty and suffering would be solved;

(c′) reject tradition as a ground for a favoring judgment on an institution or mode of conduct, and are ready to accept quick, drastic and extensive social change if this recommends itself on rational and utilitarian grounds.

In a particular individual the three attitudes belonging to each of these sets are ordinarily found together, along with several other typical and similarly contrasted elements which will be discussed in later chapters. Using a term from medicine, we may call such a set of elements or symptoms that often (though not always) occur together, a *syndrome*.

The first political syndrome here analyzed in part, defines, recognizably, the men (or attitude) generally called *conservative*. The name for the men (and attitude) defined by the second syndrome is not so generally agreed to, and is particularly subject to dispute because it covers a wider range of practical positions on politics than does the first—a range that includes both John Stuart Mill and Lenin. *Progressive* is in many ways the most satisfactory term, but in the United States (though not elsewhere, and with little historical justification) this has been superseded by *liberal*. I shall accept the latter usage. "Conservative" and "liberal" will mean what has been made explicit by this section, together with what will later on be added to these preliminary definitions.

The attitude toward tradition probably furnishes the most accurate shibboleth for distinguishing conservatives from liberals. We may put the question this way: does the fact that a particular institution or mode of social conduct has been established for some while create a presumption in favor of continuing it? To this question a conservative will answer with a definite Yes; and a liberal with No, or "very little." This does not mean that a conservative never, and a liberal always, wants to change what is. For the conservative, there might be considerations cogent enough to call for a change in prevailing ways, in spite of the presumption in their favor; and the liberal is on occasion content to let well enough alone. It is the nihilist, not the liberal, who thinks everything to be wrong; and the reactionary, not the conservative, who wants nothing altered (unless, perhaps, in order to return to the past).

In Congress the chairmen of standing committees are drawn from the majority party on the basis of seniority. Although some rational arguments can be offered in favor of this practice, they are on the whole less convincing—judged from a purely rational point of view—than the many arguments that can be and have been brought against it. It is a practice, however, of ancient lineage, which without ever having been formally debated or much thought about became fixed very early in the history of Congress. Many liberals in and out of Congress do not feel this long tradition to be of any weight; and every year there are proposals to change it, such as have been made in the past decade by ex-Senator Lehman, Senator Humphrey, Senator Douglas and other liberal members. Nevertheless, on this matter the conservative tendency in Congress has up to now prevailed without much difficulty.[11]

The electoral college system in the form under which we have chosen our chief executive since the adoption of the 12th amendment (1804) is open to, and has received, a variety of rational criticisms. In this case many conservatives as well as liberals find the arguments[12] sufficiently convincing to believe that the system should be changed. But it is noteworthy that many liberals, reasoning deductively, wish to abolish it altogether and to have the President chosen by an all-national direct election, or plebiscite. In nearly every session of Congress for many decades, a proposed amendment to this effect has been introduced by liberal members.

11. Not merely the selection of committee chairmen but the procedures and organization of Congress are in general governed by seniority. It is perhaps worth remarking that this is true also of all other legislative bodies (state and municipal) in the United States, though it is only in connection with Congress that the issue has excited much public debate.
12. The opinions of professional politicians on this matter are often related more to a calculation of probable party gains and losses under a different system than to argument.

The conservatives favoring change propose not an abandonment of the electoral college system but one or another modification that would be designed to remove certain contingent consequences of its present form that they deem undesirable: the possibility of minority Presidents, the heavy weight given to the big states by the statewide bloc vote (which also, it is argued, "disfranchises the minority"), etc. The "indirect" system of election would be retained in the conservative proposals. Actually, the present form does not work precisely as intended by the Founding Fathers (who expected the electors to be "uninstructed") or as handled in early Presidential elections (wherein many states had local district, not bloc, voting). Some conservatives urge, as a liberal would never do, that their proposed alterations would bring the electoral system more intimately in line with basic American traditions.

The two contrasting attitudes toward tradition could readily be illustrated by a hundred other instances, drawn not only from major issues of government and social policy, but from religion, morality, family and personal life. But there is a puzzling question not yet stated. How long does an institution or mode of conduct have to last before it becomes "traditional"? One year, ten or a hundred or a thousand? More directly related to our inquiry: if we say that so-and-so is "part of the American tradition," how far back must we be able to trace it? For how many years can we continue to argue that such-and-such is "counter to the American tradition"?

These are not mere closet questions. Conservatives and liberals agree that some at least of the features of Franklin Roosevelt's New Deal (compulsory social insurance, as one instance) were major and abrupt changes in what had been the American tradition up to 1933. Some of these have been dropped, but others have endured for what is now a generation. Can they still be regarded as counter to the tradition, or must they now be accepted as themselves part of the tradition?

These questions cannot be answered in the neutral, intersubjective way of mathematics and physical science. To answer them requires sensibility, tact, character and insight as well as knowledge and rational method. They are more complicated versions of the same sort of question that arises familiarly in personal life. A gentleman or a peasant knows that some things just aren't done, and some must be. If he is reflective he may be able to articulate—not fully but in some degree—the principles of the implicit tradition within which his life has been formed, and in terms of which his judgments of manner and conduct are made. But the tradition will contain conflicting trends, and will not cover all contingencies. Therefore at times his conclusions will seem—and will be—arbitrary; it will not be clear whether such-and-such is or isn't "done."

A similar arbitrariness in some judgments of what is or is not in accord with a national (or other historical) tradition is one factor persuading those who accept the ideology of science to disregard and reject tradition. From the point of view of the ideology of science, it is not proper that the "subjective" character, sensibility and training of the judge should be thought to bear on the "objective" accuracy of his decisions—that Winston Churchill, say, should be wiser about English tradition than a Chinese scientist equipped with an equal quantity of facts. To a conservative it would probably seem ridiculous even to suggest that any Chinese or Indian or Arab scientist could possibly comprehend English tradition as well as Churchill, or as any Sussex farmer tilling the land of his ancestors.

In order to avoid for a while some of the more debatable problems, I shall base my discussion in the remaining chapters of Part One primarily on our tradition prior to 1933. Much of the description holds through to the present. On the other hand, some important changes relevant to the main theses of this book started early in the century, and several might be dated more correctly from Woodrow Wilson's than from Franklin Roosevelt's administration. But the line must be drawn somewhere.

A change does not necessarily violate tradition. There are always changes. The change and the way it is brought about may be within the general form and spirit of the tradition, and thus be themselves, one might say, "traditional." For our army to adopt machine guns or trucks when technology shifted, or to enlarge its ranks in an emergency through a selective draft, did not go counter to the broad historical tradition; but total disbandment of armed force or "universal military service" (whether or not justified on other grounds) undoubtedly would. Thus, by jumping a generation to keep our initial survey focused on somewhat older ways, we will be more favorably located to judge whether the post-1933 changes broke or fulfilled the American tradition.

III

THE PARADOX OF
SOVEREIGNTY

T HERE ARE many proofs, among which Jean-Jacques Rousseau's is the most famous, that political sovereignty must be
one, and can be neither shared, divided, nor delegated. The
sovereign (whether a single person or a collectivity) is by definition
the supreme power. By delegating his power or sharing it, he ceases
to be supreme and is therefore no longer sovereign; he contradicts
his own essence.

Reasoning from the theorem that sovereignty must be one, with
the corollary that "dual power" is impossible, Leon Trotsky, in a
brilliant chapter of his *History of the Russian Revolution,* interpreted
the 1917 path that led to unmixed Bolshevik supremacy in Russia.
With the sovereign Czar out of the way, political sovereignty strad-
dled between the Duma (the old parliament) and the Soviets of
Workers' and Peasants' Deputies. But this could not be; one or the
other but not both could be supreme; and in November, through
the Soviets' conquest of all-power under Bolshevik leadership, the
contradiction was removed.

Sovereignty cannot be divided or shared or delegated; but in
many nations, and in our nation more than in any other, it is. In this
respect also, existence, time and tradition overcome a paradox of
abstract reason.

What is the address of the political sovereign of the United States?
Where exactly is he located? In England we will find the sovereign
by entering the hall of the House of Commons; in the Soviet
Union, by knocking at the gates of the Kremlin; in the France of

1957, across the river from the Place de la Concorde, up the steps of the Chamber; in Ethiopia, within the imperial palace. But where do we apply at home? At the door of the White House? the chambers of Congress?—and which chamber? the bench of the Supreme Court? the forty-eight capitols of the forty-eight states? or perhaps the guarded offices of the Joint Chiefs of Staff? A single answer cannot be given, and even a multiple answer is never quite complete.

The rigorous application of any systematic political ideology—monarchist, aristocratic, racist or democratic—tends toward the concentration of sovereignty. If a monarchist formula—such as "the divine right of kings," let us say—is carried out all the way, then sovereignty comes to rest in and only in the monarch. A strict aristocratic principle is expressed in a patrician or oligarchic rule like that of Rome in the period following the overthrow of the kings, or the Venetian Republic, where sovereignty was unambiguously located in the Senate or Council. The racist and democratic ideologies are more complex, because it is not literally possible for an entire race or people to be the functioning sovereign. But each of these, also, has the same tendency toward focus. One leader or assembly is taken to express the will of the race or people, and acts as the operative sovereign.

A division of sovereignty in practice is inconsistent with the reign of a single ideology in theory, although this inconsistency may not be acknowledged. A parliament exercising some functions of government while the king still rules without formal challenge is witnessing the breakdown of the strict monarchic formula and the intrusion of a formula justifying a sharing of the power by "the people"—at any rate by substantial, tax-paying people. In ancient Egypt and for long in China a bureaucracy of wise men (priests or mandarins) shared sovereignty with hereditary despots, a division which no single-principled ideology or political formula could encompass.

I do not want to suggest too close a parallel between theory and practice here. On the one side are the facts of how sovereignty is actually exercised within a nation or empire. On the other are the theories (ideologies, principles of legitimacy, political formulas) by which power or sovereignty is justified and explained. I am noting not an exact coincidence but a tendency. There tends to be a rough correlation between the practical concentration of sovereignty in a single person or agency, on the one hand, and the theoretical prevalence of a single systematic political ideology or formula, on the other. When sovereignty is broken up, divided or shared among many persons and agencies, then there tends to be a breakdown also in the theoretical sphere, with the intrusion of alternate ideologies, or the piercing out of the dominant ideology with scraps that cannot be harmonized with the original pattern. Conflicting aristocratic and democratic ideologies may be pasted together; or the holes in a democratic formula may be covered with aristocratic or racist patches.

2

The Founding Fathers were unanimous, or nearly so, in wishing to prevent a concentration of governmental power, of sovereignty. They believed, although this is not self-evident, that such a concentration would lead inevitably to despotism; and they were determined to resist domestic despotism in the future as they had fought what they had held to be the King's despotism in the past.

They were faced with the dilemma that we have examined. Convinced that the government under the Articles of Confederation was too impotent to endure, they wanted a new government that would be strong enough to defend America against the threat of foreign enemies and domestic disorder; and strong enough to collect taxes and enforce a sound fiscal policy. But a government of that strength would be strong enough, also, to destroy domestic justice and liberty; and, since men are governed more by passion and interest than by reason and conscience, such a government would be not only able to destroy justice and liberty but would in fact do so.

Was there any way out of the logical impasse? Drawing on their own experience, on history (some of it—as in the case of their understanding of the British constitution—garbled), and on their preferred philosophers, the Fathers concluded that they could grasp both horns of their dilemma if, while assigning a full reservoir of power to the new government they prevented its concentration, if sovereignty were spread over a compartmentalized and divided governmental structure.

Under this conception, the idea of "the government" of the nation becomes in some degree a semantic fiction. It is almost as if the nation were to be ruled by "governments," overlapping but not wholly fused.

Though the government (or governments) would possess in all a power sufficient to institute a despotism over the citizens, and though the nature of the governors would lead them to wish to do so, liberty and justice would be preserved because some of the power would be dissipated by balance and conflict among the interrelated but divided segments of the governmental structure itself.

These ideas of "division of power," "check and balance"—so familiar but so difficult to comprehend fully—are at the ineradicable core of the American governmental tradition. It is not that the ideas of the Fathers on these points were exactly carried out. In fact, the Fathers were wrong in many of their formal expectations. None of the three branches[1] behaved as they envisaged. The Electoral College never was an uninstructed gathering of impartial men who after sober discussion selected as Chief Executive the nation's most meritorious citizen. The Senate was never a non-partisan council of non-partisan wise men vigilantly checking the passions of the people as reflected in the House. Within a decade the Court and the executive were unlike

---

1. In the older literature the legislature, executive and judiciary are usually called the "departments" of the government. I shall use the familiar term, "branches," in order to avoid confusion with the executive "departments."

anything mentioned at the Philadelphia convention. Special protective devices, like the restriction of the initiative of revenue bills to the House, proved of small significance. None of the Fathers had any preliminary inkling of the kind of party system that started to form within a month of the new government's inauguration.

But the Fathers had wrought better than they knew in detail. The substance of their formal doctrines about "separation of powers" and "checks and balances" was in accord with the experience and sentiment of the nation. Madison may have been using the language of 18th century European theorists when he said at Philadelphia: "If it be a fundamental principle of free government that the legislative, executive and judiciary powers should be *separately* exercised, it is equally so that they be *independently* exercised." Still, his central meaning—that in order to secure liberty and civil justice, power must be not focused but divided and diffused—was the feeling of his countrymen then and thereafter.

No written constitution could have been of itself an absolute guarantee against the centralization of power: men can always bend words to their passions. A nation that does not want liberty will not preserve it. But the Fathers did provide us with a framework marvelously apt for blocking the concentration of governmental power (sovereignty) in any single agency, if that is what we as a nation, or most of us, choose to use it for. If the Fathers were mistaken in some details, and wrong about just how some provisions would function, their main structure did externalize their key objectives, and was closely enough in accord with our continuing tradition to have survived without basic rebuilding longer than any other governmental structure now functioning anywhere in the world.

How then was the dilemma to be solved, and a government formed that would be neither too strong for the liberties of the people nor too weak to maintain its own existence? The answer of the Fathers, and of our enduring national tradition, has been: by granting government a sovereignty ample enough to perform its protective purposes, but dividing that sovereignty among a variety of officers and agencies having a relative independence of each other:

> To what expedient, then, shall we finally resort, for maintaining in practice the necessary partition of power among the several departments, as laid down in the Constitution? The only answer that can be given is, that as all these exterior provisions are found to be inadequate, the defect must be supplied, by so contriving the interior structure of the government as that its several constituent parts may, by their mutual relations, be the means of keeping each other in their proper places. . . .
>
> In order to lay a due foundation for that separate and distinct exercise of the different powers of government, which to a certain extent is admitted on all hands to be essential to the preservation of liberty, it is evident that each department should have a will of its own. . . .
>
> But the great security against a gradual concentration of the several powers in the same department, consists in giving those who administer each department the necessary constitutional means and personal motives to resist encroachments of the others. . . . Ambition must be made to counteract ambition. The interest of the man must be connected with the constitutional rights of the place.[2]

3

The Fathers, while accepting power as an essential expedient in human affairs, distrusted all power. What is distinctive about this distrust, distinctively confirmed by the American tradition, is its

2. *Federalist*, No. 51.

universality. It is not just a king or an "entrenched aristocracy" that will, given an opportunity, tend to despotism. Any class or group of men, any institution, will tend to become despotic if it is able to concentrate power to its own disposition, if it is not counterbalanced by other depositaries of power. There can be a tyranny of merchants as well as of landlords; of debtors as well as of creditors; of the workingman as well as the lord, the poor and lowly as well as the rich and well-born. There are military and priestly and executive despotisms; and legislative and judicial despotisms also.

The idea, familiar in much of the rest of the world, that there is a messianic class or individual, that some particular group of men or some one unique man or some special sort of institution is politically pure and undefiled, immune from the temptations of power and able to rule the state with serene disinterest, is alien to the American tradition. In practice as firmly as in theory, Americans have always been convinced that no one can be trusted with the unchecked exercise of governmental power. We have always clung to institutional as well as moral guarantees against the centralization of power.

Throughout our history there may be observed a kind of counterbalancing swing of community sentiment whenever power seems to be flowing too amply into a particular class or institution, governmental or private. Within the governmental framework proper, for example, executive encroachments, which almost inevitably develop in wartime, excite a shift of popular support to the legislature. The kind of judicial usurpation that has sometimes occurred leads after a few years to strong pressures against the Court, and backing for a President or Congress that finds ways to reduce the Court's pretensions. In spite of formal theory, no agency is given "the last word" in the American political process. A judge can write a Dred Scott or a Pollock decision; but that cannot forever preserve slavery or block the levying of an income tax. Analogously, outside of the governmental framework, popular pressure has in the past always swung in due course against any social group—slaveholders or industrialists or financiers—that has threatened to gather to itself an inordinate share of social power.[3]

4

It was the aim, then, of the Founding Fathers to devise a governmental structure that would be a permanent bulwark against any of these diverse special threats to liberty and justice. But the Fathers were as anxiously concerned with the more general threat from what they called "democracy." The records of the Philadelphia convention do not show the presence of any open defender of "democracy."[4] The delegates differed in the degree of heat with which they attacked it, but they were unanimously agreed that they were there to establish not a "democracy" but a "republic." Some, like Hamilton (who hankered somewhat after monarchy) and Elbridge Gerry of Massachusetts even had their doubts about republics:

> The evils we experience [Gerry remarked on May 31] flow from the excess of democracy. The people do not want [i.e., lack] virtue, but are the dupes of pretended patriots. In Massachusetts it had been fully confirmed by experience, that they are daily misled into the most baneful measures and opinions,

3. My primary reference continues to be our history prior to 1933. I leave open here the question whether this traditional balancing process holds into the present with respect to the agencies that in our day are the leading competitors for all-power: the President and the bureaucracy (within the governmental framework); the industrial managers and trade union bureaucrats outside of government.

4. Thomas Jefferson, who in certain senses might have defended "democracy," was, of course, not present, nor were any of the "Jacobinic" figures of the Revolution, such as Thomas Paine or Samuel Adams. In some of the debate, James Wilson reasoned from democratist ideology, but even he softened his logic when it came to practical decisions.

by the false reports circulated by designing men, and which no one on the spot can refute. . . . He had, he said, been too republican heretofore: he was still, however, republican; but had been taught by experience the danger of the levelling spirit.

Roger Sherman, in the same day's debate, was fully agreed: "The people, he said, immediately, should have as little to do as may be about the government. They want [lack] information, and are constantly liable to be misled." William Livingston of New Jersey asserted bluntly that "the people have ever been and ever will be unfit to retain the exercise of power in their own hands." Edmund Randolph of Virginia observed that "in tracing these evils [under which the United States labored] to their origin, every man had found it in the turbulence and follies of democracy."

Just what did the Fathers mean by these terms "democracy" and "republic"? In its pure form, they understood "democracy" to be the direct rule of all the people (presumably, all free adult males) exercised by majority vote in some sort of common assembly. In a nation of any size there naturally could not be a unified common assembly. There could, however, be decisions on leadership or on laws made by a general direct plebiscite—a majority vote of all the people. A chief executive, a parliament (or Congress) and even judges could be selected in this manner. Indeed, the executive and parliament are in fact so selected in many countries that are nowadays called "democratic." Such a government is "representative," and therefore "impure" from a strict democratic standpoint; but it retains to a maximum practicable extent the democratic tendency. It is perhaps most accurately called a "plebiscitary" government.

Whatever the particular form taken by the representative institutions, it follows from the logic of democracy that a majority vote of "the people" is binding on the entire community with respect to all political matters. Since ultimately only a majority vote of the people can decide what matters are and what are not political, it actually follows that the majority, in theory at least, binds the entire community with respect to any matter whatever. The principle that "the voice of the people is the voice of God" is strictly correct as an interpretation of the meaning of democracy; or, at any rate, of "democracy" as understood and attacked by the Fathers.

Under this ideological conception of democracy—which I shall hereafter call "democratism"—the technical problem of government is to provide institutions and procedures designed to translate as directly, accurately and quickly as possible the opinion of the popular majority.

The Fathers' idea of a "republic," since it is not derivative from a monolithic ideology, is not so neat, unequivocal and systematic as "democratism." A republic, like a democracy, was (as they understood it) a government that rejected monarchic and hereditary principles. Like democracy, too, a republic finds its ultimate sanction in the will of the people. But it is not the function of the representative institutions of the republic to try to act as the immediate expressions or agents of the unrestricted will of the popular majority. For that matter, "the people," in the assumptions of the Fathers, included only "responsible" citizens—free, male, adult, landowning or in other ways taxpaying.

Moreover, in the republic that the Fathers were founding even the responsible and narrowed "people" were limited in both the manner and scope of their function. A strict compact (or constitution), as well as religious and social tradition, excluded many areas of public life from political jurisdiction. When the people spoke, they would be able to do so only indirectly; the voice of the demigod was to be filtered through layers of mediating institutions that calmed its changing passions and plugged the gaps in its knowledge.

Thus the republican government was not to be a small-scale simulacrum of the people, a mere technical device for carrying out as sensitively and directly as possible the majority will. The republic "represented" the people only in a very general dependence on popular consent. A method was provided through which the launching of the republic by adoption of the basic compact could receive popular sanction. Procedures were defined whereby the officers of the republic, and through them their record, could be periodically submitted to popular approval or rejection.

At no point in the national structure that the Fathers devised was popular approval interpreted to mean a general plebiscite. There is no law, officer or agency of the government of the United States under the Constitution that is determined by a direct vote of the entire enfranchised population of the country. In every case the decisions are indirect. In fact, there has never been within the United States an all-national vote (national plebiscite) on any question, not even on the adoption of the Constitution. The mechanisms of our government are so arranged that the voting population is always broken up into states, congressional districts, or some other subdivisions.

The most "logical" place for a plebiscite is in the election of the President. It is revealing to discover that at the Philadelphia convention the only delegate who argued at any length for direct popular election of the President was the one ideologist of democratism there present, James Wilson of Pennsylvania,[5] who, carrying out the same democratist logic, spoke also against a Senate in which states were to be equally represented regardless of population. Even on the Presidency, the decision was against a plebiscite and in favor of a method that not only permits the occasional election of a minority President but, by dividing the electoral process along state boundaries, clouds the "mandate" and hinders the development of a unified "national will."

5. He was supported feebly on one or two occasions by Daniel Carroll of Maryland and Gouverneur Morris of his own Pennsylvania delegation. (Morris may have been ironic in the matter.) None of the three ever discussed the precise mode of popular election they had in mind, and it may not have been a true plebiscite. Moreover, in Wilson's case his democratist ideology was at least in part a convenient formula for defending the interests of the large states against the small. What he wanted to prevent was a method of electing the executive that would have given the small states control. Consequently, he acceded readily to the final electoral plan.

With respect to "democracy" the American tradition has not, of course, carried out strictly the intentions of the Fathers. No one questions that the long-term curve of the nation's history has been toward more democracy. This is a tendency which will undergo more stringent analysis in Part III. Here let us note that, though we have traveled far along the democratic road, we have by no means completed the journey. With residence and literacy and poll tax and unspoken restraints still in effect, the franchise is less wide than it is formally supposed to be. In spite of the partial opening of the Senate gate by adoption of the 17th amendment, the structure of the central government has not yet been altogether submerged in the democratic flood. The government of our republic remains indirect, and mediated by a complex set of "independent but inter-related" agencies. It is still true that no law, officer or agency is determined by national plebiscite.

That such a political structure as ours should have somehow endured, even in these late generations during which the whole drift of the world has been so much against it, shows how well the Fathers built, but proves also that this is what most Americans have wanted. Not merely a fixed document but living tradition have protected our republic from democratist[6] subversion. We just don't seem to trust each other well enough to wish to put our fate unrestrictedly into each others' hands. Even when and where we do turn authority over to others, we tangle it up in such a maze that it never finds a clear and open road.

---

6. Of course, we now call our government a "democracy" rather than a "republic," speak of "democracy" as "our way of life," and so on. This, however, is partly a change in rhetorical habit. We as a nation are not yet consistently democratic in the full ideological sense, as our democratist ideologues daily remind us.

IV

THE DIFFUSION OF POWER

HOW WERE the individual states to be related to the new central[1] government? This problem was the primary axis around which the Philadelphia debates revolved. And this problem posed in stark outline the kind of formal contradiction that always arises, we have seen, in connection with government.

Were the states or the new central government to be sovereign? They could not both be: sovereignty cannot be divided or shared. On both sides the proponents were adamant. William Paterson of New Jersey, in his demand that the states retain their individual and ultimate sovereignty, was no less firm than James Wilson in his belief that all sovereignty must come to rest in the central government. Time and again the convention was on the verge of flying apart under the centrifugal push of this impossible problem.

In the end, through the "great compromise" initially promoted by Roger Sherman of Connecticut, the problem was solved by thrusting the contradiction deep into the body of the new government. The contradiction was neither avoided nor surmounted—to attempt either would have been illusory. It was accepted. The sovereignty, the governmental power, was divided, or more exactly, diffused over both central government and states. The new society was to be both one and many, both a nation and a federation. To those who proved that this cannot be, the reply was made: "To argue

1. The government established under the Constitution has been known as "federal," "national," "union," "united"—the choice of adjective reflecting political doctrine. I shall call it by the neutral descriptive term, "central."

upon abstract principles that this coordinate authority cannot exist is to set up supposition and theory against fact and reality."[2]

The Fathers understood what they were doing. Writing just before the convention started, James Madison (himself at that time a nationalist) had formulated the contradiction, and recognized that it would have to be accepted. He wrote in a letter to his friend, Edmund Randolph: "I hold it for a fundamental point, that an individual independence of the states is utterly irreconcilable with the idea of an aggregate sovereignty. I think, at the same time, that a consolidation of the states into one simple republic is not less unattainable than it would be inexpedient."

They knew also how closely their answer to this problem was related to their general objective of forestalling that concentration of power which they believed led inevitably to despotism. John Dickinson of Delaware was voicing more than the prejudices of a small-state representative when he argued on June 7: "The preservation of the states in a certain degree of agency is indispensable. It will produce that collision between the different authorities which should be wished for in order to check each other."

In the usual account of our history, it is explained that the great compromise was unworkable. It proved true in fact as well as in logic that there could be only one master in the house. The decision as to whether it was to be the states or the central government was only postponed by the convention, to be settled finally not by lawyers' paragraphs but by a civil war that established once for all the central government's unchallenged sole sovereignty.

No one will deny that during the course of our history the relative weight of the central government has progressively, and mightily increased; the relative share of the states in the total reservoir of sovereignty, grossly declined. We may nevertheless question whether the process has been so straight-line or so fully completed as the standard account affirms. Granted, the states are not what they

2. *Federalist*, No. 34.

were in the old days, but as political realities they have proved more resilient than theory would lead us to expect. Even crushing victory in civil war by the side that fought in the name of national unity did not destroy the reality of the states. Within a decade the states that had been totally defeated were expelling the nationalist political invaders from their borders. Today it is those same states that are the least humble in asserting a practical autonomy. To be defeated after fighting well does not always lose so much as not to have fought.

It may be that the scholars who record the decline and end of the states spend too much time with documents in libraries. The states are realities that can be seen and felt—still seen and still felt—by one who travels widely over our land. They look and smell different. No one will mistake the rocky, never regular, island-dotted shore of Maine for the flat sandy shelf of the Carolinas; the desert and mesas and sunsets of Arizona, for the black fields of Iowa; Colorado's Rockies for the green mountains of Vermont; the rolling hills of southern Ohio for the chopped hills of West Virginia; the stretching horizon of Montana for the closed scenes of Connecticut; the lakes of Michigan for the rivers of Mississippi. The differences are also in detail, and to the loving traveler in America it would seldom be necessary for him to need a sign to tell him that he had crossed a state boundary.

It is not only the land: the people who have settled it, their houses and cities and roads, their industries, their customs and churches were, and still to an amazing extent are, diverse from state to state. The German dairy farmers of Wisconsin; the Swedish farmers of Minnesota; the Yankee farmers of New Hampshire; the Shaker farmers in eastern New York; the stockmen of Texas; the planters and sharecroppers of South Carolina or the Louisiana delta; the Japanese truck farmers of California; the transplanted Massachusetts farmers of Ohio; the Scotch-Irish farmers of Tennessee; the Poles of Buffalo, Irish of Boston, Jews of New York, Italians of Providence, Mexicans of San Antonio, Creoles of New Orleans, Slovaks of Pittsburgh: each ethnic community helps to make the distinctive larger community of each state. Frame house or stone or brick; bungalow or skyscraper; villages huddled around a green or stretching out over the prairie; ranch house and mansion: the typical architectural forms are located in both time and space. Industries and occupations serve to define the states further, and we so designate them: mining states, wheat or corn or cotton states, cattle states, big industry states, inland states, maritime states.

We live in an age that tends toward the levelling of these and all differences in human society, but they are not levelled yet, and they are still considerable. Even in laws the states, in spite of practical inconvenience and logical confusion, are stubbornly unlike. They differ in their rules about how old you must be to marry or work; about what justifies divorce or mayhem; about punishments for crime and what constitutes crime; about safety and hygiene; about taxes and inheritance and drinking and the speed of travel. A bigamist in one state is an honest husband in another; a chiropractor is a legitimate doctor on one side of a state border but a fraud when he crosses it.

Of course it is true that only the central government can make war or peace or treaties with a foreign power, coin money, or define and punish piracies and felonies committed on the high seas; and true that the taxing power of the central government reaches deep into our pockets. But though such things are much written about, wars and treaties and piracies are rather minor elements in most individual lives, the problem of money is not so much who coins it as who gets it, and the central government has no monopoly on our pockets.

It is the state—or its subdivisions of county and municipality—that is continuously with us from birth to death, both of which are officially admitted by state, not national registration. We are married under the laws, regulations and licensing of the state; and divorced also under the laws of the same or another state. The state puts out our fires, educates us, guards our property, licenses our profession or business, certifies our plumbing and heat and electricity, decides how fast we can go in our cars. With only rare and infrequent (though much publicized) exceptions, it is the state that arrests us, fines us, puts us into jail or sends us to death in modes that the state defines. There are few attributes of sovereignty more categoric than the right and ability to take away liberty and life.

It is the state, within a given negative framework, that certifies me as a voter. I can vote, even in an election for officers of the central government, not by virtue of being a citizen of "the United States," but only because I am a certified citizen and voter of Illinois or Utah or Oregon.

Each state has its own autonomous and sizeable political structure: a chief executive and legislature; a complicated court system; police and an army (the National Guard) subject to the state executive's call; many regulatory agencies and a numerous bureaucracy— all sustained by big taxes and a large state debt. This structure, by its very existence, both expresses and tends to maintain the states' share of independence and sovereignty.

The surest way to become convinced of the continuing reality of the states is to live for a while in a nation where sovereignty is exclusively lodged in a centralized government. Not only in a fascist Italy or Nazi Germany or communist Russia, but in France or Spain or even England, it is impossible to avoid the always visible hand of the central government. It touches the citizen or stranger at each turn of affairs. Every paper, document, stamp, bureau, official, permit, ticket that in any remote way is related to the political, traces back to the one central sovereignty. You cannot get an automobile driver's permit, a glass of beer, or a license to shine shoes without an act of the national government.

The great compromise of the Philadelphia Convention was, then, not mere wish. In the American tradition, in spite of 170 years of encroachment by the central government, a civil war fought over the issue of state independence, and several generations of ideological attack by those in whose doctrine state autonomy is an absurd and injurious anachronism, the states have been sturdy enough to survive. By surviving they have continued to function as a critical if crumbling flank in the bulwark of diffused power that the American tradition has so far maintained against despotism.

2

The fund of sovereignty is then shared, though unequally, by the several states and the nation. But in the structure of the central government (as in the state governments too, for that matter) the allotment of sovereignty is further partitioned among the "departments" or "branches."

The Founding Fathers were at their most doctrinaire in some of their statements about the "natural" or "essential" division of power into "legislative," "executive" and "judicial" elements. They drew their rhetoric from popular authorities:

> In every government there are three sorts of power: the legislative; the executive, in respect to things dependent on the law of nations; and the executive, in regard to things that depend on the civil law. . . . The latter we shall call the judiciary power. . . .
>
> When the legislative and executive powers are united in the same person, or in the same body of magistrates, there can be no liberty. . . . Again, there is no liberty if the power of judging be not separated from the legislative and executive powers.[3]

The more learned of the Philadelphia delegates never tired of echoing that famous passage. Rufus King of Massachusetts (on July 19) referred to it, indeed, as "the primitive axiom": "that the three great departments of government should be separate and independent;

---

3. Montesquieu, *The Spirit of Laws.* In the concrete, Montesquieu argued for a form of government combining both aristocracy and monarchy, not for a republic.

that the Executive and Judiciary should be so as well as the Legislative; that the Executive should be so equally with the Judiciary." James Madison himself appealed often to "the maxim" that "required a separation of the Executive, as well as the Judiciary, from the Legislature and from each other."

The Fathers were not, however, in this or other matters reasoning as ideologues. It was only the rhetoric, the phrasing that was doctrinaire and second-hand. The actual tripartite governmental structure that they built into the Constitution was not a deduction from an abstract system of ideal government, but part of their solution for the problem that they had set themselves of combining strength, justice and liberty in the developing nation. They did not find the specific answers in Montesquieu or Locke, but in the experience of the colonies become states, of the mother country, of the still wider history with which they were acquainted, and in the adjustment of the practical and in part conflicting interests which they themselves quite consciously represented.

In a later chapter there will be some discussion of the fact that by the terms of the Constitution itself, and even more through traditional practice, sovereignty is rather "diffused" than "divided" or "separated" among the three branches. Whichever term is the most accurate, it was the intent of the Fathers—successfully fulfilled, moreover—to devise a structure that would break up the sum of governmental power, and would provide lasting barriers to its concentration. To this end they were most particularly concerned to bolster the independence of the branches, to give each a political base that would enable it to defend itself against the inevitable attempts at encroachment by the others. "If it be a fundamental principle of free government," Madison summarized, "that the Legislative, Executive and Judiciary powers should be *separately* exercised, it is equally so that they be *independently* exercised."

The branches are selected by three altogether diverse mechanisms: the legislature by a popular election according to states and local districts; the executive through the electoral college process; the judiciary by executive appointment, confirmed by one house of the legislature. Once in office, the members of one branch are virtually immune from direct coercion by members of another, except under rules so framed as to be not only complicated but most difficult to apply. The members of the legislature are immune from arrest, indictment or prosecution for any official acts. The executive is also immune in the courts, and subject only to a process of impeachment that is almost impossible to carry out. Neither legislature nor executive can get rid of each other. Members of the judiciary, though dependent on the other two branches for appointment (a much lesser dependence than if on one only), are thereupon emancipated through the life extension of their terms, subject only to a possible impeachment for gross misconduct.

The degree of independence possessed by each branch has been more extreme than in the government of any other modern nation. It is symbolized by the revealing and extraordinary fact that each of the branches can, independently of the others, put a citizen in jail—a primary attribute of sovereignty.[4]

Each branch can and does claim to speak with the authority of the national government of the United States. This means that there can be, in a particular case—the return, let us say, of fugitive slaves across a state line, or the definition and punishment of sedition—three conflicting pronouncements on the law and policy of the land: by Congress, the President and the Court.[5] Logically this is another of those impossibilities that are nevertheless solved by the shaping hand of time.

4. Congress has not in fact put more than a couple of persons in jail since 1857, except by going to the courts under a law passed in that year. Its right to do so directly, however, has never been challenged or relinquished.

5. "The Congress, the Executive, and the Court must each for itself be guided by its own opinion of the Constitution," said Andrew Jackson, in his message vetoing the bill to charter the second Bank of the United States.

The provisions of the Constitution might have prevented, but of themselves they could not have guaranteed, an independent footing for the three branches. Independence in practice required a mutual restraint on the part of the officers of government in each of the three modes; and such restraint could rest for long only on a general public approval of the structural relations—only, that is to say, on a living, active tradition. This restraint and this approving tradition marked our national history through 1933, within which term the general comments of this chapter are limited. Indeed, the sense of the nation proved stricter than the intentions of the Fathers.

The Constitution had, for example, offered the device of impeachment as a potential means for destroying the independence of either the executive or the judiciary. In practice, under the pressures of national opinion, the resort to impeachment has been so sparing that it has failed even of its intended effect as a method of correcting gross fraud or misconduct. When Thomas Jefferson and his Republicans ousted the Federalists from control of the executive and Congress, they had expected to use impeachment proceedings in order to purge the courts so that they might appoint new judges from their own ranks.

> Jefferson's supporters were inclined to take an extremely broad view of the impeachment power. By the more partisan Republicans impeachment was considered a proper instrument for removing from office judges who had fallen too far out of step with public opinion. This conception made impeachment purely a political proceeding in which any judge could be removed from office should both the House and the Senate think it expedient to do so.[6]

After the confused affair of Judge John Pickering, who turned out to be insane, the test case came in the 1805 impeachment of

6. Alfred H. Kelly & Winfred A. Harbison, *The American Constitution* (New York: Norton & Co., 1955), p. 232.

Supreme Court Justice Samuel Chase, which was voted by the House and tried before the Senate (Vice President Aaron Burr presiding), and which there fell short of the necessary two-thirds vote. "It was generally recognized both in the presentation of the evidence and in the arguments of the case that the vital issue concerned the proper scope of impeachment under the Constitution. . . . Failure convinced Jefferson and many of his supporters that impeachment was 'a bungling way of removing Judges,' 'a farce which will not be tried again.' "[7] And in fact, the result in 1805 led to the abandonment of impeachment as a political weapon against the judiciary.

Similarly, the impeachment proceedings against President Andrew Johnson in 1868, though under the fiercely partisan circumstances they failed by only a single vote, both expressed and consolidated the nation's traditional support of executive independence. As for the insistence on congressional independence (where impeachment is not applicable), we may note how the "strongest" and most popular Presidents have failed—even in these late years of disrupted traditions—to persuade the electorate to purge Congressmen for having excited executive displeasure.

Self-evidently, the three branches of the government cannot be altogether and merely independent. If so, they would be simply three different governments. They are inter-related in a complex and ever shifting equilibrium, wherein each continually rises or falls in the relative power scale. Justice Robert Jackson described the equilibrium in a decision[8] that blocked one attempt to abolish it:

> The actual art of governing under our Constitution does not
> and cannot conform to judicial definitions of the power of any
> of its branches based on isolated clauses or even single articles

7. *Ibid.*, pp. 234–5.
8. Youngstown Sheet & Tube Co. *v.* Sawyer, by which the Court overruled President Truman's seizure of the steel companies.

torn from context. While the Constitution diffuses power the better to secure liberty, it also contemplates that practice will integrate the dispersed powers into a workable government. It enjoins upon its branches separateness but interdependence, autonomy but reciprocity.

3

There is nothing remarkable in the inevitable fact that the elements of the government are inter-related. What is distinctive and astonishing in the American tradition is the degree to which they have been able to maintain, for so many generations and through so many periods of social crisis, war and economic panic, a real as well as formal independence. An account of the principal branches of our governmental structure would be inadequate if it rested with the three-part division formally established by the Constitution. In historical practice a fourth branch of the government has developed; and a fifth, though non-governmental in origin, has been grafted onto the main governmental trunk.

The fourth branch is the permanent *bureaucracy.*

The only governmental officials directly provided by the Constitution itself are the members of Congress, the President and Vice President, the members (the number being left for statutory determination) of the Supreme Court, and "Ambassadors, other public Ministers and Consuls." All other offices are established by congressional statute. From a formal standpoint, the governmental bureaucracy that thus comes into being is not considered to be a separate branch of the government, but merely the extension, "the arm" of the executive. According to the Jacksonian conception of the Constitution, the President is constitutionally responsible for the entire executive establishment, and it is he who is acting and speaking through his Cabinet, the bureau chiefs and their subordinates, and through the military hierarchy. This theory rests on the contention that the Constitution vests "the executive Power" in the President alone, and charges him to "take care that the Laws be faithfully executed." It follows that every member of the bureaucracy, from top to bottom, holds office by will of the President, and is subject to immediate dismissal by the President with or without cause.

The contrary theory has been that Congress, by the statutes establishing each office, may impose whatever conditions it chooses about qualifications, duties, term of office and mode of dismissal, and may take steps to assure itself that these conditions are met. These two views have been in frequent practical conflict from June 1789 on. It may be added that the Supreme Court managed to avoid taking direct sides with respect to them until 1926, and that its pro-executive decision of that year (Myers v. United States) was quickly counterbalanced in part by an opposing decision (Humphrey v. United States, 1935).

Both views agree that the bureaucracy—the administrative apparatus of the government—is, in general, part of the executive branch; and both agree that in establishing the various offices by statute, Congress has the right to define duties, qualifications and mode of appointment. Most of the specific disputes have arisen over the executive's right of dismissal and the legislature's right to satisfy itself that a particular officer fulfills the law as the legislature understands it.

This traditional conflict is a phase of the wider conflict between the executive and legislative branches of our government—a conflict, foreseen and intended by the Fathers, which so long as our traditional structure of government endures will never be finally settled. The President and Congress contend for control over the governmental bureaucracy. Is the bureaucracy "the arm of the President" or "the creature of Congress"?

Meanwhile, however, over the course of our history the bureaucracy gradually achieved a status of its own, and thereby became more and more independent of both the contending constitutional branches.

When there were only a few hundred government employees, the President and his Cabinet members could be personally acquainted with most of them. There was a fairly direct sense in which they could be regarded as only the administrative extension of the Chief Executive. Even when there were some thousands, the whip of the Spoils System could keep the bureaucracy closely in line with the executive will. But the bureaucracy came to number hundreds of thousands and then millions. It took on hundreds of technical and continuing functions in the life of the nation. Beginning in 1887 it came to include the permanent semi-legislative, semi-judicial "administrative tribunals" such as the Interstate Commerce Commission, Federal Trade Commission, Federal Power Commission and Federal Communications Commission. Most decisive of all, the Civil Service Act of 1883 together with its subsequent extensions applied the principles of a permanent professional civil service to all but the upper ("policy-making") levels. Through these developments, the main body of the bureaucracy has acquired an autonomous social reality of its own, its own momentum, its own will and interests which are not identical with the will and interests of either Congress or the President.

In theory there has been no constitutional change. The bureaucracy remains formally as it was, operating under the laws of Congress by the administrative direction of the President. In theory the President exercises his administrative will through his Cabinet members and other policy-making officials, not subject to civil service, whom he appoints and dismisses just as he sees fit, subject to Senate confirmation.[9] But in practice the President cannot possibly

9. Congress has never named fixed terms by statute for department heads and other high policy-making officials (outside of the administrative agencies); and has never in practice tried to interfere in their dismissal on administrative grounds by the President, although defenders of congressional predominance have claimed the right to do so in the case of all officials whose appointment requires Senate confirmation.

maintain close control over such a vast number of diversely occupied persons, ninety per cent of them protected from sharp discipline by both law and custom. Even on major issues it has in recent times become difficult to determine when a President (under the law or beyond it) has commanded the bureaucracy to carry out this or that policy, and when the bureaucracy has, almost insensibly sometimes, imposed a policy on the President.

The development of the bureaucracy into a fourth branch of the government is not of itself counter to the broad pattern of the American tradition. True enough, the Founding Fathers did not foresee it, and it is outside of the words of the Constitution. But a partially independent professional bureaucracy, sharing in the sum of governmental power and able to stand on its own political feet, is in accord with the principle of the diffusion of sovereignty. A sturdy bureaucracy might, in fact, be an effective prop to that principle.

It could be argued that in a sense that does not apply to the other three branches, the bureaucracy is politically irresponsible. Its actual role is not explicitly covered by law or charter; being permanent, it is not compelled to undergo a periodic confrontation of the voters. However, in this respect the judiciary is even more irresponsible; and the American system, as we have stressed, is not based on direct democracy or any facsimile thereof. Congress and the President (and the courts where relevant) have sufficient means to check and counterbalance even today's bureaucracy, if they chose to use them.

If the bureaucracy swells in relative power to a level from which it is able to challenge, even dominate, the other branches, then of course the American tradition will have been violated, and the American system of government will be in mortal danger. Since the mid-1930's that level has been closely approached.[10]

10. In this discussion of the bureaucracy I have not held to the 1933 limit that I earlier set for the purpose of describing certain features of the American political tradition. The most spectacular rise of the bureaucracy in both numbers and power has been since that date. However, from at least as early as the Civil

4

If we seek to analyze the actual rather than the merely formal structure of the American government, we must add to our account a fifth branch, or semi-branch: the organized lobbies. No mention of "lobbies" is to be found in the Constitution, nor does any statute declare them to be a governmental unit. Nevertheless they have over the course of time come to function as an active part of the American government in operation. The Federal Registration of Lobbying Act of 1946, generalizing bills enacted from 1935 on,[11] is an implicit legal recognition of their governmental role.

Within every nation the spokesmen for various interests hover around the seat of government in order to influence its deliberations and acts. But in no other nation has this natural practice become so extensive, so systematized, and so integrally related to the whole process of governing. Professor Henry Steele Commager speaks of lobbyists as at work even in pre-Constitutional America: "The immediate impulse for the Ordinance of 1787 came from a group of land speculators, members of the Ohio Company of Associates and of the Society of the Cincinnati, who wished to establish colonies in the Ohio country. The spokesmen for these groups were the Rev. Manasseh Cutler, Samuel Parsons, and General Rufus Putnam. These men succeeded in lobbying through a moribund Congress the famous Ordinance establishing a government in the Northwest territory."[12] Charles Beard popularized the idea that half of the members of the Philadelphia Convention itself were, in effect, lobbyists for the speculators in land and depreciated government paper.

Service Act (1887) the bureaucracy was beginning to function as a "fourth branch." (See further, Chapter XI, Section 2.)

11. In the states, regulation of lobbying began in the 1870's.

12. *Documents of American History,* edited by Henry Steele Commager (New York: Appleton-Century-Crofts, 1949), p. 128.

Since the term "lobbying" was not introduced into the language until 1829,[13] this may be jumping the gun by a generation or two, but in any case the American lobbying system had begun to emerge in its distinctive shape well before the Civil War. With the railroad lobbies of the late 19th century it started a still uninterrupted period of flourishing growth.

The registered lobbies include nearly all significant interest groups of the nation: industrial, financial, trade-union, religious, veterans, racial, and so on; special associations formed for particular purposes—prohibition, tax reduction, disarmament and what not; and many minor groups formed, through enthusiasm or money, for eccentric or episodic purposes. The representatives of the lobbies are for the most part physically located, along with Congress, the President, the Supreme Court and the bulk of the bureaucracy, in or near the District of Columbia.

The lobbies become widely publicized, as a rule, through scandalous or near-scandalous behavior: contributions to campaign funds; spectacular parties; indirect handouts to Congressmen or bureaucrats; mink and vicuña coats. In routine fact the lobbyists are daily and intimately active in the processes that result in laws passed or rejected, government contracts let or hindered, policies pushed or forgotten. They are testifying before congressional committees as well as wining and dining individual Congressmen, advising bureau chiefs on technical and market problems as well as playing golf with them. As the American government actually works, it is thought entirely normal, and neither scandalous nor odd, that the text of a law on veterans' pensions should have been prepared by the American Legion; that the American Medical Association should be consulted on a Health Act, or the American Federation of Labor as well as the National Association of Manufacturers on the wording of amendments to a labor relations law; that represen-

13. According to Dr. Karl Schriftgiesser in his book, *The Lobbyists* (Boston: Little, Brown, 1951).

tatives of the aircraft manufacturers should advise the Pentagon on bomber design.

Like the bureaucracy, the lobbies are suspended between the legislature and the executive, and Dr. George B. Galloway includes both in what he calls a "Third Chamber." Unlike the bureaucracy, however, the lobbies have their roots deep in the organized life of the community, and thus constitute a specifically representative and responsible institution.

> Congress represents the people on a territorial basis, whereas the lobby represents them on a functional basis, according to their occupations as members of organized groups. . . . It has become increasingly difficult for a member of Congress to represent all the varied interests of his constituents, and so other representatives have been added in the "Third Chamber." . . . The Third Chamber, *i.e.,* the lobby, has now become a respectable institution. It participates in the legislative process. . . . It collaborates with the executive branch.[14]

In spite of all the abuse that has for so long been heaped on the lobbies, their place in the traditional American system cannot be questioned. It is fully sanctioned by time, for the lobbies in one or another form have always been with us. Their significant share in the governing process is a creative application of the basic principle of the diffusion of sovereignty.

5

Within the American system, then, sovereignty—governmental power—is divided (unequally of course) between the central gov-

14. George B. Galloway, *The Legislative Process in Congress* (New York: Thomas Y. Crowell, 1953), pp. 496–7. Dr. Galloway apparently believes that the bureaucracy is also representative, and speaks "for the public interest and the common man." These two entities are very hard to identify in practice.

ernment and the state governments; and the share of sovereignty possessed by the central government is in turn diffused among the five major branches: legislature, executive, judiciary, bureaucracy, lobbies. If we consider social power quite generally rather than sovereignty in a limited sense, we find it to be further divided between the governmental structure and what the Tenth Amendment calls "the people"—that is, the inhabitants of the nation considered in their non-governmental aspects. In those aspects also the principle of division and diffusion of power holds. American society has always been characterized by an unprecedented plurality and diversity of "interest groups," each with a share in the sum of social power.

We speak of Church and Business and Labor and Agriculture. In reality there are churches, not a Church, each with some independent power and influence, each separate from the state and separate in organizational life from the others. And so with business, the trade-unions, the varied and diverse farm associations. The American tradition has favored the autonomy, the diversity, and even the clash of these groups. It has resisted their absorption or domination by government; and it has resisted also the tendency of any one of them to become so singly powerful as to threaten to dominate the others.

We may add also that American political parties have developed as another mechanism for maintaining the diffusion of power. Unlike the parties of most countries with parliamentary governments, our parties have never been, except episodically, strict ideological or class organizations—labor or monarchist or landlord, socialist, peasant, communist, industrialist or fascist. They have been loose, shifting coalitions of many geographical regions and interest groups that join on a limited basis for the practical purposes of conducting elections and forming a government. Each party always contains elements from all social levels. Within the parties, as within the government and the society as a whole, power is divided and diffused. Candidates are the resultant of negotiated compromise. The victory of a party in a national election is never an unequivocal "mandate" whereby a cohesive majority is in a position to impose its will on the minority, and to take full charge of the nation in the service of a particular class or ideology.

The Founding Fathers deplored parties (or "factions," as they called them), and hoped that the country would be preserved from them. In actuality the parties, once they began to develop in the distinctively American manner, became guardians of the principles of the Fathers: guarantors of the diffusion of power, and a stalwart defense against the unrestrained plebiscitary democracy which the Fathers judged to be the greatest of all political dangers.

6

We now expand somewhat the earlier description of the conservative and liberal syndromes as these have been manifest in the United States.[15]

The conservative syndrome, we have seen, includes: a belief that a non-rational (providential) factor is involved in government, together with a correlative distrust in abstract political ideology; a belief that human nature is both tarnished and limited, along with a correlative distrust in ultimate solutions; a respect for tradition.

To these symptoms we may add:

(d) a belief in "the diffusion of sovereignty" and the still wider principle of "the diffusion of power";

(e) a rejection of unrestricted plebiscitary democracy in favor of a representative form of government in which a variety of indirect institutions mediate the popular will;

(f) a specific belief in "states' rights": that is, the retention by the states of an effective share in the sovereignty;

(g) a specific belief in the maintenance of the autonomy of the various branches of the central government against encroachment or usurpation by any one of them.

15. See pp. 35—36.

We noted as elements of the liberal syndrome: a confidence in the ability of rational science to comprehend and solve all problems of government, combined with acceptance of democratist ideology; a belief in the unlimited potential of human nature; an unwillingness to accept tradition as a ground for favoring an institution or mode of conduct.

We now add:

(d') a conviction that the principle of the diffusion of power, though useful against "reactionary forces," loses much of its cogency if the power concentration is into the hands of a beneficent social entity (the common man, the people, workers and farmers), and may be waived altogether in the interests of certain ideological goals (full employment, racial equality, social welfare, peace);

(e') a tendency to approve plebiscitary democracy, and to seek governmental forms that will express the majority will as directly and intimately as possible (direct popular vote for President, direct primaries, initiative and recall, popular referendum, election of judges, extension of suffrage, etc.);

(f') a feeling that state sovereignty is either unimportant (an anachronism) or actually injurious through promoting inefficiency and lending itself to reactionary manipulation (pro-segregation, anti-labor, anti-internationalism, etc.);

(g') a belief that the traditional autonomy of the separate branches of the central government hinders it from dealing adequately with the crisis problems of the modern epoch.

V

POWER AND LIMITS

I T WOULD surely be wrong to suggest that the prime object of the Founding Fathers was to work out devices by which to dilute the power of the central government. They came together at Philadelphia not to get rid of a tyrannical government (which they had done, as they saw it, some years before, by means more direct than a convention), but to acquire a strong one: strong enough, that is, for their purposes. They objected to the Continental Congress as a danger to liberty, but a danger because of its weakness, not its power. As James Wilson explained it: "Bad governments are of two sorts,—first, that which does too little; secondly, that which does too much; that which fails through weakness, and that which destroys through oppression." The central government of the newly independent states had been of the first sort, not the second.

Experience had shown the Fathers the exact points at which Congress, acting under the Articles of Confederation, was too weak to carry out those functions of government that they deemed necessary and proper. They came to Philadelphia, therefore, with precise views already formed about the additional powers that they were disposed to grant.

The government under the Confederacy could not provide securely for the common defense. It did not have a standing army ready to act on command, and could assemble a military force only slowly and ineffectively by a call, which it had no power to enforce, on the individual states. Its inability to guarantee the common defense rested on political as much as on military weakness. It could not speak with confidence in negotiating treaties with foreign powers, nor enforce them once they were signed. It could not prevent individual states from carrying on intrigues of their own with foreign powers, or even fighting their own wars. Many of the Fathers were convinced that without a change in the government's structure and power, independence would be lost by such European exploitation of state rivalries as had already been attempted in Vermont and the South.

England, after losing the War of Independence, had strung out the treaty negotiations, got better final terms than the military outcome would normally have dictated, and had then, after the treaty was signed, blithely ignored provisions that stood in the way of her interests. Both French and British were ignoring the rights of the United States in the Northwest Territory. The lower Mississippi valley, contended for by France and Spain, was an acute present danger as well as a tempting possibility. Relations, warlike or peaceful, with the Indian tribes, many of them in the pay of the European nations, were snarled by both the excesses and the defects of the states.

As for domestic tranquillity, the outlook seemed equally shaky, with Shays' Rebellion climaxing East Coast disturbances, the unpaid veterans threatening trouble in many localities, and many of the frontier regions inclined toward anarchy.

Under the Articles, Congress was unable to establish a uniform currency and a sound fiscal system, both essential, as the Fathers saw things, to the general welfare. Congress could not levy taxes, but only make unenforceable requisitions on the states. It could not pay its bills or the debt already contracted. Neither at home nor abroad could it secure the new credits that were desperately needed.

It had neither the police force nor the courts to expound and enforce the laws; it could not guarantee any individual rights of citizens, nor even a republican form of government in the several states.

Nor was Congress, under the Articles, able to undertake either positive act or negative sanction to promote the general welfare, which was in any case continuously jeopardized by the absence of a sound fiscal system. The commerce of states without good harbors was taxed and squeezed by their more fortunate neighbors: as New Jersey by New York and Pennsylvania, North Carolina by Virginia and South Carolina, Connecticut by Rhode Island. Ships at sea were not protected from the arbitrary laws of foreign powers, impressment of sailors, and seizure of cargoes. The roads were poor and the postal service unreliable.

It was seen that the public debt, rendered so sacred by the cause in which it had been incurred, remained without any provision for its payment. The reiterated and elaborate efforts of Congress to procure from the States a more adequate power to raise the means of payment, had failed. The effect of the ordinary requisitions of Congress had only displayed the inefficiency of the authority making them, none of the States having duly complied with them. . . . The want of authority in Congress to regulate commerce had produced in foreign nations, particularly in Great Britain, a monopolizing policy, injurious to the trade of the United States, and destructive to their navigation; the imbecility, and anticipated dissolution, of the Confederacy extinguishing all apprehensions of a countervailing policy on the part of the United States. The same want of a general power over commerce led to an exercise of the power, separately, by the States, which not only proved abortive, but engendered rival, conflicting and angry regulations. . . . The States having ports for foreign commerce, taxed and irritated the adjoining States, trading through them. . . . In sundry instances, as of New York, New Jersey, Pennsylvania and Maryland, the navigation laws treated the citizens of other States as aliens. In certain cases the authority of the Confederacy was disregarded, as in violation, not only of the Treaty of Peace [with England], but of treaties with France and Holland; which were complained of to Congress. In other cases the Federal authority was violated by treaties and wars with Indians, as by Georgia; by troops raised and kept up without the consent of Congress, as by Massachusetts; by compacts without the consent of Congress. . . . In the internal administration of the States, a violation of contracts had become familiar. . . . Among the defects which had been severely felt was want of an uniformity in cases requiring it, as laws of naturalization and bankruptcy, a coercive authority operating on individuals, and a guarantee of the internal tranquillity of the States.

As a natural consequence of this distracted and disheartening condition of the Union, the Federal authority had ceased to be respected abroad, and dispositions were shown there, particularly in Great Britain, to take advantage of its imbecility, and to speculate on its approaching downfall. . . . Those least partial to popular government, or most distrustful of its efficacy, were yielding to anticipations, that from an increase in the confusion a government might result more congenial with their taste or their opinions; whilst those most devoted to the principles and forms of Republics were alarmed for the cause of liberty itself, at stake in the American experiment. . . . It was known that there were individuals who had betrayed a bias towards monarchy. . . . The idea of dismemberment had recently made its appearance in the newspapers.

Such were the defects, the deformities, the diseases and the ominous prospects, for which the Convention were to provide a remedy, and which ought never to be overlooked in expounding and appreciating the constitutional charter, the remedy that was provided.[1]

How much power did the new government possess? Enough: enough to carry out the intended duties, and an ample reserve to

1. From an essay found in rough handwritten draft among James Madison's papers, and printed as the preface to his journal of the Convention.

meet the unfolding problems of a history that could not be anticipated in detail. The central government of the United States has
never lacked sufficient power to fulfill any task that could be brought
within the limits of constitutional propriety. The government has
been able to preserve the union against the smashing blows of civil
war as well as against intrigue, corruption, and the centrifugal pull
of vast and distant frontiers. It has successfully provided for the common defense against the pricks of marauding bands or the might of
the greatest world powers. It has secured the blessings of liberty and
justice, not with ideal perfection, which is beyond the attainment of
any government or any society, but as firmly as any government that
men have constructed, and more widely than any other. Within its
jurisdiction and under the conditions of life there sustained, the
general welfare has been promoted to a level beyond even the
dreams of any other society.

It might seem that to say that the American government has had
"enough" power is to say nothing: if it has in fact survived, then it
has self-evidently had enough power to survive. But the meaning
includes more than this mere tautology. Actually, for a government
even to survive for more than a century and a half is a formidable
political achievement. There are very few governments, present or
past, that have beaten this temporal record. There are, and have
been, many nations with much longer life-spans than that of the
United States, but only a handful of governments.

The government of the United States that existed in 1933 was
recognizably the same government that came into existence in
1789. It was not identical in all respects, of course. All beings that
endure through time, whether institutions or individual organisms,
change, and grow or decay; the man is not the same as the child.
But as the man develops out of the child without any breach in essential continuity, so had the American government of 1933 developed from the government established by the Fathers. The initial
framework and structure were still intact, however broadly enlarged; the great principles stated in the Constitution and bodied in

the living tradition had been stretched and adapted but not violated or broken.

Moreover, this government in fact accomplished the purposes for which it had been founded, and which continued to be accepted by the citizens living under it as the proper purposes of government.

We can see how rare this record is if we compare it to that of the nations of Central and South America. These too came into being by rebellion against European powers. But in not a single case has the government that issued out of the struggle for independence survived. In every one of these nations, and in some every few years, there have been revolutions and counter-revolutions, coups and assassinations, constitutions made and unmade, dictatorships and anarchy, elections held and suspended. Although some of the governments possessed by some of these nations have seemed for a while very strong, and some have been served by wise and honorable men, not one of them has ever had power enough to assure for any length of time a stable union, to establish justice, insure domestic tranquillity, promote the general welfare or secure the blessings of liberty; and they have precariously provided for the common defense only because the government of the United States had reinsured it. Nor have their governments ever for long fulfilled any different or lesser purposes in terms of which their citizens might have defined a government's function.

These Latin American nations and their governments are not exceptional, but rather instances of a political rule that has few exceptions on any continent. China or Spain, India and France and Germany, Italy or Java or Siam or Iraq, Russia and Poland and Palestine—none of them has found an enduring form of government strong and flexible enough to defend the nation and at the same time enable it to achieve the purposes of political life as these are in each case understood. In all of these and almost all other nations, the course of government is breached by gulfs that are not bridged but leapt across. Constitutions are not amended but abolished; basic institutions are not adapted but annihilated; not merely rulers but the kind of rule is shifted. Even in Britain of the past two centuries, the reduction of the Crown to a ceremonial function, the great Reform Bills of the 19th century, the abolition of the power of the House of Lords at the beginning of this century, the rise and disintegration of the imperial system, introduce gaps much beyond anything to be found in the history of the United States.

The defect of power is more common than the surface appearance suggests: because political power is not a mere matter of physical strength, brutality or easy triggers. The government of the French Fourth Republic weighed on the nation like a bureaucratic pyramid; but it was not strong enough to suppress an alien-directed internal conspiracy publicly vowed to treason, nor to sustain a consistent foreign policy, nor to defend the nation's possessions, nor even to collect taxes. Franco's government has looked strong enough in its police and military and censorial wrappings, but it has not been able to maintain political conditions under which Spaniards can get enough to eat. It took only small mobs and a few deaths to topple the bristling Venezuelan dictatorship of Pérez Jiménez. The Soviet government looks stronger than any other that has ever been, but concentration camps, purges, Yugoslavia and Hungary all prove it unable to preserve domestic tranquillity.

The government of the United States has survived without abrupt or essential constitutional change, with a continuous political structure and basic law. Even its civil war, one of history's most bitter, was fought (by both sides) under and for the sake of the Constitution and the political structure in which the Constitution was historically embodied. And the government of the United States has done what it was supposed to do. If it did not always do perfectly what it had to do, the Fathers and their political descendants did not expect perfection from human government. If it did not always act as quickly as this or that impatient group of citizens might have wished, the Fathers never said or implied that speed was an important political virtue. On the contrary, indeed: a whole set of brakes was built into the structure—though there were also provisions, some of them without prior example, for emergency action if it really came to an emergency. Through the remarkable device of the autonomous Executive, there could even be, as in the Roman Republic, a temporary dictatorship, if a dictator really were needed, without any break in legal continuity.

The historical record prior to 1933 offers no evidence of any lack of relevant power in the American government—power relevant, that is to say, to the proper functions of government as these have been understood in the American tradition. Granted that tradition, the record will not support the argument that basic structural changes in the American system of government are needed to enable it to attain the ends of government. This argument can be motivated only by stepping outside of the American tradition and projecting as the goals of government something different from what Americans have traditionally accepted or assumed the goals to be. It is not an argument against an automobile that it can't dig potatoes.

2

Although the American government has had, from its beginning, great power—and enough power, that power has been circumscribed, limited. Among the other governments of the world, past and contemporary, it is the limits rather than the power that are the more extraordinary. Chief Justice John Marshall, who did as much as any man to affirm the amplitude of the new government's power, insisted no less sternly on that power's circumscription: "We must admit, as all must admit, that the powers of the government are limited, and that its limits are not to be transcended."[2]

The traditional American idea, shared by the Fathers, has been that our government came into existence through, and only through, an explicit compact, or contract: the document, namely,

2. McCulloch *v.* Maryland.

that we call "The Constitution of the United States." The government that began operations in 1789 (or 1788, if we consider the election of the Congress and Presidential electors as its first operation) was a new-born being that did not exist before then, just as a business corporation does not exist before its charter is issued. Of course the new government was not in all respects novel or unique. Those men who had created it through formulating and accepting the compact had drawn on their own past and on others' experience for the materials that they were shaping. But in their conception the new government had not "evolved" or "developed" out of any preceding government.[3] It was not a child; it had no parent; metaphysically it was a creation *ex nihilo.*

It may be granted that this traditional account of the origin of our government is in some degree mythical. In historical fact the new government could not start *de novo*. It had threads linking it to the government under the Articles, which was in turn not wholly discontinuous with the British government. In strict compact theory, there would be no valid laws except those contained in the compact itself or enacted according to the procedures which it laid down. In practice this would have meant a judicial vacuum. In rendering decisions the newly established courts drew on colonial, British and even Roman law to fill in the post-Constitutional statutes.

To call the compact theory mythical is neither to dismiss nor to denigrate it. All theories of government, we have already observed,

---

3. Not even out of the government of the United States that had existed under the Articles of Confederation. The Philadelphia Convention was called to amend the Articles, but instead the delegates replaced them by an entirely new Constitution. From a formal point of view they could conceivably have offered the new compact as an amendment to the Articles. But they wanted to insist on the separate creation of the new government. That is why, also, they provided that ratification was to be by conventions of "the people," not by the state legislatures: thus the new government would not have "evolved" out of the states. And this is why the Constitution itself had to re-validate (in Article VI) the treaties already "made" by the *different* government that existed under the Articles.

are at least partly myths. These myths are able both to express and to organize reality. The citizens of the new nation saw themselves as having come to a voluntary agreement on a contract that set up and defined a common government for their joint society, and prescribed the duties and boundaries of that government. They made much of "the important distinction so well understood in America [but] little understood and less observed in any other country . . . between a Constitution established by the people and unalterable by the government, and a law established by the government and alterable by the government."[4]

Thus the prime limit on the power of the American government (as well as its first and only license) is the compact, the Constitution itself. The social scientists of this century have painstakingly proved that this idea, also, is an illusion. A verbal document has no fixed meaning, they explain. By semantic osmosis its text can be transformed over the years to mean whatever we choose to have it mean. And in American practice, it has come to mean whatever the Supreme Court says that it means.

That words alter their meaning, that sentences can be stretched to cover what was never in the minds of those who formulated them, that principles apply differently in a different age: these are obvious enough truths, doubted by few men of common sense, and well known certainly to the Founding Fathers when they wrote the Constitution. It is easy, however, to overplay their significance. The New Testament may not mean today exactly what it was interpreted to mean nineteen hundred years ago, but we can hardly conclude that Christianity would be the same if its accepted Book had been, instead, the Upanishads, the Koran, the Tao, or the Communist Manifesto.

James Madison would be astonished at the content of some Supreme Court decisions of the past two decades or at the listings in a mid-20th century Federal Budget. Still, he would not be altogether

4. *Federalist*, No. 53.

disoriented on a voyage to our day. Indeed, if the Fathers should return they would find the institutional structure of the government to be the one recognizable feature of the historical landscape.

Automobiles, big cities, electronics, aircraft, automated factories, household gadgets would all be quite beyond their comprehension. But the same two Houses of the same Congress, their members elected still for the periods originally prescribed, would be legislating in much the same old way. William Paterson or George Cabot, Thomas Benton, John C. Calhoun or Daniel Webster would be less at a loss in entering today's Congress than the average just elected freshman. Even the topics of debate and dispute would often be familiar. Already during Congress' first three sessions the perennial arguments had begun over the treaty power, executive secrecy, investigations, the power of removal, tight credit, foreign entanglements.

They would discover the chief of state to be still a President, named by an electoral college. The judiciary would still be headed by a Supreme Court, a little larger in numbers and housed in much fancier quarters. The states, though much altered, would not have disappeared, their governors and assemblies and courts and police would still be at hand. They would find no Church establishment and no titled aristocracy. Trial would still be by a jury of fellow-citizens.

They would note their Constitution still proclaimed the basic law of the land, with only a handful of short amendments, all duly introduced according to the original plan. They would search for many a day before finding a citizen ready to argue openly that the nation ought to act counter to the plain sense of its provisions.

Launched on the river of time, a structure of words does in truth become a flexible craft—and otherwise could not long endure. But this flexibility is itself held within limits established by the keel and master braces: at least, it is held within limits unless the crew decides to scuttle ship.

3

The diffusion of sovereignty, with the division of the government into branches both independent and overlapping, is a continuous and automatic brake on the power of the central government. In the past the tendency of any one branch to acquire undue power has always been slowed and in the end checked by the counter-drag of the other branches. As a power machine, the American system of government is so designed as to be incapable of operating at a high level of efficiency for any length of time. The officials manning the different parts of the apparatus are not only different individuals; they are selected by different methods at different times, and serve for different periods, with different guarantees and sanctions. It is as if an elaborate vehicle had been constructed in which the motive power were derived from a combination of horses, foot pedals, internal combustion engine and electric motor. The likelihood would be small that all the diverse sources of energy would harmoniously push for long in a single direction.

The inefficiency of the American system of government is of course a virtue, not a defect, from the point of view of the American tradition. Except to meet the most acute sort of crisis, and not wholly even then, the government is not supposed to be able to harness and concentrate the full social power of the nation. The greater part of that power is conceived to lie outside the realm of government. Even the share allocated to government is deliberately dissipated by the system's complex design.

For the central government to acquire and wield power beyond all limits that could be reconciled with the tradition, and thus potentially all-power (that is, totalitarian power), the states would have to be reduced not merely to junior units (as they were by the Civil War) but to impotence. All branches of the central government—bureaucracy and functioning lobbies as well as the formal constitutional branches—would have to be brought under the control of a single social force.[5] The members or puppets of one organized group (party, conspiracy, cabal or however called), disciplined in both action and ideology, with a unified general strategy, would have to man the Presidency, both Houses of Congress, the Supreme Court, the controlling sectors of the civil and military bureaucracy, and the major lobbies (if lobbies continued to exist). This development is conceivable, certainly, and more readily today than in 1933. A comparable situation has come about in other nations during this century. The radical transformation of traditional American attitudes that it presupposes lies in the same direction as the actual shift that has taken place since 1933.

However, apart from a molecular social drift, the political structure of the United States makes it exceedingly hard from a sheer technical standpoint to weld the governmental fractions into a single power instrument. The loose, amorphous coalitions that Americans have developed as their chosen political parties do not qualify, even potentially, for the kind of disciplined political organization that is required to carry the job through. Even if there were such an organization—whether majority or minority backed—it would be most difficult for it to gain simultaneous and enduring control of the diverse branches. There is no way to get the multiple control at the same moment, and American history shows that by the time the Court is taken over, Congress or one House of Congress will very likely be lost; the Presidency can change content quickly, but not the bureaucracy; a captured Congress can be countered by the surviving judges.

---

5. Assuming, that is, that the outward form of the traditional system of government were kept intact. The same result could be achieved more directly by destroying the form of government—by an overt instead of a hidden political revolution.

4

The power of the central government has also been curbed by a doctrine of "natural rights" that is implicit in the original Constitution, developed in the first ten amendments, and established through our history by statute, court decisions and social practice. It should be stressed that this doctrine, as originally understood, is a limitation on government, not an extension of the tasks, powers or duties of government.

In the prevailing view of the Fathers, most of the basic civil rights—freedom of religion, speech, press, assembly, petition, the freedom to bear arms, the freedom from arbitrary arrest, imprisonment and punishment—are not created by the government, by the Constitution or by statutes enacted under the Constitution.[6] These rights inhere in the individual citizen by ordinance of "nature" or of God.[7] In order that they should exist it was not necessary for the Constitution to name them. And in fact the original Constitution as

---

6. This statement does not hold for all civic and social rights. Although freedom from arbitrary arrest and imprisonment was believed to be a "natural" and thus extra-Constitutional right, the specific right to a trial by jury under certain circumstances, as the means for implementing the natural right, is not derived from nature but only from explicit definition in the Constitution, with further development in Amendments V-VIII, XIII, XIV and XIX.

7. Tracing the origin of rights to "nature" reflects a philosophic tradition dating back to Stoicism, with its doctrine of Nature as the embodiment of Universal Reason. 18th-century Deism, which influenced a number of the Fathers, often used the Stoic terminology. In terms of a personalist theology, the rights may be understood as decreed ultimately by God. However, the difference between these two views, so far as it exists metaphysically, is irrelevant to political theory. The key problem is whether the basic rights of men are mere social sanctions, subject to and modifiable by the changing decisions of political and social institutions; or whether these rights are (as a "natural" or "God-given" doctrine of rights maintains) metaphysically prior to social institutions, and therefore "absolute" in relation to society. From the latter belief it follows that their denial is not government but tyranny.

it issued from the Philadelphia Convention did not name them: not because the delegates did not believe in them but because they assumed their validity, Constitution or no Constitution—though not in the extreme and unconditional form upheld by the ideologues of civil liberty.

Moreover the first ten amendments (the misnamed "Bill of Rights") did not—except in the special case of jury trial and related judicial procedure—"establish" the civic rights, or even call on the government to proclaim and protect them. These amendments merely state certain prohibitions, certain injunctions about what the central government *may not* do. "Congress shall make no law respecting an establishment of religion, or prohibiting the free exercise thereof; or abridging the freedom of speech. . . . The right of the people to keep and bear Arms, shall not be infringed. . . . The right of the people to be secure in their persons, houses, papers, and effects . . . shall not be violated. . . ."

These rights, in short, are limits, not powers.

In the course of time this early conception has been, first subtly and then more grossly, changed. With the spread of materialist, pragmatic and relativist philosophies, the rights came to be looked on by many not as sprung from God or nature but as changing products of the legislature, executive, courts and public opinion. The central government, in all its branches, has come to consider that, since these rights issue from its existence and acts, it has the function of clarifying, expanding and enforcing its own interpretation of them, even though that interpretation may go counter to the conviction of the individual citizen or of the local community and state.

The practical relation of civil rights to government has thus been in part reversed. Instead of operating as limitations on the power of government, they are on occasion accepted as authorizations or grants of additional governmental power over the daily affairs of citizens. The ironic result is that the enforcement of civil rights becomes an instrument not of liberty but of despotism. However, this reversal is not yet complete, and the older doctrine of rights still continues, intermittently, to perform its limiting function.

The ninth and tenth amendments, though contributing nothing of specific substance to the constitutional plan, are an unequivocal expression of the theory of limited, bounded governmental power from which the Fathers proceeded:

IX. The enumeration in the Constitution, of certain rights, shall not be construed to deny or disparage others retained by the people.

X. The powers not delegated to the United States by the Constitution, nor prohibited by it to the States, are reserved to the States respectively, or to the people.

VI

PUBLIC AND PRIVATE

I N THE AMERICAN political system the accumulation of power by the central government has been further limited by what might be called *localization*. Localization of one type or another is provided by specific clauses of the Constitution, but our traditional practice has made it far more pervasive in our political life that the Constitution enjoins. This localization, moreover, is a distinguishing trait of the American system: it has been carried further in the United States than in any other major modern nation. Even of the smaller nations there are only two or three, of which Switzerland is the most obvious, that have localization built as integrally into their political structure.

The paradoxical survival of the states as political, not merely administrative units is, of course, the plainest expression of localization; and to the extent that the states retain political vitality they diminish or rather limit the power of the central government. Under the American system the states not merely function as local governments with a certain measure of intrinsic sovereignty, but significantly affect the structure and functioning of the central government.

Not only is the Senate membership allocated on an equal basis to the several states, but each Senator is chosen by, and only by, a particular state—by the state legislature until 1913, the state's voters thereafter. An individual Senator therefore does not represent the nation as such, or any quantitative fraction of the nation. He represents a given state—that is, an organic, not a quantitative part of the nation. The Senate as a whole does not represent the nation directly, but only through the states, and only on the implied premise that the states are real political organs joined in the larger organic and qualitative unity of the nation.

From the point of view of democratist ideology the Senate is a scandal. Democratism always presses toward the conclusions that all men are equal, that political differences are only quantitative, that all issues should be decided by a numerical majority, and that representative institutions should directly reflect the quantitative relations within the populace as a whole. Not even by the most ingenious sophistries can the Senate be held to conform to any of these principles. The objections to the Senate that James Wilson, at the Philadelphia Convention, drew out of the logic of his moderate democratism[1] have re-echoed and deepened ever since. "With respect to the province and object of the General Government," Wilson argued, the states "should be considered as having no existence. . . . The General Government is not an assemblage of states, but of individuals . . . ; the individuals, therefore, not the states, ought to be represented in it." Later he specifically proposed, on his ideology's quantitative assumptions, that there should be one Senator "for every one hundred thousand souls." He insisted, quite correctly, that election of Senators by states "will introduce and cherish local interests and local prejudices."

But the Representatives also are structurally linked to local interests and local prejudices. Although their numbers are proportioned (not too strictly) to the total population rather than to the states, they are elected not on national but on local tickets. Each must reside in the locality that returns him (by law in the state, and by cus-

---

1. In part Wilson objected simply as spokesman for a large state (Pennsylvania) who resented the power that the small states might wield in the proposed Senate. But unlike other delegates from the large states, Wilson was a fairly consistent exponent of democratist ideology, even apart from Pennsylvania's special interests.

tom in the election district), and must win not just a certain number of votes from the nation's population at large, but a plurality in his local district.[2] For some reason, the rarity of these strict localizing procedures is seldom remarked. Some modern nations, with strict adherence to democratist logic, pick their national assemblies by a single all-national vote for party slates rather than individual candidates. Each party is allocated the number of seats that corresponds to its percentage of the total vote (35% to the Center Party, 26% to the Communists, 21% to the Socialists, or whatever it may be), and fills them from its own party lists in the order determined by the controlling party body. Thus a citizen does not vote, except by accident, for a resident of his locality, nor does the elected official have any special political relation to any particular region. The national assembly may contain no residents at all from many or most localities—in theory they might all reside at the capital, or anywhere else for that matter.

Although the Communists and Nazis in Weimar Germany proved that this extreme democratist procedure could be easily manipulated to undermine and finally destroy republican government, it is still common, sometimes in modified versions. Even in countries where there seems to be local district representation, the appearance is likely to be deceptive. In Britain, for example, each Member of Parliament is identified as from a particular locality ("the Member from East Norwood," or wherever), and is elected by gaining a plurality within that local district. But his relation to that locality is tenuous and arbitrary. He does not have to be a bona fide resident. It is the leadership of his party that selects him as a candidate, and then assigns him to a particular election district, from any of a variety of motives: the party may want to make absolutely certain of his election by having him run in a "safe" district—or the contrary; it may consider him especially qualified to do battle with a

2. Except in the case of a small number of "Representatives-at-large" who are elected on a state basis.

known opponent; it may want to build up the party in a certain area or to please a big contributor, and so on. The local party committee must accept the candidate, thus exercising a mild veto power, but this is usually a formality. The candidate has got to win a sufficiency of ballots, and is thus not wholly exempt from local ties, but his technical position is such that these are much looser than his links to and dependence on the national apparatus.

In substance an even more remote relationship between the members of the national assembly and local districts holds in France and Italy and indeed in most countries—including totalitarian countries that have elective national assemblies. Even where the member is elected within a local district and must be an actual resident thereof, the real choice of candidates is usually made by the leadership of each national political party.

In the United States the localization has not been a mere conventional form. Representatives as well as Senators do in fact as well as form have an intimate relation to their local districts, even when they become conspicuous as national leaders also. They are widely acquainted with their local constituents and the local problems, and responsive to local pressures. From the beginning to the present day, the history of Congress shows that a member who identifies himself closely with his local district can reasonably expect to be re-elected almost as long as he wishes to run, in spite of shifts back and forth in national alignments. Congressional candidates are seldom chosen by the national party leadership; national leaders, including Presidents—as Franklin Roosevelt discovered in 1938, and Harry Truman in 1950—have seldom been successful in purging local candidates.

During the past generation there have been mounting attempts to break through these local walls, not only by Presidents, but by the ideologically motivated organizations that have been intervening in national politics: the labor federations, Liberty League, Americans for Democratic Action, Committee for an Effective Congress, Zionist groups, National Association of Manufacturers, among others. The huge sums of money needed for contemporary electoral

techniques as well as the spread of ideologies encourage this crossing of local district lines: money has no settled residence, and can be
thrown wherever it might be useful to defeat not Joe Smith of Peo-
ria, Illinois, but an "anti-labor" or "anti-Zionist" or "pro-socialist"
someone.

These attempts have had some success, but surprisingly little,
considering their scale. The feeling for locality is very deep in the
American tradition. A Senator or Representative from Iowa is an
Iowan. He looks and talks like an Iowan; he has friends and a home
and a farm or business in Iowa and in such-and-such county of
Iowa; in his Washington office he has pictures of Iowa and his home
town, Iowan secretaries and assistants. And so with Rhode Island
and Virginia and Texas and California and all the rest. Thus the national interest and national power have got to be tempered to the
power and interest of Iowa and Virginia and Texas, and Dubuque
and Petersburg and Amarillo. This is as the Fathers intended it to be.
"Mr. [Randolph] Mason thought seven years too long" as a residence requirement for congressional candidates, "but would never
agree to part with the principle. It is a valuable principle. He
thought it a defect in the plan, that the Representatives would be
too few to bring with them all the local knowledge necessary. If residence be not required, rich men[3] of neighboring states may employ
with success the means of corruption in some particular district, and
thereby get into the public councils after having failed in their own
States. This is the practice in the boroughs of England."

George B. Galloway, one of the closest students of Congress,
comments as follows on congressional "localitis":

One of the maxims of American politics is that the stream of
government can rise no higher than its source. Under the locality rule the sources of representation in Congress are all the
localities of America, with their varying values, levels of liv-

3. Or powerfully backed men, let us add.

ing, and stages of social advancement. The typical orientation of a member of Congress is toward the district or state he represents, for it has produced him, and his re-election will depend upon how well he serves its interests. He owes his nomination and election ordinarily to state or local party organizations and has probably received little, if any, aid from a national political party. . . . Each member brings the vision of his own parish to the politics of the nation and the world. Thus, under the locality rule, congressional politics in America adds up to the sum of, and interplay of, all the local attitudes of 531 members of Congress. The dominant operating forces in the system are centrifugal, pulling away from the center of national interest.[4]

Even the one all-national elective office, the Presidency, is not immune to localization, since the President is not elected by a national plebiscite, but by an indirect method in which the state constitutes the local electoral district. This fact, together with the mode of organization of our parties, ensures a role to localities in the selection of the President. A national electorate does not exist as a politically real entity. There is only an aggregate made up of local electorates.

But localization permeates the governmental structure beyond all constitutional provisions. From the earliest days the "claims of locality" have been recognized in making governmental appointments.

Another element [of what President Washington regarded as fitness for public office] was the place of residence of the candidate, the object being to secure a favorable geographical distribution, and local residence for the lesser posts. The first Cabinet [of five members] contained representatives of Massachusetts, New York, and Virginia. The first Supreme Court [with six members] contained judges from Massachusetts,

4. George B. Galloway, *op. cit.,* p. 210.

New York, Pennsylvania, Virginia, Maryland, and South Carolina. Appointments in the field service were naturally and regularly drawn from the state and locality in which the officials were to serve; local jealousy would have tolerated nothing less. . . . Washington insisted that everyone who held a federal post should have the confidence of the community in which he lived. Men who had been rejected for local office by their neighbors were under a heavy handicap.[5]

There is a double consequence of this local diffusion of federal posts. With one tendency it promotes national unity by giving the diverse localities, through their native sons, a concrete relation to and interest in the central government. At the same time it ties the central government down, submits it to the complex of local interests, pressures and concerns. In net effect, localization in the American system acts as a brake on the central government's inherent and inevitable drive toward an ever greater assumption of power.

This is indirectly attested by the fact that localization is a recurrent target of liberal attack. Localization is another of those "irrational" factors in government—irrational, that is to say, from the point of view of the logic of democratism. Like congressional seniority, it is supported by tradition and political instinct rather than by reasoned argument from a set of abstract principles. As the liberal, who is in the end a Platonist, is likely to see it, those citizens who are best—most intelligent, far-seeing, educated, progressive—ought to rule. If one locality in its backwardness is apt, if left to itself, to send an inferior representative to Congress, then money and ideas and organizers should be pumped in from enlightened areas in order to correct the vicious local balance.

As for the bureaucracy, it ought, by the liberal logic, to be manned by those best fitted for the work at hand, whether stenog-

5. Leonard D. White, *The Federalists* (New York: Macmillan, 1948), pp. 259–60, 514.

raphy or forest ranging or accounting or administering. This can be decided by adequate "objective" tests, on the basis of which appointments can be made. With tests the sole criterion, the "claims of locality" would go by the board. It could never be proved that an Arkansas girl could, by virtue of local residence, operate a typewriter better than a competitor from New Jersey, no matter how long it had been since someone from Arkansas had got an appointment as a government stenographer.

The recruitment of a permanent civil service through competitive examinations thus works counter to localization; and since 1883, when the Civil Service Commission came into being, the principle of localization has been relatively weakened. This weakening is, in fact, part of the process through which the bureaucracy has developed into a separate branch of government. However, the American civil service system leaves several loopholes. Appointments are made from the three highest candidates on the examination list; frequent excuses are found for special appointments without examination; and the generously defined "policy making" posts are exempt from the civil service procedure. Thus localization continues to have considerable play even in the bureaucracy, as it doubtless will so long as the American system of government endures.

2

In the American tradition as defined prior to 1933, what limits were there on the power of government to intervene in the economic process? The answer to this question is in dispute, and is obscured by the habit of interpreting the past in such a way as to support current views. Those who oppose the recent statist trends from a "libertarian" or what a century ago was called a "liberal" point of view often write about the early decades of American history as a *laisser faire* Paradise wherein an austere and minimum government, carefully limiting itself to police functions, acted in relation to the economy only to block gross fraud and ensure active competition. Some of the ardent champions of the welfare state[6] have lately begun to suggest that the New Deal began with Washington's inauguration, and that the United States is socialism's original home. Neither view sustains examination.

We deal here with a question not of theoretical economics but of history. Whether *laisser faire* is or ever was a true or beneficent theory of economics, it was not the theory held by the Founding Fathers, and it has never been the theory guiding the practice of the American government. By "general welfare" the Philadelphia delegates meant the nation's material prosperity. They were founding a government that would have the promotion of the general welfare as one of its explicit purposes.

Most of them believed that the protection and fostering of property were the principal objects of organized society. The substance of Gouverneur Morris' remarks on July 5 were heard a hundred times: "Life and liberty were generally said to be of more value than property. An accurate view of the matter would, nevertheless, prove that property was the main object of society. The savage state was more favorable to liberty than the civilized; and sufficiently so to life. It was preferred by all men who had not acquired a taste for property; it was only renounced for the sake of property which could only be secured by the restraints of regular government." John Rutledge, Rufus King and others at once stated their agreement that "property was the principal object of society."[7] When Thomas Jefferson amended the draft of the Declaration of Independence to have it refer to "pursuit of happiness"

6. Professor Louis Hartz, for example.
7. But on July 13, James Wilson, referring back to this earlier discussion, did, from his ideological position that was so much closer to modern democratism, disagree, with the very modern-sounding counter-argument that "the cultivation and improvement of the human mind was the most noble object [of government and society]."

instead of the more usual "pursuit of wealth" or "property," he had no intention of denying but only of enlarging the reference—material property was an essential element of Jefferson's "happiness." It was the democrat Andrew Jackson's appointee as Chief Justice, Roger Brooke Taney, who went out of his way in his first decision to declare: "The object and end of all government is to promote the happiness and prosperity of the community by which it is established."

Taney's proposition, like the preamble of the Constitution, uses the active verb, "promote," and this has always been, if in different degrees, the traditional American conception. In foreign and domestic policy, government, as Americans have understood its function, is supposed to work actively to establish conditions under which the economy will flourish. Much of the dissatisfaction with the government under the Articles derived from its inability to do just this. The Fathers wanted a common market and a sound fiscal system precisely in order to promote business prosperity. Few at any time in the nation's history were content with a tariff "for revenue only." Even those who used the slogan did not mean it literally, and were for the most part merely asking for a tariff that favored agricultural as against industrial enterprise. Not everyone agreed with Hamilton in favoring a national bank and outright government subsidies to get new businesses going, and Hamilton's party was soon overthrown; but the Jeffersonians, once in office, were not ready to allow the government to become economically passive.

Even in 1812, under the Administration that went further than any other in our history to minimize the role of government, no one disagreed with Daniel Webster's assertion, in his Fourth of July address, that the Constitution had been adopted "for no single reason so much as for the protection of our commerce." Business and government were not to be thought of as antagonists. Our commerce "has discharged the debt of the Revolution. It has paid the price of independence. It has filled the Treasury and sustained the government from the first moments of its existence to the present time. The interests and the habits of a vast proportion of the community have become interwoven with this commerce, in a manner not to be changed and that no government has the power of changing."

It is the correlative duty of government to help business, and every one of the early Presidential addresses to Congress states the government's positive concern with the well-being and expansion of the nation's economy. The openly expressed motive for founding and maintaining a navy was to aid commerce. "To an active commerce the protection of a naval force is indispensable."[8]

The Jeffersonians did, indeed, stand formally on the avowed doctrine of their leader: "Agriculture, manufactures, commerce, and navigation, the four pillars of our prosperity, are then most thriving when left most free to individual enterprise."[9] Given a generous interpretation, this was, in fact, the traditional belief of Americans of all parties. But it was never understood with doctrinaire rigidity. In the very paragraph where he formulates it, Jefferson himself goes on to say: "Protection from casual embarrassments, however, may sometimes be seasonably interposed. If in the course of your observations or inquiries they [agriculture, manufactures, etc.] should appear to need any aid within the limits of our constitutional powers, your sense of their importance is a sufficient assurance they will occupy your attention."

It was more a purely constitutional than philosophical scruple that troubled the Jeffersonians. President Madison in his Seventh Annual Message called to Congress' attention, as a "means of advancing the public interest . . . the great importance of establishing throughout our country the roads and canals which can best be executed under

8. George Washington, Eighth Annual Address to Congress. My quotations from official papers and messages of the Presidents through Grover Cleveland are taken from James D. Richardson's *A Compilation of the Messages and Papers of the Presidents* (Government Printing Office, 1896).
9. Thomas Jefferson, First Annual Message.

the national authority. No objects within the circle of political economy so richly repay the expense bestowed on them; there are none the utility of which is more universally ascertained and acknowledged; none that do more honor to the governments whose wise and enlarged patriotism duly appreciates them. . . . Whilst the States individually, with a laudable enterprise and emulation, avail themselves of their local advantages by new roads, by navigable canals, and by improving the streams susceptible of navigation, the General Government is the more urged to similar undertakings, requiring a national jurisdiction and national means, by the prospect of thus systematically completing so inestimable a work." If "any defect of constitutional authority" stood in the way of such "internal improvements," it could easily be supplied "in a mode which the Constitution itself has providently pointed out." Meanwhile, under the local Jeffersonians, state governments were going vigorously ahead with roads, canals and similar works.

Under Washington and John Adams the central government not only established a bank and actively promoted shipbuilding, foreign trade and the fisheries, but used public money for arsenals, lighthouses, beacons, commercial piers, hospitals, storehouses, land surveys, munitions factories, timber and timber-growing lands, office buildings, post coaches and Indian trading posts.[10] Under the Jeffersonians, in spite of their professed theories, the government did not withdraw from these fields.

From the beginning, the constitutional injunction "to provide for the common defence," given a broad interpretation, has been understood to sanction "internal improvements" only indirectly related to military security: dredging, damming and other work on rivers and harbors, mapping and exploration, facilities for, as well as regulation of sea-borne (and later, air-borne) transportation, the manufacture of munitions and even non-military goods for the armed services. The constitutional authorization to regulate com-

10. Cf. Leonard D. White, *op. cit.*, pp. 507–8, 519–20.

merce with the Indian tribes, "to establish Post Offices and post Roads," and "to promote the Progress of Science and useful Arts"[11] also led from the start to active government interventions in the economy.

Throughout our national history, the central government has held, through one or another circumstance, huge tracts of public lands. At all periods the government's relation to these has been economically active. The lands have been allocated for exploitation to homesteaders, and to enterpreneurs both small and large. Millions of acres were turned over to the railroad companies that opened the lines of communication across the West. Mineral and lumbering rights have been parceled out. Vast domains have been kept in government jurisdiction for military, conservation and recreational purposes.

Governmental activity in relation to the economy has varied much, but it has never, not even in the strictest years of the Jeffersonians, been content with the negative policing role prescribed by *laisser faire* dogma. In fact, government's role in the economy has never been a rigorous application of any dogma, but has followed, rather, a pragmatic, rambling script with many erasures and accidental notations.

For all the lack of Cartesian precision, however, it is possible to summarize with reasonable accuracy the American tradition—prior to 1933—that defined the powers and limits of the central government in relation to the economy. The core of the tradition is the practising belief that: (a) private, money-making enterprise is an ethically right and good human activity; (b) private, money-making enterprise is the most effective method for carrying on and developing the economy; (c) government should seek to establish political and social conditions favorable to private, money-making

---

11. All of the early Presidents, both Federalist and Jeffersonian, were enamored with the idea of a "national university," and in their annual messages to Congress repeatedly urged its establishment.

enterprise; (d) government should in addition, when relevant or needed, itself intervene actively in the economic process in order to promote private, money-making enterprise. The American economic tradition is thus neither *laisser faire* nor collectivism. Its anti-collectivism was firmly based in a continuing national conviction that it is a fine thing for individual citizens to make money— and if possible lots of money—by work and business. But the nation has never accepted the *laisser faire* view that government should be passive in the business and money-making process. The job of government is not to take over, own, or operate the economy, but to improve and expand the opportunities for successful private enterprise.

This duty the government performs in part by political means, both domestic and foreign: by getting sovereignty over the Louisiana Territory, building a Panama Canal, exerting pressures for Central American or Mideastern conditions in which American business corporations can flourish, or by enforcing internal laws that enable a business system to operate effectively. The government has also, and continuously, given direct economic help to the money-making projects of the citizens: land for farmers or railroads or lumber companies; leases for oil wells and mines; rights of way for canals, toll roads and bridges; tariff protection for domestic factories; a host of what those who disapprove of them now call "give-aways"; information services for farmers, shippers, ranchers and loggers; technical facilities—lighthouses, buoys, charts, maps, weather reports, iceberg positions, airways control—that enable privately owned ships and wagons and trucks and aircraft to travel more safely and more profitably.

From the beginning, as we have already noted, the central government has also itself owned and operated a certain number of economic enterprises that might theoretically have been in private hands. These were, however, never more than a very small portion of the economy. Many of them, started in some special or emergency situation, hung on by a kind of inertia, as in the case of many of the projects for military arming, supply and housekeeping. Even against these, and even up through the present, there is a traditional bias. The synthetic rubber plants, built by the government for the military purposes of the second World War, were sold back to private industry. In the fields of aircraft, missiles and even of atomic armament, where the military services must necessarily be the principal or only customer, complicated arrangements are devised to give civilian, profit-making business a maximum share in production. In nearly all other countries, no matter what their mode of economy is called, such fields are largely or altogether a government monopoly.

The central government has carried on other operations where it has been felt—though often rather arbitrarily—that there is some special "public" attribute adhering to the goods or services produced: postal service, for example, which was explicitly authorized by the Constitution and which has been interpreted to include transport of odd-lot freight ("parcel post"); river and harbor improvements; considerable printing and publishing; Indian and military retail merchandising. Neither on this nor on other matters does the American tradition follow the dictate of monistic absolutes. If it was felt that something had to be done, and if there were no private citizens able and willing to do it, then the central government has usually taken on the task, at least temporarily. The decentralist Jeffersonians established a Philadelphia-Baltimore and then a Philadelphia-New York stage line when privately owned stages were not providing regular enough service for mail deliveries.[12] But these collectivist ventures—though not precisely exceptions, since they are to be found from the nation's start—are out of the tradition's main current.

12. Cf. Leonard D. White, *The Jeffersonians* (New York: Macmillan, 1951), pp. 329–30. Prof. White notes that the concept of "yardstick regulation" first appears in an 1814 comment by the Postmaster General on these stage runs: the line operating, he said, "as a check upon contractors, both in repressing exorbitant demands, and stimulating contractors to a faithful discharge of their duty."

The American solution of the relation between the central government and the economy, though it cannot be reduced to a simple formula, is distinct and distinctive: a pragmatic, problem-solving mixture, with a heavy bias toward private, money-making enterprise, supplemented by a readiness to use government for the active promotion of such enterprise. Here as throughout the social structure there is a fund of ample governmental power (the power, as the Constitution announces it in this case, "to promote the General Welfare") circumscribed by limits that are enforced more by countervailing social powers and by historical practice than by explicit law.

3

Beyond any specific listing of traditional powers and limits, the United States is distinguished from other of the world's major nations, both past and present, by a peculiar and general feature of the relation between government and society. In the United States the private lives of private citizens have always been felt to be more important than the public history of the nation. This is not a mere question of abstract ideology. There have been other countries where the professed philosophies asserted the normative priority of individuals over the nation. But there has been no other great nation wherein such a belief was so pervasively expressed through day-in, day-out social attitudes and practice. No other nation has had so little feeling for *the idea of glory*.

The history of other great countries revolves around wars and crusades and incredible adventures, sacrifice and heroism in defeat, splendor in victory, Kings, Emperors, Lords and Ladies, sinister priests and ravishing mistresses, last stands and great conquerors, public crownings and funerals and births, world missions and foul deeds, despots and assassins and revolutionaries. The great men and fascinating women, the lives and careers that seem worth recording and worth living, focus in or near the centers of governmental power.

In these categories it has always been hard to write a history of the United States, and the result is always duller than a history of Persia or Greece, Rome or Spain, France or Britain. The colonists came to the future United States for practical purposes of making a better or easier living, or to arrange conditions of moral and religious observance more to their liking. It was on practical, not ideological or grand-historic grounds that after many years of attempted compromise they broke with the Mother Country. With the exception of a few clauses, their declaration of independence reads like a lawyer's brief. And it was the leading lawyers and men of affairs who drafted a brilliant contract to set up a government that would serve them and their fellow-citizens, that would answer their needs, problems and interests, and protect the kind of life that they wanted to lead. They made plain their abandonment of the whole cult of national glory by making sure that in their country there would be no king or monarch, and "no Title of Nobility."

"Divine right of kings," "holy Mother Russia," "the Great King," "the Empire on which the sun never sets," "Son of Heaven," "his imperial majesty," "his Serene Highness": phrases like these and the set of attitudes with which they are associated lie out of range of the American imagination. The American nation is not a super-being on whose altar the subject is ready to sacrifice blood, treasure and life, but a mere practical convenience the only justification for which is its ability to serve the interests of private citizens. National wars are not gallant adventures or glorious crusades, but distasteful chores or burdensome duties, to be got over with and thrust into the past.

From the beginning of the 19th century on, foreign observers of the United States have remarked on the fact that few of the nation's most ambitious and able citizens have gone into political or military life. It has been business in particular, and to a lesser extent the civil professions, that have attracted those equipped with talent, intelligence, creative imagination and even the will to power. By their preponderating choice of career, the ablest citizens have signified unmistakably the subordination of public to private concerns. Railway tracks, steel mills, oil wells, power plants, assembly lines, huge fortunes and intricate corporate structures—these have been the jewels on America's crown. With only a handful of political and military interlopers, it is the leaders of invention, industry and banking who have been her barons and heroes.

We are noting here a key trait that is critical for an understanding of the American social structure. The weighting of the traditional social balance toward private and individual life, and away from the public and national, has probably gone further in the United States than in any other large nation. What this means, as we have already noticed in another context, is that, over and above the balance of counter-checking power that obtains within the political system, there has been an equilibrium of social powers in which private life has to an unprecedented degree predominated over government. Government could not tyrannize over the citizens because the citizens, in their private capacities, were stronger than government.

4

We have previously listed seven symptoms of the conservative, and seven counter-symptoms of the liberal, syndromes. Five more details of the contrasting patterns may now be filled in.

As traditionally expressed in the United States, the conservative syndrome displays:

(h) a warmer concern with the limits than with the powers of government;

(i) a conviction that the Constitution and the American constitutional tradition state principles that are intelligible, and of permanent and binding value;

(j) a generally favoring judgment on the various devices, direct or indirect, of "localization," by which governmental power in the United States tends to be decentralized;

(k) a presumption in favor of private, profit-making enterprise as the most just and the most effective means for economic operation and development;

(l) a belief that the private life of individual human beings, as against the destiny of nation or society, is the focus of primary metaphysical, moral and practical interest.

The liberal syndrome includes as contrasting symptoms:

(h') more stress on the powers of government, together with some impatience at the limitations;

(i') a tendency to consider the Constitution a more flexible, empirical instrument, the meaning of which changes and ought to be accepted as changing with the times;

(j') an estimate that in the modern age an over-localization of American government hampers it in dealing with crucial domestic and foreign problems;

(k') a judgment that private economic enterprise frequently goes counter to the interests of people and nation, which can in many cases be better served by government intervention or even by outright government control, ownership and operation;

(l') a confidence that an expanding sphere of governmental activity—in social and cultural life as well as in the economy—is not merely compatible with but actively productive of the best mode of life for human beings.

VII

THE PLACE OF
CONGRESS

I N THE TRADITIONAL American system, power has been widely
diffused among both private and governmental institutions.
Within the complex equilibrium of the governmental structure,
power has been divided between central and local governments, and
diffracted among legislature, executive, judiciary, and the bureaucracy both civil and military. For this and the next chapter, let us restrict our attention to the three formally designated branches of the
central government.

Legislature, executive and judiciary each shares in the total fund
of power, and it was the anxious concern of the Fathers that each
should have a relative independence or autonomy: that is, that no
one of the three should be wholly subject to or dependent on one
or both of the others, that each should exercise its share of power
in and of its own right. Otherwise the intended diffusion of power
would be illusory. There would be only an administrative division
of a unitary, centralized power, without the checks, balances and
conflicts which the Fathers believed to be the only sure supports of
liberty.

If each of several institutions has its own independent quota of
power, it does not follow that the shares are of equal weight. My car
and yours may each run by its own engine, though yours has the
power of three hundred and mine of only fifty horses; my plot of
land may be truly my own, and yet the acreage may be smaller and
the crops fewer than my neighbor possesses. To decide that the judiciary shall be independent of the legislature, and the executive in-

dependent of both, is not, or not necessarily, to intend that the three should or can be equal in power.

The Founding Fathers believed that in a republican and representative governmental system the preponderating share of power was held and exercised by the legislature. Indeed, for most of the Fathers this was a belief that seemed rather a self-evident axiom than a conclusion to be argued. The two or three who might occasionally question the priority of the legislature were inclined, like Hamilton, toward a monarchic rather than a republican form of government. And even Hamilton's monarchism was more a romantic ideal than a seriously proposed solution for the new nation. When asked in 1780 by James Duane what the trouble was with the American government, then operating under the single-branch direction of the Continental Congress, Hamilton's reply was not to advocate a supreme executive, but: "The fundamental defect is a want of power in Congress." In the series of articles that he published the following year as *The Continentalist,* he proposed a national government consisting of a one-house Congress possessing full power.

In a presidential message to Congress sent May 4, 1822, James Monroe analyzed the nature of the American government:

I will now proceed to examine [he begins one section] the powers of the General Government, which, like the governments of the several States, is divided into three branches—a legislative, executive, and judiciary—each having its appropriate share. Of these the legislative, from the nature of its powers, all laws proceeding from it, and the manner of its appointment, its members being elected immediately by the people, is by far the most important. The whole system of the National Government may be said to rest essentially on the powers granted to this branch. They mark the limit within which, with few exceptions, all the branches must move in the discharge of their respective functions.

Monroe's judgment is a conclusion not of abstract logic but of a lifetime of public experience that comprised the founding of the republic. No one in 1822, or in 1789, would have disagreed with this basic evaluation, though there would have been dispute over the exact proportions.

In a nation that has left the level of automatic custom there must be a man or an institution that makes the laws. The laws (along with surviving customs and accepted moral principles) are the rules according to which the nation exists and operates as an organized community, without which it would not be. Therefore there must be a legislature—even though the legislature may be called a King or a Party Secretary. There does not have to be a separate executive and judiciary. The legislature can itself, directly or through its agents, execute its own laws and judge the issues that arise under them. This, indeed, is the mode of the parliamentary system, before the parliamentary system is transformed into the Cabinet government that prevails in most republican nations today.

The American government that declared independence, fought the war against the world's greatest power, became regularized under the Articles of Confederation, made the peace and launched the nation on its civil career, consisted of a single branch. So exclusive an attention is paid to the defects of the pre-Constitution government that its extraordinary achievements are forgotten; but the one as the other were well known to the Founding Fathers. It carried out executive functions, of course, but through Congress itself, acting in an executive capacity, or through dependent agents of Congress. And in a good proportion of its executive acts the Continental Congress did very well. It made, no one can doubt, the perfect choice for the commander to fight the war for independence, and for the man who, in spite of the fiscal chaos, could somehow finance it. The war was fought to a victory, and the victory sealed, if with wearying delay, by a peace that served to establish the new community as a nation among the world's nations. Never in our subsequent history have we been served by a set of emissaries abroad averaging so high as those appointed by the Continental Congress: Thomas Jefferson, Benjamin Franklin, John Jay, John Adams among them. Money and military aid, both essential to the victory, were obtained from Europe during the war. Loans and treaties were thereafter negotiated with Europe's major sovereigns.

Legislative supremacy was thus not a novelty for the Fathers, but a starting assumption. John Locke, from whom many of them had learned their formal doctrine of civil government, had traced the origin of a distinct executive power to the merely technical requirement that there had to be someone at hand to carry out the laws when the legislature was adjourned. "But because the laws that are at once and in a short time made, have a constant and lasting force, and need a perpetual execution, or an attendance thereto; therefore it is necessary there should be a power always in being, which should see to the execution of the laws that are made, and remain in force. And thus the legislative and executive power come often to be separated."[1]

The delegates that came to Philadelphia agreed the central government must be granted more powers than provided by the Articles of Confederation. They all assumed that most of these powers would be assigned to the legislature. Several of the delegates did not have initially in mind the creation of an independent executive or judiciary. In the Virginia Plan, submitted by Randolph and accepted as the basis for discussion, Congress was allotted an even more predominant share in the power than it finally got. Early convention votes gave the Senate the power to negotiate and adopt treaties and to nominate judges. The earlier plans for the executive provided for his (or their—many wanted a plural executive as less tending to tyranny) election by the legislature for a limited term; and, in some versions, for his legislative removal.[2] A number of the delegates were gravely apprehensive of an executive veto:

1. *Second Treatise on Civil Government*, Chap. 12.
2. *Cf.* remarks of John Dickinson and Roger Sherman, *Debates*, June 2.

Mr. [Pierce] Butler [of South Carolina] had been in favor of a single executive magistrate; but could he have entertained an idea that a complete negative on the laws was to be given him, he certainly should have acted very differently. It had been observed, that in all countries the executive power is in a constant course of increase. . . . Gentlemen seemed to think that we had nothing to apprehend from an abuse of the executive power. But why might not a Cataline or a Cromwell arise in this country as well as in others?

Mr. [Gunning] Bedford [of Delaware] was opposed to every check on the Legislature, even the council of revision first proposed.[3]

On July 20 James Wilson argued for a strengthening of the independence of the executive and the judiciary on the grounds that "the joint weight of the two Departments was necessary to balance the single weight of the Legislature."

"But it is not possible," observes *Federalist* No. 51,[4] "to give to each department an equal power of self-defence. In republican government, the legislative authority necessarily predominates." The final paragraph of *Federalist* No. 44 (Madison) declares: "We have now in papers No. 23–44 reviewed, in detail, all the articles composing the sum or quantity of power delegated by the proposed Constitution to the Federal government." But at this point in the *Federalist* series there has been no discussion at all of either the executive or judicial departments, which "are reserved for particular examination in another place."

There are a number of passages, quoted in recent years by critics of Congress, wherein the Fathers warn against the chance of "legislative tyranny." The learned James Wilson, for example, told the Convention on August 15 that he "was most apprehensive of a dis-

3. *Debates,* June 4.
4. It is not certain whether Hamilton or Madison is the author.

solution of the Government from the Legislature swallowing up all the other powers. He remarked, that the prejudices against the Executive resulted from a misapplication of the adage, that the parliament was the palladium of liberty. Where the Executive was really formidable, *King* and *tyrant* were naturally associated in the minds of the people; not *legislature* and *tyranny*. But where the Executive was not formidable, the two last were most properly associated."

The comments of Madison (*Federalist* No. 48) are better known:

> The founders of our republics . . . seem never to have recollected the danger from legislative usurpations, which, by assembling all power in the same hands, must lead to the same tyranny as is threatened by executive usurpations. . . .
>
> In a representative republic, where the executive magistracy is carefully limited, both in the extent and duration of its power; and where the legislative power is exercised by an assembly, which is inspired, by a supposed influence over the people, with an intrepid confidence in its own strength; which is sufficiently numerous to feel all the passions which actuate a multitude, yet not so numerous as to be incapable of pursuing the objects of its passions, by means which reason prescribes; it is against the enterprising ambition of this department that the people ought to indulge all their jealousy and exhaust all their precautions.

At the convention, Gouverneur Morris was also among those who warned eloquently against the possible excesses of the legislature. On July 19 he found these a telling argument for the strong and independent executive about which some of his fellow-delegates were still doubtful. "One great object of the Executive," Madison's notes report him as saying, "is, to control the Legislature. The Legislature will continually seek to aggrandize and perpetuate themselves; and will seize those critical moments produced by war, invasion, or convulsion, for that purpose. It is necessary, then, that the Executive magistrate should be the guardian of the people, even of the lower classes, against legislative tyranny."

On the next day Morris (whose sudden solicitude for "the lower classes" may have puzzled some of his colleagues) made clear to the convention the possibly tyrannical legislative acts of which he was apprehensive: "emissions of paper-money, largesses to the people, a remission of debts, and similar measures."

The warnings of the Fathers against a danger of legislative tyranny must be understood in context. They were not arguing against the political priority of the legislature, even though some of them, aristocrats and anti-democrats at heart, regretted that priority. It was precisely because they assumed that the only viable form of government for the United States was a republic in which the legislature held the principal share of power, that they were sensible of the danger: a danger, one may add, that threatened the special interests that some of them represented more plainly than the political liberty of the nation at large.

"No government could long subsist," argued James Wilson on May 31, "without the confidence of the people. In a republican government, this confidence was peculiarly essential," and could be obtained only if sovereignty rested predominantly in a legislature, "the most numerous branch" of which would be drawn "immediately from the people." It was the inevitable legislative priority that made it expedient "to divide the legislature into different branches; and to render them, by different modes of election and different principles of action, as little connected with each other as the nature of their common functions and their common dependence on the society will admit";[5] and to fortify the counterweights of an autonomous executive and judiciary. In the public debate over ratification it was tactically advisable for the Fathers to stress the hypothetical threat from the legislative branch, which ordinary citizens looked on as their direct representative and the key to republi-

5. *Federalist,* No. 51.

can self-government, in order to quiet the natural fear that an independent single executive might easily evolve into monarchy and despotism.

The Fathers were of course right in predicting, as Gouverneur Morris did, that the "critical moments produced by war, invasion, or convulsion" would be seized for the aggrandizement of governmental power; but they mistook the branch of government that would do the seizing.

2

The primacy of the legislature in the intent of the Constitution is plain on the face of that document, as it is in the deliberations of the Philadelphia Convention. It is the Constitution's first Article that defines the structure and powers of the legislature. The legislative Congress is to be the sole source of all laws (except the clauses of the Constitution itself). In the conduct of the general government, Congress alone can authorize the getting or spending of money. It is for Congress to support, regulate and govern the Army and Navy, and to declare war. Save for the bare existence of a Supreme Court, it is for Congress to establish and regulate the judicial system. All officers of both executive and judiciary are subject to congressional impeachment; but for their own official conduct the members of Congress are answerable only to themselves.

It is not surprising, therefore, that the critical issues at Philadelphia were the manner of constituting the legislature and the method for selecting its members. There was longer and sharper debate over this set of problems than over any other; indeed, almost as much debate as over all the others. Because of the prolonged failure to agree on the composition of Congress, the convention reached the edge of breakup. When the complicated "Connecticut compromise," as amended by Gerry to provide for individual voting by the Senators, was accepted, the convention's success was assured.

There were some among the Fathers who conceived the executive as only the administrative agent, "the mere creature" of the legislature. Roger Sherman, for example, stated (on June 1) that "he considered the executive magistracy as nothing more than an institution for carrying the will of the legislature into effect"; and he, as well as John Dickinson and several others, wished the executive to be made removable by the legislature. A century of constitutional experience did not altogether erase this conception. Roscoe Conkling, Senator from New York during 1867–81 explained in a speech delivered to his Utica constituents what he still held to be the settled view of his colleagues: "Congress maintains that the President is not the law-making power of the country—that he has only the power to approve or veto bills, that two-thirds of each House, without his approval and notwithstanding his veto, are clothed with the full legislative power of the nation; that it is the duty of the President to see that all laws are faithfully executed, and that except, as already stated, he has nothing to do with the composition of Congress, nor with the adoption or rejection of measures, except that he may give information, and may recommend matters to consideration." Harold Laski quotes the still stricter views that ex-Senator John Sherman of Ohio included in his *Recollections,* published as late as 1895: "The executive department of a republic like ours should be subordinate to the legislative department. The President should obey and enforce the laws, leaving to the people the duty of correcting any errors committed by their representatives in Congress."[6]

These views on executive dependency are doubtless more extreme than those held by a majority of the Fathers, laid down by the Constitution, or carried out in the practice of the government. Still, they were close enough to traditional fact and opinion to be believed by informed and conscientious citizens. The priority of the

6. Harold J. Laski, *The American Presidency* (New York: Harper & Bros., 1940), pp. 124–5.

legislature in the traditional system has rested not solely on the immense powers assigned directly to it, but also on the ability of the legislature to exert indirect pressure on the other two branches. Even if impeachment has proved a last and almost unused resort, the power to impeach—lodged solely in the legislature—is a continuously implicit threat. From a formal standpoint, congressional power over the purse is unlimited, up or down. Formally, Congress could with a single law wipe out the entire executive establishment, save only for the President and the Vice President; and could abolish all federal courts, save for the Supreme Court, which it could reduce to a single judge with a minor jurisdiction. The missions of executive agencies and the subordinate courts, as well as their mere existence, depend on congressional statute. Even the treaty power, a primarily executive function under our Constitution, is made subject to the two-thirds approval of one of the legislative chambers. The executive's veto, by which he shares in the legislative power, may in all cases be over-ridden. Through the investigatory power—which, though not explicit in the Constitution, has been asserted from the government's first years—Congress can call the executive to detailed and public account.

In the American system, moreover, the legislature is protected from what can be made the keenest weapon of an aspiring executive: the executive's power to prorogue, or dissolve, the legislature, and to force a new election. It is this power that has brought about such an ironic transformation of most of the world's parliamentary governments. Under the parliamentary system (as under our Articles of Confederation) the legislature (parliament) is in theory all-powerful, with the executive only its agent. But in fact, in most cases, the parliamentary executive[7] has gained an ascendancy over the body of the parliament, which is reduced to the function of registering or declining to register its consent to what the executive has

7. Actually, the controlling committee (or committees) of the majority party (or parties).

done or decided. In a showdown the executive, if it is sufficiently determined, can almost always get that consent by threatening an ad hoc dissolution, with a new election that can seldom be agreeable to the existing majority. This threat cannot be made under the American system. In casting his vote a Congressman does not need to worry about a surprise election held at a time and on an issue that might put him at a maximum disadvantage. The President can neither advance nor delay the fixed date.

In the view of the Fathers, the judiciary's share in the diffused fund of political sovereignty was the smallest:

> Whoever attentively considers the different departments of power must perceive, that, in a government in which they are separated from each other, the judiciary, from the nature of its functions, will always be the least dangerous to the political rights of the Constitution; because it will be least in a capacity to annoy or injure them. The Executive not only dispenses the honors, but holds the sword of the community. The legislature not only commands the purse, but prescribes the rules by which the duties and rights of every citizen are to be regulated. The judiciary, on the contrary, has no influence over either the sword or the purse; no direction either of the strength or of the wealth of the society; and can take no active resolution whatever. It may truly be said to have neither FORCE nor WILL, but merely judgment; and must ultimately depend upon the aid of the executive arm even for the efficacy of its judgments.

This simple view of the matter suggests several important consequences. It proves incontestably, that the judiciary is beyond comparison the weakest of the three departments of power.[8]

---

8. *Federalist,* No. 78 (Hamilton). A footnote to this passage quotes Montesquieu: "Of the three powers above mentioned, the judiciary is next to nothing."

For this reason, the Fathers believed it difficult to guarantee the judiciary a genuine independence, as the doctrine of the diffusion of sovereignty demanded. In partial solution, they provided in the Constitution that judges "shall hold their Offices during good Behaviour" (that is, unless convicted under impeachment proceedings), and may thus render displeasing opinions without risking dismissal. Further to the same purpose, the compensation of judges "shall not be diminished during their continuance in Office." Apart from these clauses, and from the assignment of a limited special jurisdiction to a Supreme Court, the establishment as well as the regulation of the judicial branch are left to Congress, one House of which must also confirm each judicial appointment.

3

From the standpoint of the Philadelphia Convention, then, and of the written Constitution that was its end product, "legislative supremacy"—or, at any rate, legislative priority—was of the essence of republican government. Granted the maintenance of a firmly republican system, the Fathers anticipated little danger of executive tyranny and none at all of judicial. The constitutional problem was, rather, to devise a structure wherein the executive and judiciary would not be altogether swallowed up by the legislative branch. The diffusion and balancing of power, requisite to the defense of liberty, would be secured in the first instance by the concurrent sovereignty of the central government and the several states. Within the central government the inevitable predominance of the legislature could be somewhat reduced by allotting the executive a share in the legislative process (through a conditional veto, the ability to recommend legislative measures, and the right to convene Congress in emergency session), by giving the executive the first voice in appointments and foreign relations, and by providing methods for choosing the nation's executive and judicial officers on a basis separate and independent from the procedures for electing its legislators.

In the event, the legislative preponderance in the power balance was never as much as had been assumed. From the very first administration the executive weight was relatively heavier than expected. From the time of John Marshall's appointment as Chief Justice (1801), the judiciary quickly disproved Montesquieu's and Hamilton's belief that, in power terms, it would be "next to nothing."

One important reason for the emergence of an executive relatively stronger than some hoped and others feared was the character of the men who led the first administration. The first President was himself the most respected of all the new nation's citizens, a stern and forceful man who believed that an executive should be strong and self-sufficient. His principal adviser, who became both his Secretary of Treasury and his chief deputy in liaison with Congress, inclined even toward monarchy. Their leading collaborators, who had become known as Federalists, were distrustful of popular passions and of assemblies linked too closely to the people. From a technical point of view also, they believed in vigorous, efficient administration, which they felt could be guaranteed only by a centralized executive organization sustained by clear lines of direction and responsibility.

Apart from the two elected officers, the Constitution made no attempt to prescribe the structure of the executive branch, which was left for determination by statute. Even the nature of "Executive Power," which the Constitution vested in the President, was left undefined by the Philadelphia Convention. (Several attempts at definition, as in the June 1 and 2 debates, produced no coherent or agreed results.) Nor were the boundaries of the dual responsibility clearly marked in those cases where both executive and legislative action were required, as with appointments, treaties and military affairs. Thus the practical construction of the governmental framework and the setting of the earliest precedents, both presuming a particular interpretation of the new Constitution, were influenced by men who were inclined, up to the point that they thought compatible with their republican duty, to favor the executive rather than Congress when a choice seemed to be open.

There was an analogous situation, though somewhat later, when John Marshall took over direction of the judicial branch on John Adams' lame duck appointment in January 1801. A showdown over the role of the judiciary came quickly, because the incoming President and his Republican enthusiasts, in firm control of the other two branches, were resolved to remake and repopulate the entire government structure. They struck down Adams' revisions of the Judiciary Act, and set out to use, where necessary, even the impeachment process to get rid of political opponents. But with the failure of the move in 1805 to convict Justice Samuel Chase, very much as the 1868 impeachment move against President Andrew Johnson failed, the partisan attempt to assimilate the judiciary collapsed. Under Marshall's long leadership, the Court cemented its independent political foundation.

In both 1805 and 1868 the nation spoke in the denouement through the legislative assembly which it intuitively felt to be its most authentic representative. Thereby the nation was implicitly reaffirming the priority of Congress at the same time that it asserted the American principle of the diffusion of power. Within the varying equilibrium of power, the changing relative weight of the executive and judiciary would be at once junior and autonomous.

VIII

THE TRADITIONAL
BALANCE

I T WAS NOT only the presence at the start of strong men with strong views that shored up the new government's two lesser branches. The common sense, the energetic sense of fact, that has been a traditional mark of Americans made the early citizens recognize that when acting on its own the new Congress—in this respect like the old that had been replaced—lacked initiative, vigor and speed in dealing with the problems of expansion, finance, trade, treaty, war and threat of war that were being inescapably posed.[1] For these traits, which were sometimes necessary and could at other times be made to seem so, the executive was felt to be the more appropriate agency.

It would be wrong, however, to read a 20th-century context back into that early strengthening of the executive and judiciary beyond what had been generally foreseen or by most intended. These two

---

1. Though not all were agreed on the need, much less the desirability, of initiative, vigor and speed in government. Professor Leonard White (*The Federalists,* p. 22) quotes from a speech of John Page of Virginia to the First Congress: "The doctrine of energy in Government, as I said before, is the true doctrine of tyrants . . . Energy of Government may be the destruction of liberty; it should not, therefore, be too much cherished in a free country. A spirit of independence should be cultivated.

"The liberty and security of our fellow-citizens is our great object, and not the prompt execution of the laws. Indecision, delay, blunders, nay, villainous actions in the administration of Government, are trifles compared to legalizing the full exertion of a tyrannical despotism."

branches were from almost the start stronger than expected, stronger than can be strictly deduced from the clauses of the Constitution, stronger than they might have been if another than Washington had been the first President or if there had been no John Marshall. They nevertheless remained, for more than a century of the nation's existence, the lesser branches. Not only in doctrine and in explicit constitutional definition but also in fact, in history, the legislature was prior, first among its political peers.

The two Federalist Presidents were followed by the leader of an opposition whose object was, in his own words, "to preserve the Legislature pure and independent of the Executive, to restrain the administration to republican forms and principles, and not permit the Constitution to be construed into a monarchy, and to be warped in practice into all the principles and pollutions of the Hamiltonian Federalists' favorite English model."[2] Professor Corwin observes that "Jefferson's conception of executive power . . . was more Whig than that of the British Whigs themselves in subordinating it to 'the supreme legislative power.'"[3]

It is a historical commonplace that in the course of our history the power equilibrium among the different branches of the central government has continually varied. There have, in particular, been "strong Presidents" and "weak Presidents," with a correlated shift in the balance between executive and legislature. But a distinction must be made between a "strong President" and a "strengthening of the presidential office." The strength of a President, whereby he overweighs Congress for part or all of his term of office, may be a quality of his political personality and his own special political methods rather than the result of enduring changes that his administration makes in the constitutional nature of the executive branch.

2. Thomas Jefferson, as quoted by Edward S. Corwin, *The President: Office & Powers* (New York: New York University Press, 1948), p. 20.
3. *Ibid.*

This was, very largely, the case with Thomas Jefferson as President—in spite of the Louisiana Purchase, which indeed he recognized to be un-, or at any rate non-constitutional.[4] Jefferson was a strong President because he was a strong personality and used with frequent success an intricate, often devious, method of political operation. John Marshall correctly predicted that in net result his leadership would weaken the *office* of President. Professor Leonard White describes the paradoxical transition as follows:

> The floor leader, the party caucus, the intimate personal relations between members of the two branches, the willingness of the House to accept drafts of important bills, went far to maintain effective working relations. . . .
>
> Jefferson, in short, built up a highly centralized system, operated for the most part by conference, consultation, and free discussion rather than by harsher means of leadership. The development of this very machinery was to make possible, as [Ralph Volney] Harlow has demonstrated, "a radical change in the relationship between executive and legislature." If the House leaders should get control of the machinery of caucus, floor leader, and speakership, they would be in a position to control the whole executive administration. Precisely this development was to occur as Jefferson left the stage.[5]

The most striking institutional expression of the enhanced role of Congress, which under Madison and Monroe probably went far enough to negate the principle of the diffusion of sovereignty, was the congressional nominating caucus, by which presidential candi-

---

4. Jefferson wrote to a friend that by negotiating the Purchase he had "gone beyond the Constitution." He wished to propose a Constitutional Amendment as the only proper method for purging the unlawful act, but allowed himself to be dissuaded therefrom by his Cabinet and close associates.

5. Leonard D. White, *The Jeffersonians*, pp. 52–3.

dates were named between 1800 and 1830.[6] It was the national presidential nominating convention, left as a permanent legacy from Andrew Jackson's administrations, that grafted some of his personal and popular strength onto the Presidential office. Through the device of the national party convention, the Fathers' intent that the executive should have an independent relation to the voters was institutionally reaffirmed.

The effect of Jackson's two administrations, however, once he had himself left the White House, did not so much upset as restore the governmental equilibrium. Although the presidential office probably never again dropped so low, even when the men who held it were inordinately light in weight, as during some of the Madison-Monroe years, Congress maintained a normal priority throughout the 19th century. Not one citizen in 10,000 can remember the presidential series between Jackson and Lincoln, but (until a generation ago) every schoolboy knew something of the career and policies of Daniel Webster, Henry Clay and John C. Calhoun, and most schoolboys could quote at least a paragraph or two from their congressional orations.

Abraham Lincoln was a war executive, strong both as man and as magistrate. In order to win the war and reunite the nation, Lincoln found in the Presidency new, or at any rate unsuspected powers; and he used these powers. On the ground of the emergency in Maryland and the public safety, Congress not being then in session, he was ready even to suspend the writ of habeas corpus. He contended—though the weight of qualified opinion is, or until lately has been, against him—that he had the legal right as well as the moral duty to do so. But whether legally justified or not when done, Lincoln subsequently submitted the suspension as well as his other emergency acts to Congress, which then acquitted him through enabling if considerably ex post facto legislation. Under his mandate as

6. The system of congressional nominating caucuses began to break down in 1824. It was first used, surprisingly enough, by the Federalists in 1800.

commander-in-chief, Lincoln issued the Emancipation Proclamation, but the slaves could not be free citizens until a constitutional amendment was adopted, applicable to each and all of the several states.

In the fields of economic mobilization, military law and reconstruction, as well as in emancipation and civil rights, Lincoln often acted boldly without waiting for Congress. But he did so under the spur of overwhelming internal crisis, on the authority of the war power of the President as commander-in-chief, which was recognized by all to exist constitutionally even if there was disagreement concerning its scope. It is an intended triumph of the Constitution that it provides for a Chief Executive able to react and act with the concentrated force of the nation in a supreme emergency of war or rebellion. It would not have surprised the Fathers that such action, if the emergency were deemed grave enough, should go outside and beyond the law in, as it were, a suspension of the Constitution. But if the head of the state thus acts, it must be—according to the canons of constitutional government—at his own risk and peril. The emergency ended, he and his actions must be brought back within the frame of the law, and there judged, and acquitted or condemned.

Lincoln's conduct as commander-in-chief enlarged the permanent reservoir of presidential power, but the actual flow was abruptly narrowed at the war's end and his death. Congress, which had by no means been passive during the course of the war itself, regained its clear priority in the governmental scheme, and in some respects reached its highest relative status during the succeeding generation. The impeachment of President Johnson failed by only a single vote. Congress, in passing the Reconstruction Acts, "excepted" them from judicial review; and this restriction on its autonomy the Supreme Court did not challenge. As late as Cleveland's first term, at the end of the Constitution's first century, the English author of *The American Commonwealth* could conclude from his own careful observation: "In quiet times the power of the President is not great," and add: "He has less influence on legislation . . . than the Speaker of the House."

The relatively modest traditional role of the Presidency in relation to the legislature is symbolized by the history of the veto power. For Franklin Roosevelt, Truman and Eisenhower, drawing out political premises introduced by Woodrow Wilson, the veto, or its threat, is a routine instrument of presidential power through which the Chief Executive both influences and participates in legislation. For the early Presidents, the veto was a last reserve. By most of the Fathers it was intended only or primarily as an emergency safeguard against a manifestly unconstitutional act that, because of temporary passion or hasty error, might have passed through the legislative process.

Of the first sixteen Presidents, through and including Abraham Lincoln, seven (John Adams, Jefferson, John Quincy Adams, Van Buren, William Henry Harrison, Taylor and Fillmore) did not exercise the veto power even once. The others, in these first seventy-six years of the government under the Constitution, vetoed a total of only 48 of the thousands of bills that came from Congress: in most cases either because of what they thought to be a clear constitutional objection (even though in some cases they agreed with the substance) or because, as in one of Washington's two vetoes, there was a technical difficulty in the way the bill was drawn.[7]

In the generation after Lincoln there were 145 more vetoes, most of them a result of President Grant's petty squabbles with Congress over patronage. Cleveland ran up a total of 584, but this figure is deceptive in political substance, since almost all of these were directed against several groups of more or less identical "private bills" without legislative significance, which Cleveland judged improper or corrupt. Benjamin Harrison plus the seven Presidents between

---

7. I am using the figures in Richardson's *Messages,* supplemented by *The World Almanac,* 1958 edition. The various statistical summaries of vetoes differ among themselves, although not enough to affect the political implications. *The World Almanac* gives for these first seventy-six years 36 regular and 21 pocket vetoes.

Cleveland and Franklin Roosevelt vetoed 344 bills, most of them of minor importance.

The shift, both qualitative and quantitative, under Franklin Roosevelt is striking. He exercised his veto power no less than 631 times, against every sort of legislation. That is—if we discount the two or three special batches of private bills vetoed by Cleveland—Franklin Roosevelt vetoed more acts of Congress than all of the thirty-one Presidents who preceded him during the 144 years from 1789 to 1933. Moreover, Franklin Roosevelt (acting on February 22, 1944) was the first President to veto what was for so many centuries of Anglo-American political tradition the acknowledged key and peculiar power of the legislative assembly: a revenue bill. Harry Truman, with 250 vetoes in seven years, many of major bills, continued the transformed practice of his predecessor;[8] and Dwight Eisenhower, in spite of a rhetorical rejection of the Roosevelt-Truman swelled executive, piled up 98 vetoes in his first three White House years.

What the veto statistics confirm is that for the century and a half prior to Franklin Roosevelt the executive, however jealous of its own prerogatives, did not challenge the legislative supremacy of Congress nor even attempt any big expansion of the modest share in the legislative process that the Constitution had itself assigned to the executive branch. In American constitutional practice prior to 1933 (with which we are concerned in these chapters), the power and threat of the presidential veto were, generally speaking, restrained within the comparatively narrow limits that the Fathers intended.

8. In his *Memoirs* Mr. Truman writes: "I never hesitated to veto any bill presented to me when I was convinced that it failed to serve the best interests of the majority of the people in all parts of the country. I found it necessary to veto more major bills than any other President, with the possible exception of Grover Cleveland." (Harry S. Truman, *Memoirs*, Vol. II, p. 479; New York: Doubleday & Co., 1956; copyright 1956 by Time, Inc.)

2

The frequency of Supreme Court decisions declaring acts of Congress unconstitutional, and therefore null, follows a curve rather similar to that of the presidential vetoes, though—because of the mode of appointment of judges—lagging somewhat behind. Prior to the Civil War there were only two such decisions. There were another twenty through to the end of the 19th century. During the first four decades of the 20th century they came noticeably oftener—forty-nine in all.[9] After 1940, as the judiciary came under the influence of the same political forces that had earlier taken over the executive branch and the bureaucracy, these judicial vetoes, like the presidential, became more or less routine.

The idea, widespread today, that in the American system the Supreme Court is the ultimate and only constitutional arbiter, so that the system is actually one of "judicial supremacy," is no more borne out in American tradition than in the written propositions of the Constitution itself. "From 1803 to 1930 the Supreme Court nullified acts of Congress in some sixty cases, but less than a dozen of these were of major importance and few, if any, of them imposed lasting limits on the law-making power of Congress."[10]

A due estimate of the role of the judiciary in the American constitutional system is often obscured by two fallacies. One of these involves the meaning of "finality of judgment." With respect to the decision on a particular case at issue that falls within its jurisdiction, the Supreme Court has always insisted[11] that its determination is "final" and not subject to review by any other court or by the legislature. This finality, it is held, appertains to the nature of "judicial

9. These figures are from *The Constitution of the United States of America*.
10. Galloway, *The Legislative Process in Congress,* p. 464.
11. Explicitly so insisted from the first occasion—Hayburn's Case, 1792/3—in which the problem was raised.

power." But finality with respect to a particular case[12] is quite different from finality with respect to a general rule or principle: that is, a law. The Court, when rendering a decision about the particular case before it often does, of course, have something to say (in what are called *obiter dicta*) about the rules, principles and laws. But neither in theory nor in historic fact does the finality of the particular decision carry over automatically to the *obiter dicta*—however earnestly some judges may believe so.

There is a second fallacy—of "verbal fetishism"—whereby the verbal order is mistakenly thought to correspond exactly to the temporal and causal order of real events. Often, at any given stage of constitutional development, the Court pronounces "the final word" on a law. That is to say, the Court gives explicit, systematic verbal form to an operative interpretation of a statute or common law principle. This does not necessarily mean (though it might mean) that the Court has "made" the law or been active in changing its substance. The Court may be (and usually is) only recording, giving verbal form, to changes that have been caused in primary part by the legislature, the executive and perhaps by still other social institutions. A Town Crier was not supreme over the Mayor just because he had the last word in telling the citizens what must be done, nor does a ghost writer necessarily run a corporation because he writes the president's speeches. The process of judicial determination is, certainly, more creative than the Town Crier's mere passive repetition, and no doubt more active in substance than the usual ghost writer's verbal exercise. And sometimes, we know, the Court does make law, even on a massive scale. But without further examination we cannot assume that in the case of laws and principles the "finality" of the Court's words means anything more than "latest in time." In a totalitarian state also, the courts, as a rule,

12. Even the finality with respect to a particular case is in the American system subject to the pardoning power of the executive, and the power of the legislature to indemnify damages assessed through the judicial process.

speak the final word, but no one will argue that we can deduce therefrom that in Nazi Germany or communist Russia there is judicial supremacy.

Montesquieu, Hamilton and Madison were correct in their observation that the judiciary, on its own independent resources, must inevitably be "the weakest of the three departments of power." Chief Justice Marshall repeated the same conclusion, essentially, when he declared in 1824: "Judicial power, as contradistinguished from the power of the laws, has no existence. Courts . . . can will nothing." And Justice Owen Roberts echoed in 1936: "All the court does, can do, is to announce its considered judgment upon the question. The only power it has, if such it may be called, is the power of judgment."

And is this not really obvious? The act of a court (including its pronouncement of *obiter dicta*) is a judgment, and this judgment can be rendered only on an individual complaint that is brought—after the event—before it. The court cannot directly compel anyone to initiate the complaint or to accept its findings. Police and army— the means of coercion—are under command of the executive, not the judiciary. The courts cannot even assure the material conditions of their own existence: the taxing and appropriating powers belong to the legislature.

The judiciary can gain (or seem to gain) preponderate power only with the support or compliance of the other two branches, only in what might nowadays be called "a united front" with one or both of them. In the long run, as American history abundantly proves, the judiciary must inevitably lose in a direct conflict with the executive and the legislature—if, it should be added, they choose to fight.

The judiciary has sometimes been able to delay, but it has never permanently blocked the other two branches in a course upon which both of them are determined and for which they have the backing of the electorate; nor on the few occasions when it has been tried has the judiciary been able, in any major matter, to coerce the two sister branches into a line of action that both of them opposed.[13] John Marshall could pronounce his finding that Congress possessed all the implied powers, but this meant little while Congress was under the control of Jeffersonian legislators who were not disposed to exercise implied powers. Chief Justice Taney could deduce a judicial solution of the problems of slavery and States' Rights; but the Dred Scott decision in which he announced it, accepted by neither President nor Congress nor the states, faded away without ever having entered into the active life of the nation.

The Constitution, as we have noted, provides for only the barest minimum of the American judicial system, with all else left for Congress to determine. The Constitution decrees "one supreme Court" (its composition unspecified), but only "such inferior Courts as the Congress may from time to time ordain and establish." These inferior courts—their numbers, kinds, jurisdiction, funds, duties, rules, their powers to issue writs and injunctions and orders—exist only by virtue of congressional statutes that begin with the basic Judiciary Act passed by the first session of the first Congress.

Although the Supreme Court does exist by constitutional, not statutory fiat, it is not exempt from congressional restriction and control. The number of its members, its budget, even where and when it meets, are subject to the legislative will. The Constitution assigns it original jurisdiction only in "Cases affecting Ambassadors, other public Ministers and Consuls, and those in which a State shall be Party." In other federal cases, the Supreme Court holds appellate

13. Whether the 1954 and subsequent de-segregation decisions will be accepted by the nation is not yet known. Although it is true that in this set of related decisions the Court has gone further than ever before in making law, and in doing so by positive action rather than negative interpretation, nevertheless the Court is not acting wholly on its own. Its policy is in accord with the will of the executive, and a considerable portion of Congress, the states and the people. Otherwise Brown v. Board of Education would by now be deader than [Dred] Scott v. Sanford. At that, it is not very lively.

jurisdiction "with such Exceptions, and under such Regulations as the Congress shall make."

In 1849 the Supreme Court ordered the Wheeling & Belmont Bridge Co. to destroy its bridge over the Ohio River as an "unlawful" obstruction to navigation. The company, disregarding the decision and a subsequent injunction, turned to Congress, which in 1852 passed a statute declaring the bridge to be "a lawful structure." The Court, accepting, noted that although the bridge "may still be an obstruction in fact, it is not so in the contemplation of law."

In 1868, when *Ex parte McCardle*—an action that implied a challenge to the constitutionality of the Reconstruction Acts—was actually before the Court, Congress passed (over President Johnson's veto) a rider repealing the Supreme Court's jurisdiction in all cases arising out of the relevant statute. The Court then dismissed the case. Under Franklin Roosevelt, the workings of the wartime Price Control Act were similarly exempted from Supreme Court scrutiny.

In conflicts with the Supreme Court, Congress has often threatened to use, and has a number of times actually used its power to alter the number of Justices. Under the original Judiciary Act there were six Justices of the Supreme Court. As episodes in the Jeffersonians' struggle to control the judiciary, Congress changed the number to five in 1801, then back to six in 1802. The number was raised to nine in 1837 (to water down the influence of John Marshall), and to ten in 1863 (to give the North a safer majority); dropped to seven in 1866 (to prevent Andrew Johnson from making any appointments), and voted back to nine in 1869, when Grant could name the new members—who, as expected, brought a reversal of the Court's previous finding against the Legal Tender Act. There were thus substantial precedents for Franklin Roosevelt's "Court packing" proposal. Though this last was never adopted by Congress, its threat, combined with Roosevelt's manipulation of public opinion and Willis Van Devanter's forced resignation, brought the Court around to acceptance of the New Deal measures.

The Court can always be corrected by amending the Constitution, a process in which it has no role. Amendments XI, XII and XV were, in fact, specifically designed to overrule Supreme Court decisions. Impeachment—within the sole power of Congress—is also always a formal possibility, although it has not been attempted for Supreme Court Justices since the Jeffersonians failed against Salmon Chase. Still, even the latent possibility of impeachment serves as a psychological curb on the judiciary.

Let us also note that the Justices do not grow Topsylike from the Bench. They are selected by the Chief Executive and confirmed by one House of the legislature. Though the Justices, like other men, can change through the years, and though because of their permanent appointment they run no risk from changing, they and their Court usually reflect the basic opinions and values of those who have chosen them.

By these observations I do not intend to dismiss as negligible the traditional share of the Court in the complex whole of American sovereignty, nor to deny that this share proved to be considerably larger than was conceived by the Philadelphia Convention. I wish merely to moderate the exaggerated theory of "judicial supremacy" which, by an overly formalistic reading of the record, sees the Court as the major or even majority partner in the national directorate. Under the American system the Court does undoubtedly hold an autonomous share in the nation's power, a bigger share than that of the judiciary in most other nations; but neither the intentions of the Fathers, the provisions of the Constitution, nor the actual history of the nation's political development confirm the theory of the Court's preponderance.

Even in the narrower field of "constitutional interpretation" it is not true that the Court has had the sole and final word. Faced with a striking decision that goes counter to their own conviction on an issue that much concerns them, political analysts fall back on the aphorism: "The Constitution means what the Supreme Court says it means." Like most aphorisms this one is inexact and over-simplified. The Constitution means in the first instance its own explicit words, the intent of which is in some considerable measure unchallengeable and unchallenged. And it means, in gloss on that source, what the Congress and President, and also the states and public opinion, say it means, as well as what the Court says. We find here as throughout the American system an actual resultant that obtains from the dynamic clash and balancing of divided and autonomous powers.

The Presidency, from Washington's first day in office, and Congress from the first action of the first session of the first Congress, have been interpreting and applying the Constitution. We have already observed that the executive veto power has always been understood, and sometimes exclusively, as a negative device for protecting the integrity of the Constitution. No important debate in Congress neglects the constitutional bearing of the questions at issue. For every statute that the Supreme Court has nullified on constitutional grounds, a score have, on the same grounds, failed of congressional enactment. There are many more words, and as cogent words, of constitutional analysis in the journals of Congress as in the opinions of the Court; and there are not a few, also, in the messages of the Presidents.

Throughout the 19th century the great constitutional debates raged, and for the most part were acted on, in the halls of Congress, not in the courts. The judiciary seldom intervened, and then never decisively, in the supreme issues of slavery and union. In the development of the meaning of the commerce clause, the war powers, and regulatory functions, the role of the judiciary, though real, was by the nature of the case secondary; the initiative, the historical as distinguished from the formal decisions, could only come, generally speaking, from the President or the Congress.

In the present century, undoubtedly, the Court has enlarged its share in the power. By its more frequent decisions nullifying congressional acts or creating new laws under the guise of interpreting the old, the Court has shown more openly what has always been true: that in the American system the highest court is not a merely judicial bench but one among the integral "political departments." But even in its boldest encroachments, the Court has not been able to overleap the all but inevitable limits of the judicial function. The Court cannot indefinitely prevail against the united view of executive, legislature and public opinion. Certainly up through 1933 (to which period our conclusions are still restricted), "judicial supremacy"[14] was more a polemical metaphor than a historical description of the American system.

Traditionally the American governmental system has been in fact what it has been customarily said to be: a changing equilibrium of dispersed, balancing and conflicting powers. If within that system any one of the diverse elements has traditionally been, on the whole, of relatively more weight than the others, it is, as the formal scheme of the Constitution plainly suggests, the legislature, the Congress. If we have had—or have—any sort of special supremacy, then it has been a congressional supremacy.

3

That the traditional form of the American government was in fact "congressional supremacy" was the conclusion of one of the most famous analysts of the American system, to the proof of which he wrote his first and best known book in the concluding years of the nation's first century. The young Woodrow Wilson selected the title of *Congressional Government*[15] to make unmistakable the meaning of

14. The idea of "judicial supremacy" was first popularized around the turn of the century by Marxist and semi-Marxist historians who viewed and attacked the Court as the most reactionary influence in American society. Cf., for example, Gustavus Myers, *History of the Supreme Court of the United States,* and Charles A. Beard, *The Supreme Court and the Constitution.*

15. Woodrow Wilson, *Congressional Government* (Boston: Houghton, Mifflin, 1885).

his central thesis. He was very scornful of those who mistook "the 'literary theory' of the Constitution" with its doctrine of elaborate checks and balances for "the actual machinery" (p. 12), who confounded "the ideal balances which are to be found in the books" with "the rough realities of actual practice" (pp. 39–40). Studying these realities "in a light unclouded by theory," we will find that "for all practical purposes . . . Congress [is] predominant over its so-called coordinate branches . . . Congressional government [is] the real government of the Union" (pp. 52–3).

In his introductory chapter Wilson laid down and applied his methodological principles:

> The leading inquiry in the examination of any system of government must, of course, concern primarily the real deposi-taries and the essential machinery of power. There is always a center of power: where in [the American government] is that center? . . . The answers one gets to these and kindred questions from authoritative manuals of constitutional exposition are not satisfactory, chiefly because they are contradicted by self-evident facts. It is said that there is no single or central force in our federal scheme; and so there is not in the federal *scheme,* but only a balance of powers and nice adjustment of interactive checks, as all the books say. How is it, however, in the practical conduct of the federal government? In that, un-questionably, the predominant and controlling force, the center and source of all motive and of all regulative power, is Congress. All niceties of constitutional restriction and even many broad principles of constitutional limitation have been overridden, and a thoroughly organized system of congres-sional control set up. (pp. 10–11.)

The courts have proved ineffective as brakes on the legislature. Even the doctrine of implied powers, though "given out, at length, with the sanction of the federal Supreme Court," and containing, by

Wilson's interpretation, "in its manifest character as a doctrine of legislative prerogative, a very vigorous principle of constitutional growth," had the inevitable effect of reinforcing Congress as "the dominant, nay, the irresistible, power of the federal system" (p. 23). And it is Congress that holds the initiative. "The legislature is the aggressive spirit. It is the motive power of the government, and unless the judiciary can check it, the courts are of little worth as balancewheels in the system. . . . [But the courts] have naught to say upon questions of policy. Congress must itself judge what measures may legitimately be used to supplement or make effectual its acknowledged jurisdiction" (p. 36).

As for the executive, "the prestige of the presidential office has declined with the character of the Presidents. . . . I am disposed to think, however, that the decline in the character of the Presidents is not the cause, but only the accompanying manifestation, of the declining prestige of the presidential office. . . . Its power has waned because the power of Congress has become predominant" (pp. 42–3).

The Senate of itself, indeed, is more than enough to browbeat the President:

All through the direct dealing of the Senate with the President there runs this characteristic spirit of irresponsible dictation. The President may tire the Senate by dogged persistence, but he can never deal with it upon a ground of real equality. He has no real presence in the Senate. His power does not extend beyond the most general suggestion. The Senate always has the last word. . . . It dictates to another branch of the government which was intended to be coordinate and coequal with it. . . . It was not essentially different in the early days." (pp. 238–9.)

In a still earlier essay, Wilson had decided that the President is "merely the executor of the sovereign legislative will," and is not to be judged the first citizen of the republic. "The most important, the most powerful man in the government of the United States in time of peace is the Speaker of the House of Representatives."[16]

These statements were exaggerations, of course, even at the time when Wilson was writing them, and in general Wilson cannot be accepted as a scrupulous, unbiased observer. He was from the start something of an ideologue, with a reformer's zeal and, beneath his rather Sunday-school appearance, a passionate will to personal power. He was more interested in scourging congressional abuses than in merely describing congressional power. Like many who love words, he tended toward a rhetoric of superlatives. Still, to the many thousands of readers of *Congressional Government*,[17] the picture was recognizable and convincing, even if drawn in heavy lines.

It is invariably pointed out by scholars, nowadays, that Wilson was writing in 1883–84, toward the end of a post-Civil War Reconstruction Period, when the Presidency had fallen on feeble days, and both the power and the corruption of Congress were relatively mighty. But Wilson was a young man more of books than of affairs. He had read as much, probably more, of the nation's pre- as of its post-Lincoln constitutional history. He did not temper his generalizations. If he found Congress predominant, supreme even, through the administrations of Ulysses Grant, Rutherford Hayes and Chester Arthur, there is nothing to suggest that he did, or could have reached a different conclusion concerning the administrations of a Zachary Taylor, Franklin Pierce, John Tyler or James Madison. In

16. "Cabinet Government in the United States," published in the August, 1879 issue of *The International Review*. The quotations from the article are taken from *The Politics of Woodrow Wilson*, selections from his speeches and writings, edited, with an introduction, by August Heckscher (New York: Harper & Bros., 1956).

17. There were fifteen printings by 1900, and a number of foreign translations.

fine, though Woodrow Wilson was exaggerating, he was exaggerating a truth. The relative power of the three great branches of the federal government had been in a continually shifting equilibrium. The power of the executive had had temporary spurts, principally under three extraordinary circumstances: the beginning of the nation with the Father of his Country in the chair; the advent (in Andrew Jackson) of an amazing personality that at the same time expressed the political emergence of new social and geographical forces; and the Civil War. Nevertheless, in the broad curve of American political development Congress had been, Wilson accurately understood, predominant.

In writing a new preface to his book in 1900, and in the 1908 Columbia lectures that became his *Constitutional Government in the United States,* Wilson added postscripts to his earlier assertions, without repudiating their application through the year when he had written them. In 1900 he found that, as a result of the war with Spain and the greater part that foreign affairs were playing in national policy, "a greatly increased power and opportunity for constructive statesmanship [had been] given the President. . . . There is no trouble now [as there had been throughout much of the 19th century] about getting the President's speeches printed and read, every word." He concluded his preface with authentic prophecy: "It may be, too, that the new leadership of the executive . . . will have a very far-reaching effect upon our whole method of government. It may give the heads of the executive departments a new influence upon the action of Congress. . . . It may put this volume hopelessly out of date."

By 1908 he was ready to declare to his audience that the President "is also the political leader of the nation, or has it in his choice to be. . . . A President whom it trusts can not only lead it but form it to his views." But by 1908 Wilson was jumping a bit ahead of history, perhaps because he was shifting from the rhetoric of a historian to that of a candidate.

4

By adding one more element, we may not complete the description of the conservative and liberal syndromes, *genus Americanum,* that has been built up through the discussion in these chapters that constitute the first Part of this book.

In addition to the twelve symptoms previously listed, the conservative syndrome—as at present manifest in the United States—characteristically includes:

(m) a tendency to favor the relative power of Congress within the diffused power equilibrium;

and the liberal:

(m') a tendency to distrust Congress, and to favor the relative power of the executive.

The difference here (as with many of the other symptoms) is not absolute, but in tendency, emphasis or bias. Both conservatives and liberals accept, or claim to accept—whatever might be the actual consequences of the full triumph of one or the other view in practice—the basic American principle of a diffusion of sovereignty. The issue is that of relative weight within the balance. The conservatives feel that in the present equilibrium, Congress has, in general, dropped too low; that, as a practical political matter, the prerogatives of Congress should be defended and restored, and its powers strengthened; that the executive should be curbed. The liberals are not dismayed by the relative decrease in Congress' weight within the political system or by the accretions to the executive. In general, the modern liberals judge as desirable a political order in which the executive would be even stronger, and the legislature even more restricted in function, than obtains today in the United States.

We must note, however, that these contrasting attitudes toward the roles of legislature and executive, unlike most of the other elements of the conservative and liberal syndromes, are temporary and perhaps somewhat opportunistic symptoms. It cannot be held that an American conservative always and necessarily favors the legislature; and an American liberal, the executive. Today this is so, but it has not always been and may not forever be. In the early decades of our national history conservatives[18] tended to favor a strengthening of the executive as against Congress; and the "liberals" of those years (if we may extend the term by analogy) on the whole wanted to fortify congressional power. Throughout the 19th century many European conservatives expressed particular admiration for the Supreme Court as against both Congress and the President. It is thus suggested that the attitude toward the various branches of government is a secondary or derivative symptom. Primary allegiance shifts from executive to legislature to Court as this or that branch seems the most likely to foster the *other* elements of the political syndrome.

However, it is at the present time a fact, not likely to change for some while to come, that American conservatives tend to favor Congress; and American liberals, the President. It has been my aim to define the conservative and liberal syndromes—the respective political attitudes of present-day American conservatives and American liberals—in what might be called "existential" terms. That is, I have tried merely to describe summarily and to list the political ideas, beliefs and tendencies that are *in fact* held (though not always consciously articulated) by those present-day Americans whom most of us recognize as "conservatives" and those others whom we call "liberals."

Now it is possible to approach this problem of definition by another mode of analysis, which will be found to yield similar though

18. Since I am defining "conservatism" and "conservatives" in "traditionalist" terms, and am concerned specifically with the "American system" as developed through the history and tradition of the United States as an independent nation based on the 1789 Constitution, there is some vagueness about the meaning of "conservative" in the early decades. If a "respect for tradition" is part of the essence of conservatism, there was not then an established American national political tradition to be respectful of; though of course the American tradition relates back, in many respects, to pre-Constitutional history.

not identical results. We can define conservatism and liberalism by reference to certain philosophical principles, and from the two sets of principles deduce the position that each holds on this or that political and social issue. But there is a dispute about these defining principles. Some hold, for example, that conservatism is based ultimately on an individualist philosophy; others, that it rests on an "organic" view of society; still others, that its roots are theological. Similarly, some claim and others deny that liberalism logically presupposes a materialist or relativist metaphysics. Even if we could agree on the philosophic criteria, these are not enough to guide us to the practical, operative meaning of the two attitudes. The decisive political and social issues upon which our opinions divide are products of history, tradition and present circumstance as well as of metaphysical dichotomies. We cannot always deduce a citizen's specific position on these issues from his general philosophic principles.

I have therefore chosen a more humble, descriptive method. Using the traditional (pre-1933) American political system as an orienting background, I have charted the conservative and liberal attitudes as these actually exist in the United States today, as expressed or implicit in the political behavior of those whom we do in fact call conservatives or liberals. Any other observer may check the accuracy of the charts from his own experience, and may, if the evidence requires, introduce corrections.

In the remaining two Parts of this book I propose to use the terms "conservative" and "liberal" in the meanings that have now been defined. In order to keep them freshly and fully in mind, let us sum up the two lists as briefly as possible, while recognizing that the brevity brings a certain amount of distortion.

THE CONSERVATIVE SYNDROME

C-1. Belief that government involves a non-rational factor; distrust of abstract political ideology.

C-2. Belief that human nature is limited and corrupt; anti-utopianism.

C-3. Respect for tradition.

C-4. Belief in the diffusion of sovereignty and power.

C-5. For representative, mediated government; against plebiscitary democracy.

C-6. For States' Rights.

C-7. For the autonomy of the various branches of the central government.

C-8. Greater solicitude for the limits than for the powers of government.

C-9. Belief that the American constitutional tradition embodies principles that are intelligible, and of permanent value.

C-10. For decentralization and localization.

C-11. Presumption in favor of private economic enterprise.

C-12. Primary philosophic concern with individuals in their private capacity, rather than with nation or other collectivity.

C-13. Presumption in favor of Congress as against the executive.

THE LIBERAL SYNDROME

L-1. Confidence in the ability of rational science and democratic ideology to comprehend and solve all problems of government.

L-2. Belief in the unlimited potentiality of human nature.

L-3. No presumption in favor of traditional usage.

L-4. Willingness to waive principle of diffusion of power if thereby progressive forces or goals are furthered.

L-5. Tendency toward plebiscitary democracy.

L-6. Minor concern with or even disapproval of States' Rights.

L-7. Belief that the autonomy of the branches of the central government hinders solution of major contemporary problems.

L-8. More solicitude for the power of government to accomplish progressive goals than for limits on government.

L-9. Interpretation of the American constitutional tradition as instrumental, its meaning wholly dependent on time and circumstance.

L-10. Belief that decentralization and localization often interfere with solution of modern problems.

L-11. Critical attitude toward private economic enterprise, and positive belief in government economic control plus some measure of government ownership.

L-12. Belief that expansion of governmental activity aids the attainment of the good life.

L-13. Presumption in favor of executive as against Congress.

By saying that these lists designate two "syndromes" I mean that each of these two groups of thirteen elements or symptoms tends to hang together: that is, to occur as a group, not merely at random. Whether the cause of this linkage—which is not absolute, of course—is metaphysical, social or psychological we do not need to decide in order to observe that it exists. If a citizen exhibits symptoms C-3, C-5 and C-11, for example, we will usually discover him to possess most or all of the other C's, and few if any L's. A belief in expanded governmental activity (L-12) seldom is found without fairly optimistic confidence in human potentialities (L-2), a pragmatic theory of the Constitution (L-9), a lack of major concern with States' Rights (L-6) or decentralization in general (L-10), and indeed most of the other L's. We seldom discover anyone who stands strongly for private economic enterprise (C-11) and at the same time for, say, plebiscitary democracy (L-5).

In other words, we might say that conservatism and liberalism as here defined are social facts in contemporary American society. The greater part of the American citizenry tends to divide as conservatives or liberals—a division which, however, does not coincide with that between Democrats and Republicans in our political machinery.

For the special problem of this book—the role of Congress in the American political system, in particular its present and future role—

the division can be put crudely but not inaccurately. Conservatives tend to be *for* Congress—for Congress as an institution, that is, not necessarily for each of its actions; to wish to defend, strengthen and preserve it. Liberals, when the institutional relations are at issue, tend to be *against* Congress; to be inclined to attack and weaken it. The further chapters will note many engagements, of both practice and theory, in this conflict that in its outcome will prove so decisive for the future of our Republic.

PART TWO

The Present Position
of Congress

*It need hardly be pointed out that in modern states, which are far larger in
size than the ancient and have their complicated organization, their bureaucracies, their standing armies, no revolution can be achieved with a dag-
ger thrust in somebody's back, with a well-laid ambush, with a
well-planned attack on a public building. When modern revolutionists take
their cue from the practices of their ancient predecessors, they fall into gross
errors of anachronism.*

GAETANO MOSCA, *The Ruling Class*

IX

THE FALL OF
CONGRESS

FROM 1825 to 1829 John Quincy Adams had been President of the United States. In September 1830 several of his Massachusetts neighbors inquired whether he could be induced to stand for election to the House of Representatives from the Plymouth district. Adams replied that he had "in that respect no scruple whatever. No person could be degraded by serving the people as a Representative in Congress." He was elected by a large majority, and thereafter served continuously in the House until his death in 1848.

In the summer of 1843 Adams traveled through upper New York and much of Ohio, to Cincinnati, where he laid the cornerstone of an astronomical observatory, the first built in America, which he had long promoted. The New York side trip had been planned originally for the merely domestic end of his daughter-in-law's health, but it turned quickly into a triumphal journey. In Buffalo, Albany, Rochester and Utica as well as in Cleveland, Columbus and Cincinnati, there were delegations of leading citizens, "immense crowds . . . , people shouting . . . , guns firing, bells ringing," parades and receptions. Crowds and leading citizens were alike welcoming not the dean of living ex-Presidents, but the many-termed congressional representative, public defender of the Constitution and the right of petition. After his first election to Congress in 1830, Adams had himself written in his diary: "My election as President of the United States was not half so gratifying to my inmost soul. No election or appointment conferred upon me ever gave me so much pleasure."

It certainly cannot be said that John Quincy Adams' career or person was typical of his own or any other period in our national history. However, although no other President, at any time, became a Congressman after his tour as Chief Executive, it is only in our day that such a shift in office has become simply unthinkable. The office of President has grown too vast. We have lately had two Presidents who after leaving the White House have lived on through many vigorous, alert and public-minded years. A naive friend or editorial has now and then sighed that one or the other of them ought to be able, for his country's sake, to run for the Senate. (No one has been so naive as to mention running for the House.) Most citizens have understood that this is out of the question, not from any mere personal aversion, but because of the institutional disparity.[1] A man whose person has embodied the power now pertaining to the executive office cannot become just one unit of the group in which rests the legislature's remaining share. In fact, even the reflected glow over the Vice Presidency makes the shift almost impossible. In 1832 John C. Calhoun resigned the Vice Presidency to get elected to the Senate. In 1952 Richard Nixon resigned from the Senate to get elected Vice President.

We do not have an exact quantitative gauge to measure the percentages of power adhering to the several branches of the central government. We do not need an exact gauge to inform us that—relative to the executive, the bureaucracy and for that matter the judiciary—the legislature's share has during the past generation not merely somewhat declined but dropped to an altogether different level. The difference is not merely a change but an overturn. Throughout most of our history there has been congressional predominance within the central government. Since 1933, Congress

---

1. In December 1958 Harry Truman remarked one jovial evening that he might run for the Senate in 1960. When to his astonishment some humorless reporters took him seriously, he had to explain publicly that he was "only joking."

has not been even the peer of the executive, but a mere junior partner. To understand what is happening to the political structure of American society, we need to keep both facts in mind: that the legislature was, traditionally, predominant in theory and practice; and that it is no longer so.

The equilibrium among the different branches is continually changing, of course, and a curve displaying the relative power of Congress would have its peaks and valleys. We could compare the Congress of 1923, say, or even the Congress of early 1939 with the Congress of Washington's third year or Andrew Jackson's first, and find that nothing had changed very much. But the peaks and valleys, like those in the stock market curve or the daily climate charts from a temperate zone city, have a net direction. It is not that Congress has already lost all power, or is no longer capable of even brief revival, but that its over-all, standard or mean function has dropped to a new range.

Also as in the stock market curve, there is a Black Friday, a 1929 when a base was deeply penetrated—though the analogy is not complete, since the legislature's bear market has never turned up again except for what market operators would call episodic "technical corrections." Before and after 1933; before and after Franklin Roosevelt and the New Deal—these mark the crossing of the political line.

There were earlier auguries of the shift in the trend of many events from the beginning of this century, more deliberate in the administrations of Theodore Roosevelt and Woodrow Wilson. Theodore Roosevelt was a very strong personality and a fairly strong President. He had positive and often quite detailed ideas about a number of things that the government ought to do and the laws that Congress ought to pass so that it might do them. Certainly the presidential office was more formidable under his weight than under that of his timid predecessor. But Congress met him, in collaboration or conflict, at least as an equal. Theodore Roosevelt never cowed or supplanted Congress; Congress continued to be the lawmaking and for the most part the law-initiating body.

Woodrow Wilson went further than Theodore Roosevelt, and in theory—for he was a theorist—very far. Wilson had not only described and analyzed congressional supremacy, but condemned it. As teacher and as candidate he had set himself the quite conscious aim of aggrandizing the office of President. This he symbolized at the outset by addressing Congress in person, as no President had done since 1800. Although in the first two years of Wilson's "new democracy" and in 1917–18 the Presidency did advance to a level of more varied prominence than ever before in the nation's history, this was not yet either pervasive or secure. Congress did not accept his structural innovations, many of them modeled on his rather academic idea of British parliamentarism. Though Congress went along for a year or two with the economic and fiscal proposals from the White House, and acceded to the more than Lincolnian enlargement of the executive office through interpretation of the commander-in-chief clause, there was a sharp reversal before the war had ended. By the time of the League of Nations debate, Congress was re-asserting control not only in domestic but even in foreign policy, traditionally its most precarious field.

Under Warren Harding, with postwar lethargy and then corruption eroding the executive office, the curve of relative congressional power jumped upward. Calvin Coolidge and Herbert Hoover were by no means the "weak Presidents" that they are ordinarily pictured by post-New Deal historians. Hoover is, as Coolidge was, a man of decided intellectual convictions and a firm moral outlook, with a lofty notion of a President's responsibilities as well as his prerogatives. As President, neither hesitated to fight back vigorously against whatever he took to be a legislative encroachment on the executive function. With some allowance for an expanded role of government in American society, we may say that during their administrations the equilibrium among the branches held within the traditional range. It was in 1933 that a new zone was penetrated.

2

The shift from legislative to executive predominance—in Wilson's terms, from "congressional government" to "presidential government"—is recorded in the sensitive lists of formal society and official protocol, and mirrored in popular literature and art.

Until a generation ago, there were always a number of Senators and often some Representatives also, who kept "fashionable houses" in Washington, points of interest in conducted tours of the city, to which it was a social distinction, duly chronicled, to be invited. Today the congressional dwellings have sunk into the anonymous obscurity of a large city. It is the houses of a Secretary of State or War, or the head of this or that bureau, along with the embassies and public buildings, to which the guides point. Congressmen must be content to be mentioned in the society columns as among the guests of the administrator of a great agency. On 1957's confidential protocol charts as well as in the Social List that instructs the hostesses of Washington, not only all Cabinet members but a personal assistant of the President as well as two bureau chiefs outrank all members of Congress except for the Speaker of the House. No one in Washington society would give an extra heartbeat at a dinner invitation from a member of Congress. There are very few so assured that they would decline the bidding of the chief of a department or special agency.

In May 1882, *Harper's Weekly* published an informative article for their untraveled readers on "The City of Washington." Its first two sentences imply a contrasting attitude that today is close to unintelligible. "Strangely enough, Washington is contemplated by the press and people of America simply as the capital of the republic. In fact, its distinctiveness was fixed long ago in the public mind as the temporary abiding-place of Clay, Webster, Adams, Benton and Calhoun, and as the seat of law-making power." It is implicit that [John Quincy] Adams won his place on this list of the great and defining Washingtonians not as once-President but as the many-termed Congressman.

In Washington, as elsewhere, the ratings of formal society are usually accurate, since formal society is simply a mechanism for objectifying and systematizing the real relationships of power, influence and prestige within a community, without reference to subjective, individual qualities. Journalism and art are mirrors that are as likely to distort social reality along planes of desire and myth as to reflect it accurately. But the desires and myths, if they are shared by those who shape the opinions of the nation, can themselves become a transforming force. And contemporary journalism, literature and art, no less than protocol and etiquette, proclaim the fall of Congress.

As pictured by the two most influential political cartoonists of recent years—Herblock and Fitzpatrick—a member of Congress has been standardized as a kind of humanoid monster: overweight, baggily clothed, coarse featured, unshaven, cruel, stupid, greedy, and motivated by a hatred of all that is good, true and beautiful. The Senator of Al Capp's "Li'l Abner" comic strip, like the Congressmen of radio and TV serials a variant of the same stereotype, is accurately described by Professor H. H. Wilson as "a gross, groggy creature who woke from his nap only at the sound of the gavel and, after voting an invariable 'Nay', immediately went back to sleep."[2]

The magazine, *The New Yorker*, makes a regular feature of quotations from the *Congressional Record* under the heading, "Wind from Capitol Hill Department." This congressional wind that stirs *The New Yorker's* spirit of patronizing irony has frequently its source in one of the Capitol's traditional rituals, courtesies or formalities. It is instructive to contrast the impression that these same forms made a

2. H. H. Wilson, *Congress, Corruption and Compromise* (New York: Rinehart, 1951), p. 2. The mythological origin of the stereotype is most obvious in its picturing of Congressmen as plug-uglies in appearance and manner. As anyone with any personal acquaintance with members of Congress knows, most of them are personally attractive, friendly, and often charming—not unnaturally, in a profession that depends on pleasing people.

century and a quarter ago on an observer whose eyes and pen were as sharp, in general, as a *New Yorker* editor's:

> I rode to the Capitol. Being Monday, the states were successively called for presentation of petitions; a most tedious operation in the practice, though to a reflecting mind a very striking exemplification of the magnificent grandeur of this nation and of the sublime principles upon which our government is founded. The forms and proceedings of the House, this calling over of the states for petitions, the colossal emblem of the union over the Speaker's chair, the historic Muse at the clock, the echoing pillars of the hall, the tripping Mercuries who bear the resolutions and amendments between the members and the chair, the calls of ayes and noes, with the different intonations of the answers from the different voices, the gobbling manner of the clerk in reading over the names, the tone of the Speaker in announcing the vote, and the varied shades of pleasure and pain in the countenances of the members on hearing it, would form a fine subject for a descriptive poem.[3]

It would be hard to find any mid-20th-century commentator whose review of a congressional proceeding would resemble in either content or feeling what we rather often find in Adams' Journal:

> Schenck, of Ohio, had the floor from Saturday and made an hour speech of unrivalled eloquence in that department of debate which one of the Athenian orators called the Shears—cutting up the arguments of the adversary. His manner is cool, firm, unhesitating, with conscious mastery of his subject; his voice clear and strong, his elocution neat and elegant, with a swelling vein of sarcastic humor, which more than once made the hall ring with shouts of laughter. He had got hold of

3. John Quincy Adams, *Diary*, Feb. 20, 1832.

Douglas, and was shaking him as a bull-dog shakes between his teeth a dead rat, when his hour expired. (Jan. 8, 1844.)

There is little evidence that the conduct of Congressmen is very different today from what it was in 1844, when those notes were written. There is a world of difference in the way in which the congressional conduct is seen and felt and valued.

The Congressmen who stalk through stories and plays of the past twenty-five years do not differ, essentially, from the Congressmen of the contemporary cartoons. In *State of the Union,* the very successful play by Howard Lindsay and Russel Crouse that was based on the Wendell Willkie campaign for the Presidency, Senator Lauterbach, symbolizing Congress as a whole, is a foolish "tool of the interests," summed up as one who "prefers Martinis before dinner and a steady diet of highballs after."

In *Deep Are the Roots,* a widely acclaimed drama by Arnaud d'Usseau and James Gow on "the Negro question," produced on Broadway in the 1945–46 season and in little theaters from then on, Senator Ellsworth Langdon (Ret.) is a racist imbecile, violent and heavy drinking. His racial bitterness drives him to rudeness and·disloyalty. He rails at American Negro soldiers who, in the war, have "drawn their bayonets through white [*i.e.,* Nazi] flesh." He refuses to shake hands with the returned Negro war hero, Lieut. Charles Brett, deliberately frames Brett on a false charge of watch-stealing, and tries to provoke his lynching.

In Garson Kanin's *Born Yesterday,* another well-known postwar play that was popular in first production and perennially revived, Senator Norval Hedges is presented as the cringing, bribed hired hand of the coarse millionaire, Harry Brock. The farcical elements of *Born Yesterday* do not soften the satirical bludgeoning. "You know what a Senator is to me?" asks Brock, and replies to himself: "a guy who makes a hundred and fifty bucks a week." At the end of one scene the Senator is ordered to leave Brock's hotel suite and to return promptly the next morning; and the dialogue continues:

Senator Hedges. "I want to thank you, Mr. Brock. For everything."

Brock. "Call me Harry, Senator, will you?"

But when the Senator is late arriving the next day, Brock curses him and shouts: "You better get moving or I'll butcher you."

As in *Deep Are the Roots,* the plot is arranged to show that the Senator is disloyal and unpatriotic. On Brock's orders, Senator Hedges is pushing through Congress a bill that will enable Brock to make millions out of war scrap. The hero of the play, Paul Verrall of the Washington staff of *The New Republic,* explains to the heroine (Brock's blonde mistress, whom Paul is transforming into a liberal ideologue) that "selfishness" like that of Brock and Senator Hedges is "fascism." The play's final speech is a toast in which "sons of bitches" like the fascist twins, Senator Hedges and Millionaire Brock, are placed in eternal opposition to the common men and women "who thirst for freedom—and search for the truth—who fight for justice—and civilize each other."[4]

Senators as presented in such movies as *Giant* and *The Great Man* are fit, if somewhat less crudely drawn, colleagues of Senator Hedges.

Until the end of the 19th century, Congressmen (and Presidents) very seldom figured prominently in plays;[5] and in fact, even in this century's literature of political and social "significance" there are not many American novels or plays about political leaders. We certainly can find nothing comparable to these theatrical Senators of the past two or three decades in American literature prior to the first world war. In such a novel from the 1890's as, for example, *Congressman John and His Wife's Satisfaction,*[6] we come upon John Fairfax as not only a Congressman but the book's hero. Congress is por-

4. Armand d'Usseau and James Gow, *Deep Are the Roots* (New York: Scribner's, 1946); Garson Kanin, *Born Yesterday* (New York: Viking, 1946).
5. There were a few early plays with Washington as hero, and a couple, one of them an attack, with Andrew Jackson as principal character. That is about all for nearly a century.
6. By Emma W. MacCarthy (New York: G. W. Dillingham, 1891).

trayed as, on the average, considerably less than superhuman, but with brilliant as well as conscientious members in its ranks. As in the passage quoted above from John Quincy Adams, there is a plainly serious attitude toward the Speaker of the House, the Chaplain, and the traditions of Congress that are kept alive in the talk and procedures. At a theatrical performance, Congressmen are listed as "among notable personages." There is a pleasant, sympathetic attitude toward congressional informality, the jokes and smoking and cloakroom gossip; and an approving account of the train journey north from Washington to New York on the day of adjournment, with the cars adorned by Senators and the "brilliant lights of the House. . . . The most pessimistic moralizer may take heart; the country is safe with the men who laugh."

At the book's end, John Fairfax's faithful wife declares to her husband: "You have demonstrated that an assemblyman and a Congressman may be a statesman, a patriot, and an honest man"—an assertion that is implicitly denied, even in this hypothetical form, by many of our own day's cartoonists and writers.

From the beginning the members of Congress have of course been targets of criticism, as all elective officials in a free society must always be. But during the 19th century the usual general criticisms—apart, that is, from issues of specific policy—charged Congress with being overly factional, lazy, or personally corrupt. In January 1829, the *New England Weekly Review*, recalling that for some years the "crying sin of our National Representatives" had been their "party politics and personal jangling," found them shifting into a phase of indifference, "laziness and dissipation."

Are such things to be endured forever? Are individuals to be denied the liquidation of their just claims against the nation, and public business to stagnate, that the lazy or dissolute propensities of our legislators be gratified? Our legislators are our hired servants—we pay them individually eight dollars per day for their labor—they are bound to diligence by an express stipulation—and those of them who receive the wages without performing the labor, are neither honorable nor honest. Every day of the session of Congress costs the country two thousand dollars.

These were the standard complaints, and as the lobbyists proliferated in the second half of the century, the problem of personal corruption became more prominent and acute. It should be remarked, however, that the 19th century did not understand corruption quite as we have come to do. Without risking anything worse than factional attacks by political opponents, Congressmen could accept money or its equivalent under circumstances that would bring both legal and moral condemnation in our day. *Harper's Weekly* of Feb. 25, 1882, for example, finds in a story it retells occasion only for admiration:

> Mr. CORCORAN is the only Washington banker who has "come to the rescue" of great statesmen at the right time and in an imperial way. After Mr. WEBSTER had delivered his famous 7th of March speech, which provoked from WHITTIER his equally famous poem, "Ichabod," Mr. CORCORAN inclosed to Mrs. WEBSTER her husband's note for $10,000, loaned to him by Mr. CORCORAN. WEBSTER met Mr. CORCORAN at an entertainment that evening, and grasping his hand, said, "That was a princely action of yours, CORCORAN." Mr. CORCORAN still preserves the beautiful letter of thanks written by WEBSTER.

The tone was not always so congenial; the criticism of Congressmen by disappointed suitors or ardent reformers was sometimes sharp, and exceedingly picturesque during the years when Sam Ward, Cyrus McCormick, Samuel Colt, Alexander Hay and Commodore Vanderbilt applied their inventive genius to the art and science of lobbying. But the range and depth of the attack was always limited. Individual Congressmen were shown as stupid, provincial or dishonest; specific acts of Congress were opposed; some congressional practices were criticized as wasteful, or injurious to the conduct of the nation's business. The role of Congress as an institution was never brought into question, nor even its accepted primacy within the American system of government.

The attitude toward Congress that is mirrored in much of the journalism, cartoon-making, popular arts and even academic writing of the past generation is radically different. Even where this is not made explicit, we sense a rejection of Congressmen and Congress as such, as an institution. A typical member of Congress is not merely ignorant and silly; he is vicious, depraved, quite possibly disloyal, dedicated to a subversion of the true interests of the nation, a saboteur of the executive and of the dedicated administrative officials who seek to lead the country onward into an era of peace, prosperity and social justice. When Professor Wilson writes[7] of the "deep distrust," the "terrible cynicism" of our generation toward its inherited institutions, of the "nation-wide contempt for Congress" and its whole traditional set of procedures that, as he italicizes it, "*must* be revised," he is of course not so much describing fact as expressing his own left variant of liberal ideology. But that same ideology, with this same attitude toward Congress, has been common to so many of the verbalists and opinion-moulders of the past generation that it has become itself an historical fact of the first order in determining Congress' present place and role.

The meaning of this shift in attitude toward Congress has been fully grasped by a group of observers whose account of the contemporary scene is more serious than is supposed by those who are acquainted with it only by hearsay. The best of the science fiction writers use a method of what they call "extrapolation" to draw out, in the form of their fables, the logical implications and probable historical consequences of trends in the existing situation. As prophets

7. *Op. cit.*, pp. 2, 6, 12.

they have made some spectacular hits, as we all know by now, as well as many a miss. But in reality their stories are more interesting and more relevant as a critique of the present than as predictions of what is to come.

On Congress they are ironically unambiguous. "I don't know what good Congress is anyway, except to plague honest bureaucrats," comments the protagonist of Poul Anderson's story, *Sam Hall.*[8] In the novel, *The Space Merchants,* the protagonist, a couple of decades hence, is having a drink with a dwarf space explorer in the Washington airport restaurant: "I looked down at him across the table and looked away through the window. Off to the south the gigantic pylon of the F. D. R. memorial blinked its marker signal; behind it lay the tiny, dulled dome of the old Capitol."[9]

3

In this century there has been a rough temporal correlation among three structural developments within the American system: first, the relative expansion of government both quantitatively (as measured by numbers of persons on the government payroll, or by the budget) and qualitatively (as shown by the scope of the intervention of government in social life); second, the increasing centralization of government; and third, the fall of Congress—the decreasing relative weight of Congress in the power equilibrium.

Most political scientists assert, or assume, that there is a causal connection among these three; and, in particular, that the fall of Congress is a consequence of big and centralized government. The proof that the relation is causal is less than complete. During the 19th

---

8. Included in *Science Fiction Thinking Machines,* edited by Groff Conklin (New York: Bantam Books, in arrangement with Vanguard Press, 1954/55).
9. Frederic Pohl and C. K. Kornbluth, *The Space Merchants* (New York: Ballantine Books, 1953).

century the central government expanded substantially in relation to the rest of society—about five times as measured by per capita government expenditures in standardized (1926) dollars.[10] Northern victory in the Civil War meant a jump in the relative power share of the central government. Nevertheless, these shifts did not lead to a decrease in the relative power of Congress within the central government. The predominance of Congress continued throughout the 19th century, and it was in the decades after the Civil War that its power reached its highest point since Monroe's administration.

After their sharp rise in World War I, the operations of the central government—as measured by per capita expense, number of employees and variety of activities—leveled out on a plateau that was much higher than any point reached in the 19th century,[11] but Congress was if not the predominant at any rate an equal partner in the government mechanism. The simultaneous explosive turn of all three curves— steeply up for the size and scope of government, as steeply down for the relative power of Congress—dates only from 1933.

There does seem to be some sort of causal correlation among the three factors, but we need to be cautious in judging just what sort. It may be not that the growth and centralization of government inevitably cause the weakening of Congress, but rather that the growth of government in general (Big Government, Statism) offers the occasion for aggrandizing the central government as against state and local governments; and that a centralized Big Government in turn offers the occasion for diminishing the role of the legislature. Human beings and human intentions may be at work here, as well as impersonal "historical forces."

Whatever its precise nature, the connection does, in our day, exist. We do have, that is to say, a central government vastly swollen

10. *Cf.* M. Slade Kendrick, *A Century and a Half of Federal Expenditures* (New York: National Bureau of Economic Research, 1955).
11. By certain indices, though not all, the Civil War peak was slightly above the 1918–32 plateau.

in size and power; and within it a Congress much fallen from its former state. The central government has a civilian bureaucracy numbering three million instead of the few thousand of a century and a half ago, and about three million more in its permanent armed forces. Its budget has risen from around $10 million to $38,000 million (in 1926 dollars);[12] its per capita expenditure (in the same notation) from $2 to more than $200.

All three branches of the central government have, of course, expanded over the years. But more than 99% (in fact, about 99.9%) of the expansion, as measured by the budget, has been of the executive branch. More than 99% (about 99.5%) of this executive expansion has taken place since 1914, about 95% of it since 1932.

During most years of the nation's first several decades, the expenditure for the legislature was actually higher than that for the civilian section of the executive (excluding, that is, military expenses and debt service). For as late as 1822, *Niles Register* gives $455,356.60 as the expenditure for Congress; and $449,465.85, for all executive costs—the office of the President, all departments, agencies and bureaus. In the late 1950's the total annual legislative expenditures were running somewhat less than $100 million (current dollars) as against approximately eight hundred times that sum for the executive.

It is true that this disparity does not in itself measure the comparative power of the two branches. The question is not merely how much money is spent on what and whom, but who controls the spending. This is not settled merely by the relative size of the respective budgets. Nevertheless, size itself is in this case of considerable political importance. In sheer human weight, the 3,000,000-man civilian bureaucracy (to which the nearly 3,000,000-man military force is an adjunct) looms like a colossus over the minuscule contingent of a few hundred Congressmen plus their few thousand[13] staff employees.

---

12. Kendrick, *op. cit.* I am rounding out the typical figures.
13. 6,554 as of June 30, 1957.

X

THE LAW-MAKING
POWER

ACCORDING TO THE 18th-century theories in which the Fathers of our Constitution were instructed, the essential expression of sovereignty is law-making. The law-making body (or person, in the case of monarchy) is peculiarly, and in the primary sense, the sovereign. We have already remarked that by John Locke's account an executive and a judiciary exist only as a practical convenience for the day by day conduct of affairs. Because the legislature sits intermittently, it is expedient in practice to have special agencies "always in being, which should see to the execution [and expounding] of the laws that are made" by and only by the legislature.

But "sovereignty is indivisible" (as they put it in the 18th century). Therefore, since law-making is the essential expression of sovereignty, Rousseau as well as Locke taught that the law-making power cannot be delegated. In Locke's words: "the legislative neither must nor can transfer the power of making laws to any body else"—a rule he derived from the more general principle, *Delegata potestas non potest delegari*.[1]

By the words of Article I of the Constitution, "all legislative Powers herein granted shall be vested in a Congress of the United States." Even in the explicit intent of the Constitution this declara-

---

1. "A delegated power cannot itself be delegated." As applied in republican theory, the people have delegated their innate power to the legislature, and only the people, not the legislature, could delegate it elsewhere.

tion is not to be taken quite literally. Through the veto power and the obligation to report on the state of the union, the executive is assigned a subordinate share in the legislative power, just as the legislature, through the provisions on appointments, impeachment, treaties, etc., shares, by plain intention, in the executive power. Moreover, we may recognize further that in practice no rigid line can be drawn between one power and another, that the executive in enforcing and the courts in expounding the law will inevitably, in some degree at least, share in making the law.

Granted these qualifications, it remains true that for nearly a century and a half Congress did keep in its own hands a clearly preponderant and seldom challenged control of the law-making power and process. This was symbolized, as we have seen, by the sparing, strictly circumscribed resort to judicial nullification or presidential veto of congressional acts. As recently as 1928 the Supreme Court (in the words of its then Chief Justice, William Howard Taft) reasserted the unrestricted doctrine of non-delegation: "The well-known maxim, '*Delegata potestas non potest delegari*,' applicable to the law of agency in the general and common law, is well understood and has had wider application in the construction of our Federal and State Constitutions than it has had in private law. . . . It is a breach of the national fundamental law if Congress gives up its legislative power and transfers it to the President, or to the Judicial branch."[2]

Traditionally the courts have often proclaimed the narrow limits of their intrusion into the field of the legislature. Judicial review of legislative acts, by a fiction that in the past was not wholly without substance, was held to be only a necessary development of the judiciary's task of declaring what the law is or means in specific cases brought before the court. If "constitutional issues" could be avoided by the court, if there was no "strict necessity" to meet them, then they should be avoided, according to the traditional doctrine. "Po-

---

2. 276 U.S. 394.

litical questions" were declared outside the judicial province. Acts of the legislature were to be presumed constitutional unless the contrary judgment was "beyond all reasonable doubt."

Another "maxim of constitutional interpretation runs to the effect that the courts are concerned only with the constitutionality of legislation and not with its motives, policy or wisdom, or with its concurrence with natural justice, fundamental principles of government, or spirit of the Constitution."[3] By the doctrine of *stare decisis,* the judiciary recognizes its obligation to precedent, the presumption against a change in or departure from the accepted interpretation of the law's meaning.

This whole doctrine of judicial restraint, no matter how elaborated, cannot remove all ambiguity from a political system in which judicial review is an accepted procedure. In the last analysis the discretion of the judges themselves and the readiness of the other branches and the citizens to accept their pronouncements must define the boundary that they are willing to recognize. But until 1937, when the Supreme Court gave way before the rush of the New Deal, the American judiciary did in fact, with only rare major exceptions, restrict its intervention into the legislative process well below the level at which it might be charged with encroaching on the role of Congress as the primary law-making body.

Indeed, the 1937 breakdown in the doctrine of judicial restraint did not at first lead to an effort by the Court to supplant Congress, but rather to the Court's backing of the political departments, of Congress and more particularly the executive, in their radical departures from the explicit statements and traditional interpretations of the Constitution. The Court made it its business to "legitimize" the New Deal. Thereby, however, it was sharing, more than ever in the

---

3. *The Constitution of the United States of America,* Edward S. Corwin, editor. Legislative Reference Service, Library of Congress (Washington: U.S. Government Printing Office, 1953), p. 564. For this section, I have drawn generally on pp. 556–66 of this authoritative compilation.

past, in the legislative process; and from 1937 on the Court's share has been expanding.

When Congress, after 1938, began to clash more frequently, and sometimes for entire sessions, with the executive, the Court found itself acting, as a rule, as the executive's ally. This combined front has continued through the changes of administration. In the school integration decision (Brown *v.* Board of Education, 1954) and in a number of subsequent decisions under the Chief Justiceship of Earl Warren, the Court, in active conjunction with the executive, has scarcely troubled to hide the fact that it has been performing a legislative rather than judicial function.

2

In our day the account of the legislative process which the press furnishes, and we accept as normal, runs somewhat as follows. During the months prior to the opening of a congressional session, the various governmental agencies, departments and bureaus, under the President's direction, prepare budgets that are assembled and funneled through the Bureau of the Budget, and draft a series of legislative proposals on matters that the President or his aides believe require statutory action—farming, labor, defense, banking, health, social security or whatever. The general budget plus the proposed laws constitute what becomes known as the "White House (or administration or presidential) program."

This program is then presented to Congress in the opening report (delivered by the President in person) "on the state of the union," and in supplementary reports (some of them also delivered in person) on the budget and on the major legislative fields. At the same time the actual text and figures of the budget—in physical, printed form—and the text of the "administration bills" are physically transported to Capitol Hill, where they are placed in the hands of appropriate congressional committees or individual Congressmen. It is assumed that the budget and the bills will then be dropped into the congressional "hopper," processed according to the established rules, and for the most part, perhaps with some modifications, finally enacted into law.

Many newspapers and news magazines have come to handle our law-making rather as they do a track meet, and to keep a running score as with the Olympic games. They draw up a kind of form sheet, listing the main items of the administration's (Eisenhower's, Truman's, Roosevelt's) legislative program. Each week the list is printed, with columns of check marks to show how each item stands: in committee; scheduled for floor debate; passed by the House; passed by the Senate; in joint conference committee; before the President for signature; safe at home—signed, sealed and delivered.

At its conclusion, a congressional session is scored: *Good*—enacted most major White House proposals without "harmful" (*i.e.*, White House-disapproved) amendments; *Bad*—enacted few White House proposals, or even (lowest grade of all) originated and passed statutes on its own that were contrary to White House desires; *Fair*—somewhere betwixt and between.

According to this account the function of Congress—bearing some similarity to the function of parliament in a modern Cabinet system—is merely to approve (perhaps with minor modifications) or to reject legislation that is initiated, formulated and presented by the executive. In fact, it has come to be widely felt that the only "positive" function of Congress is to *approve* the proposed legislation. Rejection is "negative," a sabotage of progress and the national interest.

This idea of a White House (presidential, administration) legislative program is now so familiar that it is hard to realize how recent it is in our national history, and how contrary in many respects to the traditional conceptions of the American political system.

The Constitution does, of course, explicitly assign to the President a certain share in law-making. Not only does he have the veto power defined in Article I, Section 7, but by Article II, Section 3 "he shall from time to time give to the Congress Information of the State of the Union, and recommend to their Consideration such Measures as he shall judge necessary and expedient; he may, on extraordinary Occasions, convene both Houses, or either of them, and in Case of Disagreement between them, with Respect to the Time of Adjournment, he may adjourn them to such Time as he shall think proper." Following Washington's precedent, this obligation to give information and recommend measures has led to the custom of an "annual message" from the President to Congress at the start of each session, and occasional "special messages."

Prior to the present century the annual messages, and even most of the (then comparatively rare) special messages were usually quite general in content, and sometimes very short. An annual message, after discussing the general state of the world and the nation, would single out a few problems that the President felt to be of special interest or concern: the threat of war; western territories; education and science; slavery; internal improvements; the banking system; civil service; or whatever. With respect to some of these the message might call on Congress to enact laws to correct some abuse or further some national interest. Such a recommendation was made in terms of purpose, not detail; the formal words of the message always implied that it was up to Congress, as the nation's legislature, to decide whether a law was in truth necessary, and if so to write, consider and enact it. Not seldom Presidents used the occasion of the message for reflections on philosophy and history, especially Roman history, to which many of them were prone. From 1801 to 1913, as if to insist on another formal symbol that would express Congress' law-making monopoly, the messages were transmitted in writing, not spoken in person by the President.

It was possible under the traditional system for a President to take the initiative in urging a general course of legislative policy—or, as in the case of Andrew Jackson, in blocking a particular course of legislative policy—and to become in that limited sense a legislative leader, or perhaps more accurately "a leader to the legislature." Some Presidents were and some were not active initiators of legislation and legislative policy; some were so in certain fields but not in others. Washington, for example, through his Secretary of the Treasury, initiated, shaped and shepherded the bills that established the fiscal system of the new government, but he had little to do with the critical Judiciary Act and the statutes that set up the executive departments. On the whole, moreover—because of his own unique personal position and the unique task of the nation's progenitive administration—Washington's legislative initiative, modest as it is by mid-20th-century criteria, was greater than that of his successors for more than a century.

Jefferson exercised a large and in some instances fairly detailed influence on legislation, but he did so for the most part as an individual rather than as President; and the formal distinction has here a real significance. It was as party leader and through personal relations, pressures and intrigues that Jefferson led Congress to pass legislation he wanted. Formally, he insisted on a strict separation of the executive from the legislative function. We have had earlier occasion to remark that though Jefferson was a "strong" personal leader, his mode of operation weakened the office of President, and reduced the share in the legislative power that it had seemed to be attaining under the two Federalist predecessors.

No doubt few other Presidents went so far in renunciation as the unfortunate William Henry Harrison:

I cannot conceive that by a fair construction any of [the Constitution's] provisions would be found to constitute the President a part of the legislative power. It cannot be claimed from the power to recommend, since, although enjoined as a duty upon him, it is a privilege which he holds in common with every other citizen; and although there may be something more of confidence in the propriety of the measures recommended in the one case than in the other, in the obligations of ultimate decision there can be no difference. In the language of the Constitution, "all the legislative powers" which it grants "are vested in the Congress of the United States." It would be a solecism in language to say that any portion of these is not included in the whole.[4]

Still, most of the 19th-century Presidents—with the most notable exception of Lincoln in his use of the war powers—limited the range of their legislative interventions, usually restricted them to matters of general policy, and ordinarily exerted their legislative influence in the Jeffersonian style—not by their formal conduct of the office of President, but by personal relations, bargains on patronage, and maneuvers within the political parties which, especially after the advent of national nominating conventions in 1832, became a critical element within the American system.

Prior to this century bills proposed for congressional enactment were never written by an executive official in an executive office and then transmitted to Congress, openly and with an acknowledgment of their origin, as formally sponsored administration or White House measures. Of course, bills were in fact sometimes so written in whole or part, and transported back and forth between executive and congressional offices. In preparing the text of bills, Congress sometimes asked and needed advice from experienced officers of the executive administration, and administrative officers sometimes gave advice without the asking. But the forms were preserved, and the forms expressed a political meaning. Congress had the power to make the laws, and this meant that it was Congress' job to write them.

In the post-1933 epoch probably more than half of the enacted major statutes (excluding private bills and those of purely local interest) originate, in basic text as well as policy substance, in the executive branch. The text of most of the remainder gets an executive workout before completing the legislative process.

It was Theodore Roosevelt, with his vigorous personality and his trust-busting, "progressive," conservationist ideas, who first at-

4. Inaugural Address.

tempted a major alteration in the presidential relation to the legislative function. Using not only his personal dynamism but the prestige of the office and the President's unique relation to the voters as a collectivity, he drove through Congress and its formidable committee machinery a number of statutes that even in their detailed provisions were products of his initiative and sponsorship. And after some years in office, pushing still further, he tried to leap over the formal barrier. In 1908 he had his Secretary of the Interior carry the completed draft of a White House bill to an administration stalwart in Congress, who was told to introduce it for enactment. This attempted breach was closed, however, for that decade by a slashing speech in which Senator Henry Cabot Lodge, who had been Roosevelt's political patron, denounced the Secretary's presumption and encroachment, and asserted the autonomous, sovereign legislative power of Congress. Senator Lodge's strictures were made those of the Senate as a whole by formal Senate vote.

Woodrow Wilson, operating from a more intricate theoretical base that included a vastly enlarged conception of the Presidency, went much further with, for a time, more success. By reviving the Federalist practice of delivering his principal message in person, Wilson expressed his conviction that the President ought not only to share but to lead in the legislative process. In his first annual message and supplementary special messages he laid down, with specificity, a legislative program for his "new democracy." The texts of several of the early major statutes, including the decisively important Federal Reserve Act, were largely White House productions. Then, with the coming of the war, building from Lincoln's precedents, Wilson carried presidential law-making in some instances close to what it was to become more frequently under the second Roosevelt in World War II: government by executive decree.

The departures under Theodore Roosevelt and Wilson were, however, only foretastes, largely neutralized under their immediate successors. It was not until the administration of Franklin Roosevelt that the office of President completed its constitutional transformation into a full, often leading participant in the legislative function; and this time the gear stayed shifted under the hands of the succeeding drivers of whichever party.

The annual White House legislative program is now routine. Apart from investigations, which are in a special category, the principal law-making business of Congress now consists in considering the bills that are proposed and very often written by members of the bureaucracy under the direction of the President or his subordinates. Most of the time, congressional autonomy is restricted to discussing, modifying and occasionally rejecting these White House proposals. During certain periods of this past generation even this limited autonomy has been suspended. When the New Deal was at its height, Benjamin Cohen, Thomas Corcoran, Felix Frankfurter and the other law-writers of the Roosevelt staff turned out the text of bills at an assembly line pace. Senatorial colleagues later recalled how these would be rushed to Joseph T. Robinson of Arkansas, the Democratic Party leader, on the floor of the Senate. There were instances when, without any member's having seen a word of the text, without anything more than the title being read, Senator Robinson (though, according to the memory of his friends, with a burden of humiliation on his heart heavy almost to tears) would, under suspended rules, move the adoption that would be at once and automatically voted.

It was some years later that the point of no return was even more nearly approached. The incident is described by Dr. Roland Young as follows:

> The spring and summer of 1943 [1942?] passed with Congress taking no specific action to amend the price law. Then on September 7 came the threat: the President told Congress that he would act independently if within the month Congress failed to lower the price ceilings on farm commodities to 100% of parity. The unexpected and even frightening message contained these ominous words: "I ask the Congress to take this action by the first of October. Inaction on your part by

that date will leave me with an inescapable responsibility to the people of this country to see to it that the war effort is no longer imperiled by the threat of economic chaos. In the event that the Congress shall fail to act and act adequately, I shall accept the responsibility and I will act. At the same time that farm prices are stabilized, wages can and will be stabilized also. This I will do."

The economic necessity for making such a proposal was not apparent to everyone, and in the perspective of time the threat appears to have been a rash and unnecessary challenge to constitutional procedures. Congress came within a day of meeting the President's imposed deadline, and this quick response, humiliating as it was under such goading, prevented the development of a constitutional crisis. . . .

One may well ask why the President acted as he did. . . . He got irresponsible advice from a staff that had had little experience with Congress or even sympathy with the legislative process. . . . The official administrative history of this period, published by the Bureau of the Budget, says that the President was under strong pressure to act independently of Congress and that these advisers, who are not identified, had prepared an appropriate order for his signature.[5]

It was literally a constitutional crisis that was provoked by the President's ultimatum. Franklin Roosevelt was threatening to usurp the law-making function not merely in substance—as had through subterfuge or oversight or presidential impatience been done before—but in form and official procedure as well: a step far more fatal from a constitutional standpoint. Such are the vagaries of real life that constitutions are, inevitably, violated from time to time in fact. Granted that the violations are occasional and unsystematic, a con-

5. Roland Young, *Congressional Politics in the Second World War* (New York: Columbia University Press, 1956), pp. 94–5.

stitution can survive them if it continues to be adhered to in form and procedure. But Roosevelt was striking, and striking openly, at the key formal principle of the Constitution's first article, at the vesting of "all legislative Powers" in the Congress. His threat, which was in no way hidden but rather flaunted in the message prepared by those "advisers, who are not identified," was that he, as President, would legislate, would make the law that he, as Chief Executive, would then enforce. It will be noted in Dr. Young's account that the implicit general crisis of the traditional constitutional system was solved—or, more accurately, postponed—only by the capitulation of Congress on the specific issue over which the crisis arose.

The critical issue remains suspended over the heart of the American body politic. Harry Truman, though as a person so much less impressive than Franklin Roosevelt, shared and in some respects even exaggerated Roosevelt's conception of executive supremacy. This he demonstrated in spectacular practice by throwing the nation into the Korean war without any action by Congress (even ex post facto) and by his seizure of the Youngstown Steel Company (later narrowly invalidated by the Supreme Court) through executive decree.[6] Mr. Truman acted in such cases not by impassioned whim, as

---

6. Of the steel seizure Mr. Truman later wrote: "In my opinion, seizure was well within my constitutional powers, and I had acted accordingly. The Constitution states that 'the executive power shall be vested in a President of the United States of America.' These words put a tremendous responsibility on the individual who happens to be President. He holds an office of immense power. It surely is the greatest trust that can be placed in any man by the American people. It is trust with a power that appalls [sic] a thinking man. . . . I believe that the power of the President should be used in the interest of the people, and in order to do that the President must use whatever power the Constitution does not expressly deny him." This final dictum is of particular note, inasmuch as the Constitution does not "expressly deny" the President anything.

Mr. Truman concludes with a novel gloss on the meaning of political responsibility: "The essence of government in a democracy is that it be responsible, and to me that means that the responsibilities of government be accepted and carried out." (*Memoirs,* Vol. II, pp. 472–3.)

some have imagined, but by the settled principle that he summed up in his *Memoirs:* "A wise President will always work with Congress, but when Congress fails to act or is unable to act in a crisis, the President, under the Constitution, must use his powers to safeguard the nation."[7] A reader cannot help wondering just what constitution Mr. Truman was here referring to.

Those citizens who believed that the issue faded away under the more passive dominion of Dwight Eisenhower could have been rudely undeceived by the mode of his 1958 intervention in Lebanon.

3

From 1954 to 1958 the then Republican Senator, William F. Knowland, occupied the Senate post, once informal but become officially recognized since the 1890's, of "party leader."[8] On January 13, 1957, James Reston, head of the *New York Times* Washington bureau, wrote in the course of an article on President Eisenhower: "On Capitol Hill, his Senate leader, William F. Knowland, has announced his retirement."

A few months before, Richard Strout, Washington correspondent of the *Christian Science Monitor,* had written in a review of Robert Donovan's semi-official book, *Eisenhower: The Inside Story:* "When President Eisenhower came to Washington he had the notion that

---

7. Harry S. Truman, *Memoirs,* Vol. II, p. 478.

8. I have not been able to discover written evidence of the exact date when the "party leader" began to be formally voted by the party caucus, and formally recognized in the proceedings. I base the reference here made ("the 1890's") on personal conversations with a number of persons acquainted with several generations of congressional history. I have more generally relied, for the material of this and the preceding section, on such personal conversations, of which I cite as particularly relevant those with Arthur Krock and ex-Senator Henry F. Ashurst (the first Senator from the newly established state of Arizona, which he had previously represented in Washington as territorial delegate).

the Republican Congress ought to support him and his initial program, which was modest enough. But Congress seemed more occupied with investigations. Aggravations multiplied. The Senate Republican leader, for example, was asked on a radio broadcast whether he felt America was getting 'truce with honor' by the Eisenhower Korean cease-fire. 'I don't believe so,' the President's leader in Congress coolly replied."[9]

The phrases, "his Senate leader" and "the President's leader," although they would hardly have excited the surprise or even the notice of more than a handful of readers, are a telling symptom of the change in the public understanding of the place of Congress within the American political equilibrium.

A letter from ex-Congressman William S. Bennet to Mr. Reston's newspaper, published later in 1957 (August 5) might almost have been a commentary on the Reston–Strout use of the presidential-possessive:

> I was a member of the House of Representatives in four Congresses. During my service Theodore Roosevelt, William H. Taft and Woodrow Wilson were successively Presidents. . . .
>
> In those days our conception of the relations between the Congress and the President were distinctly different and I think more constitutional than the present apparent Congressional—or at any rate public—conception.
>
> In those days the Congress was expected to form its own views, not to get them from the President. . . .
>
> I recall that John Sharp Williams, the Democratic House leader, once bitterly denounced Gerrit J. Diekema, a Republican from Michigan, alleging that he had gone to the White House to get the President's advice as to legislation, and I recall as well Diekema's indignant denial. . . .

9. *The New York Times Book Review,* July 1, 1956.

In Mr. Bennet's story the congressional party leader is so far from being "his" (*i.e.*, the President's) man that he criticizes a fellow member who merely seeks the President's opinion on a legislative problem.

According to the traditional conception a "party leader" in Congress was the head of the party group in one or the other House. The party members recognized him, and came in time to elect him formally, as their principal spokesman and the manager of the party caucus. He in turn was their representative, and was responsible to them. One of his functions was to maintain liaison with the White House, particularly if the President was, as is usually the case, of the same party as the congressional majority.

Although conflicts between executive and legislature are normal and expected in the American governmental system, its successful operation naturally presupposes that the area of cooperation between the two branches will be larger than that of dispute. This cooperation, as well as the resolution of the conflicts, requires a communication between President and Congress more active and flexible than can be carried on through formal "messages" and "resolutions." The party leader is one of the most important channels of such communication. The President can explain his views to the party leader, and through him to the other party members; the party leader in turn can inform the President about the opinions, problems and intentions of the party members in Congress.

In this relationship, as traditionally understood, the party leader[10] is not representing the President. In some degree his function bridges the divisions of the governmental structure, and cannot be reduced to any one of them. He has, by virtue of his post, a general duty to the government as a whole, which enjoins him to help maintain an effective working collaboration between the executive

10. Throughout this section I am referring to "party leaders" in Congress. In the broadest sense, the principal de facto "leader" of the party may be someone outside of Congress—often, of course, the President himself for his own party.

and the legislature. This means that he must try to understand the executive's position sympathetically and to communicate it accurately to his party caucus and to Congress in general. But he has also a special duty, and this is to his party caucus in Congress; he is its man, its representative, not the President's. He tries to mediate differences of opinion between President and caucus, between executive and legislature, when these arise; but if these prove irreconcilable, he is a member of Congress and of his party in Congress, not an appointee or agent of the President.

This notion of the role of the party leader, so different from what is implicit in Mr. Reston's phrase about Senator Knowland or in the attacks on him for "disloyalty to the President" that were so common in liberal columns during 1956 and 1957, is what can be deduced from our traditional system of government as well as observed in traditional practice. It was first breached at the same time that the traditional system as a whole showed the first big cracks: in the first administration of Woodrow Wilson. In 1913 the Democratic Party, to which Wilson belonged, had a majority of eight in the Senate. John W. Kern of Indiana was the Senate Democratic Party leader. He was the first to act in that post, and to be recognized, as "the White House spokesman." This was, of course, in accord with Wilson's long-standing and often expressed preference for "parliamentary" (or Cabinet) as against "congressional" government.

It was not merely that Senator Kern agreed with the President. Party leaders and Presidents had often been in agreement before that, either on specific questions, or more or less continuously for some years at a time, as under McKinley. But Kern's agreement was of a different sort: not a mere coincidence of views, but a subordination to the President's views. He conceived it to be his task to represent and speak for the President within the Senate, and to try to get the Senate to vote for what the President wanted. That 63rd session of Congress (1913–15) was the first in which Senators would have thought of settling problems by saying, "Find out what the President wants"; the first in which bills were introduced with such remarks as, "This is recommended by the Secretary of Agriculture," or "This is what the President proposes."[11]

The shift in the role of party leader[12] under Wilson was neither complete nor final. During the three succeeding administrations (1921–33) of Republican Presidents Harding, Coolidge and Hoover, Senators Henry Cabot Lodge, Charles Curtis and James E. Watson were successively the Republican party leaders. For that period the Presidents, the members of Congress and the general public all shared the traditional pre-Wilsonian view of their role and function. The late Hiram Bingham, one-time Senator from Connecticut, recalled[13] how, when he first came to Washington (after a mid-term election, held because of the death of his predecessor), he called on President Coolidge at the White House. He was inexperienced in Washington's ways, and he inquired what the President would like him to do in the Senate. "Ask Charley Curtis [then party leader in the Senate]," was Mr. Coolidge's reply.

It was in the Franklin Roosevelt administrations that the Senate party leader (of the President's party) came to be generally regarded not only by the President himself but by public opinion—an opinion, however, never entirely shared by Congress—as a presidential

---

11. Ex-Senator Ashurst was good enough to acquaint me with his vivid recollections of this session—where he was now sitting as one of the new state of Arizona's first pair of Senators, after his long service as territorial delegate.

12. It is the role of the leader in the Senate that is the sensitive indicator of political relations. The actual majority leader in the House is normally the Speaker, who is established as an officer of the legislature by express constitutional provision as well as continuous tradition. We noted in a previous chapter that some observers of the American system in the late 19th century judged the Speaker of the House to be the most powerful individual in the United States, more powerful than the President. Because of the greater solidity of his position, the transformation of the Speaker into a spokesman of the President has lagged behind the rate of transformation of the Senate leader. The Speaker, moreover, has never been publicly *considered* a White House spokesman even when, as for several years in the Roosevelt regime, he was in fact so.

13. In a personal conversation.

representative and spokesman in the Senate, rather than as a Senate party caucus spokesman in liaison with the executive. In the first New Deal years Senator Joseph T. Robinson, though he had been freely chosen as leader by his colleagues, became a faithful presidential spokesman through a kind of voluntary servitude induced by the national economic crisis. He remained the President's man, although his friends later reported that supporting Mr. Roosevelt through the days of the 1937 court-packing plan, which Robinson abhorred in conscience, broke first his political and then his physical heart.[14]

Alben Barkley, who succeeded Robinson as Senate Democratic leader and who served longer as leader, in all, than anyone else in the Senate's history, was the first Senate leader to be handpicked by a President. Even the sweet tempered Barkley had his moment of rebellion. When in 1944 Mr. Roosevelt wrote his unprecedented veto of the revenue bill, and did so in sharp language that insulted both the intelligence and integrity of Congress, there was enacted one of those ballet-like romantic comedies that every now and then recur in the history of parliamentary assemblies. But this comedy, like many another, made the essential points more plainly than the actors were aware.

Barkley, for the first time differing with the President, protested the veto in an emotion filled speech wherein he referred to his seven years service as a majority leader who had through thick and thin unfailingly "carried the flag" of the Roosevelt administration, and had loyally followed the President because the President was the people's champion. He proposed that Congress over-ride the veto in order to vindicate its "self respect." Whereupon he resigned as leader. By that act of resignation (which was, of course, only a pirouette in the parliamentary ballet), as well as by his description of

14. Senator Robinson died July 14, 1937. I rely for the statement in the text on the recollections of certain of the friends, made known to me in private conversation.

his leadership career, Barkley was implying the theory that the party leader is the agent and spokesman of the President. If he had thought of himself as the representative of his party colleagues, there would have been nothing unusual in his differing with the President—whether of his own or another party—and no occasion whatever for talk about resigning.

The ballet had in quick scenes its duly happy ending. The shrewd Roosevelt wrote Barkley a friendly letter, hoping that he would not actually resign his leadership, and, if he did, that his colleagues would unanimously reelect him. And, promptly and unanimously, his colleagues did so.[15]

With Mr. Roosevelt's death, the post of Senate leader slipped back into an unstable middle ground between the traditional and New Deal alternatives. In spite of his belief in executive supremacy, Harry Truman—elevated to the Presidency by the accidents of physiology and factional politics after rather routine service as one Senator among the rest—was not in a good position to treat the Senate leader as a henchman of the White House; nor would Alben Barkley, who carried over as leader, or even his pleasant but colorless successor, Scott Lucas of Illinois, have accepted from Mr. Truman the same subordinate relation that Roosevelt's personal dynamism plus the critical weight of depression and war had imposed. When Senator Lucas was defeated for re-election in 1950 it was the openly anti-Truman majority of the Democratic caucus that named Ernest W. McFarland of Arizona as the new leader.

General Eisenhower, without any clear idea of the place of the President in the American system, had to deal in his first six years with party leaders—Robert A. Taft and William F. Knowland—who were men of firm, independent principle, convinced believers in the traditional prerogatives of Congress as the supreme lawmaking body. But for all their tendency to see the leadership post in

15. I have made use of Roland Young's account of these incidents. See *Congressional Politics in the Second World War*, pp. 139–43.

the old way, as representing the party caucus in liaison with the executive, the Wilson-Roosevelt precedents had sunk too deep to be altogether thrown off. On not a few occasions—foreign policy disputes conspicuous among them—Senator Taft or Senator Knowland approached Congress not as convinced spokesman of and for his colleagues but as a messenger of the President urging acceptance of "What Ike wants." However Messrs. Taft and Knowland saw their own role, and however the rest of Congress understood it, most of the articulate voices of public opinion, and especially the liberal commentators, assumed the Wilson-Roosevelt definition; and, as we noted at the beginning of this section, condemned Mr. Knowland, as Taft before him, when in the Senate he opposed, as he sometimes did oppose, the opinions and wishes of the President. By the prevailing interpretation, the proper function of a leader of the legislature is to be the led of the executive.

XI

THE RISE OF THE FOURTH BRANCH

E VEN BEFORE the end of the 19th century, there were pre-
monitory signs of that weakening, delegation and erosion of
Congress' law-making power that have gone on so rapidly
and dramatically since 1933. One such sign is the appearance of the
first "independent regulatory agency," the Interstate Commerce
Commission, in 1887. This was followed in 1913 by the Federal
Reserve Board (now the Board of Governors of the Federal Reserve System), the Federal Trade Commission in 1915 and the Federal Power Commission in 1930. Since 1933, besides a host of
semi-independent interdepartmental agencies, six major independent agencies have been added: the Securities and Exchange Commission and the Federal Communications Commission in 1934; the
National Labor Relations Board in 1935; the United States Maritime Commission in 1936; the Civil Aeronautics Board in 1940;
and the Atomic Energy Commission[1] in 1946.

These agencies now exercise an extraordinary authority over
some of the principal concerns of our national life: air, road, rail and
sea-borne transport; radio and television; the production of electri-
cal energy; credit, investment and banking; labor unions; advertising
and commercial practices; the entire field of nuclear science, technology and manufacture. In their operations, these commissions
combine executive, legislative and judicial powers. Their decisions,

---

1. The annual budget of the Atomic Energy Commission exceeds the total
budget of the central government for any year prior to 1917.

which have a status not merely as administrative acts but as law, have direct and profound effects on life, liberty and property.

In theory the commissions are "arms" of Congress. They have been created by congressional statute, and are financed by congressional appropriation or congressionally authorized fees. Their chief officers are appointed by the President, but subject to statutory qualifications and to Senate confirmation. They can at any time, in theory, be abolished or bridled by congressional enactment, and they are subject to the inquiries of relevant congressional committees. To satisfy the doctrine of non-delegation, they are said to hold a "quasi-legislative" power only to "fill up the details" of congressional statutes, and to make findings of fact in order to apply legislation left purposely contingent on such findings.

In practice each commission, developing a political life of its own, tends to become a kind of baronial sovereign over its own special demesne. It is exceedingly difficult for Congress to supervise them actively. The technical complexity of the fields with which most of the commissions deal is itself an almost insurmountable obstacle to discerning supervision. Even some of the regulations by which Congress has sought to prevent the executive from gaining complete control over the "independent" commissions—for example, the specified appointment qualifications, and statutory instead of "executive pleasure" terms of office—have in practice the effect of releasing the commissions from dependence on Congress.

Dr. Galloway comments as follows:

> Beginning in 1887, when Congress created the Interstate Commerce Commission, more and more commissions have perforce been established . . . in many areas of economic and social activity. To these agencies Congress has usually delegated the power "to issue such regulations and orders as it may deem necessary or proper in order to carry out the purposes and provisions of this act." This practice of delegating to

administrative agencies or commissions the power to issue rules and regulations spelling out the general principles of law and applying them to specific cases has grown apace since 1912. . . . Congressmen generally recognize the need for delegating legislative powers as a means of reducing their work load and of taking care of technical matters beyond the competence of Congress. But they believe that the great growth of administrative law-making has become a menace to the constitutional function of Congress as the legislative branch of the national government. . . .

These commissions have mixed executive, legislative, and judicial powers. Taken together, they constitute a "headless fourth branch" of government.[2]

In the nature and conditions of their work, in the common civil service and security regulations, and in the shared relation to the non-governmental sectors of society, the commission bureaucracies tend to merge into the broader executive bureaucracy. It is the permanent bureaucracy as a whole that can be taken as constituting "the fourth branch."

2

No one any longer questions the fact, but only the degree and the merits of this century's aggrandizement of the executive branch within the aggrandized central government. But here we must return to the distinction that we found it necessary to make in Chapter IV, in discussing the diffusion of power within the American system. Just as the commission bureaucracies have ceased to be—if they ever were—mere delegated agents of Congress, the permanent "executive" bureaucracy is no longer a mere agent of the President.

2. George B. Galloway, *op. cit.*, pp. 10–11, 86.

The combined bureaucracy has become, rather, a fourth primary branch of the central government.[3]

In theory the permanent civil servants are only technicians, carrying out the President's will in accord with the laws enacted by Congress. They are theoretically distinguished by the protected, permanent and formalized status of their jobs from those who have a voice in policy. The policy posts remain under a spoils system, filled not by civil service examination but by specific presidential appointment (with Senate confirmation), and exposed to instant dismissal with or without stated cause. Because of their merely temporary service and their immediate, continuous dependence on the presidential will, the "policy echelon," headed by the Cabinet members, usually functions in fact as the mere agent or "arm" of the executive that it is supposed to be in theory. But, generally speaking, the huge mass of the permanent bureaucracy is not temporary, and not dependent in any direct, continuous way on the executive will; nor, in practice, is it really possible to preserve the distinction between "policy-making" and "non-policy-making" posts.

The Civil Service Act of 1883 was in part the result of decades of ideological agitation. The government, it was held, would be best served by a permanent career staff selected on the basis of training and ability, and protected by law and regulation against the vagaries of political struggle or popular passion. Apart from the ideological agitation—and without prejudice to its merits—civil service reform, with its guarantee of job security, was a natural social target for the government employees *in situ* as well as for those who might be considered to belong to the potential-bureaucratic type: citizens aspiring to careers in the government service, but more suited by nature to passing examinations and manipulating files than to the rougher, man-to-man battles of elections or the spoils system.

3. In this section I retrace, within the different context, part of the same ground covered in Section 3 of Chapter IV.

Before the event, both Congress and the President managed to persuade themselves that they might be able to gain something, in power terms, from a solid civil service system. The President could hope to get a more efficient and even more docile instrument to carry out the executive purpose. Congress could imagine that, with the governmental apparatus made secure from the arbitrary purges of a Jacksonian President, it would be more difficult for the executive to thwart the legislative will; and that, even if the permanent bureaucrats should lose their franchise by becoming residents of the District of Columbia, their job contentment would spread to their voting cousins in the hinterland.

Both Congress and the President failed to take into account the fact that the bureaucracy itself, once it had reached a certain size and was performing a variety of functions, would be a power element with interests and aims of its own, and that the protective ramparts of civil service "reform" must enhance its independent power. In our day only the very naive can suppose the civil bureaucracy, with its base peacetime number nearly 3,000,000, supported most of the time by the socially similar military bureaucracy, to be a mere agent of the President, meticulously obeying the orders of his appointive officials under the laws passed by Congress. The bureaucracy, like the Carolingian Mayors of the Palace in 8th-century France, not merely wields its own share of the sovereign power but begins to challenge the older branches for supremacy.

This emergence of the bureaucracy is a creeping growth, expressed most tellingly in the day to day, unpublicized activities of the governmental colossus, though on occasion it is more openly marked. What most plainly reveals the independent power of the bureaucracy are those cases where the bureaucrats of some department, agency or office persist in a policy that is contrary to the policy held by both Congress and the President. Under such circumstances—which are not at all unusual—it is obviously an illusion to believe that the civil servants are in reality subject to the "policy-making" appointive official who is their nominal superior, or to the laws that have been enacted by Congress. In a process well known to modern Washington, the official, who may be the Secretary or Assistant Secretary of one of the major departments, becomes the dupe or tool or front of the permanent civil servants whom he is assigned to direct.

For example, many of the permanent officers of the Public Health Service have long favored an expansion of the government's role in the field of medicine, and both inside and outside the governmental apparatus have advocated measures that, in practical effect, move toward the progressive socialization of medicine. This is natural enough from the standpoint of their own jobs and interests. Moving on the inside track, their power and influence necessarily increase with every advance in a statist direction.[4] Probably few of the permanent officers are doctrinaire socialists; but most of them tend much closer to a medical socialism, or statism, than either the President, their appointive policy-making superiors, or Congress.

A similar pattern of relations is observable in government offices dealing with education, social insurance, agriculture, electric power and housing, and from the same organic cause. It is often forgotten that governmental "social insurance," for example, whatever its objective merits, is ineluctably bound up with the incomes and careers of tens of thousands of lesser and greater bureaucrats who administer it; and, more generally, the livelihood, power and prestige of the members of the permanent bureaucracy are bound up with the state. Once the bureaucracy has grown beyond the limits within which personal acquaintance and inspection can fairly well comprehend it, once it has taken on an institutional life of its own, an average bureaucrat (whatever he may say in public for discretion's sake) cannot be expected to support measures that would lead to the decrease of government's funds, functions and personnel. An exceptional individual strongly indoctrinated in anti-statist ideology or

4. The well-known bureaucratic phenomenon of "empire building" arises not from accidents of individual psychology but out of the inner imperatives of the bureaucratic situation.

carefully watched by an anti-statist superior, might do so, but for the bureaucrat to advocate anti-statism is equivalent to asking for his economic throat to be cut. Thus the huge modern bureaucracy is both a product of statist tendencies and simultaneously a cause of the persistence of those tendencies.

The independent policy of the bureaucracy is manifest in connection not only with the general issue of statism but with a multitude of other problems as well, some of them minor and accidental, perhaps springing from no more complex cause than the ingrained ideas of a long-lasting individual bureaucrat or a particular bureau's fossilized work habits. It has been evident for some years that the permanent staff of the State Department, especially the career officers of the Foreign Service, have—besides their technical abilities—policy ideas of their own that do not readily yield to the directives of the President and the appointive heads of the department, and that are at a still further remove from the notions that Congressmen try to incorporate in laws. The independent power of the foreign affairs bureaucracy is so widely recognized that it has given birth to a special term ("Indians") to designate the bureaucratic assistants to the appointive "policy-makers." "Some high officials have in part attributed to these juniors the 'force of inertia' that unduly delays, or leaves unconsummated, the execution of presidential policy."[5] There is substantial evidence that a number of important foreign policy decisions of the past generation—on the Nazis, China, Tito, Nasser, for example—were the will of the permanent bureaucracy rather than of the President and his supposedly policy-making appointees.[6] The

5. Arthur Krock in the *New York Times,* Dec. 14, 1956.
6. The curious procedure usually employed in recent years to arrive at policy decisions automatically increases the weight of the bureaucracy. An outsider would assume that a policy-making official (or the President, if the matter were important enough) would issue a general directive, and instruct his staff to elaborate it, show how it would be implemented, etc. This is not what happens. The official instructs his staff to prepare *a policy* (on China, Yugoslavia, Germany or whatever) for him to adopt.

conduct of the independent regulatory agencies—such as the National Labor Relations Board or the Federal Communications Commission, to cite two conspicuous examples—departs still more widely at times from the intent of Congress and the President.

These observations apply to the military as well as the civil bureaucracy. In theory the President as Chief Administrator directs the civil bureaucracy, and as Commander-in-Chief directs the military bureaucracy. In practice each escapes from his control when it becomes large, technically complex, and permanent. The two bureaucracies have both common and special interests. In recent decades the power of the military has particularly expanded because of the increase in the size of the permanent military establishment, the immense sums of money put at its disposition, and the influence of military procurement on finance and industry. In spite of the doctrine of civilian supremacy, the influence of the military bureaucracy has come to be felt, and is sometimes decisive, not only in military and foreign affairs but in the domestic economy.[7]

The expanded power and autonomy of the bureaucracy is expressed in the symbols of personal conduct and social intercourse. Most citizens, lost in the mazes of tax or subsidy or license rules, have had immediate experience of that "bureaucratic arrogance" or insolence that the chroniclers of other bureaucratized societies have often described. All who have had business to do at the nation's capital will have discovered how long and perilous is the path to the desk of a high-ranking official of a departmental or agency office, and how small a chance there is that one's troubles will be promptly adjusted when one finally scales the last precipice. It is far easier, as anyone may readily confirm for himself, to get to talk with a member of Congress than with a bureaucrat of the middle or higher grades.

---

7. In *The Power Elite*, Prof. C. Wright Mills contends that the upper level of the military bureaucracy is integrally linked with the managerial group in industry to constitute the nation's now dominant stratum.

The bureaucratic arrogance has in recent years come to be directed against Congress and Congressmen as well as the lay public. For appointments between Congressmen and bureaucrats, the bureaucrats are more likely to be late than the Congressmen. In their endogamous conversations, at their parties, the upper strata of the bureaucracy do not hide their feeling that Congress is a road block that they must somehow bypass if the country is to progress, a kind of idiot boy who must be pushed, teased and cozened. Reporting to Congress, testifying before its committees, "briefing" its leaders, is, as much of the bureaucracy judges it, a painful waste of time that can do nothing but interfere with the proper—*i.e.,* bureaucratic—guidance of the nation's affairs.

This arrogance of the bureaucrat toward Congress—so significant a symptom of the altered power relations—has not been much studied in public. In order to give it a more precise specification, I shall quote from some unpublished material that has been made available to me by Anne Brunsdale. The following excerpts are transcribed "raw" (to use the bureaucratic dialect) from confidential interviews—wire or stenographically recorded—with higher level (G16–18) governmental officials whose names, by the nature of the case, must be omitted.

An official recently transferred to the Department of Agriculture from the State Department:

> You hear them talking around the department about what they can get away with. It's always a question of, given this piece of legislation and this bunch of people in Congress, what can we get by with. . . . Often a bureaucrat has got to pretend that he is representing the people—and he does it honestly, and what action he takes [against congressional sanction] *is* in the public interest. He never takes any action like this without clearing it with his counterparts in other agencies and everybody else who would have any interest in it. And generally I think he comes out with something that represents a consensus all around the place. . . .

The bureaucrat has a program to carry out that he believes in. The question of whether or not Congress has authorized it is not so important to him. He figures that if Congress really had the facts and knew what was right, it would agree with him. So he goes right ahead, getting away with as much as he can.

I've attended lots of these meetings within the department where budget questions and the like were decided, and I never heard a respectful word spoken about Congress at one of them.

A colleague, commenting on these same meetings referred to in the last paragraph:

The premise in these meetings is that Congress doesn't know what is going on over here, but it does want to save money, so if we let them they will take away every cent we have for our program—and then what would happen to the public interest? . . . Congressmen are too damn dumb. A good bureaucrat is paid to keep those bothersome Congressmen shut up and to write those letters to [quiet down] his constituents.

An official of another department:

The real hard fact about life on the hill [*i.e.*, in Congress] is that very few times does Congress, acting together and well-informed, pass the laws. . . You [an administrative official] go up there and explain to the subject-matter committee how these things work and why. We [administrators] draw up good legislation in the national interest with all the parts fitting into the whole properly, and what happens to it when it hits the hill is like a Christian among the heathen. So we spend lots of time figuring out how we can do something we want to do and think we should do, without taking a new piece of legislation over to Congress.

An official at the highest level (G-18) of the permanent bureaucracy:

> Put in simple terms, it's the problem of the layman and the expert. . . . My relationship with Congress makes me conscious of my inability to get across the problem and their inability to understand what I am saying. . . . They [Congress] can't fire us of course.

A high level (G-17) research official:

> The President is President of all the people and not just of one group. Congress is a local body in a sense. I think that most of the Presidents we have had (maybe not Hoover) have acted in the public interest. I feel you are more likely to get the public interest represented better through the President than through Congress. . . . We get better policy [*i.e.*, laws] when the primary formulation job is done by the administrators. . . . Too often Congress makes changes that aren't so good. It would be better if the administrator got his way more.

An "action official":

> The administrative arm of government is taking over and making laws and decisions that can't be made except through statistical analysis and working with the problem—and which can't be anticipated by Congress when it passes legislation. Rex [Tugwell] felt that what we needed was strong central planning and a strong President ready to back his planners. . . . Congressional supervision of administrative activities is terrible. It circumscribes our activities. It makes social science into no science at all. . . . The subject matter is too complex and diverse for any committee of Congress to know and understand.

Another, in reply to the question, "What's your estimate of the individual Congressmen?":

> They're a pretty dumb bunch. They have to voice an opinion about something they know nothing about. . . . I can't think of a more unhappy fate for me than to be put in the position of a Congressman. . . . On the other hand, most people in administrative jobs are there because they are trained for the job; they are employed in the field they are qualified for.

An official of the Post Office Department (some of whose remarks indirectly show the key role of the civil service job-guarantee in determining the power relations):

> Everything that Congress does is wrapped up with the matter of votes. Theoretically the Congressman is supposed to vote as to what is going to help the country. . . . But of course we might as well be practical and realize he doesn't do this. . . . Congress represents the selfish wishes of the people. It is concerned with getting votes, whereas the bureaucracy isn't. . . . I don't think Congress has any business supervising the activities of the administrative branch. The minute that Congress had the power to fire me, they would have a political weapon in their hands that would entirely destroy the civil service. . . . Our biggest problem with Congress is getting money and the fact that Congress is always passing laws without considering their effect upon the matter of operating the service. . . . [In an indignant tone:] We have to have a man here doing nothing but keeping up contacts with Congress, answering letters, giving Congressmen information, etc.

As a rule, the native ideology of the bureaucrats is a form of what we have defined as liberalism. Liberal commentators and publicists therefore tend to welcome the increased power of the bureaucracy, and to side with bureaucrats in their disputes with Congress or their less frequent publicly known disputes with the President and his temporary appointive agents. The occasional trips abroad of Congressmen are satirized and denounced, by a common linguistic convention, as "junkets" squandering the taxpayers' hard earned money. The constant voyages of tens of thousands of bureaucrats to an endless sequence of conferences, international gatherings, inspections and checkups—on which hundreds of times as much money is spent—are seldom even mentioned. It is taken for granted without comment that tens of thousands of government-bought automobiles should be at the disposition of the bureaucracy, thousands of them assigned individually to members of the higher echelons, but that Congressmen (except for the half-dozen chief congressional officers) are to drive their own.

In relative judgments within the administrative apparatus, it is almost automatic that the liberal attitude should favor the permanent civil servant over the appointive official. There was an entertaining and typical example of this in 1957 in connection with the appointment of Maxwell Gluck, a businessman who had contributed heavily to the Republican Party, as ambassador to Ceylon. In the Senate confirmation hearing, Mr. Gluck was not able to state the (somewhat complicated) name of Ceylon's Prime Minister. Although it is rather less than self-evident why this disqualified him from upholding American national interests as personal agent of the President— the presumed job of the ambassador—Mr. Gluck's lapse touched off a nation-wide campaign against "non-career" appointments and for the assignment of all diplomatic jobs to permanent Foreign Service officers equipped with ample funds and perquisites by due appropriation of a chastened Congress. This campaign was ably led by James Reston of the *New York Times,* who is widely believed to be an informal but cogent spokesman for the Foreign Service, and who has often found it necessary to scold both Congress and the appointive heads of the State Department for their ingratitude to the

Foreign Service corps, as well as their stubborn disregard, now and then, of Foreign Service advice.

Although contemporary liberals still keep Andrew Jackson's portrait near the center of their ancestral gallery, they have long ago transferred his notions about public office, as about most other matters, to the attic:

> There are, perhaps, few men who can for any length of time enjoy office and power without being more or less under the influence of feelings unfavorable to the faithful discharge of their public duties. . . . Office is considered as a species of property. . . . Corruption in some and in others a perversion of correct feelings and principles divert government from its legitimate ends and make it an engine for the support of the few at the expense of the many. The duties of all public officers are, or at least admit of being made, so plain and simple that men of intelligence may readily qualify themselves for their performance; and I can not but believe that more is lost by the long continuance of men in office than is generally to be gained by their experience. I submit, therefore, to your consideration whether the efficiency of the Government would not be promoted and official industry and integrity better secured by a general extension of the law which limits appointments to four years.
>
> In a country where offices are created solely for the benefit of the people no one man has any more intrinsic right to official station than another. Offices were not established to give support to particular men at the public expense. No individual wrong is, therefore, done by removal, since neither appointment to nor continuance in office is a matter of right. The incumbent became an officer with a view to public benefits, and when these require his removal they are not to be sacrificed to private interests. It is the people, and they alone,

who have a right to complain when a bad officer is substituted for a good one. He who is removed has the same means of obtaining a living that are enjoyed by the millions who never held office. The proposed limitation would destroy the idea of property now so generally connected with official station, and although individual distress may be sometimes produced, it would, by promoting that rotation which constitutes a leading principle in the republican creed, give healthful action to the system.[8]

8. Andrew Jackson, *First Annual Message to Congress,* Dec. 8, 1829.

XII

THE PURSE

ONEY AND arms are the material pillars of government. To rule, the sovereign must dispose of wealth and force. Unless he controls both he will not be able to rule, but will give way to whoever does have money and arms, the purse and the sword, at his command.

Under the Articles of Confederation the United States remained, beneath all forms, a league rather than a nation precisely because the political apparatus set up by the articles did not possess the sovereign power over money and arms. The Articles did not grant the Congress a direct power to tax individuals, nor to have a standing armed force of its own. Congress could only requisition the states for money or troops, without the means of coercing them if they failed, as they usually failed, to meet the requisitions. The several states were therefore individually sovereign, and there was no common, collective sovereign for the United States as a whole. Properly speaking, the institution set up under the Articles was not a government. It was a permanent conference of governments, through which these were sometimes able to take joint action with respect to problems of general concern.

The Founding Fathers, well aware of these realities, understood that a new government of the kind they sought would have to be equipped with both purse and sword. At the same time they believed that if any one individual or institution had unlimited control over money and arms, the result would inevitably be despotism. Moreover, neither the states nor the citizens would have agreed to give such unlimited control to a central government. As guardian of liberty, the Fathers therefore appealed to their normal principle of the diffusion of power.

This meant in the first instance a division between the central government and the states. In granting access to the purse, the terms of the division as written into the Constitution were exceedingly generous: both central government and the states were assigned a money power that was to be concurrent and all but unrestricted. The states were prohibited only from levying taxes on imports. Apart from a couple of procedural rules, the only restrictions on the money power of the central government were against duties "on articles exported from any State" and direct taxes "unless in proportion to the census or enumeration herein before directed." This latter proviso was, of course, removed in 1913 by the Sixteenth Amendment.

The division of power over arms was more complex, and about its details there was considerable ambiguity in the founding document. Save for exceptional circumstances the states were to retain their internal police powers, with the responsibility for assuring domestic order. The central government was charged with the collective defense against all foreign powers. But even to this purpose it was not anticipated by the Fathers that the central government would dispose of a large standing army. The principal armed forces were still to consist of the state militias. The new government was given the power as well as the right to summon these militias to the general defense.

How were these great new powers of the central government over money and arms to be divided among the different branches—how, in particular, between the legislature and the executive, since the judiciary is not here directly involved? The accepted doctrine of the diffusion of sovereignty and the balancing of powers led to the wish to prevent the concentration of control over money and arms in either branch. "The purse and the sword ought never to get into the same hands whether legislative or executive," as Colonel Randolph Mason put it in the debate of June 6, 1787.

In spite of the doctrine, however, the formal provisions of the Constitution with respect to money and arms are heavily weighted on the side of legislative supremacy. This is altogether and unequivocally clear for the power of the purse. There can be no doubt that the Fathers—following herein the historical tradition of parliamentary development in all nations—intended to assign the money power, and by the words of the Constitution did so assign it, to Congress. Leaving aside the vexed problem whether in other fields certain powers inhere in the executive office as such, the Constitution plainly indicates that in relation to the public purse the executive functions only as the agent of the legislature. The President cannot,[1] by virtue of his own powers, raise or even borrow a penny, nor levy even the smallest tax or impost. He cannot appropriate any moneys for any purpose. The Constitution is strict and explicit in its limitation: "No Money shall be drawn from the Treasury, but in Consequence of Appropriations made by Law." The President, true enough, is the one who spends the money (the greater part of it, at any rate), but in the constitutional conception he does so only for the purposes, and in the amounts and manners, prescribed by Congress. All his spending powers are derived, not autonomous; so far as the use of the public purse goes, he is the agent not merely of the nation, but of Congress as herein representative of the nation.

The weighting is not quite so clear-cut in the case of the power of the sword, although the constitutional forms are roughly parallel. It is Congress that is assigned the power "To declare War, grant Letters of Marque and Reprisal, and make rules concerning Captures on Land and Water." It is for Congress "To raise and support Armies"[2] and "To provide for a Navy." Congress also—in an exten-

---

1. Cannot, that is, in his capacity as Chief Executive. But in his secondary legislative functions—through his veto and his duty to make recommendations to Congress—the President is assigned a share in the money as in all other legislative powers.
2. Though even Congress cannot appropriate money to that use for a longer term than two years.

sion of authority that is by no means a self-evident part of the legislative function—is "To make Rules for the Government and Regulation of the land and naval Forces," as well as "To provide for calling forth [and] for organizing, arming and disciplining, the Militia, and for governing such Part of them as may be employed in the Service of the United States." It is only, then, within this strict and delimiting framework that "The President shall be Commander in Chief of the Army and Navy of the United States, and of the Militia of the several States, when called into the actual Service of the United States."

Formally, the Constitution thus defines the relation of the President to the sword and to the purse in much the same manner. The size, temper and target of the sword are to be decided by Congress, just as Congress is to determine the amount, source and purpose of moneys. The President wields the sword, as he opens the purse, only as attorney, steward, agent for Congress, and only through Congress for the nation and the people.

2

Lucius Wilmerding, Jr., has shown that the formal ideal of exclusive legislative control over the purse cannot be fully realized in practice, and has not been at any time in the history of the American government. In spite of what theoreticians may sometimes say, common sense must reject the notion that "no circumstance whatever—no cataclysm of nature, no risk of invasion, not even invasion itself or insurrection—can justify the executive in varying the appropriation of public money which Congress itself has directed. . . . By [Jefferson, Hamilton and most of the Founding Fathers] it was recognized that in so complicated a government as that of the United States cases must sometimes, perhaps often, arise, where it would become the duty of the executive authorities, in the exercise of discretionary powers vested in them, boldly to set aside the requirements of the legislature, trusting to the good sense of Congress, when all the facts of the case should have been explained, to acquit them of all blame."[3] Thus Jefferson in 1807, after the attack on the *Chesapeake,* ordered military purchases not sanctioned by law; Lincoln, at the outset of his administration, had the Treasury advance $2 million for military purchases; Theodore Roosevelt gave immediate aid to San Francisco after the 1906 earthquake and fire; and Coolidge in 1926 advanced funds to storm ravaged Florida farmers.[4]

Even beyond such hardly disputable occasions, Mr. Wilmerding shows by examples drawn from several periods of our history that the central government has frequently violated the theoretically accepted principle of fiscal control. For reasons of administrative expediency, as it saw them, or from its own conception of the public weal, the executive has been able, through a variety of devices, to divert public moneys from the purposes originally intended by Congress in appropriating them. Congress has never been able to develop procedures adequate to forestall wholly or to correct such fiscal usurpation. From early years, the executive found it possible to spend more money than Congress had appropriated or intended to appropriate, and to force Congress to make good. For example, a department or agency could be operated on a scale that exhausted its annual appropriation within less than the year. Congress would then have to enact a deficiency bill, or face the shutdown of a perhaps essential service. This "coercive deficiency" method was sometimes carried a stage further in a more or less accepted routine by which a part of this year's appropriation would pay off last year's de-

3. Lucius Wilmerding, Jr., *The Spending Power* (New Haven: Yale University Press, 1943), pp. 3–4.
4. *Cf. ibid.,* pp. 9–16.

ficiency.[5] Again, the executive early learned the flexible use to which could be put the unexpended balances remaining on the books of the Treasury at the end of each fiscal year.

Until a generation ago, however, most of these deviations from the theoretical norm were relatively minor. Though they broke the purist doctrine that the legislature should have exclusive control over the public purse, they did not upset the legislature's over-all fiscal predominance. Executive departures from the letter of appropriation laws seldom went so far as a reversal of basic congressional policy. It was usually a question of practical judgment in applying accepted policy, or of meeting some contingency unforeseen in the law. Most of the 19th-century examples cited by Mr. Wilderding concern the military services, especially the Navy Department. Except for a few of the navy instances—where, following the precedent of Jefferson's Secretary of the Navy, there had grown up a habit of defiance that endures to our own day—it could be argued that the executive's share in the spending power, though anomalous from the standpoint of literal, formal doctrine, was in accord with the American governmental tradition of diffused and divided sovereignty.

The general breakdown in congressional control of the purse took place during the first world war. Patched together again from 1919–32, it then went into a further collapse, from which subsequently it has never made more than partial and episodic recovery.

Of the 1917 breakdown, Mr. Wilmerding writes:

The executive insisted and Congress recognized that much must be entrusted to the current judgment and discretion of administrative officers.

The expedients adopted by Congress to give flexibility to [*i.e.,* to concede control over] expenditure were several. It

---

5. Congress has come to connive, often, at this deficiency-makeup method in order to make a public showing of an official budget at a lower figure than actual expenditures are likely to be.

made lump-sum appropriations; it authorized the departments to obligate the government in excess of appropriations; it permitted appropriations to be renewed or increased by reimbursement; it established revolving funds; and, what is even more remarkable, it allowed incorporated government bureaus to collect and disburse the public moneys with scarcely a reference to the congressional appropriating power.[6]

Mr. Wilmerding quotes a 1919 comment by Treasury Secretary Carter Glass on the fiscal significance of these incorporated bureaus, agencies, banks and commissions:

> The particular advantage (which I should rather call menace in time of peace) accruing to government functions so organized, is the freedom which they enjoy in the expenditure of public money without the legal restrictions that the Congress has imposed with respect to the usual transactions of the government. If these activities were sustained by specific appropriations and were required to withdraw their funds from the Treasury in the manner prescribed for other government establishments with the same accountability both as to disbursements and receipts, there would be little or no ground for the corporate form of organization.[7]

Of the 1930's (which he calls "years of looseness") Mr. Wilmerding observes: "All the latitudinary devices employed during the war were, it is true, revived during the depression; an even greater grant of authority—the right to transfer appropriations—was for a time conceded to the executive; resort was had to coercive deficiencies."[8]

6. *Ibid.,* p. 154.
7. *Ibid.,* pp. 158–9.
8. *Ibid.,* p. 180.

Mr. Wilmerding's meticulous study ends before the entry of the nation into the second world war, during which all the "loose" tendencies and devices by which congressional control over the purse had during the first world war and the depression moved into the hands of the executive were speeded and compounded. The "permanent crisis," cold war and little war years since 1945 have not restored the traditional ratios. At most there has been a postwar drop from the wartime peak of executive supremacy, with a somewhat slower rate of constitutional erosion. Moreover, not only Congress but the executive also have largely given up control of the moneys turned over to the new international agencies such as the International Bank for Reconstruction and Development, the International Monetary Fund, and the other United Nations agencies and auxiliaries.

It would not be correct to say that Congress has altogether lost control of the purse. Even during the second world war, Congress on a few occasions asserted an independent legislative will, contrary to the will of the executive, on issues of fiscal policy—primarily on taxation, price, salary and profits control rather than on spending, which was delegated to the executive under virtually blanket grants of authority. But the executive now shares control of the purse with Congress; and in the real substance of power Congress' share is the lesser. Of course the established constitutional ritual is still preserved. Appropriation bills originate in the House of Representatives, and are enacted by both Houses in the prescribed manner. Payments by the Treasury are formally checked by the accountants against an appropriation on the books. The tax collectors justify their exactions by ultimate reference to laws passed in the prescribed manner. But we know from the history of the Roman Imperial Senate, the Nazified German Reichstag and a hundred other shadow assemblies that these outward forms are not in and of themselves decisive signs of the realities of power relations.

3

Granted, we cannot calculate the exact quantitative proportion of the money power that has been lost by Congress, and exactly how much has been gained by the executive and the bureaucracy. Granted, even, that the executive-bureaucratic share is still somewhat less than the predominant portion that I would judge it now to be. Even so, we confront a major shift in the equilibrium of power. Not only in our own tradition, but in the world history of parliamentary development, control of the purse by parliament, by the representative assembly, has always been understood to be the key issue. The histories of parliaments are largely the accounts of how representative assemblies of the people, or some strata of the people, came to terms with kings and lords and priests by gradually acquiring control over the disposition of their own and the nation's wealth. Thus when in our generation control over the purse begins to move backward— from the representative assembly to the executive (however called)— the constitutional history of the past seven hundred years is beginning to unwind. It is the fact of this reversal of direction rather than its exact measurement that is historically crucial.

The extent to which Congress has lost control of the purse can, like the form of one of Seurat's pointilliste paintings, be judged best by a broad view of the main composition rather than by close attention to isolated details. Most of the time during the two world wars, and particularly the second, Congress did not even pretend to maintain fiscal control. Senator Joseph C. O'Mahoney proclaimed openly in 1942 that war is "an executive function; it is not a legislative function."[9] The President, the military and the civil bureaucracy were given all the money they asked for, to do with it what they thought best. The fiscal function of Congress became little more than that of an office clerk who for formal legal reasons coun-

9. Quoted by Roland Young, *op. cit.*, p. 29.

tersigns the checks. In the New Deal depression days, similarly, Congress had no real control over, or even knowledge of, what Harry Hopkins, Harold Ickes and Henry Wallace were doing with the "relief" and "public works" billions that flowed over their desks.

Let us put the question in this way. How often in the years since 1932 has Congress expressed an independent will, contrary to the will of the executive, on money matters of major importance? Of course the independent will of Congress might be expected to coincide, fairly often, with the will of the President, and on such occasions it is hard to be sure just who is in charge. But in the natural course of events over these past stormy decades, including a good number of years when one or both Houses of Congress have not been of the President's political party, Congress, if it retains an independent fiscal will of its own, might be expected to have differed with the President now and then, and sometimes basically, in what it thought the public moneys should be applied to. If Congress' independent fiscal will were also, as formal theory declares, prevailing, then some of these differences would have been translated into upsets of executive fiscal proposals; refusals to give fiscal support to entire programs, agencies and bureaus; the junking of agencies and programs by cutting off all funds; and, more positively, the use of the fiscal weapon as the means, when conflict arises, to compel the executive to accept and pursue the broad policy determinations of the legislature.

In the record of these years we find very little of this sort of thing, much less than would have been inevitable if Congress were still supreme and unchallenged in control of the money power. There has been squabbling over the budgets, true enough, but the quarrels, even when bitter, have not sunk deep. It has been a question of $2 billion or $2½ billion for work relief funds; $16 billion or $17 billion for the air force; $300 million plus or minus for a $5 billion foreign aid program; 87% or 90% of parity in farm surplus payments; this particular fiscal emphasis or that in public housing, medicine, social security, propaganda, or what not. Congress, leaving the initiative to the executive, has never posed in this post-1933 period the foundation issues: whether it should be not $3 billion or $3½ billion or $1½ billion for work relief, but $0.00; whether foreign aid or public housing or farm surplus should get not this or that sum of public moneys but nothing at all; whether it is not the size of the air force budget but the strategic doctrine and national policy behind the budget that is of critical concern; or whether, for that matter, the government should not in some cases spend much more money and perhaps set up a new agency or undertake a new function that the executive neither proposes nor desires.

Even with respect to the squabbles on secondary points, Congress has no effective means to enforce its fiscal decisions on the executive, to discover whether these have been faithfully carried out, or to punish the bureaucracy and the executive if there have been violations. By such devices as have already been mentioned—transfer of appropriations, coercive deficiencies, manipulation of unexpended balances, vaguely defined lump sum appropriations, government corporations with separate bookkeeping—plus the expanding use of contingent and discretionary funds, and the spread of secret agencies (like the Central Intelligence Agency) with deliberately concealed budgets: by these and a dozen other tools in the accountants' box, the bureaucracy has to a very considerable degree freed its fiscal operations from congressional bonds. And, finally, Congress does not even possess—if such is indeed technically possible—any mechanism for an intelligible post-audit of governmental expenditures. That is, Congress has no sure way of finding out what really has been spent, by whom and why, or of fixing responsibility for illegal or improper disbursements that are on a scale larger than personal frauds and peccadilloes.[10]

10. As Mr. Wilmerding shows, neither the General Accounting Office nor the Bureau of the Budget nor the Comptroller General nor congressional hearings carry out a general and significant post-audit, without which strict fiscal control is impossible.

Several incidents in both the Truman and the Eisenhower administrations have shown from still another perspective the decline in congressional power over the purse. According to traditional doctrine as summarized by Mr. Wilmerding: "I. It is the exclusive right of Congress to specify the several objects to which the grants for the year may be applied and to limit the amounts which may be applied to each object. II. It is the duty of the executive, *except* in cases of urgent necessity, to apply the congressional grants only to the objects and within the amounts voted."[11] It is additionally implied in the traditional doctrine that Congress has the right to specify that grants *must* be applied to designated objects, and that the executive has the consequent duty, within the limits of the grants, to secure those objects. The "objects" are prior to the grants: that is, Congress as the law-making body has the right and duty to specify, under the principles of the Constitution, the objects of governmental action. The duty of the executive is to see that those objects are achieved, if they are technically possible under the circumstances of the time and the size of the allotted grants. If the executive can achieve them with less money than appropriated, then the savings are the nation's, and the President is to be congratulated for efficient administration. But if the grant is unspent because the executive refuses to seek the object specified by Congress, then he has flouted the legislative will and violated the Constitution as traditionally understood.

Just this has several times happened in recent years, especially in connection with military matters. One publicized instance was the refusal of the Truman administration to order additional units of B-36 long range bombers that had been voted, with the necessary appropriations, by Congress. Another instance that is still more striking because of its non-technical, purely political character, was the persistent refusal of both the Truman and Eisenhower administrations to use the $100 million voted by Congress to carry out the terms and intent of the so-called Kersten Amendment to the Mu-

11. *Op. cit.*, p. 193.

tual Security Act. During congressional consideration of military appropriations in the spring of 1958, Secretary of Defense Neil McElroy stated publicly that the administration would not build more nuclear submarines than planned, no matter how many Congress might vote; and hinted that it would also refuse to start construction of the new plutonium plant that a congressional bill provided for.

4

"Congress," Mr. Wilmerding concludes, "has not yet succeeded in devising a system of procedure stringent enough to render efficacious its unquestioned right to control the public expenditure."[12] It has failed in its attempts to institute an effective auditing system for retroactive control. It has failed, equally, to assert an advance or prior financial control by the method to which it has often, though not consistently, resorted: the multiplication and subdivision of specific appropriations that are mirrored in our day by the undigestible thousands of pages of the general budget. "The specification of appropriations is carried to an extreme incompatible with the needs of administration. The purpose of specific appropriations is to limit the quantity of power which may be abused. But it is a mistake to believe that this purpose can best be subserved by an indefinite multiplication of appropriations. . . . It is . . . possible to do too much as well as too little. . . . The extreme of rigor leads to the extreme of laxity."[13] So concluding, Mr. Wilmerding has made certain proposals by which he, and others, believe that the defects might be overcome, and Congress' claims made good.

In the years since Mr. Wilmerding wrote—the years of the second world war and after—the failure, certainly, has become more

12. *Ibid.*, p. 308.
13. *Ibid.*, pp. 194–99.

gross and pervasive. An earlier distortion of the intended scheme has become a reversal. In present reality, as I have suggested, Congress is no longer fiscally predominant. The executive and the bureaucracy now have principal control over the purse, subject to some secondary checking and harassment by Congress.

We may readily agree that Congress could not uphold its right to full control of the purse by means of its present fiscal procedures. It is not so clear that a mere change in procedure would enable it to do so.

The fact is that for a century and a quarter Congress did control the public expenditure, not in every instance and every respect, not as totally as theory demanded, but on the whole, by and large, in spite of loose, inadequate and incorrect bookkeeping, accounting and general fiscal procedures. Thus its current loss of control would not seem to be a consequence of faulty procedures, nor to be recovered by improving the procedures.

One major cause of the shift is obvious enough. In the government's earlier decades, any member of Congress and any moderately literate citizen could easily comprehend the budgets, which were very brief[14] as well as very simple. Moreover, in the normal course of observation a member of Congress could get a fair idea of what the executive department was doing. The activities were not massive in either scale or variety. He would probably be or become personally acquainted with most of the officials even of middle rank. Except for acute military matters, the sums of money involved in taxes or appropriations were not too far beyond what merchants, bankers, shippers and lawyers dealt with in their civil and private business. As a fiscal enterprise the government was, like all governments, odd, but it was not at all mysterious.

The members of Congress thus could fairly well know—and many of them did know—what was going on in the government,

14. The first general appropriation act was less than a page in length; and for several decades the length was held within three or four ordinary size pages.

what the executive branch was up to. They either could not or did not figure out how to keep the navy from juggling its accounts a bit, but they knew what kind of navy it was, what major weapons it had, what sort of shape it was in. They could tell whether the departments were over or under-staffed, how sloppy they were, whether they were doing—if not what they were ideally supposed to do—at least what they were realistically expected to do.

One of the recent annual budgets of the central government, elaborated into infinite detail and in sheer physical substance too heavy for any but a wrestler to lift, is beyond any man's comprehension—quite literally, any man's. The general budget is an artificial aggregate pieced and sewed and pasted together by thousands of hands. Not even the brightest accountant of the Budget Bureau comprehends it as a whole-and it is not a whole in any organic, coherent sense. Quite probably no single person in any of the departments or major agencies comprehends even his own sub-budget.

Opaque as are the trillion-digited pages of the budget, the vast and myriad activities which these dimly symbolize, with the millions of jobs and lives caught in that world-encompassing web, are a still much darker mystery. What man can simultaneously understand and evaluate the latest nuclear reactor, the economic needs of Pakistan, the deficit in the Post Office Department, the alternative designs for a space ship, tree diseases in the Pacific northwest, the newest methods for teaching languages, mildew in tropical military equipment, computer systems for inventory control?

The central government has grown too big both quantitatively and qualitatively—that is, in both the scale and the variety of its operations—for the members of Congress to comprehend the fiscal problems in detail. The most that a single member can do is to know one or two small governmental provinces that he makes his specialty. And because Congress cannot comprehend the problems, it cannot control their solution. We no longer have the kind of government that was envisaged in the traditional fiscal doctrine and the traditional practice.

Nor will it do any good for Congress to try to solve its own members' inevitable ignorance by hiring a great staff of experts. There would have to be tens and tens of thousands—as there are in the executive branch—of accountants, lawyers, scientists and specialists of all the myriad kinds. So the mystery would be merely redoubled. Besides, by the nature of the case, the huge staff would soon metamorphose from an arm of Congress into another wing of the bureaucracy.

Granted gigantic government, the legislature cannot exercise fiscal control in detail. Formally it remains possible for Congress to cut gigantic government down to a more modest and amenable size: either by lopping off some of its multitudinous limbs, or by reducing the fiscal flow to this or that organ not by the vain attempt to prescribe in advance the exact size of each corpuscle but by setting an overall maximum flatly defined and rigorously enforced. Dozens of bureaus, offices and agencies could simply be abolished, by reducing their appropriations to zero, without any noticeably adverse effect on the ends of government as these are stated in the preamble of the Constitution. A bureau which, by one means or another, has been able to spend $100 million of the public money annually, might be told by law: $50 million, and not a cent more, from all sources—direct or indirect appropriation, deficiencies, borrowings, reassigned or reshuffled quotas, contingency or discretionary funds or whatever.

In such ways, Congress might recover not a detailed but a broad and sufficient control over the public purse. But neither Congress nor any other contemporary parliament shows a disposition to act with vigor and persistence in such ways. The truth is that the decline in congressional control of the purse, the shift in fiscal control from the legislature to the executive and bureaucracy, is equivalent to the decline of congressional power in general. Within the structure of representative government, "the money power" is not really a separate power or function, one power among others, that can be parceled out among the various branches of government according to the whim of statesmen or the accidents of time. "Money," wrote

Hamilton in *Federalist* No. 30, "is, with propriety, considered as the vital principle of the body politic; as that which sustains its life and motion, and enables it to perform its most essential functions."

The money power is not something different from the other operations of government, but is coextensive with them, since every operation has and must have its fiscal aspect or phase. Thus the increasing ascendancy of the executive (and the bureaucracy) in the governmental equilibrium necessarily means increasing executive (and bureaucratic) control of the money power.

This is why procedural changes, no matter how skillfully made, could not of themselves enable Congress to re-establish basic control over the public purse. Congress will recapture the purse only if the whole present constitutional direction is reversed, if Congress rebounds from its historic fall, and swings the governmental equilibrium back within the limits once set by charter and tradition.

XIII

AND THE SWORD

THE IDEA THAT in war time Congress sits back while the President takes charge of national affairs, both civil and military, as a kind of general dictator has become so familiar since 1941 that we tend to take it for granted as a constitutional axiom. Actually, no one ever heard of the "war power" or "war powers" of the President until the Civil War. Even in the Civil War, Lincoln discovered that he possessed a "war power" only because, it being a domestic conflict, his constitutional duty "to take care that the laws be faithfully executed" was brought into coincidence with his constitutional role as Commander in Chief.

After the Civil War, the presidential "war power" slumbered for another seventy-five years until 1940–41. In the first world war it was not the executive alone but the executive in conjunction with Congress that asserted a new, peculiar and unprecedented war power. The assignment—as in Senator O'Mahoney's declaration, cited in the last chapter, that war is "an executive function; it is not a legislative function"—of not merely *a* war power but *the* war power to the executive is an offshoot of the years since 1941, of the administrations of Franklin Roosevelt, Truman, Eisenhower, Kennedy and Johnson.

By the intent of the Founding Fathers and the letter and tradition of the Constitution, the bulk of the sovereign war power was assigned to Congress. Although the Constitution names the President Commander in Chief, it does not explicitly allot him any other element of the war power. Now it is doubtless true that a nation's first commander, particularly if the nation is actively at war, will inevitably exercise somewhat more than a technical military function. But it is certainly not the case that the Fathers thought of the President's military command as endowing him with the attributes of a general dictator, or with the legislative functions otherwise reserved to Congress. Nor were they reasoning in the abstract. The appointment of a commander in chief for a nation's armed forces was a procedure common in scores of governments of all political forms, from ancient times through their own 18th century, and did not, as a rule, subvert the normally prevailing political system. Hamilton, explaining the Constitution's war provisions in *Federalist* No. 69, writes:

> The President will have only the occasional command of such part of the militia of the nation as by legislative provision may be called into the actual service of the Union. The king of Great Britain and the governor of New York have at all times the entire command of all the militia within their several jurisdictions. In this article, therefore, the power of the President would be inferior to that of either the monarch or the governor.
>
> *Secondly.* The President is to be Commander in Chief of the army and navy of the United States. In this respect his authority would be nominally the same with that of the king of Great Britain, but in substance much inferior to it. It would amount to nothing more than the supreme command and direction of the military and naval forces, as first General and admiral of the Confederacy; while that of the British king extends to the *declaring* of war and to the *raising* and *regulating* of fleets and armies,—all which, by the Constitution under consideration, would appertain to the legislature.

The older commentators, and Court decisions prior to our day, had no doubt about where the war power was lodged. The remarks of Professor Charles W. Bacon in the once well-known textbook,

The American Plan of Government—written, significantly enough, just before the first world war—are typical of the traditional understanding:

> The framers of the Constitution turned over an ample measure of the powers of war to Congress because Representatives and Senators are delegates of the People and States of the United States whose commercial interests must be staked upon the issue of every conflict. The People pay the bill. Therefore, their representatives in Congress are of right the proper persons to control military affairs.
>
> "The war making power," according to the decision in the case of Perkins *vs.* Rogers, "is, by the Constitution, vested in Congress and . . . the President has no power to declare war or conclude peace except as he may be empowered by Congress."[1]

Today, with the experience of the first and more particularly the second world wars before us, many citizens are surprised to learn that Congress has any meaningful function of any sort in war time. "At the beginning of the [second world] war," notes Professor Roland Young in the introduction to his study of *Congressional Politics in the Second World War,* "it was widely believed that Congress need not, or should not, play a very important role in fighting a war. A modern war required that the President be given the power necessary to direct the civil and military establishments." As if explaining that a senile old codger can still walk to the dining table, Mr. Young finds that Congress "was by no means the anachronism which many—including some of its own members—predicted it would be."[2] It may be added as further comment that Mr. Young's

1. Charles W. Bacon, *The American Plan of Government* (New York: G. Putnam, 1916), pp. 152–3.
2. *Op. cit.,* pp. 3, 4.

is the only book so far published on what Congress had to do with the second world war, as against unnumbered hundreds on what was done by the two Presidents, their commanders, and the civilian officials.

Under the Constitution, it was Congress, as we have noted, that was assigned the control over the size, composition and regulation of the armed forces. Congress alone was to authorize their domestic use ("to suppress Insurrection"). And Congress alone could declare a foreign war. In the earlier (August 6) draft of the Constitution, the enabling phrase read "To make war" rather than "To declare war." This was discussed on August 17. Madison and Elbridge Gerry made the motion to change "make" to "declare." They explained that their purpose was to give "the Executive the power to repel sudden attacks"; and Gerry, in order to dispel any possible misunderstanding, declared flatly that he "never expected to hear, in a republic, a motion to empower the Executive alone to declare war." There was no dissent from George Mason's assertion that he "was against giving the power of war to the Executive, because not safely to be trusted with it." Connecticut's delegates, Roger Sherman and Oliver Ellsworth, inclined at first against the verbal change from "make" to "declare," because, though they agreed that the executive, as commander, would properly act to repel invasion, they wished to be sure that the general war power granted specifically to Congress should not be "narrowed." Rufus King explained that "make" war might be understood to mean "conduct" it, "which was an Executive function." With these clarifications, which were the sense of the assembly, Connecticut's objections were withdrawn.[3]

The distinctions can be made considerably clearer in form than in practice. Whatever the exact intentions of the Fathers and wording of the charter, in the traditional conduct of the central government the war power was fairly evenly divided between executive and

3. New Hampshire, however, still voted for the original wording. Massachusetts was absent.

legislature. The President's share was derived from his mission to command the forces and "conduct" operations, from his initiative in the conduct of foreign policy, and from his part in the governing process as a whole. Congress participated as the law-making, taxing and appropriating agency, through its confirmatory tasks in connection with treaties and with ministerial and military appointments, by its determination of the size and character of the armed forces, and by general policy decisions that affected the country's international relations.

During the past generation congressional control over the size, composition and regulation of the armed forces has largely been submerged in the same complex gigantism that has swamped congressional control of the purse; indeed, the loss of military control is largely a necessary consequence of the latter, since the primary method by which Congress can control the armed forces is through control of military appropriations. But in the case of the contemporary military apparatus, such control by Congress is nearly impossible to uphold.

The mere existence of a huge "standing army" is enough to make congressional control all but impossible. An army is under the operative orders of its commander. If the army is large and powerful in comparison with the community as a whole, then the commander is correlatively swollen, no matter what the formal limits of his jurisdiction. This the Founding Fathers comprehended perfectly, and it was for this reason that they were unanimous in their conviction that the new government ought not and would not have a large standing army in time of peace. The peacetime armed forces, such as they might have to be, were to consist, according to their conception, primarily in the militias of the several states, subject to the command not of the President but of the executives of the state governments. The decentralized militia organization of the armed forces would thus spread and fragmentize, under normal circumstances, the total military and war power of the nation, guarding against an executive tyranny springing from control of the sword. In

a major war the risk had to be run. "If the defence of the community under such circumstances [of rebellion or invasion] should
make it necessary to have an army so numerous as to hazard its liberty, this is one of those calamities for which there is neither pre-
ventative nor cure. It cannot be provided against by any possible
form of government."[4] A large force would, if the nation's defense
demanded it, come together under the single presidential command; but only for the war's temporary purpose, and subject to lawful regulation by the legislature. With the war's ending, the large
standing army would dissolve.

Among the Philadelphia delegates there were some who were
opposed to there being any standing army whatever in peacetime.
The absence of such a prohibition was, in fact, cited by Edmund
Randolph among the reasons that led him to vote against the Constitution and to oppose its adoption by Virginia. A number of
others, like Roger Sherman and Elbridge Gerry, wanted to place
explicit limits on its size. "The people," declared Gerry on August
18, "were jealous on this head, and great opposition to the plan
would spring from such an omission. . . . He thought an army dangerous in time of peace, and could never consent to a power to keep
up an indefinite number. He proposed that there should not be kept
up in time of peace more than ———— thousand troops. His idea
was, that the blank should be filled with two or three thousand." A
few days later, Madison declared as a principle that "the greatest
danger to liberty is from large standing armies"; and on September
14 he advised that "as armies in time of peace are allowed on all
hands to be an evil, it is well to discountenance them by the Constitution." In the *Farewell Address,* Washington re-echoed Madison:
"Hence, likewise, [all the parts of the country] will avoid the necessity of those overgrown military establishments which, under any
form of government, are inauspicious to liberty, and which are to be
regarded as particularly hostile to republican liberty."

4. *Federalist,* No. 26 (Hamilton).

This feeling against a large standing army was so strong in the debates over ratification that Hamilton felt compelled to devote three of the *Federalist* papers to it. Moreover, he can find no other defense for the constitutional latitude on the matter than that: (a) "the whole power of raising armies [is] lodged in the *Legislature,* not in the *Executive*"; and (b) there is "an important qualification even of the legislative discretion, in that clause which forbids the appropriation of money for the support of an army for any longer period than two years. . . .[5] The legislature of the United States will be *obliged,* . . . once at least in every two years, to deliberate upon the propriety of keeping a military force on foot; to come to a new resolution on the point; and to declare their sense of the matter, by a formal vote in the face of their constituents. They are not at *liberty* to vest in the executive department permanent funds for the support of an army, if they were even so incautious enough to be willing to repose in it so improper a confidence."[6]

2

Hamilton might seem to be writing about not so much another country as another world. In 1793 Secretary of War Knox felt called on to defend his request for an annual appropriation of $50 thousand as "not inordinate." (The total for 1791 had been only $40,306.) In the government's first twenty years, the sum of all military and naval expenses, other than pensions, was $54 million. Today our "standing army in peacetime" absorbs in a single year more than seven hundred times the total allotted during those two full decades.

Neither the size of its budget nor the numbers in its ranks reveal the full proportionate weight that the armed forces now have in our

5. *Federalist,* No. 24.
6. *Federalist,* No. 26.

national society. Through the armament and procurement programs they reach into every corner of industry, commerce and agriculture; through the posts and missions abroad they are entangled with every aspect of foreign policy; through conscription they are linked with every home and school. Moreover, the strength of the armed forces is organized, and therefore of a heightened potential in relation to the other less tightly organized social forces. And the weight of the contemporary "standing army" has almost wholly left the congressional side of the governmental balance.

With very few exceptions, Congressmen, like the lay public generally, cannot understand the technical nature of modern military equipment. The votes on all the array of nuclear and electronic and aero- and astronautical apparatus must necessarily be blind. Nor can Congress effectively judge—or, because of claims of secrecy, even find out about—the prevailing strategic doctrines upon which the security and survival of the nation must depend. Billions of dollars are spent by such secret agencies as the Atomic Energy Commission and the Central Intelligence Agency without any detailed accounting, before or after, of where the money goes; in the case of the Central Intelligence Agency, without even a disclosure of the total sum, which is concealed by deliberately falsified entries. Because of the tremendous inertia of so vast a machine as the present military force, because of the long years needed to plan, design, develop and build modern armament,[7] and because of the consolidation of predominant executive-bureaucratic power, the two-year limit on military appropriations is rendered meaningless.

In truth, Congress is deprived almost altogether of freedom of action in relation to military affairs. Almost all of its actions in this decisive field of sovereignty are coerced. Formally, Congress must be asked to renew each year, or every two years, appropriations for such-and-such type of planes or ships or missiles or bombs; but in

---

7. For modern weapon systems, the "lead time" required to go from decision to "operational hardware" ranges from five to more than ten years.

fact, once the long-term plans have been authorized, they cannot be stopped or greatly altered; and in the original authorization, Congress itself will have played a passive role. Formally, it is still congressional enactment that is deciding military policies, discipline, rules, purposes, missions; but in fact the great permanent military apparatus is a power auxiliary of the Commander in Chief and its own professional chiefs.

In the early conception, the key factor in the war power was thought to be that of "declaring" war, and this was given to Congress' keeping. The formal declaration never had quite the importance that was attached to it in theory. If it is for the commander to conduct military operations, and if it is his duty—whether or not specified by law—to repel invasion or other immediate threat to the lives and property of citizens; then he can always order fighting without a declaration, if he judges it necessary; and if the fighting spreads he can confront Congress with a *fait accompli* that makes the declaration no more than a symbolic recognition of what is already happening. From the early days (in dealing with pirates, for example, hostile Indians, or certain small nations of Africa and Latin America) the Presidents have not hesitated to order naval vessels or troops into small-scale actions without congressional authorization. All declarations of war by the United States, even the rather narrowly voted declaration of the War of 1812,[8] have come after events had already ruled out any real freedom of choice. Still, until 1917 certainly, and possibly until 1941, Congress had always shared or even dominated in the prior determination of policies that led toward and into war.[9] If the final decision was coerced, it was by the course of events, not by the executive or the military. And until the formal declaration by Congress, it was in the past always possible to

8. 79–49 in the House; 19–13 in the Senate.
9. There is no question, for example, that the fateful decision in 1898 for the United States to engage in war with Spain—the first great outward step in the nation's world imperial expansion—was forced by Congress on a reluctant President.

draw back from an approaching or even partly begun war—as on a number of occasions, starting as early as the almost-wars with both France and England in the 1790's.

But in our day the act of formally "declaring" war, losing all substantial meaning, has been reduced to a legalistic ritual without important historical or social consequence. And in this case it is not that Congress has lost a right or power to the executive, as one further phase of the over-all congressional decline. Because of the change in the nature of war itself, the right or power "to declare war" no longer has much meaning, no matter who possesses it.

The high speed and long reach (spatio-temporal compression) of modern weapons, the world-wide deployment of the forces of the major powers, the saturation blows of which weapons are now capable, and the tactical advantage possible from surprise and deception—all such factors combine to eliminate the older preparatory period to a war. Wars—wars in the physical sense—now just start; before any legal note can be taken of them they are profoundly and irrevocably joined. And this follows not merely from the wickedness of governments and leaders but from the technical imperatives of the new weapons and the correlated shifts in strategy and tactics.

There is not the slightest chance that these technical conditions will change in ways to make possible the revival of the role of formal declarations, but rather the contrary. The development of ballistic missiles means that the first blow in a major war might well cause 50 or 100 million casualties and scores of billions of dollars worth of property damage. The decision on the counter-blow will have to be given within a limiting period of a few minutes, since no more than a few minutes' time will intervene between the first detection of the approach of the enemy blow and its arrival in the target region. Not only is the idea absurd that this decision could be referred back to a congressional vote; it is improbable that the President or even the Chiefs of Staff could participate in it.

Even where the war situation permits recourse to traditional forms, the executive now tends to assume full and autonomous power. Not only do the presidential acts, as in the case of Franklin Roosevelt's moves from 1939 to 1941, make a war inevitable, so that the Pearl Harbor occasion of its open start is, like the congressional declaration, a secondary incident; President Truman further demonstrated in Korea how one of the biggest wars in our history, in terms of casualties and cost, can now be entered and conducted without any legal authority from the legislature, simply by not calling it "a war." President Eisenhower, seeking a constitutional form for the same presidential power, asked Congress to give advance authorization to any wars he might decide to make around Formosa or in the Middle East, and in July 1958 he ordered troops into Lebanon without any reference to the Congress then in session. This amounts to an assumption of the power to declare war, and is obviously not an extension but a contradiction of the traditional content of the Constitution.

Analyzed from another standpoint also, the significance of the power to declare war has evaporated. In our time the line between peace and war has largely disappeared. There is a continuous international struggle—now called "the cold war"—that is fought by varying methods with one or another degree of violence. The old fairly plain legal distinctions between war time and peace time, soldier and civilian, combatant and non-combatant, war industry and peace industry, war targets and open areas, no longer have clear applications. "Emergency" and "crisis" are not special but routine. In its daily normal functioning the nation tends, in response, to act as it did in the semi-total Civil War and the first world war: with more and more of the total social power centering in the government, and more and more of the governmental power moving into the hands of the President (and bureaucracy) conceived as exercising emergency and war duties.

The nation comes to understand that the nature of modern war is such that ordinary constitutional limitations on the scope of federal sovereignty cannot be permitted to interfere with the mobilization of the country for victory. As a consequence, the limitations inherent in the American constitutional system which in theory made it a poor instrument for waging total war have been almost totally overcome.

. . . In the Curtiss-Wright case, the Court . . . asserted that the power to wage war was inherent in national sovereignty, antedated the Constitution itself, and was not dependent upon the enumeration of federal powers in Article I, Section 8.[10]

It remained for Congress to perform the ironic ritual of formally recognizing, on the one hand, the central government's assumption of potentially unlimited power, and at the same time its own loss of a critical share in that power.

Both before and after Pearl Harbor, Congress enacted a series of critical statutes, all of which asserted vast federal powers for the prosecution of the war. These statutes were alike also in that they made tremendous grants of authority to the executive for the exercise of the powers over which Congress asserted its sovereignty.[11]

---

10. Alfred H. Kelly & Winfred A. Harbison, *The American Constitution* (New York: W. W. Norton, 1955), p. 847.
11. *Ibid.*, p. 848.

XIV

THE PROBLEM OF
TREATIES

THE FATHERS knew that the treaty power, because it could not
be securely confined by any constitutional fence, was a likely
source of trouble. The difficulty may be put as a dilemma:
either the treaty power will be too weak to meet the requirements
of a great and sovereign nation, or it will be strong enough to break
through all constitutional limits.

Under the Articles of Confederation the treaty power had been
too weak. There had been no true supremacy clause through which
treaties entered into by the United States would become the law of
the land; and no means of enforcing a supremacy clause if there had
been one. Therefore individual states could, and did, disregard
treaties and other international instruments that had been ratified by
Congress. Some states entered into international relations on their
own account, even to the extent of trafficking with the enemy. In
this as in general, the Fathers were resolved that the new government should have power adequate to secure the ends that they had
set themselves.

There was therefore never any question but that treaties, like domestic legislation, were under the new system to be the law of the
land, enforceable on both citizens and states in the courts, backed
ultimately by the force that was to be at the disposition of the new
government. It was so provided in all the preliminary documents
submitted for discussion at Philadelphia and in all the early drafts of
the instrument that became the Constitution. The resolutions introduced by William Paterson of New Jersey, expressing the small-state

outlook with its stress on the sovereign rights of the individual states and its distrust of too centralized a general government, contained a supremacy clause, applicable to treaties, that was stronger than that of the competing Virginia resolutions or the wording that was in the end adopted:

> 6. Resolved, that all acts of the United States in Congress, made by virtue and in pursuance of the powers hereby, and by the Articles of Confederation, vested in them, and all treaties made and ratified under the authority of the United States, shall be the supreme law of the respective States, so far forth as those acts or treaties shall relate to the said States or their citizens; and that the Judiciary of the several States shall be bound thereby in their decisions, any thing in the respective laws of the individual States to the contrary notwithstanding: and that if any State, or any body of men in any State, shall oppose or prevent the carrying into execution such acts or treaties, the Federal Executive shall be authorized to call forth the power of the confederated States, or so much thereof as may be necessary, to enforce and compel an obedience to such acts, or an observance of such treaties.

In Charles Pinckney's plan, though it represented the jealous views of South Carolina, the supremacy clause, though shorter, was equally unequivocal.

When such legal and political supremacy had been extended to treaties, they had been released, potentially at least, from constitutional control. The objects of domestic legislation could be stated by affirmation, implication and negation. But a treaty was an agreement of the nation in its collective, sovereign role with another sovereign.[1] There did not seem to be any way—and indeed there

---

1. Originally, treaties were, literally, personal agreements between one sovereign monarch and another. As in the analogous case of business corporations, many of the puzzling confusions in the theory of treaties doubtless arise

was no way—to specify in advance just what could and could not be included in such agreements, or to be sure just what might be the indirect effect of future treaties on the domestic affairs of citizens and states. Debating the appropriation clause on August 15, George Mason "was extremely earnest to take this power [to originate money bills] from the Senate, who he said could already sell the whole country by means of treaties."[2] And in a formal sense this was true, because it was usual for treaties to settle boundaries, and a boundary settlement could and often did cede territories. Commenting further on Mason's aside, John F. Mercer of Maryland drew from precedents in British history to confirm that "the Senate, by means of treaties, might alienate territory, etc., without legislative sanction. The cessions of the British Islands in the West Indies, by treaty alone, were an example."

Some attempt was made to delimit formally the range of the treaty power, as in Hamilton's often quoted discussion in *Federalist* No. 75:

> The power of making treaties . . . relates neither to the execution of the subsisting laws, nor to the enaction of new ones; and still less to an exertion of the common strength. Its objects are CONTRACTS with foreign nations, which have the force of law, but derive it from the obligations of good faith. They are not rules prescribed by the sovereign to the subject, but agreements between sovereign and sovereign. The power in question seems therefore to form a distinct department.

It cannot be said that this or any other positive attempt was very clarifying. In fact, there is an evident sophistry in Hamilton's dis-

---

from the effort to translate ideas derived from an actual personal relation to an institutional relation between "sovereigns" that are "persons" only by a juridical fiction.

2. The draft constitution at this stage assigned the treaty power exclusively to the Senate.

tinction. If treaties have the force of law—as under the Constitution he was defending they explicitly do—then they become, in necessary if indirect consequence, "rules prescribed by the sovereign to the subject."

Actually, although the Fathers were intellectually aware of the potential danger in the treaty power, they were only mildly apprehensive about its abuse in practice. Their reliance was not on formal, explicit definition, but on a shared commonsense understanding of the field of interest covered by treaties, on the negative limits that the charter as a whole would put on the treaty as on every other power of the central government, and on the diffused treaty-making process that they agreed to in the final weeks at Philadelphia.

The treaties with which they were acquainted were of two general types. One of these was political, concerned with problems of war and peace, with alliances, indemnities, boundary settlements, and so on: with the preparation for, protection against, conduct and conclusion of, wars. The other type of treaty (which might be included as part of the same document that also contained clauses dealing with war and peace) was economic, concerned with commerce and navigation, the privileges, rights and restrictions applicable to the international shipping and trade of the treaty nations. Under the economic and technological conditions of the 18th century, neither of these types of treaty impinged on the nation's social and political foundations, or jeopardized the basic rights of individual citizens. Of course, the central government's monopoly of an enforceable treaty power meant that the individual states lost all direct control over foreign policy and foreign commerce; but this they had given up in words even by the Articles of Confederation, and to back up those words by adequate power was a primary motive for shifting to the new form of government.

Meanwhile, both states and individuals would be protected from abuse of the treaty power by the negative restrictions on the central government that were explicit or implicit in the charter by which, alone, it existed. For the most part the subject matter of treaties fell outside the province of domestic government. The consequences of a treaty, though they might be of import to the citizens' security and well-being, did not affect, one way or another, the structure of the political system. If by mischance a treaty, or a provision of a treaty, violated a principle of the system as this was defined by the Constitution, then that treaty or provision was void.

In this interpretation, Hamilton concurred with Jefferson. "A treaty," wrote Hamilton, "cannot be made which alters the Constitution of the country or which infringes any express exceptions to the power of the Constitution."[3] Jefferson, in Section 52 of his *Manual of Parliamentary Practice,* long accepted by both chambers of Congress as an authoritative reference and still printed as part of the *Senate Manual,* comments:

> To what subjects [the treaty] power extends has not been defined in detail by the Constitution; nor are we entirely agreed among ourselves. 1. It is admitted that it must concern the foreign-nation party to the contract, or it would be a mere nullity, *res inter alias acta.* 2. By the general power to make treaties, the Constitution must have intended to comprehend only those subjects which are usually regulated by treaty, and can not be otherwise regulated. 3. It must have meant to except out of these the rights reserved to the States, for surely the President and Senate can not do by treaty what the whole Government is interdicted from doing in any way.

The Court, in its infrequent dealings with treaty questions, seems to have shared this natural enough opinion. "The government of the United States . . . is one of limited powers. It can exercise au-

3. Alexander Hamilton, *Works,* Vol. IV, p. 342, quoted by Frank E. Holman in *The Increasing Need for a Constitutional Amendment on Treaties and Executive Agreements* (Seattle: Argus Press), p. 14.

thority over no subjects except those which have been delegated to it. Congress cannot, by legislation, enlarge the federal jurisdiction, nor can it be enlarged under the treaty-making power."[4] This traditional interpretation was repeated in Geofroy *v.* Riggs (1890) when Justice Field wrote for the Court: "It would not be contended that [the treaty power] extends so far as to authorize what the Constitution forbids, or a change in the character of the government or in that of one of the States."

Finally, the treaty-making process was itself felt to be a reliable check on the undue extension of the treaty power:

> The security essentially intended by the Constitution against corruption and treachery in the formation of treaties, is to be sought for in the numbers and characters of those who are to make them. The JOINT AGENCY of the Chief Magistrate of the Union, and of two thirds of the members of a body selected by the collective wisdom of the several States, is designed to be the pledge for the fidelity of the national councils in this particular.[5]

2

Although in our day commonly thought to be so, the treaty power is not a self-evident executive function.

> Though several writers on the subject of government place [the treaty] power in the class of executive authorities, yet this is evidently an arbitrary disposition; for if we attend carefully to its operation, it will be found to partake more of the leg-

4. New Orleans *v.* United States (1836). Quoted by Holman, *loc. cit.*
5. *Federalist,* No. 66 (Hamilton).

islative than of the executive character, though it does not seem to fall within the definition of either of them. The essence of the legislative authority is to enact laws, or, in other words, to prescribe rules for the regulation of the society; while the execution of the laws, and the employment of the common strength, either for this purpose or for the common defence, seem to comprise all the functions of the executive magistrate. The power of making treaties is, plainly, neither the one nor the other.[6]

Under the Articles of Confederation, the treaty power was assigned to Congress, and we have had previous occasion to observe that the record of the pre-constitutional Congress in its conduct of foreign relations was, in the difficult circumstances of the embattled young federation, remarkably good. Judged comparatively, the achievements of the United States in foreign policy from 1777 to 1787, as well as the personal quality of the appointed ministers, are perhaps to be rated higher than those of any subsequent decade. When we recall that the start was from scratch; that Congress found powerful allies, money and arms to make possible a successful war against the mighty mother empire; that a favorable peace was delicately negotiated and signed; that loans were obtained without an established credit standing; that peacetime trade treaties were arranged with great commercial nations; and when we remember that all of these were done by a government that lacked the full attributes of sovereignty, then we can hardly contend that the legislature is by some inherent necessity unsuited for the control of foreign policy and international relations. In the conduct of foreign policy it was not Congress that was essentially at fault under the Articles (though mistakes were, as in all human enterprises, from time to time made), but the ambiguities of a charter that left the foreign policy acts of Congress at the mercy of thirteen separate sovereignties, each of

6. *Federalist,* No. 75 (Hamilton).

them in the last analysis possessed of more power than the general Congress itself.

By both the Randolph and the Paterson plans submitted early in the Philadelphia convention, the treaty power would have remained, as under the Articles, with Congress; to be exercised, it seems to be assumed, in the same way as the normal domestic legislative power. The first full draft of the Constitution, which came from the Committee of Detail on August 6, assigned the treaty power as well as the appointment of ambassadors to the Senate. At these stages, even in the August 6 draft, it was still provided that the executive was to be elected, in one manner or another, by Congress.

When in the final weeks it was decided to make the President an autonomous office with its own special mode of election, the allotment of the treaty power was modified, in accord with the pervading principle of the diffusion of sovereignty, into the method stated in the final version: "[The President] shall have power, by and with the advice and consent of the Senate, to make treaties, provided two-thirds of the senators present concur: and he shall nominate, and, by and with the advice and consent of the Senate, shall appoint ambassadors, other public ministers and consuls. . . ." But let us add that under Section 8 of Article I, Congress and not the President is assigned the powers "To regulate commerce with foreign nations" and "To define and punish piracies and felonies committed on the high seas, and offences against the laws of nations"—both of which, particularly and most importantly the first, would ordinarily be thought of as subsumed under the treaty power.

In the closing debate at Philadelphia, James Wilson, discussing the treaty clause in its new (and ultimately adopted) form, "moved to add, after the word 'Senate', the words, 'and House of Representatives'. As treaties, he said are to have the sanction of laws also [and should therefore be ratified by both chambers of the legislature]. The circumstance of secrecy in the business of treaties formed the only objection; but this, he thought, so far as it was inconsistent with obtaining the legislative sanction, was outweighed by the necessity of the latter."[7] He was voted down, with only his own Pennsylvania delegation supporting him, but not because the Convention was unwilling to provide "legislative sanction" for treaties. What the final draft in fact provided were two distinct and coequal procedures by which legislative sanction was to be obtained. A treaty was to be as much a law as any other enactment could be.

At Philadelphia and in the subsequent public debate over ratification the argument for excluding the House from the treaty procedure was based on practicality, not on principle. The large size, fluctuating composition, shorter corporate life, and less rounded experience of the House "forbid us to expect in it those qualities which are essential to the proper execution of such a trust. . . . A body so variable and so numerous" will not, in particular, display the "decision, *secrecy*, and despatch" that are required in the conduct of foreign affairs.[8] Under the regime of the Articles there had been painful troubles over secrecy. Members of Congress had leaked reports of secret negotiations with France and England, and—in a notorious scandal involving David Howell of the always difficult state of Rhode Island—with Sweden.

The Fathers believed that with election by the state legislatures and a longer term of office the Senators would be older, wiser and more responsible than the Representatives, on whom the popular breath would beat more fiercely. The leaders of the small states, seeing in the Senate the body that was peculiarly their own, welcomed an expansion of its power.

Still more practically, it was plain to practical men that a two-thirds vote in the Senate would be more difficult to get, and thus more of a check on executive aggrandizement or other abuse of the treaty power, than would be the bare majority in each cham-

7. *Debates*, Sept. 7. Wilson was here giving consistent expression to his own tendency toward democratism, which we have earlier remarked.
8. *Federalist*, No. 75 (Hamilton). "*Secrecy*" is italicized in the original.

ber that was to be the rule for ordinary domestic legislation. James Wilson, reasoning ideologically as he usually did, after having vainly argued that treaties should be subject to the standard two-chamber "legislative sanction," went on to object—accurately, of course—to the two-thirds requirement as "putting it into the power of a minority to control the will of a majority." There was considerable discussion, with Rufus King and some other delegates arguing that a process calling for the President plus a simple majority of the Senate was protection enough against malice or stupidity. But the convention, agreeing with Pierce Butler's contention that the two-thirds rule was a "necessary security against ambitious and corrupt Presidents," voted Wilson down, nine states to one.

Finally, the House of Representatives was by no means excluded from the treaty power, after all. It held a share through the commerce clause, and more generally through the constitutional principle that any appropriation that might be (as it often would be) needed to carry out any clause of a treaty must not only go through the full procedure of domestic legislation, but must originate in the House.

The issue arose sharply as early as 1796, when the House was called on to enact certain appropriations in connection with the Jay Treaty, which had been negotiated by the executive and duly ratified by the Senate. Some of the supporters of the treaty insisted that, the treaty having become the supreme law of the land through ratification, the House had no choice in the matter. However, in a set of resolutions that fixed the traditional doctrine, Madison laid down the dictum:

When a Treaty stipulates regulations on any of the subjects submitted by the Constitution to the power of Congress, it must depend for its execution, as to such stipulations, on a law or laws to be passed by Congress. And it is the Constitutional right and duty of the House of Representatives, in all such cases, to deliberate on the expediency or inexpediency of carrying such Treaty into effect, and to determine and act thereon, as, in their judgment, may be most conducive to the public good.[9]

The required concurrence of the House, and of the full domestic legislative procedure, in carrying out any terms of a treaty that reach into the public purse thus adds a reserve safeguard to the checks imposed by the treaty-making process itself.

3

It seems clear that the Fathers expected the Senate to participate as a kind of "executive council" in the negotiation of treaties and the active conduct of foreign relations. There was some brief attempt at this in early practice, but it did not work out satisfactorily. In his first summer of office, President Washington on one occasion visited the Senate in order to discuss a proposed treaty with the Senators. There are differing accounts of what happened, but it is agreed that Washington became angry at the disputatious attitude of some of the Senators, and made no further overture of the kind.

In a diary entry for Nov. 10, 1824, John Quincy Adams refers to this incident:

Mr. Crawford [Secretary of the Treasury, at a Cabinet meeting under President Monroe] told twice over the story of President Washington's having at an early period of his Administration gone to the Senate with a project of a treaty to be negotiated, and been present at their deliberations upon it. They debated it and proposed alterations, so that when Wash-

9. Quoted in *The Constitution of the United States,* pp. 418–9.

ington left the Senate chamber he said he would be damned if he ever went there again. And ever since that time treaties have been negotiated by the Executive before submitting them to the consideration of the Senate.

The President [Monroe] said he had come into the Senate about eighteen months after the first organization of the present Government, and then heard that something like this had occurred.

As Adams here observes, it became fixed in constitutional tradition that the President was charged with actual negotiating of treaties and with the active, day-by-day conduct of foreign relations. This did not, however, mean that the executive had seized monopoly control over the treaty power. By not having participated—officially—in the writing of the treaty, the Senate was not committed beforehand, and could actually retain more independence of judgment about ratifying. To make sure of the two-thirds vote, a President had to sound out senatorial opinion in advance, consult informally with Senate leaders, and keep Congress informed concerning the plans and progress of foreign negotiations.

The influence of Congress over foreign policy was meanwhile being continuously felt through the consequences of national policy decisions, the regulation of foreign commerce, the effects of tariffs, the activities of congressional committees named to overlook foreign relations, the control over appropriations, and the senatorial confirmation of ambassadors and ministers. In a few notable cases— the Louisiana Purchase, for example, or annexations of Hawaii and of Texas—the executive, acting outside all normal procedures, behaved as what the Fathers might have called a "despot." But these were generally (in the case of the Louisiana Purchase quite openly) recognized to be unconstitutional usurpations that could be justified only by acute and overriding national interest, and by their subsequent legitimization through such congressional action as voting the funds to carry them out. For the most part, until the 1940's, the nation's foreign policy, though administratively directed by the President, was a joint executive-legislative[10] enterprise marked by a fairly successful record of collaboration without subordination.

We are now so conditioned to the view that foreign policy is the executive's business, that many older comments are likely to seem outlandish. In 1818, Senator Rufus King of New York, who had been a delegate to the Philadelphia convention and later a close congressional ally of Hamilton and the "strong executive" Federalists, observed:

> In [foreign policy] concerns the Senate are the Constitutional and only responsible counsellors of the President. And in this capacity the Senate may, and ought to, look into and watch over every branch of the foreign affairs of the nation; they may, therefore, at any time call for full and exact information respecting the foreign affairs, and express their opinion and advice to the President respecting the same, when, and under whatever other circumstances, they may think such advice expedient.[11]

Woodrow Wilson's description of what he took to be the actual state of affairs after a century's development is still more startling:

> The greatest consultative privilege of the Senate . . . is its right to a ruling voice in the ratification of treaties with foreign powers. I have already alluded to this privilege, for the purpose of showing what weight it has had in many instances in

10. Until very recent years, when it has begun to concern itself with all phases of the national life, the judiciary tried to avoid intervention into the treaty province.

11. Quoted by *The Constitution of the United States* from M. Farrand, *Records of the Constitution,* Vol. II, p. 183.

disarranging [in Congress' favor] the ideal balance supposed to exist between the power of Congress and the constitutional prerogatives of the President.... The President really has no voice at all in the conclusions of the Senate with reference to his diplomatic transactions... He is made to approach that body as a servant conferring with his master, and of course deferring to that master.[12]

12. *Congressional Government*, pp. 232–3

XV

THE ESCAPE OF THE TREATY POWER

BEGINNING SHORTLY after the second world war, the status of the treaty power became the topic of a complex and continuing national debate. This was brought to a focus in 1952 when Senator John W. Bricker of Ohio first proposed a constitutional amendment for the purpose, as he explained it, of "curbing" the treaty power. After lengthy hearings, the following text of what became known as "the Bricker amendment" was approved by a 10–5 vote of the Senate Judiciary Committee:

> SECTION 1. A provision of a treaty which conflicts with this Constitution shall not be of any force or effect.
> SECTION 2. A treaty shall become effective as internal law in the United States only through legislation which would be valid in the absence of a treaty.
> SECTION 3. Congress shall have power to regulate all executive and other agreements with any foreign power or international organization. All such agreements shall be subject to the limitations imposed on treaties by this article.

This text has been changed, expanded and contracted a number of times over the years, as the issue has been argued in committee, on the floor of Congress, in the White House, and in many public forums. In 1954 the Senate failed by only a single vote (60–31) to give the then prevailing text the two-thirds majority required for congressional initiation of a constitutional amendment. This did not close the debate, however, which has continued at varying intensities, in and out of Congress and official circles. In 1956 a much simplified form of the proposal was approved by the Senate Judiciary Committee:

> A provision of a treaty or other international agreement which conflicts with any provision of this Constitution shall not be of any force or effect.

Looking back over this prolonged controversy, we may observe that a majority of the members of Congress, as judged by committee or floor votes and by their public statements, has been and remains in favor of some form of "Bricker amendment" with its formal intention of a constitutional curbing of the treaty power. When the issue moves toward a parliamentary showdown, the White House, whether under a Democratic (Truman) or Republican (Eisenhower) President, has always thrown its influence against the amendment, usually by first suggesting diversionary changes in the wording, but in the end by lining up negative votes.

Among the scores of business, civic and educational organizations that have taken a public stand on the issue, the political lineup is for the most part unmistakable. Using the terms "conservative" and "liberal" as defined in Part One, we find that the conservative groups are for, the liberal groups against, the Bricker amendment. The Chamber of Commerce, the veterans' organizations, Kiwanis, American Farm Bureau, Daughters of the American Revolution, Colonial Dames, General Federation of Women's Clubs, American Medical Association, National Association of Real Estate Boards and so on, are *For*. Americans for Democratic Action, United World Federalists, the American Association of University Women, American Jewish Congress, American Federation of Labor-Congress of Industrial Organizations, American Civil Liberties Union, have de-

244 CONGRESS AND THE AMERICAN TRADITION

clared *Against*. Groups like the state and national bar associations, which are not so clearly differentiated as either conservative or liberal, have been divided in their public views.

It is easy to become lost in the legal technicalities of the discussion[1] of the Bricker amendment. The formal points are subtle and delicate; and each word—even the tiniest connectives—in the changing texts have been painstakingly chewed and whittled. It seems fairly clear, by now, that at a formal, verbal level the basic political and historical issues cannot be seriously joined. The words, even after they have been refined and polished for so many years, cannot seem to tie down the problem.

Reflection shows the reasons for this semantic elusiveness. To require (as do some versions of the amendment) that a treaty, in order to become operative as internal law, must go through the standard process of domestic legislation[2] (majority vote of both chambers of Congress plus presidential signature) would merely eliminate the Constitution's alternate rule for making laws for the United States (presidential proposal plus two-thirds confirmatory vote in the Senate). Now it may be that the motives that led the Fathers to lay down this alternate rule in the case of treaties are no longer relevant. But eliminating them would do nothing to curb the abuse of the treaty power, if there is such abuse; and would rather, in fact, as we have already noticed, loosen its reins still further, since the two-thirds requirement in the Senate is more, not less, of a restriction than the two-chamber majority.

To declare that a treaty (or other international agreement) that conflicts with the Constitution is void, without "force or effect," is,

1. A discussion which includes thousands of pages of testimony before congressional committees.
2. Or, as it is sometimes put, that treaties should not be "self-executing." But as a matter of fact, treaties are not now self-executing in the British parliamentary sense: under the United States Constitution they merely have, after having been negotiated, a special mode for being made into the law of the land.

really, a tautology. So long as the American government is considered to derive its ultimate authority from the Constitution, then any and every governmental act that conflicts with the Constitution is void and without (legal) force or effect. This has never been disputed, and could not consistently be, unless the constitutional basis of the American government were openly abandoned. The real problem is always formulated in constitutional terms: just what is the proper meaning, interpretation and application of the Constitution in the given circumstances. No one would ever think of defending a treaty, or any other governmental act, with the argument that it is legal *though unconstitutional*.

2

The treaty power itself is anomalous for constitutional government, as we have seen, and this is why it cannot be tied down firmly with constitutional words. It could not be in 1787, and it cannot be in the 1950's.[3] But from their lack of significant verbal definition we should not assume that there are no real issues at stake in the conflict over the Bricker amendment. These real issues are expressed in, rather than defined by the words used and the formal arguments advanced on both sides. They were not evoked by the proposal for the amendment, nor will they be ended by its adoption or final defeat. For a hundred and fifty years the half-concealed treaty problem simmered quietly. Let us review those circumstances that in our day have brought it to a disturbing boil.

3. Metaphysically, the cause of the difficulty is the fact that a government in a constitutional relation to its citizens is not the same entity as a government in its corporate relation to another government. This is the distinction alluded to in the quotation from Hamilton, (cf. p. 196 *supra*). Adapting Vilfredo Pareto's language, we might say that a treaty is an act "*of* a community," not "*for* a community."

(A). The subject-matter of treaties (and comparable instruments) is no longer limited to the rather small range of items that were actively involved in pre-20th-century international relations. The speed-up and expansion of communications, transport, technology and so on have made almost everything—from atoms to air rules to radio frequencies—a matter of potential international concern, and thus a possible subject for treaty determination. In line with the general statist tendency of our times, the fact that the international or partly international problems *can* be handled governmentally is judged sufficient reason that they *should* be so handled. Big government thus draws its sustenance from international as from domestic nutriment.

Moreover, the line between foreign and domestic affairs becomes blurred. Aircraft, radio, disease quick-spread by modern transport, business concerns active over half the earth, foreign trade along with huge foreign aid and relief programs, tens of millions of travelers and exiles moving across the continents, soldiers of many nations intermingling in all regions, space satellites disregarding all political boundaries: all these are at once and indistinguishably of domestic and international bearing. They signify that treaties and foreign affairs have become continuously relevant to the private life of the average citizen.

(B). As the field of "foreign policy" swells, the President has increasingly substituted "executive agreements" for treaties. The executive agreements are not submitted to Senate ratification, or as a rule to any other form of congressional action. In some cases they are not even made known to Congress.

The use of executive agreements is not without precedent in our earlier history, and, though not explicitly authorized by the Constitution, is within commonsense limits a natural extension of the President's role in the conduct of foreign policy. Practical steps must be taken, for example, to carry out the terms of treaties or of special military undertakings. The routine activities that are a normal part of international intercourse—from visas and health precautions to landing rules at international harbors and airports—need technical understanding for which the necessarily ponderous treaty process is not well suited. It has always been assumed that within the framework of established policy, matters of such kinds are to be handled as a usual part of the executive's function. We have also noted that on exceptional occasions in the past, as in the case of the Louisiana Purchase, executive agreements have been deliberately used to circumvent not only the treaty process but the recognized restraints of the Constitution.

In summary, then, the traditional executive agreements were as a rule either normal applications of established policy (including treaties that had been duly ratified) or technical conventions. The cases in which an executive agreement meant a basic change in going policy were rare and notorious.

During the past generation the number of executive agreements has rapidly increased, and their birth rate has become more than twice that of treaties.[4] Because of the more intimate interlacing of the world, even ostensibly technical agreements now have a closer relation to domestic affairs and over-all national policy.[5] In addition, and not as exceptional but as routine practice, executive agreements have come to cover the kind of policy determination that would traditionally have been assumed to be the subject for treaties.

This shift became conspicuous during the second world war. The great wartime policy declarations, as well as the establishment of international organizations that expressed basic policy as well as military decisions, were all undertaken through executive agreements

4. According to Dr. George B. Galloway (*The Legislative Process in Congress,* p. 147), about 1,500 executive agreements and 900 treaties had come into effect through 1952.

5. As, for example, agreements on international air transport routes or radio channel allocation, which directly affect the operations and profits of domestic corporations in these fields.

unrelated to treaties. This was the case with the Atlantic Charter, the setting up of the Combined Chiefs of Staff and the Combined Food Board, and the Declaration of the United Nations. Perhaps the most decisive instance of all was the destroyers-for-bases trade with Britain,[6] arranged by President Roosevelt on his sole executive responsibility, which made the probable entry of the United States into the war inevitable. The "status of forces" understanding with Japan, under which there took place in 1957 the bitterly disputed case of William Girard, is also an executive agreement.[7]

Formally, neither Congress as a whole nor the Senate in particular has any part in either negotiating or confirming an executive agreement. Actually, Congress may have an indirect share. When an agreement is merely applying a policy already set by treaty or other law, Congress (or the Senate) will have had in substance a prior voice. In certain cases, as with the Reciprocal Trade Agreements Act, Congress enacts a law stating a general policy under which it specifically authorizes the President to enter into executive agreements. And often Congress gives an ex post facto legitimization to an agreement by making an appropriation to carry out its terms. This was done, for example, with the destroyers-for-bases trade; but in that as in other instances the appropriation was in reality coerced; it would be naive to suppose that Congress had any independent will in the matter. It is more generally true that executive agreements are a device by which the President, on his own authority, can make policy decisions of indefinite range in their domestic as well as international import.

(C). Several Supreme Court decisions from the period between the first two world wars, less noticed at the time they were handed

6. Characterized by Prof. Edward S. Corwin in a public letter as "unrestrained autocracy in the field of our foreign relations."
7. The status of forces rules for the NATO countries are, however, covered by treaty.

down than during the past decade, have made it more difficult to
obscure the peculiar status of the treaty power. The Court's dicta in
these decisions are both ambiguous and incomplete but the more
puzzling and extreme interpretations to which some analysts believe
they lead have not been repudiated.

The earliest that has become prominent in the treaty controversy is
Missouri *v.* Holland (1920). There was at issue a treaty with Great
Britain concerning reciprocal protection of birds migrating between
Canada and the United States. Under this treaty Congress had passed
a law authorizing the Department of Agriculture to regulate, subject
to penalties, the hunting of these internationally migratory birds. On
the objection that this invaded an acknowledged police power of the
respective states, Justice Holmes commented for the Court:

> Acts of Congress are the supreme law of the land only when
> made in pursuance of the Constitution, while treaties are de-
> clared to be so when made under the authority of the United
> States.[8] We do not mean to imply that there are no qualifica-
> tions to the treaty-making power; but they must be ascer-
> tained in a different way.[9] It is obvious that there may be
> matters of the sharpest exigency for the national well being

8. According to Madison's words in *Debates,* August 25, the only purpose of
the different language used ("in pursuance" and "under the authority") was "to
obviate all doubt concerning the force of treaties pre-existing." The Fathers did
not wish to nullify the treaty of peace with Great Britain or the other treaties
successfully concluded under the Articles; but these had obviously not been
made "in pursuance of the Constitution" since the Constitution had not yet
come into existence. Thus the Court in 1920 was inventing, not discovering,
the distinction to which it appealed.
9. The only intelligible meaning for this cryptic phrase, "a different way,"
would seem to be, by the doctrine of the decision, "a correspondence with what
are deemed to be imperative national interests independently of their consis-
tency with the Constitution." That is to say, the ancient doctrine that has so
often been the ideological prop of despotic government: *Salus populi suprema lex.*

that an act of Congress could not deal with but that a treaty followed by such an act could, and it is not lightly to be assumed that, in matters requiring national action, "a power which must belong to and somewhere reside in every civilized government" is not to be found. . . . Here a national interest of very nearly the first magnitude is involved. It can be protected only by national action in concert with that of another power. . . . It is not sufficient to rely on the states. The reliance is vain.

Professors Kelly and Harbison observe:

The theoretical implications of this decision were astounding. If a treaty could accomplish anything of a national character so long as its subject matter were plausibly related to the general welfare, what limits were there to federal authority, if exercised in pursuance of the treaty-making power? The decision, in fact, seemed to open a serious breach in the limited character of federal sovereignty.[10]

In United States *v.* Curtiss-Wright Export Corp. (1936) the Court carried, or seemed to carry, the doctrine of the extra-constitutional character of the treaty power a big leap forward. Justice Sutherland wrote for the Court:

The broad statement that the federal government can exercise no power except those specifically enumerated in the Constitution, and such implied powers as are necessary and proper to carry into effect the enumerated powers, is categorically true only in respect to our internal affairs. . . . The investment of the federal government with the powers of external sovereignty did

10. *The American Constitution*, p. 677.

not depend upon the affirmative grants of the Constitution. The power to declare and wage war, to conclude peace, to make treaties, to maintain diplomatic relations with other sovereignties, if they had never been mentioned in the Constitution, would have vested in the federal government as necessary concomitants of nationality.

In an early case (Penhallow *v.* Doane, 1795), counsel had pressed on the Court this same theory of the metaphysical priority of the government to the Constitution: "A formal compact is not essential to the institution of government. Every nation that governs itself, under what form soever, without any dependence on a foreign power, is a sovereign state. In every society there must be a sovereignty. The powers of war form an inherent characteristic of national sovereignty." The theory, rejected on that occasion, disappeared until this rebirth in United States *v.* Curtiss-Wright, one hundred forty-one years later.

In this same Curtiss-Wright opinion, Justice Sutherland, cutting the last links with the expectations of the Fathers, asserted unqualifiedly "the very delicate, plenary and exclusive power of the President as the sole organ of the federal government in the field of international relations." More recent decisions have still further extended and ideologically reinforced the monopoly control of foreign policy that the executive has been exercising in practice, and have formalized the reduction of the Senatorial and congressional role to little more than rhetoric and ritual.

The two cases of United States *v.* Belmont (1937) and United States *v.* Pink (1942), which arose out of President Roosevelt's 1933 executive agreements in connection with recognition of the Soviet government, repeated the Missouri *v.* Holland theory that the treaty power is not subject to the constitutional limitations that apply to domestic legislation.[11] At the same time, they seemed to elevate executive agreements—that is, international compacts made by the President alone, without any authorization, participation or ratification by the Senate or by Congress as a whole—to the same constitutional status as treaties. Under these interpretations, executive agreements would seem to be judged not merely "lawful acts"—as they had of course always been considered when entered into by the President in consonance with the Constitution and his duties under it—but as "the supreme law of the land" in the same full and binding sense as treaties formally ratified by two-thirds of the Senate. The agreements are "final and conclusive on the courts," in Justice Douglas' words. Even the fiscal terms of such agreements were held to be legally binding on the states and on individual citizens, though without any concurrence of that branch of government which had been traditionally assigned the power of the purse. "State law" as well as domestic federal law "must yield when it is inconsistent with, or impairs the policy or provisions of, a treaty or of an international compact or agreement."

The Constitution of the United States[12] explains that "the executive agreement attained its fullest development as an instrument of foreign policy under President Franklin D. Roosevelt, even at times threatening to replace the treaty-making power, if not formally yet actually, as a determinative element in the field of foreign policy." The practice of Mr. Roosevelt's successors does not indicate any lessening of the role of the executive agreement as an instrument of foreign policy. The 1957 decision of the Court in the William Girard case continued the Pink case's seeming acceptance of an executive agreement as constitutionally equivalent to a duly ratified treaty. C. L. Sulzberger has commented as follows on this shift as it applies to the supreme determinant of sovereignty, that is, to war:

11. In the Pink case, which involved the ownership of property located in New York state, the Court dismissed arguments drawn from the state's jurisdiction and from the Fifth Amendment that would admittedly have been conclusive in a normal domestic action.

12. P. 437. This volume, from which I have frequently drawn, is the official congressional annotation of the Constitution, prepared by the Legislative Reference Service of the Library of Congress.

From Truman's administration on, there has been a steadily increasing tendency by our executive branch to involve us in a condition of war (as in Korea) or to risk involving us in such a condition (as in Lebanon) without prior legislative approval. Likewise, the President, without much comment or objection, can now virtually obligate the nation in treaty commitments such as the Baghdad Pact minus the formality of Senate ratification.[13]

Thus a kind of constitutional syllogism is completed: the subject matter of treaties is handled through executive agreements: executive agreements are given the binding status of treaties.

(D). Since 1945 the United States government has entered into three treaties that are radically different from anything in the nation's previous history: those, namely, through which the United States became part of the United Nations, the North Atlantic Treaty Organization, and the Organization of American States.[14] For the United States there is a basic constitutional novelty in the United Nations, and to a somewhat lesser degree in NATO and the Organization of American States. Traditionally, the nation's commitment under a treaty has been specific and limited, in space, time and money. A treaty has been thought of along the lines of Hamilton's interpretation, as a contract between two (sometimes several) existing governments whereby they settle certain defined problems, make certain reciprocal undertakings concerning boundaries, property settlements, tariff and navigation, apprehension of criminals and similar matters, and establish certain procedures for settling

13. *New York Times,* Aug. 6, 1958.
14. The Organization of American States differs from the United Nations and NATO in having, in the Monroe Doctrine and practice, fairly solid traditional, if not legal roots.

questions that arise in application. No new, permanent political entity comes into existence through the treaty: at most there may be a temporary commission or arbitration panel or joint committee to carry out, interpret or apply the treaty's stipulations. Considered from the point of view of the United States Senate, all this meant that traditionally, in ratifying a treaty, the Senate knew fairly well what it (and through it, the nation) was getting into.

Along a different plane, the United States has also during the present century—through treaty, executive agreement or congressional legislation—adhered to several dozen continuing international bodies with technical or scientific functions: Inter-American Radio Office, International Bureau of Weights and Measures, International Whaling Commission, International Criminal Police Commission, and that sort of thing. Just prior to the first world war, the United States entered the International Court of Justice ("The Hague Tribunal"), now blanketed into the United Nations apparatus. The International Court is a continuing body with functions that go beyond the technical, but since it hears only those cases that all parties are willing to submit to it, and is not backed by any police or military power, even indirectly, its decisions lack any coercive force. Moreover, when ratifying the Hague Convention under which the Court was established, the Senate attached its own special conditions to United States participation.

But the United Nations Charter, which became operative through a multilateral treaty, is of a quite different order. The major commitments are not specific and limited, nor are they definite settlements or undertakings. The essential consequence of the United Nations treaty is the creation of a continuing, presumably permanent organization—or rather, complex of organizations—of which the United States is an integral member and part. This organization is chartered to exercise a broad, vaguely indicated variety of functions, a number of which have always been considered attributes of national sovereignty: including actions affecting war and peace, military and armament problems, police actions, industrial projects,

definition and enforcement of "human rights," fiscal appropriations
for miscellaneous purposes in many regions of the world, education
and indoctrination, and so on. Most immediate in relation to national sovereignty, independence and survival are, of course, the activities that relate to peace and war. These are still more intimately
at issue in the (also continuing) North Atlantic Treaty Organization,
as well as (though somewhat less imperatively) in the looser Organization of American States.

Now it is true that under the three treaties by which it joined
these three organizations (UN, NATO, OAS) the United States did
not formally renounce sovereign control over its own war-making
power (or any other essential sovereign power) nor alter, formally,
the procedures under which war and peace or other acts are supposed to become legal under the United States Constitution. But in
fact they do entail a decisive alteration, and are pointed toward still
more basic alterations to come.

Formally a decision of the United Nations (Security Council or
General Assembly) or of NATO (the Supreme Command or the
Council) is not binding on the United States unless the United
States chooses to accept it as so. The choice, however, is made by the
United States executive alone (acting through his agents in the UN
or NATO). That is to say, if the UN or NATO opts for war—or for
peace—the United States will go along if the President says so. Neither Congress as a whole, to which the Constitution assigns the sole
power to declare war, nor the Senate, to which the Constitution assigns an integral share of the treaty power, need have any voice in
the decision. The war-making power of the United States, and at
least a portion of a number of other significant national powers, are
now possessed in fact by the President plus any one of several international assemblies.

This is not only plain as a possibility. It has been proved in prac-
tice by the Korean war, which was decided and initiated by the
President, and ratified not by either chamber of the United States
Congress but by the Security Council of the United Nations. The

technical military situation in Europe makes it self-evident that Congress would have no part in deciding a NATO war.

Similarly, the financial adjuncts of the United Nations (the International Bank for Reconstruction and Development and the International Monetary Fund), as well as the economic auxiliaries attached more directly to the Secretariat, dispense large sums of money appropriated or lent by the United States government without any congressional share in controlling the uses to which the money is put. There is no congressional action on budgeting these moneys before they are spent, nor any subsequent congressional audit. The decisions are made at all stages by international bodies in which sit officers of the American executive but no congressional agents. United Nations action in the fields of education and indoctrination, which are considerable enough to have practical significance, are also exempt from any sort of congressional control.

True enough, the formal constitutional logic has been stretched rather than openly breached. The United States government participates in the United Nations, the North Atlantic Treaty Organization and the Organization of American States by virtue of treaties that have been duly—and overwhelmingly—ratified by the Senate. Through these treaties, it can be formally argued, the President has been "delegated" to do all that he does do in these organizations, while some undefined portion of the powers of the United States government has been "delegated" to the organizations themselves. Such formal analysis, though it has a certain importance, should not be allowed to obscure historical realities. As both Locke and Rousseau pointed out, the basic powers that are the essence of sovereignty cannot be delegated. Whoever exercises them is in fact the sovereign, whatever words are used, and anyone is sovereign to the extent that he exercises them. To "delegate" such powers as control over money, war and foreign affairs is, in reality, to renounce them, to abdicate.

3

During the past two decades, then, the treaty power—understood
in a broad sense that covers all forms of international instruments
and the general conduct of foreign policy—has suffered the following changes:

(1) The subject matter dealt with in treaties (and other international compacts) has been greatly expanded, so that it now includes
much that is of major and pervasive domestic concern.

(2) Recent treaties, in parallel to other recent tendencies, have
served to increase the relative power and to swell the functions of
the central government.

(3) The treaty power has been emancipated, probably to a greater
extent than any other governmental power, from constitutional restrictions.

(4) The congressional share in the treaty power has been so much
reduced that what remains of it is largely by presidential grace. In
this field the President can, when he chooses, operate in virtual
complete independence of Congress, with Congress invited to
chime in occasionally as an ex post facto echo.

In April 1952, the year before he became himself an officer in the
executive apparatus, John Foster Dulles summed up the present status of the treaty power in a speech delivered at Louisville, Ky.:

The treaty-making power is an extraordinary power liable to
abuse. Treaties make international law and also they make domestic law. Under our Constitution treaties become the
supreme law of the land. They are indeed more supreme than
ordinary laws, for congressional laws are invalid if they do not
conform to the Constitution, whereas treaty laws can override
the Constitution. Treaties, for example, can take powers away
from the Congress and give them to the President; they can take
powers from the states and give them to the federal government

or to some international body and they can cut across the rights given the people by the constitutional Bill of Rights.[15]

The treaty power has thus become one of the most effective and flexible instruments for accomplishing political aims, particularly those aims that entail marked and rapid changes from traditional procedures in the direction of centralization, statism and executive supremacy. Those citizens, therefore, who favor such changes, and who accept or welcome a dilution of national sovereignty into systems of collective security, international authority or embryonic world government, find the treaty power a useful political weapon for their purposes both domestic and international. Such citizens belong to the group that we have defined as liberal; and, since they have for most of the past twenty-five years controlled the conduct of American affairs, they have in fact wielded the treaty power, on the whole successfully, in pursuit of their goals.

Conservatives are opposed to these ends that can be so effectively served by use of the treaty power, and they are specifically opposed to the concentration of power in the executive to which the nearly exclusive presidential control of foreign policy contributes. If conservatives had been directing national affairs during the past generation, they need not have been overly disturbed over the treaty-power issue. They could voluntarily have held the use of the treaty power within traditional channels, or might even have used it—though perhaps somewhat awkwardly—to their own conservative purposes. Under the actual circumstances of liberal ascendancy, the conservatives have been prompted to mount a national campaign aiming to blunt and curb the treaty power, to pull it back within traditional limits. The Bricker amendment has been, in its changing forms, the central demand of this conservative campaign.

15. This did not, of course, prevent Mr. Dulles, two years later as a member of the Eisenhower Cabinet, from opposing the Bricker amendment and any comparable treaty-limiting enactment.

There is a curious feature of the liberal-conservative division on the treaty-power issue. The liberal doctrine and practice on this issue necessarily weakens the relative power of Congress in the American system of government. It would seem natural therefore that most Congressmen, except for those who were really hardened in liberal ideology, would tend—out of a mere sense of institutional self-preservation—to be for a protective curb on the treaty power. And this seems to be the case for the members of Congress taken severally and subjectively. By what they say individually, most of them favor the intended principle of the Bricker amendment. The Senators so voted by just one short of a two-thirds majority, and it took intense White House pressure to produce that one more than one-third. There is no reason to think that the division in the House is very different. Many members of both Houses frequently and eloquently lament those consequences of the contemporary use of the treaty power that we have reviewed.

Nevertheless, on the decisive occasions of these recent years Congress as a collectivity has invariably confirmed even the most far-reaching treaty operations of the executive—or at any rate, those few that have been brought before it. Although many of the Senators have, as individuals, sharply criticized the United Nations, the Senate voted 89–2 for ratification of the Charter, and few votes in either House are recorded against the annual United Nations appropriations. The votes have been overwhelming, as well, for the North Atlantic Treaty Organization, the Organization of American States, and for the most recent in this new generation of world organisms, the International Atomic Energy Agency.

The contrast could hardly be sharper between this obedient acquiescence today and the fierce battle a generation ago—over what were after all the same basic issues—through which the Senate blocked the executive's attempt to lead the country into an earlier United Nations. For an assembly or nation as for an individual, the prime mark of autonomous power, of independence, is the ability to say No.

XVI

THE INVESTIGATORY
POWER

B Y A NOT uncommon sort of irony, the governmental power that is the unique, unshared possession of Congress, that has freshened rather than withered during the past generation, and that is now the senior element in what remains of the Congressional portion of the national sovereignty, is not mentioned in the written Constitution: the power, namely, of investigation and inquiry. The omission was doubtless not from oversight at Philadelphia, but rather because the Fathers took the investigatory power for granted as implicit in the legislative function. Certainly it has been sanctioned by the active tradition of the government since its earliest years.

The tradition of the post-Constitution American government here continues, as in many other particulars, the prior tradition of the English Parliament and the assemblies of the separate colonies. Formal parliamentary investigations in England date back at least to the 16th century.[1] In the 17th century they were of fairly common occurrence, and the records of a number of them still exist. In the 1604 case of Sir Francis Goodman, Parliament gave a committee the crucial authority to summon witnesses and require the production of records. In 1681, Sheriff Acton was sentenced to the Tower of London for lying to a "Committee for the Examination of the Merchants' Business." As early as 1666 the Commons had set up a supervisory committee similar to the Senate's current Committee on Government Operations.

1. The first—into certain election disputes—is generally dated about 1571.

In 1689 the Commons appointed a Select Committee "to inquire who has been the Occasion of the Delays in sending Relief over Ireland, and particularly to Londonderry"; and in the same year a committee was authorized to investigate espionage in the Irish wars, with power "to send for persons and papers." In the years following, other committees were appointed to supervise administrative agencies and their personnel, prisons and poor relief.

The colonial assemblies in America assumed the investigatory power as a normal part of their business, and were sustained therein by the courts. Accounts of colonial investigations survive from most of the colonies, especially Massachusetts, New York, Pennsylvania and Virginia.[2] In 1722, the Massachusetts Assembly summoned a Colonel Waltin and Major Moody for questioning on the military operations in Maine. As a result, both officers were retired from the service. Still earlier, in 1691, the New York Assembly had imprisoned the French minister, Mr. Dally, for refusing to answer questions. A few years later, it imprisoned George Webb for insulting, and R. Richards for assaulting, a member. The thirteen constitutions adopted during the revolutionary period by the newly independent colonies expressed in nine cases, and in the other four implied the power of the legislature to punish for contempt.

Under the federal Constitution the first formal congressional investigation was undertaken by a select committee of the House in 1792. A military expedition under General Arthur St. Clair had been almost annihilated by an Indian ambush in the Northwest Territory. There was widespread popular concern, with a demand for some sort of public accounting. A doggerel rendering of the disaster made the rounds:

2. For this earlier history I am relying principally on Marshall Edward Dimock, *Congressional Investigatory Committees* (Baltimore: Johns Hopkins Press, 1929) and Ernest J. Eberling, *Congressional Investigations* (New York: Columbia University Press, 1928).

November the 4th, in the year ninety-one,
We had a sore engagement near to Fort Jefferson;
St. Clair was our commander, which may rememberer be,
Since we lost nine hundred men in the western territory.
The day before our battle fifteen hundred men we had,
But our old gouty general he used us very bad. . . .

The House voted an "inquiry into the causes of the late defeat of Major General St. Clair." In the discussion before the vote was taken, some members argued that it would be insulting to President Washington, and that he should be requested to conduct the investigation through the executive branch. Representative H. Smith of South Carolina, rejecting this alternative, expressed the conviction of the majority: "This House is the grand inquest of the nation."

In the hearings that followed, the Secretaries of the Treasury and of War were among the witnesses. General St. Clair was found to have displayed "coolness and intrepidity," and was exonerated of any personal guilt, but study of the testimony led to a number of changes in war department policy and procedures.

Only three subsequent Congresses have failed to initiate investigations. There had been about thirty by 1814, and, according to Professor Dimock, three hundred and thirty through 1928. Since then, as the investigatory power has increased its relative strength in the congressional arsenal, the rate has so greatly quickened that there have been more than twice as many investigations in the quarter century following 1933 as during the government's entire preceding history.[3]

It would be hard to name a topic of even the smallest public concern that has not been the target of a congressional investigation.[4] The

3. This post-1933 frequency rate of *congressional investigations* thus shows a striking numerical parallelism to that of *executive vetoes* and *judicial nullifications.*

departments and major agencies of the executive—to which investigations were confined until 1827—have all been investigated, most of them many times. Each of the nation's wars, except for the Spanish-American War (which was in a special sense Congress' own conflict), has been diversely investigated. There have been investigations of all major branches of the economy: railroads, shipping, oil, banks, housing, insurance, utilities, munitions, agriculture, mining, investment, communications, real estate, lobbying. In early days the Post Office Department, which then operated in large part through subcontracts with private individuals, was a favorite and rewarding subject, as military departments and their procurement practices have always proved to be. For a century the customs houses periodically tempted investigatory ardor. Often Congress has instituted special investigations of scandals, riots and disasters: such as the investigation of the New Orleans riots in 1866, of the Kansas disorders (1856), the Credit Mobilier scandal (1872/3), the Jay Cooke bankruptcy (1876), the Star Route mail contract scandals in Grant's administration or the airmail scandals in the 1920's, the Alaska Purchase scandal, the Teapot Dome oil contracts (1924), various kinds of racketeering in recent years, the railway strike of 1886, irregularities in Daniel Webster's books (1846), or General Andrew Jackson's conduct of the Seminole War (1818).

Nor are investigations of alleged conspiracy and espionage by any means a mid-20th-century novelty. Even before 1800 espionage in relation to France and Spain was a subject of investigation. In 1810 a committee was instructed to inquire into a reported conspiracy through which General James Wilkinson "corruptly received money from the government of Spain or its agents," and more generally into

---

4. Congress has, of course, often investigated the election qualifications of its own members, or the conduct of government officials in connection with possible impeachment proceedings. These two cases differ from other types of investigation, in that they are pursuant to explicit clauses of the Constitution which herein assigns Congress a plainly judicial function.

the relations with foreign agents. Full-scale investigations probed the Aaron Burr conspiracy (1808) and John Brown's raid (1859).

The roughest of our present-day investigators are mild enough compared to some of their predecessors. Fletcher Pratt describes Senator Ben Wade, chairman of the famous Committee on the Conduct of the [Civil] War: "barrel-chested, vulgar, shrewd, and violent, [he] kept a sawed-off shotgun in his desk . . . and tried every means he knew to provoke some of the Southern fire-eaters into calling him out, for he was a deadly shot."[5]

John Quincy Adams tells in his diary how a witness named Reuben Whitney was handled by an 1837 investigating committee:

> [Representative] Bailie [Balie?] Peyton, of Tenn., taking offense at one of his answers, threatened him fiercely, and when he rose to claim the committee's protection, Mr. Peyton, with due and appropriate profanity, shouted: "You shan't say a word while you are in this room; if you do I will put you to death." The Chairman, Henry A. Wise, added: "Yes, this insolence is insufferable." As both of these gentlemen were armed with deadly weapons, the witness could hardly be blamed for not wanting to testify again.

Of Adams' own inquisitorial abilities, a colleague admiringly observed: "He has . . . an instinct for the jugular and the carotid artery, as unerring as that of any carnivorous animal."

2

The investigatory power has been developed further within the American than within any other political system. And within the American system it is uniquely the prerogative of Congress.[6] The

5. Fletcher Pratt, *Stanton* (New York: W. W. Norton, 1953), p. 154

British government also disposes of a formidable power of inquiry, exercised through parliamentary committees, Royal Commissions and "special tribunals." In the past it was a rod often used to chasten the King and his agents; but within the structure of modern "responsible" (*i.e.,* Cabinet) government, it does not have much effect on the general power equilibrium. In non-Anglo-Saxon nations, the development of an independent investigatory power—where it exists—in all cases falls far short of the American level.

The investigatory, like the treaty power, is "an extraordinary power, liable to abuse." Although formally it is interpreted as an expression of the legislative function, in actuality it is quasi-judicial, and in some cases also of administrative—that is, executive—import. Investigating bodies cannot convict and punish a defendant for crimes of substance, but they can and often have created situations that lead to subsequent conviction and punishment. Even without later court action, investigations have been the cause of social, economic and political sanctions against witnesses. Moreover, by disclosures, threats and other pressures, investigations can indirectly intervene, sometimes rather intimately, in the administrative process.

In order to rate the investigatory power, it is important to understand the precise conditions under which that power achieves its full flexibility and amplitude. The essential conditions are three. First, the investigator (individual, committee or other corporate body) must have the power of compulsion, the power to compel the presence and testimony of persons, and the production of documents. This of course implies the power to punish a refusal to appear and to testify, or to produce documents on order. Second, the investigator must himself have personal immunity for his conduct of the investigation. He must not be subject to any legal, police or any other official reprisal for anything that, as investigator, he may do. And finally, he, or the body of which he is a member or agent, must have autonomy

6. In the central government, that is. The investigatory power is also, of course, exercised by the legislatures of the states.

with respect to the investigation: that is, must not be restricted in the exercise of the investigatory power by any other person or institution.

Congress has traditionally claimed that all three of these conditions—the power of compulsion, immunity, autonomy—hold for its investigatory power; and Congress has never formally acknowledged any limitation on any of the three. They hold, on the traditional view, for investigations into the acts of any and all persons within the jurisdiction of the United States, except possibly the President and the Justices of the Supreme Court. Even this minimum restriction has never been officially admitted, and does not in any case apply to an investigation that might be motivated by the possibility of impeachment. Nor has Congress ever acknowledged any limitation (except as may be self-imposed) on the subject-matter that may be inquired into. It has always been recognized that the strict courtroom rules of evidence and procedure do not hold for the non-punitive and necessarily looser type of inquiry undertaken by an investigating committee. In early years, in fact, some members of Congress maintained that the first ten (Bill of Rights) amendments do not apply to congressional investigations. It was more than a century before anyone suggested that a Fifth Amendment "privilege against self-incrimination" was relevant to a congressional investigation.

In 1860, during the Senate debate over the Harper's Ferry inquiry, Senator William P. Fessenden of Maine—though a Northerner and altogether out of sympathy with that inquiry's objective—asserted in unqualified terms the traditional claim of Congress to investigatory autonomy:

> Congress have appointed committee after committees time after time, to make inquiries on subjects of legislation. Had we not the power to do it? Nobody questioned our authority to do it. We have given them authority to send for persons and papers. . . . Have we not that authority, if necessary to legislation? Who is to be the judge as to our duties necessary to legislation? [The people] have made us their Legislature. . . . The

people [and only the people] have power over us.[7]

It should be remarked that this extreme interpretation of the investigatory power is rigorously logical. The first section of the first article of the Constitution vests *all* legislative powers in Congress. If the investigatory power is—as it is granted to be—a legislative power, then, in pure logic, it is for Congress and Congress alone to decide how the investigatory power is to be used. Of course, like any other power, this will be subject to the provisions (including the restrictions) of the Constitution; but—again by pure logic—it will also be for Congress to give its own interpretation to these provisions and restrictions. To submit the investigatory power to restrictions and interpretations issuing from the courts or from the executive means to deny the exclusively legislative character of this power, which is granted in the premise.

Such a rigorous, univocal application of any political premise is, however, contrary to the genius of the American tradition. In practice, rules and limits governing the exercise of the investigatory power have been gradually formed over the years. Most of these have been imposed by the two Houses of Congress on themselves. Congress has accepted others from the courts or (for inquiries concerning the executive) from the practice of the executive. In neither case, however, has Congress formally granted the right of the other branches to intervene in what it continues to assert as its own exclusive prerogative.

3

The specific power to compel testimony, by the threat of appropriate sanctions, is of the essence of a true investigatory power. Prior to 1857 and occasionally thereafter, Congress itself punished witnesses

7. *Congressional Globe,* 36th Congress, 1st session, Part 2, p. 1102.

for contempt, without turning them over to the lengthy processes of court trial and appeal. A resolution would be passed: "That the Speaker do issue his warrant directed to the Sergeant-at-Arms attending the House, commanding him to take into custody, wherever to be found, the body of So-and-So, and the same in his custody to keep, subject to the further order and direction of the House." The contumacious witness would then be brought to the bar of the House (or Senate). If he refused to purge himself of his contempt (by answering the questions that had been put to him, if that was the issue), he would be "incarcerated" in "the common jail" of the District of Columbia.

This procedure was challenged in 1819 by one John Anderson, who sued Thomas Dunn, the then Sergeant-at-Arms of the House, for assault and battery, and false imprisonment, in having brought him under duress to the bar of the House to be "there reprimanded by the Speaker for the outrage he [had] committed" in trying to bribe a member. The Supreme Court, in Anderson *v.* Dunn (1821), rejected Anderson's charges and upheld the investigatory power of Congress, though the Court maintained, plausibly, that the derivative power to incarcerate a contumacious witness lasted only until the adjournment *sine die* of the session of Congress that had suffered the contempt.

In 1857 Congress enacted a law under which witnesses in contempt could be prosecuted in the courts. Thereafter, such prosecution rather than direct congressional action became the usual procedure, and has never been challenged in principle.

In Kilbourn *v.* Thompson (1881), a case that grew out of the Jay Cooke bankruptcy, the Supreme Court asserted a limit to the right of Congress to inquire into private affairs unless these were charged with public interest. But in this decision no answer is given to the problem of who is to decide whether public interest is at stake. *In re* Chapman (1897), confirming the contempt conviction of a Senate witness, declared that a legislative intent must be presumed in a congressional investigation: "We cannot assume on this record that the action of the Senate was without a legitimate object, and so encroach upon the province of that body. . . . It was certainly not necessary that the resolutions should declare in advance what the Senate meditated doing when the investigation was concluded." As the Court further observed in United States *v.* Bryan (1947): "The exact scope of an investigation cannot always be charted and bounded in advance with the precision of a survey."

In McGrain *v.* Daugherty (1927), an aftermath of the Teapot Dome investigation, the Court summed up the traditional doctrine of the investigatory power in a sweeping affirmation of Congress' extraordinary prerogatives:

We are of opinion that the power of inquiry—with process to enforce it—is an essential and appropriate auxiliary to the legislative function. It was so regarded and employed in American legislatures before the Constitution was framed and ratified. Both Houses of Congress took this view of it early in their history—the House of Representatives with the approving votes of Mr. Madison and other Members whose service in the Convention which framed the Constitution gives special significance to their action—and both Houses have employed the power accordingly up to the present time. . . .

A legislative body cannot legislate wisely or effectively in the absence of information respecting the conditions which the legislation is intended to affect or change; and where the legislative body does not itself possess the requisite information—which not infrequently is true—recourse must be made to others who do possess it. Experience has taught that mere requests for such information often are unavailing, and also that information which is volunteered is not always accurate or complete; so some means of compulsion are essential to obtain what is needed. All this was true before and when the Constitution was framed and adopted. In that period the power of inquiry—with enforcing process—was regarded and employed as a necessary and appropriate attribute of the power to legislate—indeed, was treated as inhering in it.

Anderson *v.* Dunn, the first of these judicial reflections on the investigatory power of the legislature had found, in effect, that the protection of the rights and liberty of citizens against the abuse of that power rested, basically, not on the courts or on "the balance of powers," but on the representative and responsible nature of the legislative body: "Where all power is derived from the people, and public functionaries, at short intervals, deposit it at the feet of the people, to be resumed again only at their will, individual fears may be alarmed by the monsters of imagination, but individual liberty can be in little danger."

This same conception, which implicitly singles the investigatory power out as unique among the powers of the American government, was repeated as late as 1948 by the majority of the District of Columbia Court of Appeals: "The remedy for unseemly conduct, if any, by Committees of Congress is for Congress, or for the people. . . . The courts have no authority to speak or act upon the conduct of the legislative branch of its own business, so long as the bounds of power and pertinacy are not exceeded."[8] From a formal standpoint the investigatory power is an expression or adjunct of the legislative function. In order to determine whether a new law is needed or whether an existing law needs changing, Congress requires relevant information. But since Congress is the body charged with the making and unmaking of laws, Congress cannot—if it is to fulfill its constitutional duty—rely on any other person or body for such information. Congress must get its own information, in its own way and on its own responsibility, from whatever source seems to it appropriate; and it must have the power and resources to do so.

But a merely formal analysis of the investigatory power does not

8. Barsky *v.* U.S.

reveal its complexity, subtlety and scope. In practice only the thinnest verbal stretching can bring all the modes and aims of the investigatory power under a single semantic roof.

As the courts judge them, all legitimate congressional investigations—apart from those concerned with Congress' own members or with possible impeachment—have as their purposes: (a) to gather information bearing on the enactment, amendment or repeal of laws; (b) to check the consequences on the public weal of laws previously enacted; (c) to check the performance of the executive and the bureaucracy in administering the laws; (d) to check how public moneys lawfully appropriated are actually being spent.

This set of related purposes fits comfortably under the constitutional formalities, and it is a fact that as a direct or indirect result of its investigations Congress has enacted, amended or repealed many laws on many subjects. This has been true throughout the nation's history: from the postal contract investigations of the early 1800's that brought reorganizations of the Post Office, through the 1860 Covode investigation of graft in printing contracts that led to the establishment of the Government Printing Office, to the New Deal probes of the 1930's that prepared for new banking acts, the Holding Company Act, the Securities and Exchange Commission, the National Labor Relations Board, and so on.

Besides their relation to specific legislative problems, investigations have played a critical and pervasive role in sustaining the delicate equilibrium that marks the traditional American system of government. On the stage of a major investigation, with the Court watching from the wing and the public in the stalls, the actors of the government drama—Congress, the executive, the bureaucracy, the lobbyists, and individual citizens who are selected by accident or design to embody a force or cause—issue their challenges and defiances, cross swords, join hands also, make and break pacts with and against each other, expose wrongdoing and boast of achievement.

In particular, the investigations have been the setting for the ambivalent encounter of legislature and executive, whose eternal conflict and cooperation, wedding and divorce, are an intended and inescapable element of the American political system. Although most congressional inquiries dealing with problems of administration have been critical of the executive, others have been friendly and some, subservient. Agents of the executive have themselves requested investigation of their own departments, following an example set by Oliver Wolcott when he withdrew in 1800 as Secretary of the Treasury. The need for this or that investigation has sometimes been suggested by the executive. In Woodrow Wilson's first three years and (still more notably) Franklin Roosevelt's first six, congressional investigations became almost an operating arm of the executive in advancing the policies of the White House. This, however, indicated not so much an accord between Congress and President as a subordination of Congress to President. Still, it is a distortion to see American political history for any lengthy period as simply a conflict between legislature and executive. Without frequent conflict liberty would have been lost; but without still more frequent cooperation there would have been no government at all. If investigations have been more naturally an occasion for conflict, they have also provided a device for communication and mutual aid.

Supporting the legislative function and helping to sustain the governmental equilibrium do not exhaust the range of the investigatory power. It has been well understood from early days that the investigatory process can be used to foster political ambitions. The 1819 investigation of the Arbuthnot and Ambrister court martial, decided in Andrew Jackson's favor, launched him toward the White House. Daniel Webster used investigations to expand his fame and to try to rouse a call for his own presidential services. The "Covode Inquisition" into the Buchanan administration helped prepare Lincoln's election. Senators Thomas Walsh and Burton Wheeler made their chief public mark as inquisitors of the 1920's. Few had heard of the young Ferdinand Pecora until the New Deal banking investigation, with its roll call of the mighty, and the circus dwarf on the elder J. P. Morgan's lap. It does not seem likely that Hugo Black would sit today on the Supreme Court if he had not headed so spectacular, and so ruthless an investigation; or that Harry Truman would have been picked to run with Franklin Roosevelt in 1944 if not for his wartime record on the Senate Special Committee Investigating the National Defense Program. It was the televised inquiry into gambling and big city rackets that made Estes Kefauver known outside his native state and Capitol Hill. The frequency with which investigations have become the path toward national fame is a consequence not only of the drama to which such hearings naturally incline, but also of an intuitive public awareness of the importance of the investigatory power to our political system.

Just as investigations are sometimes used to advance the public fortunes of an aspiring inquisitor, so can they serve as a weapon against an opponent or victim. The disclosures of investigating committees can virtually compel the prosecution of exposed witnesses, or their discharge from their jobs. Without any subsequent official action, some witnesses have suffered the adverse social consequences of a battered or ruined reputation. As a traceable result of the Teapot Dome investigations in the 1920's, three Cabinet members were compelled to resign, of whom one went later to jail and one died while awaiting trial; two witnesses committed suicide; four oil millionaires skipped the country, and numerous other individuals were jailed or fined sums up to several million dollars.

This spectacular aftermath was probably a record, but on a more modest scale sanctions against individuals have been common enough. Investigations of lobbying, gambling and racketeering have led to many indictments. In the early 1950's, the committees investigating subversion developed a routine technique through which witnesses with "sensitive" jobs in defense industry who "took the Fifth" at a committee hearing,[9] would then be fired by their employers. A number of government employees—such as the State Department officials, John Carter Vincent and John Paton Davies—

lost their posts (for a while, at least) in consequence of their testimony before congressional inquisitors. The cause-and-effect relation is sometimes astonishingly abrupt: as when in 1957, M. S. Pitzele was discharged from his jobs with both New York state and the McGraw-Hill publishing company immediately after he received unfavorable publicity from his testimony before the Senate committee investigating labor rackets.[10]

When congressional investigations are made part of a process that leads to the imprisonment or fining of individuals, or to the firing or job re-assignment of employees of the government's executive branch, then the investigating committees are performing judicial and executive rather than purely legislative functions. When they injure the reputation or livelihood of individual private citizens, they become part of the apparatus by which public opinion, through its complex arsenal of social pressures, approvals and threats, tries to keep individuals within certain implicit customary and moral boundaries. By critics of the investigatory power the first two extra-legislative side-effects will be regarded as "encroachments" on the constitutional provinces of the courts and the presidency; and the third, as a form of psychological terror. However judged or pre-judged, they are further witness to the high potential of the investigatory function.

Investigations are also a principal means by which Congress exercises "the informing function," which, though not mentioned in the Constitution and never recognized formally by the Supreme Court, is so integral an attribute of the legislature of a representative government that Woodrow Wilson concluded it "should be pre-

9. That is, who refused to testify on the ground—accepted under the prevailing interpretation of the Fifth Amendment—that a truthful answer might tend to "incriminate or degrade" them.

10. In this as in many similar cases, the investigation was directed toward a factional political purpose. The committee was under Democratic control, and Mr. Pitzele was a protegé and long-time associate of Thomas E. Dewey in the New York Republican machine.

ferred even to its legislative function."[11] Even in ordinary debates, of course, Congress is incidentally carrying out an informing function which can be more deliberately exercised through an investigation focused on a subject-matter of public importance. Through public investigation Congress informs the citizens about the nation's problems at the same time that it is informing itself.

The subject-matter of investigations falls into two broad groups, often though not always linked in particular inquiries: first, the activities of private citizens or groups of citizens engaged in economic, political or social pursuits having or felt to have a public interest; second, the activities of administrative (and occasionally the judicial) officials and employees of the government itself.

With respect to the first type (into private activities), congressional investigations have often been one of the most important sources of public information concerning the great problems that have arisen in one field after another during the course of the nation's development: banking and finance, transport, communications, mining, power, education, labor relations, lobbying, subversion, shipping, charity. With respect to the second type (into governmental administration), congressional inquiry is often the only method by which the conduct of the executive and the bureaucracy can be brought into the light. In Woodrow Wilson's words:

There is some scandal and discomfort, but infinite advantage, in having every affair of administration subjected to the test of constant examination on the part of the assembly which represents the nation. The chief use of such inquisition is, not the direction of those affairs in a way with which the country will

11. *Cf. Congressional Government,* p. 303. In stressing "the informing function," Wilson was perhaps following, as he often did, Walter Bagehot, the great analyst of the British Constitution. Bagehot lists five "parliamentary functions": (1) elective (under the American system confined to Senate confirmation of certain appointments); (2) expressive; (3) teaching; (4) informing; (5) legislative.

be satisfied (though that itself is of course all-important), but the enlightenment of the people, which is always its sure consequence. . . .

Unless Congress have and use every means of acquainting itself with the acts and the disposition of the administrative agents of the government, the country must be helpless to learn how it is being served; and unless Congress both scrutinize these things and sift them by every form of discussion, the country must remain in embarrassing, crippling ignorance of the very affairs which it is most important that it should understand and direct. . . . The argument is not only that discussed and interrogated administration is the only pure and efficient administration, but, more than that, that the only really self-governing people is that people which discusses and interrogates its administration.[12]

This last sentence of Wilson's suggests that through its inquiries the legislature is not merely informing itself and the citizens about the nominal subject-matter, but is carrying on an active dialogue with the citizens and also with the bureaucracy. Through the sessions of the committees, their reports and records, as well as by all the varied publicity, criticism and debate that these evoke, the citizens and their government get to know each other, and mutually influence each other. It would be superficial to judge the achievements of congressional investigations by a bare list of information garnered and laws passed. They are a vital and almost continuously active organ of the body politic.

12. *Ibid.*, pp. 299, 303.

XVII

THE ATTACK ON
INVESTIGATIONS

I N THE PAST, congressional investigations have been intermittently and sometimes sharply attacked. The 1923–24 investigations into the oil industry and the Departments of the Navy and
Justice were condemned by Owen J. Roberts, speaking before the
American Bankers Association, as mere "propaganda for national-
ization." The *Wall Street Journal* dismissed them as a "political
smokescreen." The *New York Times* declared that Congress was
"investigation-mad," and was trying to introduce "government by
clamor [and] hole in corner gossip." The *Times* (in February 1924)
upheld Attorney General Daugherty as a sturdy patriot who was defending "decency [and] honor . . . , the honor which ought to prevail among gentlemen, if not among politicians."[1] In the same
month the Communist *Daily Worker* created the label, "smelling
committees."

A few years earlier Walter Lippmann, in his book, *Public Opinion*,[2]
had described investigations as "that legalized atrocity . . . where
Congressmen starved of their legitimate food for thought, go on a
wild and feverish man-hunt, and do not stop at cannibalism." In 1925
the influential legal authority, J. H. Wigmore, characterized the investigators as "on the level of professional searchers of the municipal

---

1. Within six months Daugherty had resigned in disgrace, after the investigators had shown that during his two and a half years in Washington on a $15,000
salary, his personal holdings had shifted from a $19,000 debt to a $100,000
fortune.
2. Published in 1922.

dunghills." The investigators to whom Wigmore was thus referring (Senators Walsh, Wheeler, Borah and LaFollette) were also termed, in the contemporary press, "scandal-mongers," "mud-gunners," "assassins of character." Their inquiries were described as "lynching bees," "poisoned-tongued partisanship, pure malice, and twittering hysteria," and "in plain words, contemptible and disgusting."

A decade later the New Deal inquiries into investment, banking, utilities, and munitions were the targets for denunciations comparable in content though less colorful in rhetoric. Long before, congressional investigating methods had been eloquently criticized even from the floor of Congress itself. In 1860, during the course of the Senate inquiry into John Brown's raid on Harper's Ferry, Senator Charles Sumner defended a contumacious witness, Thaddeus Hyatt, who had been "incarcerated in the filthy jail" for having refused to answer the committee's questions:[3] "To aid a committee of this body merely in a legislative purpose, a citizen, guilty of no crime, charged with no offense, presumed to be innocent, honored and beloved in his neighborhood, may be seized, handcuffed, kidnapped, and dragged away from his home, hurried across State lines, brought here as a criminal, and then thrust into jail."

Senator John P. Hale of New Hampshire, agreeing with his colleague from Massachusetts, declared: "I ask . . . if there ever was a despotism on earth that could define its position more satisfactorily than that? . . . If Louis Napoleon has more than that I think he would be willing to give it up readily."

Sumner's rhetoric, in antiphony, swelled still higher: "For myself, sir, I confess a feeling of gratitude to the witness [Hyatt], who, knowing nothing which he desires to conceal, and chiefly anxious that the liberties of all might not suffer through him, feeble in body and broken in health, hardly able to endure the fatigue of appearing at your

3. Here and below, the quotations of the Harper's Ferry debate are taken from *Congressional Globe*, 36th Congress, 1st session, March 12, 1860, pp. 1100–09; and Part 4, June 15, 1860, pp. 3006–7.

bar, now braves the prison which you menace, and thrusts his arm as a bolt to arrest an unauthorized and arbitrary proceeding."

Generally speaking, as these prominent instances suggest, it has been the gored ox that has bellowed. Whether well-grounded or not, vigorous congressional inquiries usually threaten institutionalized as well as individual interests. The spokesmen and friends of these interests, along with the individuals directly involved, fight back as best they are able. Usually the best defense, in a public polemic, is to drop the question of one's own private concern out of sight, and to counterattack either with *ad hominem* grapeshot or with seemingly general considerations of propriety, morals and political philosophy.

It was natural enough that the *Wall Street Journal,* the American Bankers Association, the *New York Times* (as edited in the 1920's) and the Hearst press (with large Hearst mining interests in the background) should look with initial disfavor on a probing of oil leases by a partisan and already suspect Public Lands Committee. The established banking and investment interests, the utility holding companies, and the great industrial corporations that had armed the nation for the first world war could not, even though cowed by the long depression, welcome the inquiries of the 1930's into their carefully unpublic ways. John Brown was a martyred hero of the abolitionists, who had provoked and financed his raid on Harper's Ferry. The abolitionist Senators from New England could hardly have been expected to further an investigation, headed by a Senator from Virginia, which was likely to confirm the formal case against Brown and to uncover the links in the conspiracy. It was no doubt natural also that the committee chairman from Virginia, James M. Mason, and Senator Jefferson Davis from Mississippi made the replies that Senators Sumner and Hale might have formulated if the interests at stake had been reversed.

Jefferson Davis. How shallow the plea is, when a witness is brought here for great purposes, that he should say his conscience was too tender to tell the truth. What criminal, or what man who had been in a conspiracy, criminal in all its ends and aims, would not shelter himself, when commanded before a Committee to testify, if his tender conscience at the last hour, when steeped in crime and treason, might plead against the right of a Committee to know from him the truth? . . .

James Mason. The matter inquired into here . . . was matter affecting the very existence of this government—treasonable purposes; and if there is any citizen in the land who can give information on the subject, he is bound by every obligation of honor, of duty, of loyalty to his country, voluntarily to come; not to seek to avoid this duty by evasion, or subterfuge, or pretense that his conscience will not allow him to give his testimony.

Hugo L. Black, writing in 1936 when he was an investigator and not a Supreme Court Justice, summed up the natural response: "The instant that a resolution [authorizing an investigation] is offered, or even rumored, the call to arms is sounded by the interest to be investigated."[4]

2

I do not mean to suggest that all of these past criticisms of inquiries have been subjectively biased or hypocritical. It may be presumed that Dean Wigmore was concerned primarily with the investigative procedures that are too coarse and unrestrained for so judicially oriented a mind as his was. Mr. Lippmann has been long and persistently critical of investigations differing widely in

4. Hugo L. Black, "Inside a Senate Investigation" (*Harper's,* February, 1936).

subject-matter and political direction. For that matter, most of the critics have doubtless been sincere enough when they voiced their criticisms.

At the same time we may note that until recent years, most of the attacks on the investigations, like the defending replies, seem to be part of the general political struggle in the nation over issues and problems that have successively arisen. The impetus of the attacks has been specific: against this particular inquiry or related set of inquiries. The legislative inquiry as an accredited institution of the American political system has not been in dispute. The critics did not question Congress' autonomous right to investigate, with adequate compulsory sanctions, in its own way and on its own sovereign authority. In the Senate debate over the Harper's Ferry inquiry, the critics made their appeal for gentler treatment of Hyatt to the Senate itself. They did not suggest that there was an relevant recourse to the courts or to the executive. Senator Hale, recognizing that he and Sumner would lose the vote in the Chamber and not questioning its power to act as it saw fit, directed his words to what was logically the only supreme tribunal of a sovereign legislature: "You may imprison him; you may lock him up; you may make his bars and his bolts fast, and turn your key upon him; but I tell you that the great *habeas corpus* of freemen, the ballot, will reverse your judgment, and pronounce sentence of condemnation, not on him, but on you."

During the past decade the attack on the investigations has assumed a very different character. Although it has arisen primarily out of inquiries dealing with Communism and other forms of subversion, it is no longer specific or limited. In fact, it is no longer an attack on investigations, but on the investigatory power, and it has come in waves from all directions: from journalists, cartoonists, publicists and academicians; from the courts; from the executive; and even from within Congress itself.

As pictured by the most influential liberal cartoonists, led by Herblock and Fitzpatrick, the typical congressional investigator is either a gangster, a Star Chamber hanging-judge, or a rubber-truncheoned fascist. Thousands of editorials, articles, monographs, lectures and sermons have condemned the investigating committees, their methods, their results and their most prominent members. In 1955 two general books—Alan Barth's *Government by Investigation* and Telford Taylor's *Grand Inquest*—broadened the adverse critique that had been undertaken by such preliminary studies as Robert K. Carr's *The House Committee on Un-American Activities*. A number of organizations—among them Americans for Democratic Action, the American Civil Liberties Union and the Committee for an Effective Congress—have in these recent years made the defects of investigations and investigators a principal element of their public agitation. For several years prior to his death in 1957, the figure of Senator Joseph R. McCarthy of Wisconsin became the symbolic target for this massive campaign against the investigatory power—a campaign which began, however, before McCarthy's entry on the national stage, as it continues after his exit.

3

The opponents and critics of congressional investigations do not explicitly call for the abolition of the investigatory power; that is, they do not state that Congress should be altogether deprived of the right and power to make investigations. They argue, rather, that the investigations should be curbed, limited and controlled in such ways as to prevent violations of rights, demagogic exploitation, encroachments on the executive or judiciary, and other excesses. The restrictive proposals go along such lines as the following:

(A.) *Some topics should be outside the purview of investigations.* These prohibited subjects would include all private affairs, rather broadly defined.[5] It has also been urged that all the varied matters included under "espionage" and "subversion" should be put under the exclusive jurisdiction of the Federal Bureau of Investigation and other security agencies: that is, should be shifted wholly out of the legislative into the executive branch.

(B.) *Investigating committee proceedings should be governed by detailed rules for the protection of the rights and privileges of witnesses, similar to the rules governing judicial actions.* Witnesses should have right to counsel, to confront accusers, to cross-examine, to call rebuttal witnesses and submit rebuttal evidence, to obtain full transcripts, and so on.[6]

It should perhaps be added that many of the rules proposed by the critics—such as the requirement of a committee quorum for all hearings and for all decisions in preparation of hearings—are virtually impossible under the real conditions of congressional activity. Others, drawn from courtroom practice, are inappropriate to an investigation, which by the nature of the case, is partly a "fishing expedition" in which the issues are not known fully in advance—unlike a court action, where the issue is defined in the indictment. And it is seldom remarked that the loose investigatory procedures, though they undoubtedly sometimes violate what would generally be regarded as individual rights and are often disturbing to individual pleasure and convenience, at the same time frequently offer witnesses unusual liberties that they do not possess in the courtroom: to make long statements; to argue with interlocutors; to bring in hearsay, subjective

5. Thus extending a principle recognized by the Supreme Court in the Kilbourn case.
6. Actually, many such procedural rules have in fact been adopted by the committees, either through customary practice or on formal action. The House Committee on Un-American Activities—to cite one of the most controversial instances—operates in accordance with a printed list of fourteen rules in addition to the governing rules of the House itself.

motivation, mitigating circumstances; to delay and repeat; to become the accuser and to counterattack.

(C.) *The self-incrimination clause of the Fifth Amendment should have total application to inquiry proceedings.* That is, a witness, without any motivating explanation on his part or any objective indication that the refusal is well-grounded, should have the right to refuse to answer any question whatever on the ground that by answering it he risks possible incrimination. This blanket restraint on the investigatory function seems to be accepted at present by the courts and by Congress. It is further and persistently being proposed that the grounds for a refusal to testify should also include the First Amendment guarantees of freedom of belief and speech. Historically there is no foundation for applying these amendments to congressional inquiries. "These guarantees," observe Messrs. Kelly and Harbison, "were historically associated almost entirely with the business of the courts. And the substantive guarantees of the Bill of Rights—freedom of speech, press, and the like—appeared to apply to the content of congressional legislation, not to the mode of enacting it."[7]

(D.) *All phases of congressional investigations should be subject to review and adjudication by the courts.* For a hundred and fifty years the Supreme Court shied as far away as it could from intervention in the legislature's investigatory power, finally summing up its traditional recognition of legislative autonomy therein by its sweeping decision in McGrain v. Daugherty (1927). In the late 1940's, by refusing to review three lower court decisions that reasserted congressional autonomy in investigations,[8] the Court held fast to McGrain v. Daugh-

---

7. Alfred H. Harbison and Winfred A. Kelly, *op. cit.,* p. 908.
8. United States v. Bryan (1947), United States v. Josephson (1948), Barsky v. United States (1948). In the latter two decisions there had been a sharp division in the Court of Appeals.

erty against the rising liberal clamor. Then, in a series of decisions that began with Christoffel *v.* United States (1950) and reached a high point in Watkins *v.* United States (1957), the Supreme Court asserted what would be by implication its general right to define the rules, limits, methods, scope and sanctions of the investigatory power. On the meaning of the Watkins case, which reversed the decision of both the District Court and the Court of Appeals, dissenting Justice Tom C. Clark wrote that the Supreme Court was appointing itself "Grand Inquisitor and supervisor of congressional investigations."

(E.) *Congressional investigators who get out of bounds should be disciplined.* This proposal, a frequent exhortation of the critics of Congress, is difficult to apply, because of the explicit words of Article I, Section 6 of the Constitution: "[Senators and Representatives] shall in all Cases, except Treason, Felony and Breach of the Peace, be privileged from Arrest during their Attendance at the Session of their respective Houses, and in going to and returning from the same; and for any Speech or Debate in either House, they shall not be questioned in any other Place." Since these words seem to put members of Congress, so far as their official acts go, out of reach of the courts, traditional doctrine has left their due punishment to the ballot. As a disciplinary supplement, the new critics urge—though so far unsuccessfully—that too savage investigators might be tamed by being deprived of committee chairmanships, or even of membership on committees that conduct investigations.

The temporary focusing of the problem in Senator Joseph McCarthy provoked a novel, and momentous sanction. In 1954, through combined pressure from a liberal-led public opinion and the executive branch, Congress was induced to turn its investigatory power against itself; and then, by the Senate vote of an unprecedented censure against one of its own members, to make common cause with its critics.

In the winter of 1953–54 the Senate's Permanent Subcommittee on Investigations, under Senator McCarthy's chairmanship, was conducting a free-wheeling inquiry into various of the Army's affairs. This exploded into a volcanic scandal after a bitter clash between McCarthy and Major General Ralph Zwicker, who had been called as a witness in the case of a drafted dentist-officer, Irving Peress, who had been routinely promoted in rank after having refused, on the ground of the Fifth Amendment privilege, to declare whether he had been a communist.

By a sudden coup,[9] the subcommittee's inquiry into the Army was transformed into an investigation of the countercharges that the Army brought against McCarthy—that is, against a member of the Senate, and by plain extension, against the Senate itself and its investigatory power. Under Senator Karl Mundt, who replaced McCarthy as chairman, televised hearings continued for months, solidifying emotions but not clarifying many facts. These hearings led to the appointment of a special committee under Senator Arthur Watkins to consider the complaints against McCarthy. The report of this special committee, though it was accepted only in part, prepared the way for the Senate's 67–22 vote of condemnation on December 2, 1954.

As the bitterness and crudities on both sides of the McCarthy controversy recede into the tranquillizing past, it takes its historical place, from a constitutional point of view, not as a great battle either of the war against communism (as Senator McCarthy's admirers saw it) or in the struggle for human rights (as it appeared in his enemy's eyes), but rather as a symptomatic episode in the erosion of congressional power. This was plainly recognized by relentless critics of Congress, such as General Telford Taylor, who, writing in early 1955, summed

---

9. The full history of this coup has never been publicly disclosed. According to most accounts, it was the result of an informal bipartisan agreement among part of the White House staff, some Pentagon officials, and several Senators of both parties, prominently including Senators Stuart Symington (Dem.) and Charles E. Potter (Rep.).

up his own analysis in the rhetoric of executive supremacy: "The essence of the constitutional crisis of 1954 . . . is *the effort of some legislators, notably Senator McCarthy, to destroy the President's effective control of the executive branch and bring it under their own domination.*"[10] This corresponds exactly, when rhetorical translation is made, to Senator McCarthy's declaration in the midst of the Zwicker-Peress explosion that the basic question was "whether the Army as agent of the executive branch is supreme over the Congress . . . and the American people, and can enjoy special dictatorial immunity in covering up its own wrongdoings."

At the last moment, however, the Senate, diverting the battle into its purely personal channel, avoided formal surrender of any part of the battered investigatory power, and thus suspended the constitutional issue. "It is especially noteworthy," General Taylor comments sorrowfully, "that Senator McCarthy was not censured for his misuse of the Senate's investigatorial prerogatives, for his attack against the executive branch, or for his treatment of anyone other than his fellow-senators."[11]

We have seen that a true investigatory power cannot exist unless the investigator (individual or institution) is equipped with immunity, autonomy, and the power of compulsion. The public critique and the Supreme Court decisions since 1950, though not openly directed against the investigatory power itself, have attacked and much weakened these three conditions of its effective operation.

The power of compulsion is meaningless unless there is assured, speedy punishment for contumacious witnesses. Such punishment, under the now prevailing court rulings and congressional practice, is neither sure nor speedy. It can be postponed indefinitely when it is

10. Telford Taylor, *Grand Inquest* (New York: Simon & Schuster, 1955), p. 112. The italics are in the original.
11. *Ibid.*, p. 134.

not avoided altogether, by legal technicalities, the plea of civil rights, or Congress' own unwillingness to pursue the matter vigorously. Thus, with very little personal hazard, witnesses may defeat the ends of a current inquiry: there will be a new Congress with new interests, before the question of punishment is decided one way or the other.

The investigator's immunity and autonomy do not mean that he can properly do anything that he wishes, but that the major decisions about what he can properly do will be his. More specifically applied to congressional investigation: that Congress shall itself decide when an investigation has a legislative purpose, what sort of evidence is relevant to that purpose and from whom, how evidence and information may be most fruitfully gathered. Quite possibly this is too great a license to be granted without restriction to any single institution. That is not here at issue, but merely the historical observation that in recent years the investigatory power of Congress, at the same time that it has emerged as the first among the remaining congressional powers, has been shorn and blunted by a many-sided and continuing attack.

4

The public controversy over the investigatory power has often failed to distinguish between two types of inquiry that are profoundly different in their political meaning: investigations into the activities of private citizens, associations and institutions, on the one hand; and on the other, investigations of the administration of the government—that is, of the executive branch and the bureaucracy. A particular inquiry may bridge the two types (as in a study of the relation between a government regulatory agency and the industry it is supposed to regulate), but the functional distinction remains clear.

Most of the formal arguments that are advanced against investigations concern, primarily or exclusively, the first type. It is alleged that the civil rights or personal life of private citizens who appear as witnesses are violated, and that the protection of these private rights is a duty that takes precedence over the possible public gains from investigating this or that subject-matter. That is to say, the argument is cast in the form of: individual liberty *vs.* despotism.

For Americans, an argument in this form has roots in both tradition and rhetoric. It is persuasive to many citizens even apart from their opinion on the particular content of the investigations which provoke the controversy. And it is a fact that an unchecked investigatory power always threatens and sometimes subverts what Americans wish to regard as inviolable individual rights.

But inquiries into the doings of the executive and the bureaucracy are of a different order, in which private and individual rights are only coincidentally at stake. By making an artificial amalgam between the two types of investigation, we smear the second with the doubtful or negative feelings attached to the first. Objectively, the principal similarity between the two is the mere fact that both express the investigatory power of the legislature.

Traditionally it has never been questioned, either in doctrine or practice, that the legislature possesses the power, as it was put in early years, "to inquire into the honesty and efficiency of the executive branch." Under the American system it is this that is the heart of the investigatory power. It is conceivable that, without a major constitutional transformation, Congress could cede all investigations of the affairs of private citizens to the executive and judiciary. But if it lost the power to investigate the executive, Congress would retain only the name of legislature.

The late Senator George Norris, once the dean of liberals, accurately remarked during the controversies of 1924: "Whenever you take away from the legislative body of any country in the world the power of investigation, the power to look into the executive department of the government, you have taken a full step that will eventually lead into absolute monarchy[12] and destroy any government such as ours."

Woodrow Wilson's distaste for the practices of Congress did not lead him to obscure the basic relations:

> Quite as important as legislation is vigilant oversight of administration. . . . An effective representative body [ought] to serve as [the nation's] eyes in superintending all matters of government. . . . There is some scandal and discomfort, but infinite advantage, in having every affair of administration subjected to the test of constant examination on the part of the assembly which represents the nation. . . . Congress is the only body which has the proper motive for inquiry. . . . It is the proper duty of a representative body to look diligently into every affair of government and to talk much about what it sees. It is meant to be the eyes and the voice and to embody the wisdom and will of its constituents. Unless Congress have and use every means of acquainting itself with the acts and the dispositions of the administrative agents of the government, the country must be helpless to learn how it is being served. . . . The only really self-governing people is that people which discusses and interrogates its administration.[13]

Professor McGeary has put the situation still more bluntly: "An administrator's knowledge that at some future time he and his activities might be subjects of congressional investigation has probably

---

12. In the traditional American vocabulary, "absolute monarchy" was the term often used to refer to "despotism."

13. Woodrow Wilson, *Congressional Government*, pp. 277–303 *passim*.

been the principal external deterrent to wrong-doing in the executive branch."[14]

Scholars who have taken refuge in the United States from totalitarian regimes have been still more deeply impressed with the crucial role of legislative investigations into the operations of the executive. Dr. Henry W. Ehrmann, a refugee from Nazism, concludes that a lack of this power was a prime factor both in the failure of German pre-Nazi parliamentarism and in the bureaucratic sclerosis of the French political system.[15] He recalls the judgment of Germany's great sociologist, Max Weber: "In his criticism of the political situation in Imperial Germany, [Weber] attributed greater responsibility for the unsatisfactory results of constitutional life to the lack of parliamentary investigation than to any other single factor. The German parliament was condemned to dilettantism as well as ignorance."

Under Weber's influence, a right of parliamentary inquiry was introduced into the Weimar Constitution, but, as in the case of the inquiry function in France, there was no real power of compulsion to back it up. In both countries it could therefore have only minor political significance. "The unsatisfactory results in both France and Germany can easily be explained by the insufficient powers obtained by the parliamentary committees."

It is against this background that we may evaluate the progressive undermining of the investigatory power during the past decade by the executive as well as by liberal publicists and the courts. The executive under Presidents Franklin Roosevelt, Truman, Eisenhower, Kennedy and Johnson has challenged the investigatory power in the

14. N. Nelson McGeary, "Historical Development," a contribution to the symposium on congressional investigations in *University of Chicago Law Review,* Vol. 18, No. 3, Spring 1951; p. 430.
15. Henry W. Ehrmann, "The Duty of Disclosure in Parliamentary Investigation: A Comparative Study" (*Univ. of Chicago Law Review,* Vol. 2, No. 2, Feb. 1944), pp. 117–53.

most direct of ways: with respect to an ever expanding mass of data, it has simply refused to supply information to the investigating committees.

These refusals have been formally motivated by: the doctrine of "the separation of powers"; the need for secrecy; various laws, and in particular a "housekeeping act" of 1789 originally passed to authorize executive departments to set up files and records; an alleged traditional practice within the American system. These considerations were systomatically stated in a memorandum submitted in May, 1954 by Attorney General Herbert Brownell to President Eisenhower, and countered by a Staff Study of the House Committee on Government Operations, dated May 3, 1956.

The executive's argument from tradition is undoubtedly specious. It is true that a number of Presidents, beginning with the first, have denied the universal right of Congress to call for testimony and documents from the executive branch. Among them have been Presidents otherwise so various as Andrew Jackson, John Tyler, Abraham Lincoln, Grover Cleveland and Calvin Coolidge. Washington would seem to have declared—in theory—a complete executive immunity to the investigatory power: "The executive ought to communicate such papers as the public good would permit and ought to refuse those, the disclosure of which would injure the public." Jackson, when Congress wished to look more closely into the working of his Spoils System, replied indignantly: "For myself, I shall repel all such attempts as an invasion of the principles of justice, as well as of the Constitution; and I shall esteem it my sacred duty to the people of the United States to resist them as I would the establishment of a Spanish inquisition." Even Calvin Coolidge denounced with unwonted sharpness the investigatory feelers directed by the Couzens committee at Secretary Andrew Mellon's administration of the Treasury Department.

But if we look more closely at the offered precedents in the pre-Franklin Roosevelt past, we will learn that they have little bearing on the executive practice that has become established since 1933. In the first place, the earlier incidents were exceedingly rare. Attorney General Brownell's memorandum[16] states at the outset that "American history abounds in countless illustrations of the refusal, on occasion, by the President and heads of departments to furnish papers to Congress, or its committees." In fact, however, he cites only twenty-six instances in all, of which fifteen are from the Franklin Roosevelt and Truman administrations.

Moreover, nearly all the pre-1933 instances have certain common characteristics. They almost invariably concern either treaty negotiations or appointments. The papers or information that the executive refuses[17] are the record of confidential, often informal discussions and reports—in which, as a rule, the President has himself been personally involved—that have entered into preliminary stages of treaty negotiations, appointments, or diplomatic missions. Constitutional niceties aside, the Presidents were taking a reasonable and common sense position when they argued that administration of the public business, or of any business, would be impossible if the chief administrator could not have confidential preparatory discussions with his immediate subordinates and agents.

The same message from Washington, quoted above, that claimed an executive privilege to withhold certain material, explicitly recognized that Congress "might call for papers generally." Grover Cleveland had more of a contest on this score than any other pre-1933 President, but in the incident concerning appointments that Mr. Brownell cites from his administration, Cleveland declared in his formal communication to the Senate: "The Senate is invited to the fullest scrutiny of the persons submitted to them for public office. . . . I shall furnish, at the request of the confirm-

16. The memorandum is reprinted in *The Federal Bar Journal,* Vol. XIV, No. 1, Jan.–Mar. 1954, pp. 73–86.
17. Or merely claims the right to refuse. In several cases, including one of the two that Mr. Brownell cites from Washington's administration, the President, having made the claim, supplied the data nevertheless.

ing body, all the information I possess touching the fitness of the nominees placed before them for their action." He objected only to the transmittal of "letters and papers of a private and unofficial nature."[18]

This earlier occasional practice—which like so much in the older American tradition commends itself to ordinary common sense—has now been blown up into a polished routine. By an administrative fiction, the "confidential" relation between President and subordinates—which in the past meant a literal personal relation between man and man—has been extended to the entire bureaucracy, so that the executive now claims a right to order any official or employee of the bureaucracy to refuse to testify to an investigating committee, or to withhold almost any sort of document or record pertaining to any department or agency.

In explaining Congress' 1958 attempt to restore the traditional interpretation of the 1789 housekeeping act as a mere authorization to preserve public records, Representative John E. Moss of California commented:

The "housekeeping act" has been twisted and tortured by federal officials seeking to withhold information from the public and from the Congress. . . .

A few of the recent examples of misuse of the act include the withholding by the Treasury Department of information about imports and exports; the attempt by the Agriculture Department to impose censorship as the price for cooperation in the making of newsreel and television films about agricultural subjects; the withholding of information by the Farmers' Home Administration and the Rural Electrification Administration on loans of public money.

18. Richardson, *Messages & Papers of the Presidents,* Vol. 8, pp. 377, 381–2.

Mr. Moss added a revealing datum: "Each of the ten Cabinet departments opposed this amendment to restore the traditional interpretation."[19]

With the shibboleths of secrecy, security and "classification," the executive has still further darkened the screen constructed out of the claims of constitutional privilege and separation of powers. Whenever the executive (or the bureaucracy) wishes to hide information from congressional scrutiny, it is only necessary to declare it "classified." Sometimes, granted the conditions of our age, this procedure is justified—as, for example, in the case of advanced military experiments, or the Federal Bureau of Investigation's "raw" (*i.e.*, unevaluated) security files on individuals[20]—but the secrecy labels have been extended over a considerable portion of the nation's ordinary business, which thus becomes removed from congressional (and thereby also from public) scrutiny.

The results are sometimes curious, from a traditional point of view. The executive, for example, will call on Congress to vote appropriations for foreign aid, but will decline to furnish the information about what has been, is being and is intended to be done with the foreign aid. On the basis of a special commission study, like the 1957 "Gaither report," the executive will demand certain armament funds; but will not show Congress the report which supplies the motivation. The executive will insist on Senate confirmation of a military treaty, like those establishing the North Atlantic or the Southeast Asia treaty organizations, without disclosing the commit-

---

19. *New York Times*, Aug. 17, 1958.
20. Common sense would agree that it would be improper to turn over such files to a large and factionally minded congressional committee. But even in this case there are solutions other than total executive immunity: *e.g.*, the British practice of showing the confidential material to a small parliamentary committee of authoritative and trusted members. Something of this sort was done in Washington during the 1953 conflict over the appointment of Charles Bohlen as Ambassador to Moscow.

ments that the treaty entails. Thus, inevitably, the weakening of the congressional investigatory power leads to a correlated further weakening of the congressional share in the power of the purse, the war power and the treaty power.

It would be wrong to exaggerate the stage that the contest has reached. The investigatory power is bruised and shaken, but it is still vigorous. In fact, it is just because the investigatory power is so vigorous, because it retains more vitality than any other of the congressional powers, that it is so sharply under attack. It becomes easier to see why Dr. Ehrmann, reflecting on the experiences of many nations, concluded the study to which we have made reference with the summary judgment: "Certainly 'government by investigation is not government,' but government without investigation might easily turn out to be democratic government no longer."

XVIII

THEORETICAL
GRAVEDIGGERS

THE POLITICAL fall of Congress has been correlated, as is usual in such cases, with a verbal critique proving that the victim amply deserves his unhappy fate. This critique is doubtless both cause and effect of the historical process through which the relative power of Congress within the American system has been weakened. "Advanced opinion," translating the theoretical attacks on Congress into the rhetoric of schoolroom, pulpit and market place, helps to undermine the public confidence without which a political institution cannot flourish in a republican society. Then, when they think that they have spotted the loser, routine commentators add their verbal blows.

Although no one has yet made an open call for the abolition of Congress, the contemporary critique differs basically from the past. It might be said that the criticism of Congressmen has turned into an attack on Congress. In older days, as we have noted, Congressmen were often enough denounced for laziness, ignorance or corruption. Specific laws or proposals were, sometimes most fiercely, condemned. But the criticism was not driven deeply into the institutional core of Congress. Only a few eccentrics brought into question, even indirectly, the role of Congress within the American system. During the past generation, in contrast, the criticism of Congress has been generalized, and has often been directed at features of congressional conduct that are essential to its continued functioning in anything like the traditional mode. Full acceptance of the charges—and the prescribed remedies—would mean the overturn of the traditional equilibrium of the American system.

Woodrow Wilson's early book, *Congressional Government* (written in 1883–84), and his youthful articles, "Cabinet Government in the United States" (1879) and "Committee or Cabinet Government" (1884), sounded a premature prelude to the generalized criticism of Congress. If we examine his argument closely, it turns out to be both doctrinaire and circular. The young and rather provincial scholar was a passionate admirer of what he believed to be the British parliamentary (or cabinet) system, and of its contemporary flowering (as he judged it) under Gladstone. He was much influenced by the recently published masterpiece of Walter Bagehot,[1] in which the British constitution comes off so markedly better than the American. Moreover, Wilson was both an intellectual and a southerner. To most intellectuals, then as now, the ways of Congress are unsympathetic and indeed all but impenetrable; and it is certainly plain from *Congressional Government* that Wilson did not really understand what Congress does or tries to do. As for southerners in the 1880's, they were still seeing in Congress the vindictive despot of the reconstruction era.

Wilson's argument strips down to the following. The American political system is in bad shape. This is because it has become "congressional government," which is in practice equivalent to government by the chairmen of the standing committees plus the Speaker of the House. Such a form of government is basically different from the parliamentary system, or government by a responsible cabinet that defends its policies openly on the floor of the assembly. The American system should therefore be changed to the parliamentary system, or something similar to it. The parliamentary system is in good shape. This is because it is not the congressional system. Thus the circle is completed. Along with occasional insights and some interesting reflections on general problems of political philosophy,

1. The American edition of *The English Constitution* was first published in 1877.

Wilson has done little more than express his personal preference for cabinet over committee government.

The real tendency of Wilson's criticism became clear in the second half of his career. The notion of remaking the American into an English-model parliamentary system was quietly dropped overboard. As his ideas and ambitions shifted, Wilson discovered the native antidote to the blight of congressional predominance in the office of President. The balance could be righted, or rather reversed, by swinging from congressional to executive predominance—more exactly, to executive supremacy. Though what Wilson produced in his own lifetime was only a rehearsal rather than the first act of the constitutional drama that opened its professional run in 1933, his verbal finger was prophetically pointed.

2

Some of the most effective essays in the verbal denigration of Congress take the form not of polemics, argument or critique but of historical study and analysis. Many historians and political scientists, both lay and academic, have found recent occasion to report, as the result of their researches into the American past and present, that: (a) save for one or two exceptional and lamentable periods, Congress never had much power in the American political system; and (b) Congress still, to our sorrow, possesses the predominant power, and is more than ever encroaching on the constitutional prerogatives of the executive and the judiciary. Although these two assertions very nearly contradict each other, they are often put forward, on different pages, by the same author. Whatever their logical interrelation, they are felt to give joint historical backing to a single conclusion: namely, that congressional power is a bad thing.

The *Federalist* warnings against the possibility of "legislative despotism," and Thomas Jefferson's comment in his *Notes on Virginia* that "173 despots would surely be as oppressive as one," have been quoted in a thousand books and articles of the past decade, with the suggestion that the primary object of the Fathers was to introduce a benevolent autocrat as chief, who would block the tyrannical impulses of the representative assembly of the people. Congress is impressionistically sketched as passive and helpless from the beginning, good on its own for little more than sporadic interference with the wisdom of the Chief Executive. Congress best serves the national interest by waiting to be told by the President what to do, and then obediently doing it.

Professor Arthur N. Holcombe, writing in *The Yale Review* of March 1956, blandly summarized this creative trend in historical reconstruction: "After all, the function of Congress under the Federal Constitution is not to dictate legislative policy to the President. It is rather to insure that the policies of the Administration will not be carried into execution without substantial evidence of the consent of the people in different parts of the country." (In these contexts it is not thought relevant to recall that Jefferson's reference to "173 despots" was part of a passage in which he criticized the Constitution on the ground that by its terms "all the powers of government, legislative, executive, and judiciary, result to the legislative body.") At the Philadelphia Convention, declares Professor Clinton Rossiter in his study of the Presidency, "all arguments over the executive . . . were resolved in favor of power and independence."[2]

But the admirers of a strong Presidency are not content to find that in the past Congress never had and was never intended to have much power anyway. They add the clinching discovery that the present power of Congress is inflated to a usurping level that puts the nation at the verge of the legislative despotism that was once averted by the vigilance of the Fathers. Each timid effort by Congress (foredoomed in almost every case to failure) to get plain information from a truculent bureaucrat, to fix some sort of limit on

2. Clinton Rossiter, *The American Presidency* (New York: New American Library, by arrangement with Harcourt, Brace & Co., 1956), p. 60.

executive discretion in spending public money, or to correct the
Court's deliberate misreadings of Congress' own intentions, is denounced as a subversive encroachment on administrative or judicial
functions. The indignation is not confined to the liberal columnists
and editorial writers of the daily journals. Professor Rossiter announces the academic findings as of 1956:

> Congress is busy asserting control over [the laws'] execution,
> and there is evidence to support the charge that Congress has
> roamed farther out of bounds than the President in the past
> ten years. . . . Congress . . . does not have the right [to] direct;
> and this—straight-out direction of various agencies and offi-
> cers—is what Congress has been doing too much of in recent
> years. The result has been disorder, dissension, indecision, and
> disruption of morale. . . . Concern over improper meddling in
> the business of the executive reached a peak of indignation in
> the heady days when Senator McCarthy was asserting with
> implausible gall his right of espionage in the executive branch.
> It did seem for a while as if he and his friends might do per-
> manent damage to those vague but visible lines drawn by cus-
> tom between President and Congress.[3]

It is Walter Lippmann who has performed the most remarkable
feat of historical acrobatics. In *The Public Philosophy* (1955), he revealed the basic political development of the 20th century: the fact
that, beginning with the first world war, "the old structure of executive government with the consent of a representative assembly was
dismantled."[4] On Mr. Lippmann's interpretation, that is to say, the

3. Clinton Rossiter, *ibid.*, p. 146. It will be noted that by implication Professor
Rossiter shares the conclusion we reached earlier, that the relation between
Congress and the executive bureaucracy was primarily at issue in the McCarthy
affair.
4. Walter Lippmann, *The Public Philosophy* (Boston: Little, Brown & Co. and
Atlantic Monthly Press, 1955), p. 12.

form of the traditional political structure was not merely executive predominance, but "executive government"—that is, executive supremacy. The political function of the representative assembly (for which "legislature" would be a palpable misnaming) was to signify popular assent to what the executive had done, did, or proposed to do. The constitutional revolution of our day is defined by Mr. Lippmann to consist in the fall of the executive, with the correlative rise of the assembly to predominance and supremacy. "Congressional government," as Woodrow Wilson wrote about it, was no more than a faint foreshadowing of the congressional despotism of Mr. Lippmann's present.

By deduction from the axioms of a world that could never have heard of Caesar, Bonaparte or Hitler, or of contemporary statism, Mr. Lippmann derives the generalization that he needs to support his political views: "Congenitally [in democratic states] the executive, when dependent on election, is weaker than the elected representatives. The normal drainage of power in a democratic state is away from the governing center and down into the constituencies."[5] His summary of "the democratic disaster of the twentieth century" is a triumph of ideology over observation: "The power of the executive has become enfeebled, often to the verge of impotence, by the pressures of the representative assembly and of mass opinions."[6]

5. *Ibid.*, p. 48.
6. *Ibid.*, p. 55. In *The Public Philosophy*, Mr. Lippmann is writing, sometimes with much passing insight, about the contemporary "revolt of the masses" and its destructive effect on society and civilization. Such is the obsessive power of ideology over even a mind so well informed as Mr. Lippmann's that he somehow fails to observe the fact—obvious to the point of self-evidence—that this revolt expresses itself through triumphant Caesar ("the strong executive"), over the crushed political body of the representative assembly.

3

It is not possible to take these two theses—of past congressional impotence and present congressional usurpation—very seriously as historical and political analysis. For that matter, their sponsors, most of whom contradict them as often as they assert them, hardly bother to hide the fact that they belong rather to rhetoric than to science.

It is true, of course, that in the United States under the Constitution Congress has never been all-powerful. The Fathers at Philadelphia did not intend to set up a government by Congress, but a dual and limited government, dividing sovereignty between states and central apparatus, and further diffusing the portion of the central apparatus among its several overlapping but semi-autonomous branches. Under the Constitution Congress has never governed the country, except as one element in the many-headed leviathan of state and national authorities, of legislature, executive, judiciary, bureaucracy and lobbies. There has seldom been even the degree of congressional supremacy that is alleged and attacked in Wilson's *Congressional Government*.

Experience did soon show that the Chief Executive would assume certain powers and more power than expected or intended by most of the Fathers. If from no other cause, this followed from administrative need and convenience. The Senate was never able to exercise its generally expected share in the active conduct of foreign relations. More generally, experience showed that in the complex American structure the initiative, including the initiative toward new legislation, would often—though by no means invariably—come from the President. "Steering a novel course between the great powers of the English king and the feeble powers of most state executives, the Convention recommended" and tradition confirmed "a chief magistrate strong enough to lend energy . . . to the general government" but "'bound by law,'"[7] and responsible in both

7. Leonard D. White, *The Federalists,* pp. 15, 16.

specified and customary ways to the legislature as well as to the Constitution and the people.

It may be that in some sentences of this book I have exaggerated the traditional power and the present weakness of Congress, and it is plainly impossible to determine either with quantitative accuracy. Nor is it necessary. In order to know that Jean Paul Getty is richer than the corner filling-station operator, and that certain significant conclusions follow therefrom about their social potentials, we do not have to have all figures on their respective balance sheets. The coarse fact about the position of Congress in the American political system is simple enough: Congress once held a large, quite probably the largest, share in the total sum of power possessed by the central government; and now it holds a share that is not merely smaller but so much smaller as to be of a different order of magnitude. This is equivalent to saying that in the American governmental system a constitutional revolution has taken place, through which Congress has been reduced from a co-ordinate or predominate to a secondary and subordinate rank.

This is the evident enough fact. When not affected by the heat of polemics, everyone knows it. In sober discussion, few scholars would disagree with the conclusion reached by Dr. George B. Galloway, one of the most meticulous contemporary students of congressional history and behavior, after his survey of the "Original Design of Congressional Powers and Functions":

> The architects of the Grand Design of 1787, keenly conscious of the incompetence of Congress under the confederation, expressly vested the primary powers of the new national and federal government in the Congress of the United States. From the place of prominence they give it in the fundamental framework and the vast powers they conferred upon it, the framers evidently intended to make Congress the central department in the new republic.[8]

8. George B. Galloway, *op. cit.*, pp. 6–7.

Of the thirty-one Presidents prior to Franklin Roosevelt, the partisans of executive supremacy do not claim, at most, more than seven: Washington, Jefferson, Jackson, Polk, Lincoln, Theodore Roosevelt and Wilson. Of these seven, two—Jefferson and Theodore Roosevelt—though of strong individual personalities, did little (in Jefferson's case, less than nothing) to strengthen the *office* of President; while Polk, though he believed in high prerogatives for the office, was too inconsiderable a personage to affect its character. And in the nation's first administration as compared with the pre-Constitutional government, it would be more accurate to say that *both* President *and* Congress were strong; there was no precedent by which to gauge their relative strength. Now the primary meaning of "strong" and "weak" as applied to Presidents refers to their strength or weakness in relation to Congress; and thus, by the most presidentially oriented accounts, Congress was relatively strong during the incumbencies of from twenty-four to twenty-eight of the first thirty-one Presidents.

Professor Rossiter, though in some of his pages seemingly anxious to clothe his own ardent admiration of executive power with the traditional authority that only the past can confer, is at last quite candid:

> The Presidency today has the same general outlines as that of 1789, *but the whole picture is a hundred times magnified.*[9] The President is all the things he was intended to be, and he is several other things as well. . . .
>
> [The Presidency today] is distinctly more powerful. It cuts deeply into the powers of Congress; in fact, *it has quite reversed the expectations of the framers* by becoming itself a vortex into which these powers have been drawn in massive amounts. It cuts deeply into the lives of the people; in fact, it commands

9. My italics here and below (J.B.). It would be hard to prove the exact figure, but we can follow the rhetorical intention.

authority over their comings and goings that Hamilton him-self[10] might tremble to behold. . . .

The outstanding feature of American constitutional devel-opment is the growth of the power and prestige of the Presi-dency.[11]

Professor Rossiter also makes the converse explicit: "The long decline of Congress has contributed greatly to the rise of the Presi-dency. The framers, as I have explained, expected Congress to be the focus of our system of government."[12]

The second thesis—that the American governmental system is today marked by a gross expansion of congressional power over that of the other branches—is so ridiculous if interpreted as an assertion of historical fact that it cannot be meant in that sense. Both theses are in reality pseudo-statements. They are not empirical generalizations about American political history and structure, but rhetorical weapons wielded in a massive, persistent verbal attack on Congress. In a dispute over political and social affairs, it is always desirable to have the prophets, the sacred texts and the sanctions of custom on your side. Therefore those who, approving the fallen state of Congress, wish to keep Congress weak or to weaken it still further, read the present situation and their own wishes back into the intentions of the Founding Fathers, the text of the Constitution and the nation's tradi-tional practice. They do so, at any rate, in their polemic moods. Many of them, knowing a good deal about American history, do not try to sustain the historical nonsense in their calmer moments.

10. Though not, it would seem, Prof. Rossiter.

11. *Op. cit.*, pp. 60–62, *passim.*

12. *Ibid.*, p. 65. It is a tautology to write that the decline of Congress "has con-tributed" to the rise of the Presidency. In terms of the mechanics of the polit-ical equilibrium the decline of the one is the equivalent of the rise of the other, like the simultaneous rise and fall of the opposite ends of a see-saw—if, at any rate, we understand by "Presidency" not the President alone, but the President plus the executive office and the bureaucracy.

Similarly: when your opponent is down, your best chance to keep him that way is by persuading the onlookers that he will be a dangerous threat not merely to you but to them, if he so much as tries to lift a little finger. Thus with Congress, whenever it gives an outward hint of reviving political vigor.

About the broad outline of the facts concerning the relative place of Congress in the American political structure, past and present, there is, then, no real doubt. Whatever its rhetorical form, the actual dispute is about, not the facts, but their evaluation. What does the fall of Congress presage for the future of the American system? Is the fall a victory or a defeat? Is it good or bad? And in whichever case, what, if anything, can and ought to be done about it?

XIX

THE CASE AGAINST CONGRESS

ACCORDING TO THE most familiar set of charges, Congress is slow, inefficient, archaic, horse-and-buggy in its methods, "out of touch with the 20th century." By the 1950's, remarks Dr. Galloway, "Few any longer regarded [Congress] as the keystone of the federal arch. With Congress overwhelmed by its great responsibilities, operating under its ancient ritual, the streamlined age of the Giant Clipper, radar, and the atomic bomb seemed to have passed it by."[1] "What the framers did not reckon with," Professor Rossiter feels, "was the astounding growth of the republic, which has turned Congress into a cumbersome, overstaffed pair of assemblies that speak in a confusion of tongues."[2]

The accuracy of this description seems to almost everyone, both friend and foe of Congress, to be self-evident, quite too obvious to require any proof beyond the mere statement. Somehow the slowness and inefficiency of Congress just seems to leap to the eye. What could be slower reading than the *Congressional Record*, no skipping permitted? What could be a more inefficient way of getting business over and done with than entrusting it to two divided Houses, the infinitely complicated parliamentary rules, the long rigmarole of committee referrals and hearings and studies, the circumlocutions of

1. George B. Galloway, *op. cit.*, p. 8.
2. Clinton Rossiter, *op. cit.*, p. 65. "Overstaffed"—as applied to Congress' poor little supporting platoon alongside the multitudinous corps of the executive bureaucracy—is an adjective that Prof. Rossiter's unconscious must have slipped by his scholarly censor.

debate, the amendments and joint conference committees? What, compared to the streamlined charts of a jet-age firm of management consultants, could be more outmoded than the congressional "table of organization"?

Yet when anything seems all that obvious we ought to suspect that some factor may have been dropped. A whale would look slow on the Santa Anita racetrack, but in his ocean he can beat any horse in the stable. An octopus would be clumsy at a computer console, but he does well enough on his rocks. It is necessary to check both the meaning and relevance of the terms we use. Congress is "slow" and "inefficient"? Compared to what? And if so, why not?

Cost for work done is considered one measure of efficiency. For the legislature of the richest nation of the world, the congressional budget seems modest enough by today's standards: about a hundred million dollars annually for the whole legislative establishment—a fraction of one percent of the executive budget, and much less than the expenses of hundreds of private corporations. Members of Congress, most of whom work from twelve to sixteen hours daily, are paid the salary of junior executives in a small company, less than Cabinet members or Supreme Court Justices, less than a tenth that of the chief officers of a big corporation. The professional staff of Congress (legal, research, and administrative aides) is as competent as the average in comparable jobs, and turns out more work at lower pay.

Is Congress slower and less efficient than the bureaucracy? The comparison can be made only where the operations are more or less similar. With respect to these, no one who has much acquaintance with the ways of Washington will rule Congress too far behind in the race. Generally speaking, a citizen can get a letter or appointment or advice from a congressional office in much shorter time than from an executive bureau. A congressional committee and its staff can turn out a competent report on an urgent problem at least as quickly as an executive agency. Congress cannot, by the nature of the legislative procedure, take more than a year on military budget problems that may have been five years crawling through the Pentagon.

The stereotyped contrast between a creaking, horse-drawn Congress and a streamlined, jet-propelled administration is a myth without much substance. The huge executive bureaucracy is a swollen, arthritic, half-paralyzed cripple, about a third of whose time is spent taking care of itself (on "housekeeping," as it is called) and another third in ducking responsibility. The congressional "decision process" is cumbersome enough compared to an ideal model, and rather more cumbersome than it could be in practice, but it does not suffer when compared to the bureaucratic decision process, which can take up to ten years to order production of a new weapon system or a change in the type of pen on post-office desks.

Neither the Fathers nor the philosophers before and after them ever listed speed and efficiency among the virtues of a representative assembly. They wanted "energy and dispatch" in the executive, but "in the legislature," they believed, "promptitude of decision is oftener an evil than a benefit. The differences of opinion, and the jarrings of parties in that department of the government, though they may sometimes obstruct salutary plans, yet often promote deliberation and circumspection, and serve to check excesses in the majority."[3] White-haired, slow speaking Nestor, not the impulsive Achilles, the aged Priam and not passionate Troilus, are the archetypes of the legislator.

What is it that Congress is supposed to be so speedy about? Is the efficiency of Congress measured by the average number of laws it turns out, or dollars it appropriates, per hour? Naturally, a bureaucrat asking a doubled appropriation for his agency, a lobbyist needing an industry-favoring bill to get his contract renewed, a newspaper reader hopped up by sensational headlines and the cry of "crisis" that has become endemic to our era, get impatient with what from their standpoint is congressional slow-motion. And one

3. *Federalist*, No. 70.

very good reason why tradition has built up its elaborate procedures is to resist such impatient pressures until they can be sorted and weighed.

Many who complain about congressional slowness and inefficiency have not stopped to reflect that many of the ways in which Congressmen "waste their time" are apt methods for accomplishing the tasks of a representative legislature in a democratic republic: by the chats and correspondence with constituents, the encounters with the press, the lunches with experts from the bureaucracy and even the cocktails with the lobbyists, the informal hours with each other and the staff professionals, the lecture trips to cities and universities, the travel junkets at home and abroad, the members are not merely helping to get themselves re-elected (which is also part of a legislator's business in a democracy), but getting to know—or, better, to feel—the myriad problems and interests, the competing needs and desires, complaints and demands, that the legislature, if it performs its function, must try to weave into some sort of working resolution.

For an intellectual, the right or wrong of a bill on foreign aid or prices or housing or subversion is likely to be the product of a few minutes of deduction from ideological premises. Every Congressman, after a few months' service, knows that it can seldom be that simple. The political equations are too complex; there are too many values and wants and problems simultaneously at issue; and in a democracy, laws and policies must meet the test—very subtle to determine in advance—of sufficient public acceptability, whatever else may be their merits. That perennial cartoon subject, the last-minute rush of laws at the end of the session, which an intellectual despises as a symptom of laziness and sloppy method, is only an appearance: the final votes are the Q.E.D. of theorems that have been developed step by step over the months preceding. And in the elaboration of that sort of political theorem the Congress of the United States is a mathematician of remarkable delicacy.

When the legislative function is limited, as it normally should be, to issues of principle and broad policy, there is seldom any real need for immediate action. Even when quick action might seem abstractly desirable, there are usually compensating advantages— through, for example, the achievement of a wider public consensus—from legislative delay. For the most part, the circumstances that call for quick action fall within the province of the executive, and the American Constitution is marvelously designed to permit executive firmness and speed—although in practice the executive has often failed to display either when they have been most in order. The speedy rendering of justice is, or should be, a duty of the executive and the courts, not of the legislature. It is for the executive to repel a sudden invasion, suppress domestic insurrection, or communicate to the legislature and the nation any sudden grave turn in international or domestic affairs. When a President has convincingly shown the existence of an emergency requiring congressional action, Congress has usually responded; but Congress, and much of the nation besides, have grown a little skeptical of perpetual crises.

No convincing evidence has been offered to show that the United States Congress is slower or less efficient than other representative assemblies in other free nations. The workings of the congressional machinery, the moves and squabbles and countermoves, are more open to the public gaze than in the British sort of parliament, but this does not mean that in Britain and the Commonwealth there is no grinding of the hidden wheels. Dr. Ernest S. Griffith, the brilliant director of the Legislative Reference Service of the Library of Congress, who is as intimately acquainted with the operations of Congress as any man outside its own senior ranks, has stressed this point:

The fact that Congress, as well as the American people, makes up its mind in public has much to do with the appearance of indecision. The reaching of decision is a process over

which the British throw a veil of secrecy. There is little or no
evidence in recent years to indicate that the United States is
any less slow or more slow in arriving at an answer than is
Britain.[4]

If we are looking for modern, streamlined speed and efficiency in
assemblies, there is one and only one place to find it: in the operations of the assemblies—no longer either representative or legislative—of the authoritarian states: Hitler's Reichstag, the Kremlin's
Supreme Soviet, Franco's Cortes, Mao's and Mussolini's and Tru-
jillo's Chambers. No delays, no confusions, no upsets in running a
resolution through the prescribed procedures. But even that speed is
deceptive, if we look beyond the ritualistic ceremonies to the governing process as a whole:

> The revelations of the inefficiencies, lost motion, internal fric-
> tion, and other errors of the dictatorships of Italy, Germany,
> and Japan are now a matter of record, exposed so that he who
> wishes may read and ponder. They apparently are at least equal
> to the errors made by the democracies and may well exceed
> them by an appreciable margin. . . . Every report of any real-
> ity that comes out of the Soviet Union carries the same story
> of inefficiency and waste through terror, lack of incentive,
> cynicism, suspicion, and espionage. Yet, however inefficiently
> these dictatorships may in fact have administered their soci-
> eties, it is important to remember that for many years they
> gave the appearance of effectiveness, both to their own people
> and to others. They could cover up their mistakes and liqui-
> date their critics.[5]

4. Ernest S. Griffith, "The Place of Congress in Foreign Relations" (*The Annals of the American Academy of Social and Political Science,* Sept. 1953.).
5. Ernest S. Griffith, *Congress, Its Contemporary Role* (New York: New York
University Press, 1956), pp. 190–1.

It may be just as well to recall, now and then, that the American system of government has been more successful, in practice, than any other in history.

2

At the beginning of this century the muckrakers set a liberal precedent, more lately followed by historians, political scientists, popular journalists and President Truman, for the opinion that Congress is anti-democratic, reactionary, and servile to "the interests." Granted a suitable definition of terms, this charge—or let us say, this description—is true.

When Congress is called anti-democratic, the reference is partly to the fact that its structural forms and its procedures distort the purely quantitative, plebiscitary relations which, according to democratist ideology, are the ultimate sanction of sovereignty. Many of these distortions are obvious. It is a distortion, to begin with, to have a bicameral legislature with each chamber elected according to different rules. The representation in the Senate, with two members from each state of whatever size, is grossly out of line with population mathematics. But election from local districts (instead of national slates) and the well-known "overrepresentation of the rural districts" keeps the House also much short of the democratist ideal.

Congress operates through its committees, and especially through the committee chairmen. From the standpoint of democratism, the seniority system of selecting chairmen is a scandal that provokes regular denunciation. Unquestionably, as a glance at any session's roster of committee chairmen proves, seniority upsets the plebiscitary relations in favor of age, of social stability in the constituencies, of southern and normally one-party states against more volatile regions, and of farming or small-town districts against the big cities.

In the House, the power of the Speaker, of the Rules Committee, and of the exceedingly complicated procedural rules can be used to steamroller the majority as well as minorities. In the Senate the right of almost unlimited debate permits and almost invites a minority thwarting of the chamber's majority. And for certain very important purposes—such as the confirmation of treaties, the overriding of a veto, and the initiating of a constitutional amendment—a two-thirds vote is required instead of the simple majority that by the logic of democratism ought always to be binding.

Because of its many-layered, labyrinthine, non-democratic internal structure, Congress seldom gives direct or isomorphic expression to the raw popular will. As it passes through the congressional processes the popular will is filtered, sifted, blunted, organized and reorganized, fitted into a pattern that retains a still recognizable but only indirect connection with its source.

As a result of this non-democratic structure, the localizing principle of representation in Congress, and the lively play of semi-autonomous forces in American life, individual members of Congress, informal groups of members, and in some respects Congress as a whole do often represent what are called "the interests": that is to say—if the term is to be assigned a definable meaning—the needs or wants of organized groups and institutions within the community. From the point of view of rigorous democratism, this is a grievous fault, because a government ought to represent or express only the "common," "national" or "general" interest.

Part Three will undertake a fuller analysis of the relation of Congress to "democracy" and "the interests." Let us here remark that, while it is true that Congress is in some degree non-democratic and representative of the interests, these are, of themselves, morally neutral facts. They are not "faults" or deficiencies of Congress, or charges against Congress, except within the framework of certain assumptions, values and principles: the assumptions, values and principles, namely, of what we defined in Part One as liberalism. And it is of course liberals—including some liberal members of Congress—who bring forward these two characteristics as items in their indictment of Congress as it presently functions.

It is also liberals who declare Congress to be "reactionary"—an epithet which they assume to be adverse. The goals of modern liberalism are, by definition, "progressive." Therefore, whatever goes counter to these goals, or slows their realization, is reactionary. Now it is a fact that Congress, though it has more or less drifted along toward the progressive liberal goals (welfare statism, egalitarianism, internationalism, and so on), has shown a good deal less than the bureaucracy's zest for the journey, and has been at times downright mulish. A fair number of individual Congressmen are in their own minds squarely opposed to the progressive goals; not a few others tend to stray out of line. The liberals have never forgotten the dread example of the Senate murder of the League of Nations in 1919, which touched off a fourteen-year revival of congressional power and national reaction.

"In point of fact," as Professor Rossiter puts it, "the struggle over the powers of the Presidency as against Congress, fierce though it may seem, is only a secondary campaign in a political war over the future of America." And he adds, in a self-identification with history typical of the liberal syndrome: "The cause of the opponents of a strong Presidency . . . is ill-starred because they cannot win a war against American history. The strong Presidency is the product of events that cannot be undone and of forces that continue to roll. We have made our decisions for the New Economy and the New Internationalism."[6]

Although the total context is too different for an exact comparison, the political relations here are roughly the reverse of those that held during the nation's early years. Then it was, by and large, the conservatives who supported an executive sufficiently strong and independent to counterbalance what they feared would be the overly

6. Clinton Rossiter, *op. cit.*, pp. 150–1. Professor Rossiter is generally called, by himself as well as others, a "conservative"—specifically, a "new conservative." By our definitions, however, he is of course a liberal, though not of the extreme democratist variety.

democratic forces working through Congress. It was the liberals of that era—"Left" Jeffersonians, who were not so much for States' Rights as for a social radicalism in the mode of the French Jacobins—who wanted congressional supremacy and a weak President.

But this comparison in reverse, though attractive as a historical exercise, cannot be pressed too far. Except for a few extremists in the early years, who were true Jacobins or Tory monarchists, the citizens in all factions entered under the new constitutional dispensation with a common belief in the principles of diffused sovereignty and of coordinate, counterbalancing governmental departments. No one then conceived that the legislature should be subordinate to the executive, and most assumed that the legislature would be the determining and predominate arm. The disputes were over questions of degree—just how far the executive should have an independent role apart from his duties as administrator of the laws passed by Congress—and not, as today, of the political essence. Whether regarded as heresy or revelation, the idea of executive supremacy is, so far as American history goes, a product peculiarly of our time.

XX

THE REFORM
OF CONGRESS

THE PROPOSALS for the improvement, reform or remaking of Congress are naturally designed to correct what the proposer thinks to be wrong with it. They can be classified as technical, democratist, and British.

Not even the warmest admirer of Congress denies that its operations might, with advantage, be technically improved. Quite apart from theories about the proper place of the legislature, a change would be an improvement if through it Congress were enabled to do better whatever it might be that it was in fact doing. For example, nearly everyone will agree that any change enabling Congress to know more about what it is doing is an improvement. Congressional intelligence methods have, in actuality, been much bettered in recent years by the strengthening of the more or less permanent professional staff and the development of the Legislative Reference Service, by the use made of lay experts and research organizations, by the greater seriousness with which many members of Congress take the inspection side of their travels, and so on.

If Congress is to continue to have even a minor voice in matters of the public purse, it needs a clearer, more systematic knowledge of expenditures than it now possesses. A number of plans that might serve to this end have been put forward during the past decade.

No matter what is considered the proper political relation between the executive and the legislature, better means of communication among the White House, the bureaucracy and Congress are desirable, and such communication is in part a technical problem.

Again, it is generally agreed that a simplified committee structure, further along the line begun by the Reorganization Act of 1946, would be an aid to the accomplishment of any kind of congressional business. There are also a number of simplifying procedural changes that seem both sensible and ideologically neutral.

Through the 1946 Reorganization Act and subsequent special bills, some technical improvements have been carried out. Others have been convincingly urged by reports of the Hoover Commission and by qualified experts both within and outside Congress, although it is always a long process to get any of them adopted by a body so set in its procedural ways. In any case, such merely technical reforms should be carefully distinguished from proposed changes that would, if carried out, affect not simply Congress' methods of operating but its political essence, and in particular its basic political relations to the other branches of government and to the electorate.

Many of this latter type are what I have been calling "democratist," and are designed to change those features of the congressional organism that are inconsistent with the ideology of democratism. The seniority system is a perennial target of liberal attack, along with the privileges of the House Rules Committee and the virtually unlimited debate privilege in the Senate. Democratism inclines toward statewide (Representatives-at-large) instead of district elections of Representatives, and there is a growing tendency to give a national extension—by funds, publicity, and organizational support—to key congressional contests. But for democratism, the Senate itself as an institution remains a scandal even after the shift, by virtue of the 17th Amendment, to popular election. Therefore there are recurrent proposals for the elimination of the Senate. These usually take the form of a demonstration that bicameralism is outmoded and should give way to a unicameral legislative system.

Dr. Galloway, at the conclusion of his study of the legislative process in Congress, sympathetically records the widely held contemporary belief in "the obsolescence of the traditional functions of the Senate," and the view of "bicameralism as an anachronism, a relic of the days when checks and balances were needed to prevent tyranny." He quotes a monograph by Dr. Harvey Walker arguing for a one-chamber legislature as "the only permanent solution" on the ground that: "Adequate and careful research has demonstrated that the moth-eaten argument that two houses are needed so that each may act as a check on the other is an illusion."[1]

The idea of abolishing the two-chamber legislature is analogous to the proposal, at a more fundamental level, to eliminate the separation between legislature and executive. This proposal has two divergent sources: the ideology of democratism on the one hand; and on the other, that fascination which the British parliamentary system has exercised on so many educated Americans, almost from the morrow of the founding revolt. During the past generation, constitutional reformers of almost opposite species have managed to come together on a program for a change in the American system to a "responsible" cabinet-parliamentary-party type of government. On this conservatives like Henry Hazlitt and David Lawrence have clasped theoretical hands with the liberal Thomas Finletter and the late Harold Laski, avowedly Marxist as well as liberal.

In such a program the ideal, seldom put forward because rather obviously beyond practical possibility, is a chief executive chosen not by a separate electoral process but by the ruling party (or coalition) of the legislature. Usually, more modest proposals are made: the selection of the Cabinet from Congress; granting Cabinet members a voice on the floor of Congress; adding such parliamentary devices as a "question period." To lessen the chance of the political deadlocks between legislature and executive that the critics consider to be a

---

1. George B. Galloway, *The Legislative Process in Congress,* p. 584. The Walker quotation is from *The Annals of the American Academy of Political and Social Science,* "Communication in the Legislative Assembly," March, 1947, p. 66. Scholarly rhetoric is often puzzling. It would seem that "to prevent tyranny" is no longer a problem in the 20th century. And it is not easy to imagine just what kind of "research" can demonstrate Dr. Walker's normative conclusion.

fatal defect of the separate powers system, other suggestions would provide: the same term of office for the President and all members of Congress; a plebiscitary electoral method for both President and Congress that would guarantee that the President and the congressional majority were of the same political party; some method of dissolving a Congress or getting a new President if a deadlock came about.

Professor Laski discovered "an incoherence and irresponsibility in the relations between executive and legislature." Elaborating, he discloses in passing the reason why liberals are uneasy at the traditional separation of powers:

> An institutional system framed for a negative state cannot easily be adapted to the needs of a positive state. The legislative program in the latter type of organization needs an integration and a coherent continuity that it cannot attain under the American system. . . . No democracy in the modern world can afford a scheme of government the basis of which is the inherent right of the legislature to paralyze the executive power. . . . The modern state requires disciplined leadership; the American system leaves no assurance of its continuous availability. It is, indeed, built upon foundations that are inherently suspicious of leadership as such.[2]

Even Dr. Galloway, whose social views are far distant from Laski's collectivism, traces the constitutional separation of powers back through Montesquieu to Newton's *Principia* and ideas of physics which with "their derivative political and economic theories have become obsolescent. . . . The doctrine of the separation of powers and the system of checks and balances have become a serious handicap to that constant, confident collaboration between Congress and

2. Harold J. Laski, *The American Presidency* (New York: Harper & Bros., 1940), pp. 162–3.

the executive required by the new circumstances of public affairs in the middle of the twentieth century."[3]

Those who draw from the parliamentary, and more particularly the British, system their projects for basic repair of the structure of the American government would seem to be overlooking the essential historical dimension of time, and to be disregarding the ineluctable concreteness of political facts. The problem is not simply whether the British system is, at some level of abstraction, "better" than the American. (Actually, the British system doesn't look so very healthy of late; and it may be that the other, Anglican shore appears, even to many of its former admirers, less green than once it did.) An actual, operating political system is a function of time, practice, custom—in short, of tradition—as well as of abstract schemes and ideas. The excellences of each political system are after the manner of such a system as it is. Attempting to graft certain structural features of the British on to the American system—on the doubtful assumption that this is even possible—would not make the American system more British, and still less would it transfer to the United States any special political virtues that the British system possesses. The British parliamentary system works the way it does at least as much because it is British as because it is parliamentary: because it issues from the many centuries of England's national and imperial past, out of her economic and class relations, religion, education and culture and temperament, out of her wars and triumphs

---

3. *Op. cit.*, pp. 438–9. Dr. Galloway's admiration for the British system, here an implicit background, is undisguised in the comparative study, *Congress and Parliament* (Washington: National Planning Association, 1955), that he prepared after a special journey of observation and inquiry in England. Dr. Galloway, on the staff of the Legislative Reference Service, is probably the leading expert in the field of congressional reform both technical and substantial. He was chiefly responsible for the two most influential documents so far produced: the 1946 report of the Joint [Congressional] Committee on the Organization of Congress, and the report on *The Reorganization of Congress* by the Committee on Congress of the American Political Science Association.

and disasters, out of the accidents that fortune has thrown across her path. Just so the American, out of America's past, her society, her people and her luck.

In practical effect, any major changes along supposedly parliamentary lines (other than purely technical reforms, which in some cases are transferable) would merely reinforce the democratist tendency toward the unchallengeable supremacy of the administrative bureaucracy. This explains the paradox that both conservatives and liberals, even of rather extreme wings, are found among the supporters of British reforms of the American system. The conservatives allow themselves to be deceived by a nostalgic sentiment. The liberals accept rhetorical inconsistencies with their own ideology, out of a shrewd calculation of the practical effect.

In the context of the present period, it is in general the case that any basic congressional reform of the kind we have called "democratist," and any major new political linking of President and Congress, can serve in practice only to weaken still further Congress' already so much weakened strength, and to place sovereignty still more entirely in the grip of the executive and the bureaucracy. To shift the electoral basis of congressional representation toward a more national and plebiscitary foundation would make Congress a creature of the same mass of which the Chief Executive—"the leader"—must be the principal expression. The democratist reorganization of congressional forms and procedures would destroy fences that still permit Congress to retain a remnant of autonomous political will, and would expose the members of Congress to the full pressure of the political managers operating on behalf of the executive. The political history of the past generation, in the world as well as in North America, shows plainly enough that in our day a fusion between the executive and the legislature can mean in practice only the assumption of legislative power by the executive. Not for nothing does Professor Rossiter, in his rhapsody on the Presidency, include "Chief Legislator" high in the Presidential Litany.

2

Technical problems apart, the complaints against Congress, the listing of its faults, and the proposals for its reform amount in net effect, however intended, to a broad political attack on Congress. If carried out, the suggested changes might make Congress a better oiled, more smoothly meshing machine, but would cut still further its role as an organ of government. Indeed, the mere verbal agitation, long sustained, tends to weaken Congress politically. The academic and journalistic critique of Congress that has been mounted so aggressively during the past generation has undermined public support of Congress, fostered a growing *mystique* of the Presidency, and marred the confidence even of some members of Congress in their own corporate institution. Thus the critique, while reflecting the political decline of Congress, has also been one of the causal factors bringing it about.

Suppose that we shift to an axiomatic basis very different from that of either the liberal or the formalistic critique, and assume that what the American governmental system now needs is not a streamlined, "responsible" or docile, but a very considerably strengthened Congress: strengthened in the political sense of gaining (regaining, in historical fact) increased relative weight within the political equilibrium. On this assumption also, the performance of Congress will be judged much less than stellar. The shift in viewpoint does not remove the technical defects that have been charted by such careful analysts as George Galloway, Ernest Griffith, Robert Heller and Lucius Wilmerding. But the bill of political complaint will be drastically revised.

From this pro-Congress assumption (as it might be called) the main charge is that Congress has itself conspired in its own 20th-century decline and fall, has in short abdicated. Undoubtedly, the executive, the courts and the bureaucracy have striven to enhance their own power at the expense of the power of Congress—to struggle for power is after all the meaning of politics. Undoubtedly,

powerful segments of public opinion have been in one degree or another anti-Congress. That too, in our age especially, was only to be
expected. But Congress cannot slough all blame for its troubles onto
the shoulders of others. Congress has failed to fight stoutly and in-
telligently back; and through that failure it has been not only
Congress but our traditional system of government that has so
grievously lost.

The abdication of Congress has taken a double course. One has
been indirect. Congress has accepted—even if sometimes reluctantly—the growth of a gigantic, centralized, pervasive welfare state
that tends to swallow up Congress itself along with the state governments in the integrated rule of the administrative bureaucracy. If the
welfare state (as Americans and Englishmen prefer to call a centralized, bureaucratized statism) is carried through to its logical limit—
that is, to totalitarianism—the legislature necessarily loses all serious
political significance. Much short of that limit it becomes difficult for
the legislature to maintain autonomous operations. The growth of
statism puts one after another card in the bureaucracy's hands. This is
an automatic, spontaneous tendency. It might be held in check up to
a certain point in the statist growth, but only if the legislature were
continuously alert to the threat, and resolutely active in devising protective barriers against the political backwash of the statist expansion.

But neither on this nor on the more traditional fronts has
Congress been either alert or active in resisting the executive, the bureaucracy and the Court in their cumulative encroachment on its
own powers. Congress has thus moved toward abdication along a direct as well as an indirect route. It is not that all Congressmen have
approvingly watched congressional power draining away to the other
branches. Time and again it has been made clear on the floor of
Congress and clearer still in private discourse that most Congressmen
have opposed and resented the executive, bureaucratic and judicial
usurpations, the arrogant disregard of the legislative will assigned to
Congress by the Constitution, the free-wheeling executive commitments in foreign relations, the Court's undisguised distortions of

congressional intent, the bureaucratic refusal to supply Congress with information that is slipped to every favorite in the press corps, the bureaucratic and judicial contempt for the investigative power, the loss of congressional control over the nation's armed force and its purse strings. The opposition and resentment have been present, but they have been largely dissipated in verbal complaints and rhetorical grumblings, which fizzle out in petty amendments of administration projects. Congress has been shadow-boxing, not fighting.

The final test of freedom is the ability—and the willingness—to say No. Congress continues to utter little Noes now and then, but it would be hard to name a big No since 1933. Every important treaty proposed by the executive—though many have been denounced in Congress both before and after—has been confirmed. Every decisive economic and military power asked for by a President has been granted. The new agencies invented by the Presidents have been voted, and wartime agencies established by presidential decree have not been protested. Congress has not liquidated on its own initiative either any major agency or any major governmental activity, no matter how "temporary" or "emergency" its founding guise.[4] The revival of congressional power, if it ever does come about, will be outwardly and unmistakably marked for the nation by a shattering congressional No.

A number of the proposed technical reforms could make of Congress a keener, more flexible political instrument, and could thereby aid its struggle for political survival. But these are secondary, like armament in the wars between nations. With institutions as with individual men, survival is impossible if the will to survive has been lost.

4. Unless we include a few New Deal relief agencies, whose functions were, on one scale or another, transferred rather than abolished. In 1943 Congress, on its own, did kill the National Resources Planning Board, but in that war year, when all power was being thrust into Franklin Roosevelt's receptive hands, this particular No was a small one; and in any case the Board was administratively superfluous, since its activities had several other bureaucratic homes.

PART THREE

The Future of Congress

There is a tendency in constitutional governments of every form to degenerate into their respective absolute forms, and in all absolute governments into that of the monarchical form. But the tendency is much stronger in constitutional governments of the democratic form to degenerate into their respective absolute forms than in either of the others because, among other reasons, the distinction between the constitutional and absolute forms of aristocratical and monarchical governments is far more strongly marked than in democratic governments. The effect of this is to make the different orders or classes in an aristocracy or monarchy far more jealous and watchful of encroachment on their respective rights, and far more resolute and persevering in resisting attempts to concentrate power in any one class or order. On the contrary, the line between the two forms in popular governments, is so imperfectly understood that honest and sincere friends of the constitutional form not unfrequently, instead of jealously watching and arresting their tendency to degenerate into their absolute forms, not only regard it with approbation but employ all their powers to add to its strength and to increase its impetus, in the vain hope of making the government more perfect and popular.

JOHN C. CALHOUN, *A Disquisition on Government*

XXI

DEMOCRACY
AND LIBERTY

O UR AGE IS strewn with wounded words, among which few
have more grievously suffered than "democracy" and "democratic." There are popular democracies in communist-
ruled Eastern Europe, a democratic dictatorship in Russia and
China, parliamentary democracy in monarchic Britain, republican
democracy in the United States, one-party democracy in Mexico
and 35-party democracy in post-Perón Argentina, guided democracy in Indonesia, authoritarian democracy in Turkey, and prophetic
democracy in the United Arab Republic. Nazism expressed "the
democratic will of the German folk" just as the proletarian dictatorship, according to its founders, is "the most democratic form of government in the history of mankind." Beyond these forms of
democratic polity, there are economic democracy, social democracy,
educational democracy, democracy in housing, business and religion,
the democratic mind and the democratic way of life.

Plainly, "democracy" has become a verbal shell that spreads its
shot over a wide target. If we want to get much penetration we shall
have to tighten up the pattern.

Everyone today, of course, is democratic, pro-democracy. No one
would dream of defending a proposal or institution by calling it
"anti-democratic." That is to say, one important current use of the
word "democratic" and its associates is to express a positive evaluation, a sentiment of approval. Institutions and developments that we
frown on are likely to be, in our accepted vocabulary, anti-
democratic. Our enemy, being wicked, is against democracy.

This expressive or emotive meaning of the terms "democratic" and "democracy" figures prominently in contemporary political disputes both private and public, though it is irrelevant to the cognitive problems which are here under analysis.

We will exclude also that very broad and very vague use of "democratic" through which the term is made to apply to almost every field of human activity: the economy, sports, education, religion and what not. It is seldom clear, rationally speaking, what is meant by democracy in any such cases—as is indicated by the fact that an ideal "economic democracy" has been defined both as a maximum of *laisser faire* with absolute freedom of consumer choice and also as a maximum of collectivism ("primitive communism"). Usually (though not always) democracy in this broad sense implies some kind of egalitarianism, and this does constitute a partial link with the more restricted meanings which are the particular concern of these chapters.

The more restricted meanings are political: "democracy" may be taken—and in the past was normally taken—to refer to a certain political structure or mode of political procedure. But if we examine the actual usage of the term we will discover that in this century, though not prior thereto, even this political meaning is ambiguous. "Democracy" can, in fact, signify either of two quite different sets of political phenomena.

"Democracy" may refer, first, to a structure of government in which ultimate rule, authority, sovereignty rests, or is said to rest, in the community in general—"the people," "the general will," "the popular will"—outwardly expressing itself in the familiar procedures of voting, elections and assemblies. This meaning has received its most acute statement in the writings, or rather in some of the writings, of Jean-Jacques Rousseau. Those who "believe in" democracy (in this first sense) are committed to the theory that the will of the people is the ultimate sovereign, and the conviction that the only good and proper governments are those that in their behavior "express" the popular will. In its strictest formulation, this doctrine maintains that a government which is something over and apart from "the people" is inherently improper, a "chain" fastened on society (in Rousseau's metaphor). Government *is* nothing else than the general will.

In its second political meaning, "democracy" refers to a structure of government in which there obtains, or is thought to obtain, a "rule of law," certain "rights" that are in some sense basic and inalienable, and a "juridical defense" that protects the citizens through forms of "due process" backed by the underlying rule of law. A government of this kind is often called summarily a "constitutional government" although the constitution need not be written.

"Liberty" may be considered the special virtue of a constitutional government: "the prevalence of law and public decrees over the appetites of particular men," in the words of the Italian Renaissance historian, Guicciardini. "Freedom," however, straddles the two meanings of "democracy." If a government is believed to express the people's will, then it is sometimes said to be "free"; and thus a popularly supported revolution or even a military action from the outside that overthrows a monarchic or aristocratic government is often called "liberation"—*i.e.,* "making free." However, "freedom" is used in other contexts as if synonymous with "liberty," thus referring to the political presence of the rule of law, juridical defense, protected rights and due process.

It may be argued that only the first of these two political meanings has any right to the word "democracy," and this argument can be supported by both etymology and long tradition. In its Greek roots, "democracy" means "rule (or authority) of the people." Until rather recently this was the accepted sense, although it was never very easy to determine whether or to what extent the people were in fact ruling. But if we examine contemporary usage in English-speaking countries, we find that the second meaning, though without any etymological justification, has come to rival and sometimes supplant the first.

We (we in the English-speaking countries, that is) call the totalitarian regimes of our time—the regimes of Hitler, Mussolini, Stalin and Perón—"dictatorships"; we insist that they are non- and anti-democratic. In practice we make this judgment concerning a regime when we observe that under its authority juridical defense, civil rights and the rule of law disappear. We disregard any popular voting procedures that may characterize it. Indeed, we usually refuse even to consider the question whether the totalitarian regimes may express the popular will as significantly as do the governments of the United States, Great Britain, Canada, Switzerland, France or West Germany. In this determination, therefore, we are using the rule of law, civil rights and due process as the touchstone of what we mean by "democracy." At other times, we shuttle ambiguously back and forth between the two meanings, without making clear which of the two, or what combination, we have in mind in any given context.

In order to avoid such ambiguity I shall restrict the reference of "democracy" to the first political meaning, oriented on the ideas of "popular rule," "popular sovereignty," "the general will," "the people's will," and so on. For the second meaning I shall use the term, "constitutional government," although this is not altogether satisfactory, and will have to be understood in the sense developed by the discussion.

The democratic principle of popular rule manifested in elections and similar procedures is an example of what Gugliemo Ferrero called "principles of legitimacy"; and Gaetano Mosca, "political formulas." These principles, or formulas are, in Ferrero's language, the Guardians of the City. They may be monarchic, aristocratic, oligarchic or democratic; but whichever they are, each formula is able to offer an explanation for the problem of government that in Chapter I we saw to be rationally insoluble: why some men, these particular men, should rule over others. When a community believes one of them or a combination of several, then a government sanctioned by the formula is "legitimized," and accepted as right and proper.[1]

1. I am here summarizing an earlier discussion in Chapter I.

It is not necessary that the formula be empirically true, that in actual fact rule should be, in the given case, centered in a king or a nobility or a priesthood or in the populace at large. The formulas may in reality be myths.[2] It is only necessary that there should be an accepted belief in them, and an acceptance of known political procedures as embodying them.

If I and the rest of the community believe that the first-born male descendant in a certain family properly rules, or believe in an aristocratic principle whereby the right to rule descends in the biological line of a certain group of families, then I have an adequate explanation why that man or these men should rule over me and the others. Then the City can be internally at peace. So also, if I believe that landed property or command of magic or a majority count of ballots cast according to certain regulations, confers the right to rule.

The democratic principle is the predominant, and very nearly the only professed, political formula of our age. Let us now inquire briefly how there has come about an association, or confusion, between it and the constitutional principle.

2

Between the democratic formula and the constitutional principle there is no logical relation whatever. From the idea of popular sovereignty, of the political primacy of the general will, it is impossible, without introducing additional assumptions, to deduce a doctrine of juridical defense, rule of law, civil rights and due process. If the general will is supreme, if the people are the sole and absolute sovereign, then it is up to them to decide whether the established law, rights and due process are to be cherished, tolerated or liqui-

---

2. As I believe all of them to be. In *The Machiavellians* (New York: John Day, 1943), I have explained my reasons for agreeing with Robert Michels' conclusion that all governments are in fact oligarchies.

dated. The general will has no obligation to conduct itself in a sober constitutional manner if it prefers some other style.

Moreover, the democratic formula and the constitutional principle are empirically as well as logically independent of each other. There have been governments largely or altogether exempt from the democratic formula that have nevertheless been undeniably constitutional: reasonably solicitous (as governments go) of human rights (though not, perhaps, the exact list written into 18th-century constitutions and declarations); anxious to respect the law; and careful to observe due process. Such were the Roman (aristocratic) and the Venetian (oligarchic) republics over several centuries of their respective careers, the British monarchy for a century and a half after 1688, Poland when both independent and feudal, the French monarchy under kings like Louis IX, even (if we judge candidly and comparatively) the Austro-Hungarian empire in its last decades. Conversely, there have been governments, whose claim to being democratic can be denied only by begging the question, under which civil rights, due process and constitutional rule have withered or disappeared: the regime of Pisistratus in Athens, let us cite as an example, of Perón in Argentina, or of Bonaparte as First Consul and, for the early years, as Emperor.

How, then, have so many persons come to associate the ideas of democracy and liberty—liberty, that is, in the constitutional sense of juridical defense, civil rights, due process and the rule of law? Partly it would seem to be from a carry-over of the emotive meaning of these words. "Democracy," "liberty," "rights," "law," all express favorable emotions; we feel them all to be "good"; and therefore—by a usual sort of fallacy—we conclude that there must be some objective connection among them, that they must "go together." Democratic government is good; the citizens' liberty is good; therefore the citizens' liberty is assured under democratic government. The undistributed middle is bridged by the common feeling of approval.

But there is also a historical cause of this association of ideas. Although there is no necessary or general historical connection between the democratic formula and constitutional government, it is nevertheless a fact that in Europe and America from the 17th to the 19th century—and in some nations, most notably England, even earlier—many persons were struggling simultaneously both for more democratic and for more constitutional government. The two aims, often united in past practice, are today mentally confused in retrospect.

During the 17th, 18th and 19th centuries, the merchants, factory owners, lawyers and one-crop commercial farmers—in short, the middle class—were rapidly enlarging their numbers and their role in society. The lawyers, together with the politicians and philosophers, were occupied with the theoretical as well as the practical problems which the rise of the middle class posed. The active members of these middle class groups, confident and ambitious, sought power and status as well as wealth. Their freedom of both economic and political action was hampered, however, by laws, customs and interests linked with the social ascendancy of hereditary monarchs and a hereditary aristocracy.

The monarchs, selected by biological destiny, claimed to rule by Divine Right. This claim means that the monarch asserted his personal supremacy to any law of human origin. The only check on his rule was the will of God, and with respect to secular government the monarch alone could interpret the will of God. From the point of view of his subjects this is equivalent to saying that there is no check—or only an arbitrary, unpredictable and uncontrollable check—on his rule; that the monarch is in the last analysis a despot. Where the rule of a hereditary order of nobles prevails, the political conclusion is the same, except that a divinely appointed (and biologically revealed) corporate body rather than a single individual is in question.

In the struggle to free itself from the fetters on its growth and to get control of the governmental power, it was natural enough and expedient, for the middle class to deny the doctrine of Divine Right[3] as well as any doctrine which holds that the right to rule is biologically inherited. The most effective counter to such doctrines is, or seems to be, the belief in the supremacy of the general will. This belief was adopted, in one or another form, by the middle class ideologists, though without their following it through (except for Rousseau) to its full logical conclusions, and without any expectation that it would ever be carried out fully in practice.

For them, "the people," whose will ought properly to be sovereign, means in particular themselves. "The people" were the burghers, the town-dwellers, the lawyers and business men and commercially minded squires—those who thought of themselves, with much reason, as "the productive classes." Neither the aristocratic idlers nor the vagabonds, peasants and artisans were included among the ranks of "the people." Nevertheless, the attractive power of the myth of the popular will was not exclusive. It found an answer also in the hearts of those who were at first left outside. Many peasants, artisans and vagabonds supported the attack of the middle class on hereditary and, later, on Divine right. It was with their help that the middle class won its fight to tame or destroy the power of aristocrats and kings.

The democratic formula, with its myth of the general will, thus served the political objectives of the middle class, but more was needed in order to solve their social, economic, and moral problems. Tied to the older monarchic and feudal government, was an elaborate network of rules and restrictions that braked the development of a secular, business society appealing not to status but to

3. The actual historical development was more complex than is here suggested. In the 16th century, many middle class ideologists were defending the doctrine of the Divine Right of kings; just as, in practical politics, kings were often in a de facto alliance with middle class forces against the nobility. It was only in subsequent phases (at different rates in different nations) that nearly all the middle class ideologists swung against all versions of hereditary (biological) doctrine in favor of one or another variant of the democratic formula.

negotiated contract. From the standpoint of the middle class, many of these rules and regulations were discriminatory. Moreover, where a king or a bloc of nobles was in fact supreme the middle class had no sufficient protection—no juridical defense—for what it claimed as "rights," or against actions by the sovereign that it felt to be arbitrary and even "unlawful." In the English colonies of North America, in most of which the feudal rules had never become rooted, it was in particular this arbitrariness that became intolerable. The English government, parliament as well as king, went beyond any law that the colonists could recognize. The English interventions in the colonies, as the Declaration of Independence itemizes, came to seem not the rule of law but the arbitrary will of despotic men.

The solution could not be found in the democratic formula. This threatened, if extended all the way to "the mob," a still wilder and more arbitrary despotism. The appeal had to be made to the constitutional principle, and to the practical embodiment of that principle either in older institutions (like the parliaments and certain of the courts) remade, or in newly devised assemblies, courts and magistrates, all of these charged to declare and enforce the law according to the axioms of a charter written or implicit. The supreme executive, whether called "king" as of old or by the new name of "president" or "prime minister," would be constrained by a stable order of law that could not be altered by his will, and to which he like all citizens would be bound.

The account here is oversimplified, but we may accurately say, at a minimum, that from the 17th through the 19th century—and on into the early years of the 20th—many influential persons in Europe and America did in fact seek both democracy and liberty, both a more democratic and a more constitutional basis for government. Though they were on the whole more successful in smashing the old regimes than in building the new in accord with their formal ideals, it is also a fact that in a number of nations there was a considerable advance toward both goals, which reached its combined high point in the great parliamentary-representative governments that flourished in the second half of the 19th century, most fully in the Anglo-Saxon countries but in some measure within other of the west and central European nations.

It is this historical coincidence, the historical fact that the democratic formula and the constitutional principle—democracy and liberty—did for a limited historical period come together in both intention and achievement, that has led many persons to the fallacious conclusion—to which they were already emotionally predisposed—that between the two there is a necessary connection.

XXII

THE LOGIC OF DEMOCRATISM

T HE DEMOCRATIC formula seems simple enough in words: democracy means rule by the people. The trouble comes when we try to carry the formula into operation.

In ultimate ideal, democratic government presumably coincides with the will of each and every member of the community: that is, the community's unanimous opinion. Then and only then do the people, both severally and collectively, unequivocally rule. This ideal may have been realized by some primitive tribes and religious communities, in which the members have so fully shared common customs, rituals and values that in the conduct of their affairs they have thought as one.

However, a rule of unanimity is usually felt to be unrealistic for groups of any size or complexity. Nearly everyone will agree that a decision may normally be considered democratic if it is affirmed by a numerical majority (50% + 1). Plausible as this modification seems, we should remark that it entails a shift in the meaning of the democratic formula. Clearly the non-unanimous decision is not the will of the minority in the same way that it is the will of the majority; and it is not, therefore, without qualification the will of the people. Still, if a less than unanimous decision is to be accepted as democratic, then the rule of a simple (50% + 1) majority would seem necessarily to follow. Under that rule, it at any rate follows that a minority cannot negate a group decision.

Primitive tribes and unanimity apart, a government is said to be a "pure" or "direct" democracy when decisions are made by a majority of an assembly that comprises all the adult citizens. Such were the governments, during part of their careers, of some of the ancient Greek cities, Athens most prominent among them. On local affairs, our New England towns were also, and on some matters still are, pure democracies.

Actually, the purity here is in practice less than 100%. The citizens are only a portion of the whole community. In the Greek cities, minors, women, slaves, criminals, and residents not enrolled in an accredited tribe were excluded from the citizen ranks. There have been similar restrictions, including property qualifications, in the case of the New England town meetings. These or any other exclusions run plainly counter to the democratic imperative.

Again, it is not quite clear what to conclude when there is no majority on an issue—when, that is, there are three or more opinions no one of which receives an affirmative vote equal to a numerical majority of the entire assembly. To accept a plurality of less than 50% may be the only way out, but it means that the conduct of the supposedly democratic government is then being determined by a minority, against the expressed will of a majority. This is an inescapable and fateful paradox in applying the democratic formula. It suggests that the formula runs into difficulty unless the issue can be put as a binary Yes–No choice.

Except in a very small community, the assembly cannot be in continuous enough session to decide all problems. Therefore it must delegate powers, as did the Greek cities, to magistrates and courts, and thus dilute the purity of the democratic procedure.

As the size of the community expands, so that it becomes physically as well as politically impossible for the entire citizenry to meet, the democratic formula must be elaborated by corollary rules of representation. According to the doctrine, the people still govern and the general will remains sovereign. But the people now, for practical convenience, choose an assembly and other institutions and officers that will "represent" their sovereign will. Sovereignty, according to the doctrine, remains in the people; it is still the people ruling. But they rule through and by means of the representative institutions.

The representative relation is a difficult one to explain in any but the most metaphysical terms, the terms preferably of an objective idealism of the type of Hegel's or Fichte's. The representative institution cannot be thought of as merely the delegate or attorney of the people—the relationship that comes most readily to an Anglo-Saxon mind. As Rousseau convincingly proved, sovereignty is the one attribute that by its nature cannot be delegated: to delegate it is equivalent to giving it up. And it is a contradiction in terms to think of particular wills substituting for the general will.

Therefore the representative assembly (or other institution) must be conceived as in some rather mysterious sense "expressing" the general will, as constituting a kind of microcosm of the citizens with respect to their political will. Let us say that there are 150,000 citizens who choose a 150 member assembly on a 1 to 1,000 basis. These 150 are supposed to be a fairly accurate 1 to 1,000 scale map of the citizens' political topography, to distill and concentrate the political essence of the whole community. Thus a 100 to 50 vote in the assembly will be roughly equivalent to a 100,000 to 50,000 vote of the full political community. According to this sort of interpretation—and only thereby—the democratic formula can be preserved intact: the assembly is expressing the general will exactly as if the vote were taken at a meeting of the entire 150,000.[1]

James Wilson, the Philadelphia Convention's most consistent exponent of the democratic formula, anticipated this curious metaphysic of representation. According to the *Debates,* during the session of June 6 Wilson said that he "wished for vigor in the

1. A perfected method of "scientific sampling" of the Gallup Poll type would thus be close to an ideal representative democratic institution (as some of the promoters of such polls are not modest in claiming), short of a central computer fed by an electronic network, through which every citizen could transmit his moment-to-moment political choices.

government, but he wished that vigorous authority to flow immediately from the legitimate source of all authority. The government ought to possess, not only, first, the *force,* but second, the *mind or sense,* of the people at large. The Legislature ought to be made the most exact transcript of the whole society. Representation is made necessary only because it is impossible for the people to act collectively."

In the early phases of modern (post-medieval) history it was the assembly (Cortes, parliament) that appeared as the principal—though still partial—embodiment of the democratic formula. The power of king, nobles and Church was traced to non-democratic roots. However, as the democratic formula gradually or catastrophically supplanted its rivals in both doctrine and practice, all governmental institutions accepted as legitimate came to be thought of as in one way or another expressing the people's will. Not only the assembly, but the executive, courts, bureaucracy, and local political bodies were, or should be, representative democratic institutions.

As plotted under the expanded democratic formula, the governmental structure is imagined as a pyramidal hierarchy. The people—*demos*—constitutes the broad base upon which the whole frame rests. At the apex is the sovereign executive, the doer, the active agent of the people's will. The assembly, courts, electoral colleges, local bodies, situated between apex and base, may be called in general the *intermediary institutions.*

Of course in the earlier stages many of the governmental institutions expressed the democratic formula only inadequately, and with manifest distortions. For a long while the executive and the courts continued to embody leftovers of the doctrines of Divine Right and the right of blood. In court decisions and governmental action, appeal was frequently made to principles of natural law and morality that could point to no sanction from the popular will. The medley of intermediary institutions, new and old, with their differing origins, functions, support, and modes of election, tended to confuse and delay the direct and speedy expression of the general will.

2

Starting with the Jacobins in the French Revolution, those who felt a total commitment to the democratic formula drew out its implicit logic step by step, and pressed continuously to rid society of its non-democratic blemishes. It is this total, monolithic commitment, this obsessive wish to annul the influence of every other political formula or principle, that transforms the philosophy of democracy into the ideology of democratism.

Democratism amounts to a theory of the Divine Right of Demos, of Everyman. In a manner strictly analogous to the sister doctrine of the Divine Right of kings, democratism holds that sovereignty in its entirety, with all of its attributes, adheres solely to the general or popular will. The law is thus the expression of, or rather identical to, the popular will. There is no independent law, human or divine; or, if there is, there is no source other than popular will that can proclaim, interpret and judge it.

Handled with logical rigor, democratism entails the conclusion that all "intermediary institutions," as I have called them, are perversions of the general will. They are split-off sub-wills that break up the general will, levers by which minority wills can distort, oppose and subvert the undifferentiated general will of the sovereign people. They are—again in Rousseau's words, written at the very beginning of his great and fatal treatise—"chains fastened by society upon man born to be free." The prophets of democratism are driven to seek modes for the direct, immediate expression of the general will. "Pure democracy" becomes the political ideal, by which image they strive, in a historical reprise, to transform the giant governments of the modern age.

Whatever its merits as science and morality, there can be no doubt that this ideology of the general will has an extraordinary historical dynamism. If it cannot in truth free the masses, it can certainly help to rouse them; and during the late 18th and the 19th centuries, democratism played its effective part in nearly all social crises. But prior to the 20th century, it remained generally linked, except in the Marxian and anarchist salients, with the belief in rule by law, and with the social ascendancy of the comparatively sober mercantile and industrial middle class. "The old democracy," José Ortega y Gasset wrote in his prophetic masterwork, "was tempered by a generous dose of liberalism [in the European sense of juridical defense and limited government] and of enthusiasm for law. . . . Under the shelter of liberal principles and the rule of law, minorities could live and act. Democracy and law—life in common under the law—were synonymous."[2] In practice, the extreme consequences of the democratist doctrine were not drawn. Monarchs, nobles and priests were dethroned or tamed. But the popular will had to be content with a dispersed embodiment in the rather haphazard structure of intermediary institutions.

Nevertheless, democratism was present as an epochal sentiment, and continued to have a cumulative effect in the sense of its internal logic. Successive refinements sought to squeeze the lumpy political structure more and more tightly inside the strict democratist formula: toward the political shape that Ortega calls, "hyperdemocracy."[3]

In the 18th century, for example, it occurred to hardly anyone that all members of the community properly belonged to the electorate. Diverse qualifications as to age, sex, birth, property, color, belief, occupation, education limited and thereby defined operationally the meaning of the sovereign "people." But no such qualitative restrictions can be ideologically justified. One after another, in accord with the logic of democratist sentiment, they were modified or altogether lifted, in a process that continues into our own day. Women have been entering the electoral fold only within the last two generations. In the United States, restrictions based on skin

2. José Ortega y Gasset, *The Revolt of the Masses* (New York: W. W. Norton, 1932), pp. 17–18.
3. *Ibid., loc. cit.*

color are right now under particular attack. Age is as "arbitrary" as any other specific qualification; and in the 1952 election campaign the successful candidate declared for a lowering of the voting age from twenty-one to eighteen.[4] But why eighteen?

For a while the formula was appeased by the selection of more and more officials, judges as well as executive and legislative magistrates, by direct popular election rather than appointment. In the United States the direct popular primary for choosing party candidates made successful headway in many states, and found impassioned advocates for national adoption. Similarly derived from the internal logic of the formula are the schemes for popular initiative, recall and referendum, and for proportional representation. These have been not only propounded but adopted, on a national scale in many nations and locally in the United States. The conceived effect of popular initiative, recall and referendum is to bypass or short circuit the intermediary institutions, and thus to permit the general will to express itself in a purer, less distorted manner. The result of the referendum is taken to be a more exact equivalent of the vote by the common assembly of all citizens in the mythical ancient city. Along similar lines of reasoning, or rather feeling, proportional voting is proposed as a mechanism for guaranteeing that the elected assembly shall exactly mirror the conformation of the general will.

The omnipresent trend toward political centralization develops from and along the same logical lines. Centralization means the weakening and finally the destruction of whole series of intermediary institutions, especially those originally based on geographical divisions, that clutter the channels of the general will.

Experience has proved, it may be parenthetically remarked, that the actual effect of these measures has been very different from what was advertised by ideologists who affirmed their desirability on the basis of the logic of democratism. The popular election of

---

4. In the states of Georgia and Kentucky the voting age has, in fact, been reduced to 18.

judges serves only to bring the courts under the influence of the same political forces that operate in the election of legislative and executive officials. Centralization does not make the government more responsive to the people, but strengthens the ramparts which divide an intrenched bureaucracy from the people. Under the weight of massive bureaucratic procedures centralization does not even produce the technical efficiency which it was claimed would self-evidently result from the elimination of overlapping agencies. Far from giving a more concrete significance to the popular will, the initiative and referendum, as well as proportional representation, tend to diffuse and break up what genuine popular consensus does exist. Even the extension of the suffrage seems to have had little positive effect in bringing government closer to the real interests and desires of the governed. At the moment its principal influence in the United States seems to be to furnish the premises for government by television.[5]

3

The democratist ideology is, however, not a rational theory but an obsessive sentiment. It has not been shaken by an estimate of actual results, but has persisted undismayed in the course which was set several centuries ago. In our own day we are able to see its final goal and resting place, the end-term of the process which it sets into motion. This end is: *Caesar.*

To those who are content with the verbal surface of politics, it seems paradoxical to say that Caesar is the end and goal of what they understand to be democratic doctrine, that despotism (of a special

5. Totalitarian governments not only have the widest possible extension of suffrage, but change the *right* of suffrage into an enforced *duty* which a subject ignores at his peril—whence results the 99% turnouts for totalitarian elections.

kind) is not the contrary but the fulfillment of democracy.[6] Yet this conclusion is established by analysis as surely as it has been shown in our day through historical experience.

"The people," the people in general and in mass, cannot rule. The obsessive conviction that they can, should and must rule—that the general will can and should prevail—leads to the progressive destruction of the intermediary institutions. The intermediary institutions always appear to be incomplete, distorted and obstructive expressions of the general will. Through them are expressed the interests of classes, local regions, industries, churches, races, or other sub-sections of the people as a whole. Not only do the intermediary institutions appear in this way partial. The appearance is not deceptive: it is a fact that they are expressions of only parts or elements of the general will and interest. It is precisely through these intermediary institutions that the otherwise formless, politically meaningless, abstract entity, *"the people,"* is given structure, and becomes articulate, organized, operationally significant. But this the intermediary institutions accomplish only by making hash of the metaphysical carcass of "the general will."

On the negative side, the rule of Caesar is equivalent to the destruction of the intermediary institutions, or at least of their independence. Positively, Caesar is the symbolic solution—and the only possible solution—for the problem of realizing the general will, that is, for the central problem of the democratist ideology.

How can the general will, in its totality, find a political expression? None of the intermediary institutions—inevitably partial, distorted, fragmentary—and no mere amalgam of the fragments, can satisfy the democratist specifications. But Caesar, unique and integral, drawing on the perennial anthropomorphism that stretches back into prehistory, can become the summary mythic symbol for

6. Our conclusion here restates, of course, the classical theory shared by Plato, Aristotle and Aquinas.

the entire nation, the general will incarnate. The mass of the people and the individual Caesar, with the insulation of the intermediary institutions removed, become like two electric poles. The great spark of the general will seems to leap from the one to charge and illumine the other.

The intermediary institutions are abolished, rendered impotent, or harnessed to Caesar's chariot. Everyone, young and old, black and brown and yellow and white, top dog and bottom mongrel, the lame, the halt, the blind and the feeble-minded, votes—and, moreover, must vote—in elections which are transformed into plebiscites the function of which is to acclaim Caesar. The vote is reduced to the primitive Yes—No, and as Caesar's rule deepens, the outcome circles back also to the primitive unanimity.[7] The assemblies become a sounding board for amplifying Caesar's voice, and a ritual machine for recording his decisions. The courts are made the administrative agents of his will. Caesar: that is to say, Napoleon, Mussolini, Stalin, Hitler, Perón, Franco, Khrushchev. . . .

The advance of Caesar and his popular despotism, however, is not confined to a few localities or exceptional cases. If not literally world-wide, the process seems in our century to be proceeding within most nations that have achieved a certain degree of industrial development, as well as some that have not. The causes of this political transformation must, therefore, lie very deep, and I have elsewhere tried to analyze them as the political phase of the ascendant world social transformation of our time that I have called "the managerial revolution."[8] For Caesar, of course, is a myth and a symbol as well as a person and a fact. Politically he is more creature than creator, and behind his back rise the serried ranks of the managerial bureaucracy.

Because Caesar's advance is often slow, by almost imperceptible steps, it is often more easily observed from without than from

7. The prophetic first of the modern democratist plebiscites, in 1804, named Bonaparte emperor by a vote of 3,572,329 to 2,569.

8. In *The Managerial Revolution* (New York: John Day Company, 1941).

within. Thus a Frenchman like Amaury de Riencourt has traced the American road more sharply than any American writer:

> Familiarity breeds contempt, dulls perception and under-standing. What is familiar has to become unfamiliar and strange before we can truly grasp its full meaning. We must see in the President of the United States not merely the Chief Executive of one of the Western democracies, but one already endowed with powers of truly Caesarian magnitude. . . . Caesarism is . . . the logical outcome of a double current very much in evidence today: the growth of a world empire that cannot be ruled by republican institutions, and the gradual extension of mass democracy, which ends in the destruction of freedom ["liberty," by our definitions] and in the concentration of supreme power in the hands of one man. This is the ominous prospect facing the Western world in the second half of the twentieth century.
>
> The evidence is all around us today, but to see it in its full magnitude we must step back into history and look at the present from a distance. We shall then have a clear perspective of the road on which we have been traveling . . . and a glimpse of the road that lies ahead. We shall then notice that . . . it is our leftist leaders who, whenever they are in power, . . . have quite unconsciously been driving us around in a century-wide circle, back to the point from which our ancestors started when they revolted in the name of liberty against the tyranny of absolute monarchs.[9]

There are other modes of despotism than Caesar's. The most familiar today as throughout history has been the military dictatorship resting on directly applied force. And there are theocratically de-

9. Amaury de Riencourt, *The Coming Caesars* (New York: Coward-McCann, 1957), p. 6.

rived despotisms in which traditional beliefs as well as force sustain the despotic, though sometimes also benevolent, rule of an absolute monarch. But Caesar's is the typical despotism of our time. It is an illusion and a deception to suppose that the great tyrannies of the 20th century are a conspiracy of warriors or a plot of financiers, re-actionary cliques and feudal remnants. Our tyrannies—Nazi, fascist, communist, socialist and welfare statist alike—are popular tyrannies, liberal and leftist tyrannies. They are not the contradiction of de-mocracy, but the logical end-term, the fulfillment, of democracy, if democracy is understood in terms of a monolithic doctrine of the general will.[10]

All the great modern despotisms use the rhetoric of democracy, and appeal for final sanction to the democratic (or more strictly, the democratist) principle. In Caesar's drive for power, he and his deputies call the masses into the streets and into the market place. From hall, camp, courtroom or office, Caesar speaks over the heads of judge and parliament to the masses below and outside. Even Bonaparte, first of our modern Caesars, anointed his imperial crown with the sanction of an overwhelming plebiscite. Our more recent Caesars symbolize the destruction of the intermediary institutions and the triumph of the unformed, undifferentiated mass by colossal outward signs: they dissolve the Constituent Assembly at gun point, march on the Capital, burn the House of Parliament, and recreate the symbolic pure democracy of the ancient city by gathering the masses together in vast squares and arenas.

Many find it a puzzle and mystery that the modern despotisms call themselves "workers' states," "people's states," "people's democracies," "welfare states." To many, this seems a mere propa-ganda trick. They cannot understand how such a deception can be put over, and believe that it can be dissipated at the counter-touch

10. "I have long been convinced," wrote Macaulay in 1857 to the Philadel-phian, Henry S. Randall, "that institutions purely democratic must, sooner or later, destroy liberty or civilization, or both."

of semantic magic. But it is not a mere trick or deception. Caesar's despotism is in truth popular and democratic, and he supports it persuasively by democratic arguments. Those who share his ideological premise find in the end—as President Eisenhower found in his memorable encounter with Soviet Marshal Zhukov—that they are as hard put to meet his logical as his physical attack.[11]

11. President Eisenhower at his July 25, 1957, press conference, reported: "I was very hard put to it when [Zhukov, in a Berlin encounter soon after war's end] insisted that [the communist] system appealed to the idealistic, and we completely to the materialistic, and I had a very tough time trying to defend our position."

XXIII

CONDITIONS
OF LIBERTY

LET US TURN back to the second meaning that for many persons today is also somehow attached to the word "democracy": constitutional government, the rule of law, the preservation of certain rights, among them the right of legitimate minorities not to be crushed by or dissolved into the plebiscitary majority—in short, political liberty.

The essence of the constitutional principle (which will here be taken to cover the various related notions of rule by law, juridical defense and political liberty) is the idea that the law is not, necessarily and ipso facto, what the sovereign does or proclaims, not necessarily identical with the sovereign's will. From the standpoint of the constitutional principle, it is always at least possible that the sovereign in his active or executive capacity is acting unlawfully, counter to the law; just as it is the essence of the contrary despotic principle that the actions of the sovereign are lawful if he says they are, or simply because he does them.

From a doctrinal standpoint the constitutional principle thus entails the belief that there is some standard for the law, other than or in addition to the will and conduct of the sovereign. The separate standard has been variously identified: the Divine Will; natural law; the law of reason; custom or tradition; a charter or constitution, written or unwritten. Granted some such standard, however obscure or disputed may be its content, it becomes logically possible to make a distinction between the law and the conduct of the sovereign, whether the sovereign is a monarch, a special class or the people at large. The sovereign's act is just and lawful when and only when it is in accord with the Tables handed down from on high, the wisdom of the ancients, the conclusions of right reason, the provisions of the charter, or whatever the standard is taken to be. Might—to reduce the theory to its most familiar terms—does not of itself make Right.

A society may believe simultaneously in several such standards, arranged, perhaps, in an order of priority. In the great tradition of Western civilization the Divine Will has been considered the ultimate standard; but the Christian doctrine of the West assimilated also the Stoic belief in a natural law of reason. Except in irrationalist philosophies of the Tertullian—Kierkegaard type, the natural and divine laws have been held to be consistent and for the most part identical in their injunctions. Theistic and rational standards may be further reinforced by custom, ancestral teaching and the terms of an accepted social charter.

2

Logically, then, the constitutional principle presupposes the existence of an autonomous standard, a standard by which the conduct of the sovereign can be critically judged. *Operationally,* however, the standard will have no practical meaning unless there is an institutional check on the sovereign. There may be a general belief, shared by the sovereign, in an objective standard for the law; but if the sovereign in his executive capacity claims an exclusive right to interpret and apply the standard, and if there is no one in a position to gainsay him, then the standard has no operational significance. In practice it is still the case that the law is what the sovereign, specifically the executive, says it is.

The executive—that is, the sovereign in his executive capacity—may under normal circumstances acknowledge the objectivity of the law and his own subordination to it, but keep in reserve a theory of a "dispensing power" (as the English call it) or of "residual powers" or "executive prerogative" (as it is alternatively known in the United States) that may be drawn on for unlimited authority in cases that he defines to be an emergency or crisis. *Salus populi suprema lex,* the executive and his apologists will declare in the professed emergency. Since it is he who has decided both that the safety of the people is at stake and also what must be done to preserve it, the supreme law has been made identical in practice to his subjective will.

The forerunners of Caesar have, indeed, a special fondness for the aphorism, *Salus populi suprema lex,* and they take full advantage of the ambiguity in the meaning of the "*lex*" that figures here. In former times this *lex* was not so commonly confused with the *lex* which is the law that appears in charter and statute, the law that is the guardian of the liberty of the citizens. What the aphorism really meant was that in an extreme and critical emergency, where the safety of the people was literally at stake, then it might become necessary for the executive to violate the law, to act unlawfully. The distinction is much more than a quibble.

In a great emergency, the executive carries out an extraordinary action, not foreseen in the established law. He does so in order to save the people, because he believes that without the extraordinary action the people will be lost. If he and the community recognize that he has acted extra-legally, outside of and even against the law, then the law itself remains supreme, objective, inviolate. The proper law-making bodies can, if they see fit, approve his act ex post facto, and indemnify him for the consequences of its illegality.

But if the sovereign claims that his extraordinary action is itself lawful, becomes lawful by the very fact that he has taken it for the sake of what he alleges to be the people's safety, then we slip from liberty to despotism.

The distinction may be illustrated by a pair of examples.

On April 8, 1952, President Harry Truman directed Secretary of Commerce Sawyer to seize possession of the nation's steel mills. He did so through an executive order (No. 10340) that made no reference to any specific law or statutory authority. He based his action on his own declaration on December 16, 1950 of "a national emergency," his own finding that a threatened steel strike "would immediately jeopardize and imperil our national defense," and his own assertion of a general—undefined—"authority vested in me by the Constitution and laws of the United States, and as President of the United States and Commander in Chief of the armed forces." Several statutes governing the seizure of property were on the books, but none of them authorized seizure in the case of labor disputes. In fact, when passing the Taft-Hartley Act Congress had formally rejected labor disputes as a ground for seizure. In April, 1952, moreover, Congress was in session, and could have been asked by the President for any additional statutory authority that he considered necessary for the public safety. The executive did not, however, make such a request or demand of Congress. Essentially, the executive rested his case on the prerogative and residual powers that derive from the *Salus populi* doctrine.

This motivation, with its implied denial of the constitutional principle, expressed the substance of democratic despotism. The sovereign executive claims to embody the will and interest of the people, bypassing any intermediary institution. The executive decides whether an emergency exists. If he so decides, he acts as he sees fit to solve the emergency. Such an action so taken becomes lawful, without regard to any previously existing law. It follows, therefore, that the executive can legally do whatever he decides to do, provided he states his decision in a proper formula.

Let us consider the steel seizure against the background of an 18th-century incident.[1]

Our Founding Fathers and their British and European forebears of course recognized that sudden emergencies affecting the public

1. For an acquaintance with this incident I am indebted to Lucius Wilmerding. Mr. Wilmerding made reference to it in an essay that will be found in *Political Science Quarterly,* Vol. LXVII, No. 3, September 1952 (p. 332, note).

safety did arise in the course of events, that some of these would not be foreseen in law or constitution, and that the executive might feel impelled to act to solve them in a manner outside of or even counter to the law. They granted also that such action might be morally and politically justified. But these men, for whom liberty was the highest political value, insisted that such action, whether or not worthy of approbation, was illegal, was not the law. The executive or one of his officers was perhaps heroic to act so, but his action was at his own risk and peril. He did not change the law by acting as he deemed necessary. He remained formally subject to all the fines and punishment that the law provided. The proper law-making body—parliament or assembly or Congress—had to indemnify him against such penalties by formal act, before he could be regarded as legally purged.

Sophisticated and perhaps too refined as the distinction here may seem, it is not really unfamiliar to common sense. In driving an automobile, for example, emergencies arise from time to time that require me to swerve to the left side of the road. I assume that I am humanly justified in doing so. If it came under review, I would expect the authorities to excuse my action, provided that I could prove to them that the emergency was in fact such as to have required the deviation. But I would not claim that the emergency had changed the law of the road, which proclaims that the only legal side for driving is the right side. I would recognize, if I thought about it, that I had broken the law. In this way, both the supremacy of the law and the partly unforeseeable claims of the public weal are preserved. Similarly, a military commander, in order to save his army, often acts knowingly outside the law. Later the law-making body, if it finds his action to have been necessary to the performance of his military duty, will step in to indemnify him for any damages and suits which he may legally suffer as a consequence of his admittedly unlawful acts.

The 18th-century incident took place in England. In 1766 a statute was in effect by which the government was prohibited from placing an embargo on the export of wheat. A bad harvest had brought near-famine conditions. Because of market relations, part of the scarce home wheat began to be exported. Serious famine immediately threatened. Lord Chatham's government, disregarding the statute, placed an embargo on any further export.

It may be noted that the circumstances by which this incident differed from the steel seizure case of 1952 would seem to be on the side of executive justification. Parliament was not in session, and it took forty days for Parliament to be convened. It was universally admitted that a national emergency did in fact exist, that it could be solved only by an embargo, and that the embargo had to be imposed at once to be effective.

When Parliament did subsequently meet, Chatham's government took the same position as President Truman's administration in the steel seizure. Chatham's spokesmen claimed that the embargo was legal, and based this claim on "the dispensing power." But Parliament, though not questioning the practical necessity for the government's action, rejected both the claim and the argument. Parliament refused to admit a dispensing power, and insisted on passing an Act of Indemnity, even though the Ministry neither asked for nor wished to accept indemnity. In the preamble to the Act, the illegality of the embargo was explicitly noted.

Rising in the House of Lords, Lord Temple spoke for Parliament:

... We are, as it were, surprised into a debate upon the dispensing power, and what astonished me still more, we are got, at least some of us, into a vindication and defense of it—a thing I had long thought so odious in its very name, but so settled in the notions of it, and so exploded in theory as well as practice, that nobody ever thought of it, but to hate it, and to thank God it was utterly exterminated out of the pure solar system of the English government, and English liberty.

One noble lord has told us, he rose in this debate not as a patron of liberty, in the modern phrase, as he was pleased to call it, but as a patron of law. Modern phrase did the noble lord say? I hope it will never cease to be a modern phrase; though it is an ancient, and has in all countries been a glorious title. Our ancestors were patrons of liberty at the cost of their lives; but they secured our liberty by protecting the law against a dispensing power, which they resisted unto blood. . . .

One of the ministers had observed satirically that if the government's action had been tyranny, it was only a forty days' tyranny at worst, because by then Parliament was back in session. Lord Temple continued: "Forty days tyranny! my lords; tyranny is a harsh sound. I detest the very word, because I hate the thing. . . . A noble lord has said, as it became him to say, forty hours, nay forty minutes tyranny is more than Englishmen will bear."

In 1952 as in 1766 the law, and thus the constitutional principle, were in the end vindicated. Although Harry Truman reasoned like Caesar, he was one of Caesar's precursors, not Caesar. Although Congress remained collectively silent, neither accepting nor rejecting the seizure by any formal legislative act, the Supreme Court of that day, by a vote of six to three, rejected the executive's claims and upheld an injunction that nullified the executive's action. The clarity of the 18th century was not to be found, however, in the Court's reasoning, which was spread into six technically concurring but philosophically so far from consistent opinions that Messrs. Kelly and Harbison are constrained to remark in scholarly understatement: "How decisive and far-reaching was the check to emergency executive power, however, is a matter of some uncertainty."[2] This confusion is a measure of the distance that the nation has advanced along Caesar's road.

4

In both 1766 and 1952 the constitutional principle was upheld in practice only because there was an institutional check on the exec-

2. Alfred H. Kelly & Winfred A. Harbison, *op. cit.,* p. 888.

utive, able to contest the executive's claim to act with the full sovereignty of the nation. There were what we have called "intermediary institutions" between the executive—the sovereign in his active, dynamic capacity—and the nation. Such intermediaries have been historically various: councils of elders or of priests; local political subdivisions arranged on a federal plan; two or several chambers within the assembly; independent courts; a tribunitiate; an oligarchic or aristocratic "estate." The forms may be thus variable within wide limits, but some intermediaries, with at least a certain amount of autonomy, there must be if the constitutional principle is to survive.

Given the existence of the intermediaries, the executive's declaration of the law can be challenged, whatever the ultimate source of the law is believed to be—God, nature, reason, custom, the general will, or mere resolve expressed in a charter. An operational meaning is given to the contention that an act of the monarch, President, Duce or Vozhd is "illegal," "unjust": the citizens so contending can appeal to an assembly, courts, council or tribunes that are not themselves mere creatures of the executive. The subjects—become citizens because of this very fact—thus have means, some means at least, of juridical defense against arbitrary and apodictic decree, some measure of due process, of protection of even those rights and interests that are currently inconvenient in the executive's eye.

The Founding Fathers and the political genius of the American nation were unclear about the doctrine but very clear about the operation. By the American charter, supplemented by traditional practice, the political structure was spread into the unsymmetrical network of diffused and divided powers, the differing procedures of selection, the concurrent local and central jurisdictions, the appointed as well as elected judges, the two-chambered central assembly with its local-district base and its stiff rules, by the electoral college and the unique system of two amalgam parties stubbornly resistant to ideological fusion—by all this maze of political ramparts the nation is provided with juridical defense in depth. The constitutional principle is so intricately protected that it is often upheld in reverse, even by those seeking to attack it.

The doctrine accompanying this operational triumph has been confused, or mixed. The Fathers themselves took for granted that there was a pre-existing standard of law and justice. Most of them traced this back to the Divine Will; and all of them, in keeping with 18th-century enlightenment, felt that it was also established by the natural law of reason and the consensus of the responsible members of the community—the rich, well-born and able. The Declaration of Independence sought formal justification, in keeping with these philosophic convictions, in "the Laws of Nature and of Nature's God." But the Constitution makes no overt appeal to any standard beyond itself. In the American tradition, by one of those magical acts of historical creation on which the first chapter of this book reflected, "the Constitution" itself, given meaning not only by its own words but by the whole organic course of traditional practice and belief, becomes the objective standard and thus the doctrinal bulwark of liberty.

At Philadelphia the Fathers repudiated—though not without regrets on the part of some of them—both the monarchic and the aristocratic principles of legitimacy. No explicit appeal was made to any legitimizing principle except the democratic; and under the circumstances of the recent revolt from the English monarchy, no other could very well have been openly attempted. In its preamble, the Constitution announces itself—according to the democratic formula—as issuing from "We, the people." In defending the majority position that ratification must be referred to special elected conventions instead of to the existing state legislatures, George Mason declared:

> He considered a reference of the plan to the authority of the people, as one of the most important and essential of the Resolutions. The Legislatures have no power to ratify it. They are the mere creatures of the State Constitutions, and cannot be

greater than their creators. And he knew of no power in any
of the Constitutions . . . that could be competent to this object. Whither, then, must we resort? To the people, with
whom all power remains that has not been given up in the
constitutions derived from them. It was of great moment, he
observed, that this doctrine should be cherished, as the basis of
free[3] government.

The logical situation was thus curious. From an abstract, Platonic
point of view the Fathers, like their Constitution, were manifestly
inconsistent. They asserted the democratic formula and denied it:
used it as an indispensable part of the foundation of the new government; but refused to erect the whole structure in monolithic
conformity to its mechanical imperatives. They added blocks from a
different mold entirely, non-democratic or even anti-democratic;
and they counterbalanced, masked, checked and limited the thrust
of the democratic elements.

But this abstract inconsistency is in reality the sign, merely, that
the Fathers were not ideologists or fanatics. In the well-known passage of *Federalist* No. 71, Hamilton wrote with that moderating
good sense that the Fathers so commonly displayed: "The republican principle demands that the deliberate sense of the community
should govern the conduct of those to whom they intrust the management of their affairs; but it does not require an unqualified com-
plaisance to every sudden breeze of passion, or to every transient
impulse which the people may receive from the arts of men, who
flatter their prejudices to betray their interests." In their political
philosophy there was an honorable place for democracy (though
they preferred, as here Hamilton, to call it "republicanism"), but
none for democratism. They did not believe that the rich and varied life of a human society should be wholly squeezed into the nar-

---

3. This use of "free" carries the ambiguity to which reference was made in
Chapter XXI.

row cylinder of a formula interpreted with a doctrinaire, obsessive rigidity. And they were not prepared to sacrifice liberty to any rhetoric, no matter how beguiling.

The diffusion and limiting of power have been of the essence, not a dispensable decoration, of the American system of government. The reasonable, humane and fruitful inconsistencies of the Founding Fathers prove how entirely they would have agreed with the conclusion reached by Gaetano Mosca, which we have already had occasion to note:

> The absolute preponderance of a single political force, the predominance of any over-simplified concept in the organization of the state, the strictly logical application of any single principle in all public law are the essential elements in any type of despotism, whether it be a despotism based upon divine right or a despotism based ostensibly on popular sovereignty; for they enable anyone who is in power to exploit the advantages of a superior position more thoroughly for the benefit of his own interests and passions. When the leaders of the governing class are the exclusive interpreters of the will of God or of the will of the people and exercise sovereignty in the name of those abstractions in societies that are deeply imbued with religious beliefs or with democratic fanaticism, and when no other organized social forces exist apart from those which represent the principle on which sovereignty over the nation is based, then there can be no resistance, no effective control, to restrain a natural tendency in those who stand at the head of the social order to abuse their power.[4]

4. Gaetano Mosca, *op. cit.*, p. 134.

XXIV

WHAT IS A
MAJORITY?

S UPPOSE THAT we accept the democratic formula, its representative corollary, the simple majority (50% + 1) rule, and some
working definition of who belongs to the electoral community.[1] There still remain many slips between doctrine and operation.

For example, just how do we calculate the majority? This seems
arithmetically self-evident, but if we translate the arithmetic into
political procedures we find that there is no single or easy answer
to the question. The trouble arises over the choice of parameters for
the calculation: that is, in terms of political procedures, the choice of
the district or grouping within which the votes will be taken.

One solution is to take the largest possible district, the complete
unit to which the given sovereignty extends. In the case of national
sovereignty, this district is the entire nation,[2] and it would follow
that the nation's basic political decisions (in particular, the choice of
chief magistrates) should be put to a direct vote or plebiscite of the

---

1. The arbitrariness of such definitions is well illustrated by the provision in Article I, Section 2 of the Constitution, which apportions representatives according to a numeration in which a slave counts as $\frac{3}{5}$ of a unit and non-taxed
Indians zero, with the further implicit understanding that on the basis of state
laws neither will be actual voters.
2. In theory, the "ideal democracy" would be world-wide (or even universe-
wide, if there are intelligent beings on other planets), with the entire world
taken as the basic electoral district. We thus find that those persons who have a
plebiscitary approach to *national* government are the most likely recruits to the
goal of "democratic *world* government" based on "the suffrage of mankind."

entire national electorate. Such a plebiscite method may be called "direct"; and a majority yielded by it, a "first level," "direct," or (in John C. Calhoun's terminology) "numerical" majority.

This solution seems to be arithmetically the most "natural," and the ideology of democratism favors it in both theory and practice. If strictly adhered to, it imposes rather narrow limits on the adaptability of the electoral process, which is the prime ritual of a government that may properly be called democratic. A direct, all-national vote in which the electorate, treated as a single political entity, is not subdivided except for technical purposes of counting the result, tends to become a binary plebiscite: *For* or *Against* a particular leader, slate or issue. *Yes* or *No.*

An all-national vote can also be conducted, as has been the case from time to time in a few European nations, according to the rules of "pure" proportional representation. This, however, results in such a fractionalizing of the political structure that the government is no longer able to function effectively. It collapses altogether or gives way to a plebiscitary system—as happened in Germany in the transition from the proportionally representative Weimar republic to plebiscitary Nazism, and seems to be happening in France (as I write) with the interment of the Fourth Republic.

In both logic and history a binary plebiscite is the ideal form of the direct, all-national election. The entire national electorate is confronted with a single, simple and apparently unambiguous question: do you sanction Bonaparte's being named Emperor? Hitler's becoming Chancellor of the Reich? this official slate's assuming office? our two countries (Egypt and Syria, let us say) joining into one? In mature plebiscites conducted under the auspices of democratism, the nominal choice is often illusory, of course. The result approaches a foreseen unanimity. At earlier stages in the democratist–Caesarist development, the voters may be free to choose between two names (or two slates) on the all-national ballot—though often, as in Mexico or Portugal in recent decades, the extra names will have been added primarily for decorative effect.

When there are two (or more) names, moreover, the real meaning of the plebiscite is almost always *For* or *Against* one particular name: the charismatic name of Caesar or Caesar's forerunner.[3]

Of course all nations that we call democratic have some procedure for "consulting the national electorate." Under non-plebiscitary rules, however, this is not done by an undiluted, direct, all-national vote. Such a vote may be approximated in various ways—as it is in a parliamentary "general election" or in the American election of the President—but the differences have a real as well as symptomatic political import. Under the American system, we had an earlier occasion to recall, there has never been a direct, all-national vote for any magistrate or issue, not even on adoption of the Constitution.

2

There is a second method, or set of methods, for calculating the majority. Instead of taking the entire nation as our electoral unit and establishing directly, through our voting process, a national majority and minority, we can subdivide the nation in any of a number of ways, and determine the majority and minority within each subdivision. We may then define a national majority, which can validate national political decisions, as consisting not of the directly ascertained popular majority, but of a majority of the subdivision majorities. This second kind of majority may be called "indirect," "second level,"[4] or (again in Calhoun's terminology) "concur-

3. In France, the September 28, 1958, plebiscite was nominally on the question of the new constitution. In political reality, even thus disguised, the plebiscite was *For* or *Against* the charismatic name of Charles de Gaulle.

4. There could be and in some systems actually are still higher levels. Indeed, a prime minister elected by a cabinet that is elected by an assembly elected by local districts is a "fourth level" magistrate—if the process is genuine, and not merely a nominal form in which the initial voters have really elected a chief who has predetermined his assembly majority and who selects his own ministers.

rent."[5] It is usually calculated according to the vote of persons—such as the members of a parliament or electoral college—who have themselves been named as representatives by first level majorities.

Suppose that in an election there were 900 votes. According to the first (plebiscitary) solution, the majority would be determined by a vote of the entire 900 as a unit; and 451-449 would give the decision. But the 900 might be subdivided into three groups—A, B and C—of 300 voters each. The initial vote could then be taken within each separately, and the overall majority would now be constituted by any two of the groups against one.

Arithmetically the consequences are by no means identical, and in fact can in some circumstances be contradictory. Suppose that the vote is for chief magistrate, and that X and Y are the candidates. If the outcome were 200X to 100Y in group A; 140X to 160Y in group B; and 130X to 170Y in group C; then X has won a direct majority of 470 to 430, but has lost the indirect majority, one group to two. This is the arithmetic possibility that resulted in the effective choice, by a majority of the second level Electoral College, of two United States Presidents—Rutherford B. Hayes and Benjamin Harrison—whose opponents had received direct majorities, and one other—Abraham Lincoln—who, though having a popular plurality in 1860, was in a direct minority as against his three rivals.

The Electoral College in the American system is not, of course, though it was originally intended to be, a genuinely "representative" body. It is merely an accounting device which registers on a state-by-state basis the summation of the results of the separate state plebiscites on the choice of President and Vice President.[6] Nevertheless, even this accounting procedure, since it operates not with

5. Strictly, Calhoun's "concurrent majority" means the *unanimous* consensus of the majorities of the subdivisions. However, I shall use his terms in the wider sense here indicated.
6. Under the prevailing rules, the two offices are inseparably linked, so that only a single choice is involved.

the national vote directly, but with the subdivisions (the states) taken as discrete units, dilutes the plebiscitary character of the presidential choice. Not only does it occasionally name a candidate who has lost in the direct plebiscite; it always yields a result in the Electoral College vote that is proportionally very different from that in the direct vote. Moreover, the state-by-state subdivision of the presidential vote and the fact that the presidential campaign coincides with state-based campaigns for local and congressional offices, permit local pressures to exert more influence than they could wield if there were a single nation-wide presidential ballot. It is for such reasons that consistent democratists have long advocated replacement of the Electoral College method for choosing the President by a direct nation-wide popular vote, or plebiscite.[7]

Second level representative institutions, and very particularly the American Congress, diverge much more sharply from the direct plebiscite. Most members of the House of Representatives are chosen by a majority (or plurality) of a relatively small subdivision, of which the candidate must be a resident. Because of gerrymandering, partial disenfranchisement and other irregularities in many regions, the electoral units vary considerably in population as well as area.

For the selection of Senators, the individual states are the subdivisions, with populations ranging from 150,000 to 15,000,000. Thus the sheer arithmetic of the arrangement means that there is no close correspondence between voting ratios in Congress and the presumptive ratios in the electorate at large, even assuming that each member of Congress voted in accord with the majority opinion in his constituency—an assumption which is difficult to verify in any specific case. Arithmetically speaking, measures can pass Congress

7. Democratists *tend*, ideologically, toward a presidential plebiscite, but some of them draw back, because of certain practical advantages that the Electoral College method is presumed to give them in pursuit of certain democratist objectives: in particular, because of the key role of New York state in the Electoral College ballot, and the key role of democratist-minded minorities in controlling New York state politics.

or be defeated through the decision of members representing a minority of the voters. Measures can be decided, in fact, by a Senate majority which formally represents only a very small minority of the national electorate.[8]

At this second (or higher) level of the representative democratic process, where each of the political actors rests ultimately on the majority of the voters of a subdistrict at the first level, the political aim may not be satisfied by reaching a simple arithmetic majority. Even if not reflected by the formal vote in which the process must end according to the rules of the democratic formula, the deeper effort may be to get as close as possible to a voluntary agreement or consensus rather than a majority, to seek a political result that will be reasonably satisfactory to as many as possible, even all, of the representatives of the first level majorities. This is not by any means the same as the near-unanimous outcome of a direct plebiscite. It is a subtler undertaking in which both majorities and minorities play a continuing role, to establish the "concurrent majority":

> There are two different modes in which the sense of the community may be taken: one, simply by the right of suffrage, unaided; the other, by the right through a proper organism. Each collects the sense of the majority. But one regards numbers only and considers the whole community as a unit having but one common interest throughout, and collects the sense of the greater number of the whole as that of the community. The other, on the contrary, regards interests as well as numbers—considering the community as made up of different and conflicting interests, as far as the action of the government is concerned—and takes the sense of each through its majority or appropriate organ, and the united sense of all as the sense of

8. Theoretically as small as one-sixth, if the Senators from the 25 smallest states made up this majority; and much less (as small as one-twentieth) if the quorum were at the permissible minimum of 50 Senators.

the entire community. The former of these I shall call the numerical or absolute majority, and the latter, the concurrent or constitutional majority. I call it the constitutional majority because it is an essential element in every constitutional government, be its form what it may.[9]

Even a bare arithmetic analysis shows the ambiguity in the notion of the "democratic majority," not to mention the dizzying and indeed insoluble problem of a "democratic plurality." A direct majority of the total sovereign political unit is not mathematically identical in meaning with an indirect majority based on a summation of the majority votes of sub-units. In reaching political conclusions, the two can yield not merely different but altogether contrary results. However, this mathematical, quantitative disparity is of secondary importance for political analysis. Politically and philosophically, as this quotation from Calhoun suggests, the difference is qualitative, and momentous.

9. John C. Calhoun, *A Disquisition on Government,* etc., edited by C. Gordon Post (New York: Liberal Arts Press, 1953), pp. 22–3. What Calhoun here calls a numerical majority is what we have designated a direct, first level or plebiscitary majority. His assertion that constitutional government presupposes a concurrent majority coincides with our conclusion that constitutional government (government by law) cannot exist without intermediary institutions.

XXV

LEADER OF THE MASSES, ASSEMBLY OF THE PEOPLE

WHEN WE believe that a specified political group can make valid political decisions by taking a poll among its members, we are implicitly assuming that with respect to political decisions all the individuals belonging to the group are qualitatively identical, and thus equal; differing only quantitatively, only as one numerical unit from another. Without this assumption, in fact, we could not add up the vote. You cannot add two oranges plus three apples, two monkeys plus three horses, or two carpenters plus three merchants. Only like units can be added together: two fruits (unspecified) plus three fruits; two animals plus three animals; and two voters (qualities unspecified) plus three (also qualitatively unspecified) voters. In 18th-century doctrine this is the assumption referred to by the term, "political equality," and the sentence, "All men are created [politically] equal."

Considered philosophically, the assumption of qualitative political identity is very radical indeed. When it is carried out all the way to its logical limit, as in the democratist drive toward an unlimited franchise, it implies that no qualitative differences[1] whatever among human beings—not knowledge, sex, education, wealth, experience,

---

1. Except, perhaps, the negative criteria of undue youth, obvious insanity and major criminal record; though these too, as we have noted, are not easy to defend objectively on democratist grounds. It may be mentioned in passing that this democratist assumption of political equality is leading to some really weird election procedures in the new Afro-Asian democracies.

religion, race, talents, color, character, reputation, intelligence—
have any relevant bearing on their ability and right to make fundamental political choices. What this means, logically, is that *homo
politicus,* "political man," who is the ultimate actor in the political
process as conceived by democratist doctrine, is the Common Denominator of all the actual, living, real individuals belonging to the
group. Let us call him "political CD."

Political CD is, of course, a statistic, not a real human being. Real
human beings are complex individuals, defined in their existential
concreteness by the host of specific qualities, experiences, hopes,
occupations, possessions, beliefs and what not, that make each
human being an individual, qualitatively different in some and often
considerable degree from any and from every other human being.

No political process can, true enough, take into account the specific individuality of every human being. (To believe so is the
utopian illusion of anarchism.) But the distortion brought about by
the rule of political equality is not too gross when the group is moderate in size and when most individuals within it are fairly homogeneous with respect to those attributes that have most relevance to
political decisions: religious faith, for example, morality, general culture, deep taboos, beliefs about what is important and desirable. A
true community then exists, and CD still retains as a qualitative filling the common fund of interests, beliefs, outlook and ideals. In
1800 the enfranchised voters of the United States, like those of England, constituted communities of this kind.

When the group expands into scores and even hundreds of millions of individuals, and when at the same time the organic cultural
homogeneity breaks down into an amalgam of eclectic heterogene-
ity fused by mechanical regimentation, then political CD evolves
into an ever emptier statistical abstraction. He wants security, material comfort, sense gratification and easy amusement; but beyond
that, CD is and must be a cipher: neither Catholic nor Protestant
nor Jew nor pagan nor atheist; neither man nor woman; neither
black nor white nor yellow; neither rich nor poor, saint or libertine,

learned or simple, tax payer or pauper, farmer or artisan or banker, teacher or taught, patriot or subverter.

Political CD has become, in short, *the mass-man;* the people have become "the masses," or more precisely, "the mass." *Democratism-Caesarism-the masses:* all three are elements of the same political equation.

The advance of the masses to the front of the 20th-century political stage has been studied by many historians and sociologists. It was earliest remarked and particularly stressed by those writers holding some sort of cyclical or "morphological" theory of history.[2] In their description of the nature, role and import of the masses, there is general agreement among analysts otherwise so diverse as Oswald Spengler, Georges Sorel, Vilfredo Pareto, Max Weber, Arnold Toynbee, Pitirim Sorokin, José Ortega y Gasset.

> The multitude has suddenly become visible. . . . Before, if it existed, it passed unnoticed, occupying the background of the social stage: now it has advanced to the footlights. . . .
>
> In those groups which are characterized by not being multitude and mass, the effective coincidence of their members is based on some desire, idea, or ideal, which of itself excludes the great number. . . . The concept of the multitude is quantitative and visual. . . . The mass is the assemblage of persons not specially qualified. By masses, then, is not to be understood, solely or mainly, "the working masses." The mass is the average man. In this way what was mere quantity—the multitude—is converted into a qualitative determination: it becomes the common social quality, man as undifferentiated from other men, but as repeating himself in a generic type.[3]

2. Probably because the *democratism-Caesarism-the masses* equation has been manifested at other periods of history, notably and most familiarly in the Roman Empire, which is the theoretical "model" for most Western historians.

3. José Ortega y Gasset, *op. cit.,* pp. 13–14.

The masses, anonymous and undifferentiated by definition, are the natural electorate for the vast binary plebiscites into which the prevailing democratist ideology of our age tends to transform the democratic process. Mass-man can make no detailed qualitative distinctions, but like the transistors of a huge electronic computer, he can register the simple 0 or 1, *Yes* or *No.* And for the masses, a representative assembly whose members meet to discuss, inquire, debate, compromise and bargain, is an incompatible, even impossible, political device. The political function of an assembly issuing from the masses can only be—like Hitler's Reichstag or the Supreme Soviet—to affirm with an unmixed voice the general mass will. The quintessential political expression of the masses must be a single symbolic individual, the charismatic leader linked by direct magic to the mass: Caesar, fronting for the bureaucrats of the managerial state, is the end phase of the process, though as the end nears, the masses will seek to transmute even a haberdasher into a mask of Caesar.

When we take the entirety of a large nation or empire—or even, in projection, the world—as our election district, then the election tends to become a plebiscite, and the electorate reduced to the political Common Denominator, to "the masses." But of course it is not the arithmetic of the electoral process that creates the masses. It is, on the whole, the other way around. Through the operation of many historical causes, ranging from the unintended effects of industrialization to the deliberate tactics of ideologues and demagogues, the masses are created, and come forward. The undivided, maximum-scale plebiscite is then found to be the most appropriate form for the masses' political performance.

2

Real human beings in their existential setting are not statistical abstractions, not political Common Denominators. They make a living by this or that kind of work, occupy house or palace or apartment or shanty, dwell in mountain or plain or city, belong to this Church or that, like change or stability, seek glory or wealth or peace or pleasure. Each in his specificity is different from every other, but with respect to the problems, ends and interests that are most frequently at stake in the political process, they tend to fall into rough groupings which, though variable and overlapping, form traceable patterns. As Madison summarized during the debate over the democratic formula that took place June 6 at the Philadelphia Convention: "All civilized societies would be divided into different sects, facts, and interests, as they happened to consist of rich and poor, debtors and creditors, the landed, the manufacturing, the commercial interests, the inhabitants of this district or that district, the followers of this political leader or that political leader, the disciples of this religious sect or that religious sect."

Let us call the citizens of a nation as thus defined in the living context of their major activities and attitudes, "the people," thus distinguishing "the people" from "the masses," "citizen" from "mass-man," who cannot be other than a "subject." It is possible that the same individuals, comprising the population of a given nation, should function in one political perspective as "the masses," and in another as "the people." However, in a large, cosmopolitan and industrial nation, regimented by economic and political mechanics, and imbued with egalitarian and democratist ideology, their political reality as "the masses" tends to become dominant over, or to supplant altogether, their reality as "the people."

The masses can be thought of as a homogeneous, uniform substance like a loosely set gelatin without inner structure, that sways and bends under pressure, and assumes the shape dictated by the external system of forces playing on it. "The people" are heterogeneous, complex in geometry, intricately articulated, formed and yet dynamic, adapting to external forces in part through an inner determination: in short, possessing the varied unity of a living organism, not the merely material sameness of "the masses."

If we reject democratist ideology, it becomes evident that the people, in contrast to the masses, cannot be represented by or "embodied" in a single leader. Granted the doctrine of Divine Right or some similar monarchic assumption, a single leader might *rule* the people, but then it would be not as their but as God's representative. Under a republican formula a single person might be named—by a general popular vote, direct or indirect—as the ceremonial "head of state," symbolizing the nation's continuity and tradition; and this is done in some nations. But a head of state is not, like the head of government, an active political magistrate.

The people cannot be represented by or embodied in a single leader precisely because of the people's diversity. Their representation, if it is to be more than a masquerade, must have some sort of correspondence to their diversity. The political will of the people must therefore be projected through a multiplicity of representatives and of representative institutions, both formal and informal. Only in this way can the irreducible variety of the people's interests, activities and aspirations find political expression. The undifferentiated masses, by a plebiscite, give a "mandate" to the leader to act as their unrestricted proxy. The minorities—just by being minorities—have lost their political rights. For the duration of the mandate, minorities do not exist politically. The people, in contrast, by many kinds of election for many kinds of officer and assembly, impose on their magistrates the duty of representing the political interests of intertangled, concurrent majorities that are also, in their relation to the whole, minorities.

3

Judged by the intentions of the Fathers, the most surprising development of the American political system has been the emergence of the Presidency as the primary democratist institution. The Fathers expected the democratist impulse (which they called "democratic")

376 CONGRESS AND THE AMERICAN TRADITION

to operate through Congress, in particular through the House of Representatives; and so, of course, it has in part done. Most of the Fathers feared "the turbulence and follies" of the democratic "mob," and felt "that some check therefore was to be sought for, against this tendency of our government."[4] "The people immediately," in Roger Sherman's opinion, "should have as little to do as may be about the government." The Presidency, like the Senate and the courts, would serve not to express but to check and restrain the democratist general will that would find some outlet in the House. The Electoral College, functioning as a senior council of responsible citizens—of the rich, well-born and able—would protect the choice of President from the harsh direct clamor of demos.

A number of the Fathers feared and some predicted that the President would become a despot (or "monarch," as they put it), but it did not occur to them that he might develop into a *democratic* despot. He might, they thought, usurp despotic power as a military dictator (under his grant as Commander in Chief), by manipulating appointments, by securing the succession to his descendants, or in some other way violating the democratic principle: not by fulfilling it.

Today nearly every student would agree with Professor Rossiter's gloss:

Henry Jones Ford, in his perceptive *Rise and Growth of American Politics* (1898), was the first to call attention pointedly to the one giant force that has done most to elevate the Presidency to power and glory: the rise of American democracy. Most men who feared the proposed Presidency in 1787 were prisoners of the inherited Whig assumption that legislative power was essentially popular and executive power essentially monarchical in nature. The notion that a democratic President might be pitted against an oligarchical legislature occurred to few at the time. . . . Since the days of Andrew Jackson the

4. Edmund Randolph, *Debates,* May 31.

Presidency has been generally recognized as a highly democratic office. It depends directly on the people for much of its
power and prestige. . . . American democracy finds in the
President its single most useful instrument. Small wonder,
then, that he stands as high as he does in the mythology and
expectations of the American people.[5]

Actually it was not Henry Jones Ford but the Presidents themselves who were the first to call attention to the democratic—and
democratist—potential of the presidential office. The whole succeeding development is foreshadowed in the presidential messages of
Andrew Jackson. "We are *one people*," he proclaimed with his own
italics in 1832, "in the choice of President and Vice-President." Calling in his first annual message to Congress for the replacement of the
Electoral College by a direct presidential plebiscite, Jackson stated the
classic democratist case against intermediary institutions:

To the people belongs the right of electing their Chief Magistrate; it was never designed that their choice should in any
case be defeated, either by the intervention of electoral colleges or by the agency confided, under certain contingencies,
to the House of Representatives. Experience proves that in
proportion as agents to execute the will of the people are multiplied there is danger of their wishes being frustrated. Some
may be unfaithful; all are liable to err. So far, therefore, as the
people can with convenience speak, it is safer for them to express their own will. . . .

In this as in all other matters of public concern policy requires that as few impediments as possible should exist to the
free operation of the public will. . . .

5. Clinton Rossiter, *op. cit.*, pp. 66–67. We may translate the above passage into
our terminology by reading "democratism" for "democracy," and "masses" for
"people."

> I would therefore recommend such an amendment of the
> Constitution as may remove all intermediary agency in the
> election of the President and Vice-President.

The circumstances of his time as well as his own States' Rights
predilections prevented Jackson from drawing out the practical consequences of his theory of the Presidency. A brief comment of Professor Corwin's shows how close this theory went toward three of
the key ideas of democratism and potential Caesarism: the bypassing
of the intermediary institutions; the interpretation of the executive
as the expression or embodiment (rather than as the mere representative) of the citizens; the insistence that the chief executive, and
only he, expresses the true general will divorced from local or other
special interests. "Jackson became the first President in our history
to appeal to the people over the heads of their legislative representatives. . . . His claim to represent the American people as a whole
went to the extent of claiming to embody them."[6]

The doctrine that the President alone embodies or in some unspecified manner represents "the whole people" became a favorite.
It may be found repeated by so far from personally Caesarean a President as James Polk (in his Fourth Annual Message): "The President
represents in the executive department the whole people of the
United States, as each member of the legislative department represents portions of them." The naive and personally weak McKinley
discovered, after the Spanish-American War had begun: "I am now
the President of the whole people."

Woodrow Wilson, in the 1908 Columbia lectures[7] that abandoned his earlier belief that Congress had won permanent ascendancy in the American system, was rhapsodic on the President's
potential:

6. Edward S. Corwin, *The President: Office and Powers* (New York: New York
University Press, 1956), p. 23.
7. Published as *Constitutional Government in the United States.*

The President is also the political leader of the nation, or has it in his choice to be. The nation as a whole has chosen him, and is conscious that it has no other political spokesman. His is the only national voice in affairs. Let him once win the admiration and confidence of the country, and no other single force can withstand him, no combination of forces will easily overpower him. . . . He is the representative of no constituency, but of the whole people. When he speaks in his true character, he speaks for no special interest. If he rightly interpret the national thought and boldly insist upon it, he is irresistible. . . . [The country's] instinct is for unified action, and it craves a single leader. . . . A President whom it can trust can not only lead it but form it to his views.

And Wilson stated also, from his ideological perspective, the significant contrast: "There is no one in Congress to speak for the nation. Congress is a conglomeration of inharmonious elements; a collection of men representing each his neighborhood, each his local interest."

Actually, Wilson had come to this doctrine through Grover Cleveland, who had given it careful formulation in his essays on *Presidential Problems*.[8] Prior to publication, Cleveland had delivered two of these as lectures at Princeton, where Wilson, as the university's President, presumably heard and discussed them.

In the scheme of our national Government the Presidency is preeminently the people's office. Of course, all offices created by the Constitution, and all governmental agencies existing under its sanction, must be recognized, in a sense, as the offices and agencies of the people—considered either as an aggregation constituting the national body politic, or some of its

8. Grover Cleveland, *Presidential Problems* (New York: The Century Company, 1904).

divisions. When, however, I now speak of the Presidency as preeminently the people's office, I mean that it is especially the office related to the people as individuals, in no general, local or other combination, but standing on the firm footing of manhood and American citizenship.[9]

A study of such passages will show how closely, in developing a "theory of the Presidency," they follow the lines of democratist ideology. Democracy is interpreted as the unmixed sovereignty of the general will. The general will operates through direct, nation-wide elections, and is embodied in the plebiscitary choice of the leader whom "it craves." It is only the President, the plebiscitary leader, who embodies the true general will, who represents "the whole of the people," who "speaks for no special interest." The President is "the Voice of the People," through which is heard "clearly and unmistakably . . . the will of the people—the General Will, I suppose we could call it,"[10] writes Professor Rossiter, revealing much in his use of capitals.

The President's expressive function is performed the more perfectly, the more immediate is his relation to "the will of the people." Intermediary institutions only block and distort the expression of the sovereign general will: "as few impediments as possible should exist to the free operation of the public will." When the President, boldly shortcircuiting the intermediary institutions, maintains a direct contact with "the whole people," "he is irresistible." And, finally, we discover that "the whole people" is understood in terms that define what we have called "the masses": "no special interest," "no general, local or other combination," "standing on the firm [but qualitatively empty] footing of manhood and American citizenship"—that is, not the people in their existential reality, but the abstracted political Common Denominator.

9. *Ibid.*, "The Independence of the Executive," pp. 10–11
10. Clinton Rossiter, *op. cit.*, p. 22.

Thus, during the century preceding 1933 there was a doctrinal preparation not only for the shift to executive-bureaucratic supremacy that set in with Franklin Roosevelt, but for the popular despotism (Caesarism) into which this shift, if the prevailing tendency continues, must inevitably lead. The ideological apology for the breakdown of constitutional government, the fall of Congress and the rise of the democratic despot is plainly there. If the general will is sovereign, and the President its sole authentic embodiment, then the intermediary institutions, and Congress as the chief of the intermediary institutions, are distorting impediments to democracy. At best, they interfere with the communication between the people and their leader. If they contradict the President, then they are necessarily contradicting the general will, and their actions are antidemocratic. The general will alone legitimizes; what is in accord with the general will is lawful. The President is the voice of the general will; therefore the law is what he proclaims, the law is what he says it is. Harry Truman, drawing, as the logic of despotism always does, on the cry of "emergency" and the rule of *Salus populi suprema lex,* put the essential meaning into his flat prose: "The President . . . represents the interest of all the people. . . . When Congress fails to act or is unable to act in a crisis, the President . . . must use his powers to safeguard the nation."[11]

The democratist ideology is a myth, of course, not a scientific hypothesis. No one who puts it forward ever specifies how one man can represent, embody or express a vast multitude, or even what it would mean for him to do so. No one explains what has happened to the opposing minority—often not much smaller than the majority—when the one man speaks so totally for "the whole people." No one has ever told where any actual individuals may be found who are defined solely by "manhood and American citizenship." Indeed, the

11. Harry S. Truman, *Memoirs,* Vol. 2 (New York: Doubleday, 1956), p. 478. In the passage from which these phrases are taken, Mr. Truman is justifying the steel seizure.

rhetoric of image and metaphor, into which democratist phraseology almost automatically slips, shows plainly that we are dealing with myth.

The full democratist doctrine was only latent in America during the 19th century and the first years of the 20th. The general condition of the body politic did not yet favor its active development. The community was smaller, and still organized spiritually through the structure of traditional beliefs, values and distinctions. The masses existed only embryonically. The intermediary institutions, including the complicated state governments, were still vigorous. We must understand the early statements of the doctrine not as describing the political reality of those times past, but as prophecy and preparation.

4

The office of President is coming to be the embodiment of the citizens of the nation in their aspect as *the masses.* Congress, supplemented by the lobbies, which we earlier named as the fifth branch of the governmental structure, and by the non-ideological political parties, continues to represent the citizens in their aspect as *the people.* The President is the political resultant of a process approximating a plebiscitary, direct, all-national election. Congress is the second level resultant of hundreds of limited elections. The President is the choice of a single numerical majority; Congress, of a multitude of concurrent majorities.[12]

These parallel propositions are not true without some qualification, but they are roughly accurate in the distinction to which they point. The President is the selection of the non-plebiscitary party machinery as well as of the almost-direct popular vote; and the peo-

12. In some cases, strictly speaking, pluralities rather than majorities. But I will not overburden the analysis with the bewildering problem of pluralities.

ple as well as the masses continue to be felt through the parties. On its side, Congress both expresses and exploits, in some degree, simplistic impulses that well up from the masses. The contrast, that is to say, is not black-and-white; but there remains a marked difference between the grays.

From a formal standpoint, Congress represents the concurrent majorities (or pluralities) of local subdivisions defined according to geographical criteria: the states in the case of Senators and the Representatives-at-large; election districts of the states in the case of most members of the House. However, the principle of division is not in fact merely geographical. The local populations of the states and the congressional districts usually have an internal cohesion in other than geographical ways. They are particularly characterized by race, religion, occupation, ethnic background, degree of literacy, density of population, even language. Some districts are occupied by the people of the desert; others by the people of mountain, plain, woods or seacoast, the old stock or the new. The Congressman from New Mexico is also Congressman of the Mexican-Spanish stock; the member from Boston, of the urban Irish, as the New Yorker of the urban Jews. The gentlemen from Montana, Nevada and Colorado can speak for the mining industry. Through the Cleveland or Pittsburgh or Gary member, Congress hears the voice of the steel mills. The auto workers can send their ambassadors from Detroit or Flint. The tall corn and fat hogs are not forgotten by the Congressmen from Iowa.

Congress is neither a unitary embodiment nor a numerical analogue of the mythical general will. It represents the nation by representing *the people*—in the rough, inexact sense that representation is possible at all—in their active actuality: that is to say, as beings living and thinking and working in terms of certain specific interests, goals, values, ideals and sentiments. Except in an empty formal sense, the political process that goes on in Congress is not a plebiscite even of the congressional membership, not a counting of noses. True enough, a ballot is taken at the end, and a *Yes-No* count records a numerical score which announces the decision. But under normal circumstances that count is not in the least like a plebiscitary mandate from the "numerical majority."

Woodrow Wilson felt that Congress demonstrated its low estate in the fact that matters were seldom settled by great speeches and debates from the floor. In Britain, "the whole conduct of the government turns upon what is said in the Commons. . . . The parliamentary debates . . . determine the course of politics in a great empire. The season of a parliamentary debate is a great field day on which Liberals and Conservatives pit their full forces against each other, and people like to watch the issues of the contest. Our congressional debates, on the contrary, have no tithe of this interest, because they have no tithe of such significance and importance."[13]

There have been a fair number of exceptions to this generalization about the unimportance of congressional debates—as Wilson was himself to learn from his sickbed in 1919—but it is true that formal debates have had, as a rule, less importance in Congress than in the British and many other parliaments. Wilson, analyzing Congress through his own perspective as intellectual and verbalist, failed to grasp the way in which Congress conducts its basic business.

When it deals with an important issue, Congress carries out a prolonged, complex process of negotiation: an adjustment and balancing of needs, interests and aims. This process—a task of extraordinary delicacy in its own mode—Congressmen are peculiarly fitted to carry out precisely because they are the representatives of "the interests" of the nation and thus of the people.

In Chapter XIX we considered the scornful criticism that Congress, after dawdling its time away, crowds most of its major enactments into the last few days of a session, and we found that the vote is only the formal conclusion to the lengthy, wide-ranging journey. Congress—when operating in its own style rather than under executive dictation—feels its way slowly through the tangled

13. Woodrow Wilson, *Congressional Government*, pp. 94–101.

political thickets, trying to figure out just what the issues really are, just what is at stake beneath the shadowy words; trying to discover how the relevant interests line up; negotiating compromises here, adjusting differences there; adding this clause to reconcile one group, and dropping that clause to reconcile another. The vote records only the finish of this political safari over untracked and irregular terrain, a trip of which the occasional floor debates mark, but seldom decide, certain stages. And the numerical vote is often deceptive. Even when the vote is nearly even, the decision is, generally speaking, less close than it seems. For party and election purposes, the opposition must put the *Nays* on the record. But in most cases the members of the minority as well as of the majority have left their mark on the measure. The minorities have been granted a kind of veto, through which any provisions that they have found really intolerable have been eliminated.[14] The final bill is, at least to some degree, a joint product of the *Yeas* and *Nays*.

The necessary consequence of taking the sense of the community by the concurrent majority is, as has been explained, to give to each interest or portion of the community a negative on the others. It is this mutual negative among its various conflicting interests which invests each with the power of protecting itself, and places the rights and safety of each where only they can be securely placed, under its own guardianship. Without this there can be no systematic, peaceful, or effective resistance to the natural tendency of each to come into conflict with the others; and without this there can be no constitution. It is this negative power—the power of preventing or arresting the action of the government, be it called by what term it may, veto, interposition, nullification, check, or balance of power—

14. Of course, such an adjustment is impossible when the differences become absolutely irreconcilable, as they did—or were made to do—in the issue of slavery. When that happens, the congressional process, and the American system, break down.

which in fact forms the constitution. They are all but different names for the negative power. In all its forms, and under all its names, it results from the concurrent majority. Without this there can be no negative, and without a negative, no constitution. The assertion is true in reference to all constitutional governments, be their forms what they may. It is, indeed, the *negative* power which makes the constitution, and the *positive* which makes the government. The one is the power of acting, and the other the power of preventing or arresting action. The two, combined, make constitutional governments.[15]

For the most part Calhoun analyzed his doctrine of the concurrent majority in general terms, without stating exactly how he would apply it to the American situation. His primary immediate concern, of course, was the problem of slavery and the ever widening division between the North and the South. Taking this as the political fulcrum, he proposed the creation of a plural executive, with two co-Presidents, one elected by the North and the other by the South. Thereby he hoped that "the presidential election, instead of dividing the Union into hostile geographical parties—the stronger struggling to enlarge its powers, and the weaker to defend its rights, as is now the case—would become the means of restoring harmony and concord to the country and the government. It would make the Union a union in truth—a bond of mutual affection and brotherhood—and not a mere connection used by the stronger as the instrument of dominion and aggrandizement, and submitted to by the weaker only from the lingering remains of former attachment and the fading hope of being able to restore the government to what it was originally intended to be, a blessing to all."[16]

15. John C. Calhoun, *op. cit.*, p. 28. It will be noted that, in somewhat different language, Calhoun here summarizes also the main points of Chapter XXIII.
16. John C. Calhoun, *A Discourse on the Constitution and Government of the United States, lib. cit.*, p. 104.

The plan was not altogether fantastic. Sparta and the Roman Republic had, as Calhoun pointed out, plural executives; and Switzerland and Uruguay have them today, the former with notably satisfactory results. But in the circumstances of the mid-19th century, his two-man executive (if it had been at all possible) could only have sealed the division of the country into two nations, with at most a rather precarious alliance between them. You cannot in any case make at one stroke, apart from a revolutionary civic convulsion, so basic a constitutional change as he was proposing. Moreover, although the idea of a plural executive had been seriously considered by the Philadelphia Convention, it seems probable that the solution there adopted was inseparable from the design of the American government. A unique, autonomous chief executive is required, not only to secure vigor and dispatch, as the authors of *The Federalist* stressed, but to provide an adequate symbol of a national unity without which the country's continental domain would have dissolved into politically separated segments.

What Calhoun, obsessed with his single and quite literally insoluble problem, did not sufficiently realize was that the traditional American system itself incorporated in diverse and remarkably effective ways his principle of concurrent majorities. At the beginning and into his own day, it was the states, with their concurrent political jurisdictions, that were the primary organs of one set of parts that in their combination made up a national whole without being dissolved into it. Though by the Civil War, and the cold civil war of the post-1933 epoch, the states have been permanently weakened, they are not yet eliminated as significant political organisms.

Within the structure of the central government, the diffusion of independently based powers permits and in fact demands the operation of the principle of concurrent majorities. In the traditional American system, "[there is no] single or *one power* which excludes the negative and constitutes absolute government. [Like] all constitutional governments, [the traditional American system takes] the sense of the community by its parts—each through its appropriate organ—and regard[s] the sense of all its parts as the sense of the whole. [It is not in the mode of] absolute governments, [which] concentrate power in one uncontrolled and irresponsible individual or body whose will is regarded as the sense of the community."[17]

With the weakening of the states, it was Congress, as the assembly of *the people's* representatives, that became the primary political organ for the concurrent majorities, and thus the major bulwark of the constitutional principle. At the same time, Congress remained, and remains, as the great intermediary institution between the people and a chief executive evolving into the plebiscitary leader of the masses. By this double function, Congress gives operative meaning to the rule of a law that is not identical with the decree of the supreme executive.

> So great, indeed, is the difference between the [numerical and the concurrent majorities] that liberty is little more than a name under all governments of the absolute form, including that of the numerical majority, and can only have a secure and durable existence under those of the concurrent or constitutional form. . . . The force sufficient to overthrow an oppressive government is usually sufficient to establish one equally or more oppressive in its place. And hence in no governments, except those that rest on the principle of the concurrent or constitutional majority, can the people guard their liberty against power; and hence also, when lost, the great difficulty and uncertainty of regaining it by force.[18]

17. Calhoun, *A Disquisition on Government, lib. cit.,* p. 29.
18. *Ibid.,* pp. 46–47.

XXVI

CAN CONGRESS SURVIVE?

THE POLITICAL development of the American Congress takes place within the pattern of the long-term, world-wide historical trends that have been discussed in the four preceding chapters. The uneven, bumpy but persistent fall of Congress from the high estate described by Woodrow Wilson in *Congressional Government* began with the turn of the 20th century, and shifted to a faster rate in 1933. The spread of democratism as an ideology—called "liberalism" by Americans—follows much the same chronological schedule. Lincoln Steffens, John Dewey, Vernon Louis Parrington, Louis Boudin, Gustavus Myers, Herbert D. Croly, the young Charles Beard,[1] and Woodrow Wilson himself ushered in the first phase during the early years of the century. *The Nation,* abandoning its former editorial policy (of "liberalism" in the older European sense), and *The New Republic* moved into the ideological vanguard during the 1920's, as democratism swept toward the national ascendancy that it has since solidified and maintained.

As the democratist ideology became intellectually predominant, the liberal ideologues, and those whose opinions had been formed by the liberals, gradually took over many of the seats of national power. Their first big conquests were in the schools and in "communications"—journalism, literature, the arts, movies, preaching, and, later on, radio, television and the staffs of the great foundations. Under the New Deal they were drawn rapidly and massively into the

---

1. In later years, Beard largely abandoned democratism.

expanding governmental bureaucracy, particularly into the newer economic and social agencies. Slower processes of appointment brought them by more slowly increasing percentages into the judicial system, where the mounting influence of democratist ideology reached a critical new stage not through the avowed liberals, Presidents Roosevelt and Truman, but by Mr. Eisenhower's appointment of Earl Warren to head the highest court of the central government.

Even in Congress, liberals by training, conviction or fashion have appeared in large though variable numbers. However, Congress as an institution has been dominated by democratist ideology only when it has submitted to executive dictation. The electoral basis of Congress, and the separative effect of the diverse interests and concurrent majorities that the several members represent, have prevented Congress, in our time as in the past, from becoming solidified as an ideological institution, even when a numerical majority of its membership happens to share a particular ideology. In accordance with Calhoun's doctrine, the numerical majority does not uniquely determine the qualitative nature of the whole. The minority members, non-ideological or adhering to a different ideology, retain their political identity, and do not dissolve into the whole. Of course, on specific issues a democratist numerical majority in Congress may (though it does not necessarily) vote for a democratist bill: but Congress does not itself thereby become democratist. The democratist ideologues continue, and rightly, to characterize Congress as a "conservative" or "reactionary" body even when it is approving collectivist and egalitarian measures devised according to the doctrine of democratism.

As part of the advance of democratism in both belief and practice, a plebiscitary or numerical majority comes to seem the only proper expression of the sovereign general will. The electorate is therefore expanded toward totality by changes in custom and law. Thus, it was in 1913 that the Constitution was amended to provide for direct popular election of Senators; and in 1920 that, by the 19th Amendment, women were enfranchised. In 1958, a new statute was added to the efforts of the Court and the executive to destroy the restrictions put by custom on voting by Negroes. The Presidency, as the office most nearly plebiscitary, is more and more felt to be the primary embodiment of the general will, and thus properly dominant over all other political magistrates and institutions.

The plebiscitary axiom and the growing dominance of the President mean the progressive weakening of the intermediary institutions, which are based on the concurrent, not the numerical, majority, and represent diffusions rather than a concentration of the general will. The states and their local subdivisions lose one after another of their sovereign police, fiscal and regulatory functions to the superseding power of the central government. The states, made by the Civil War unequivocally subordinate in terms of direct force, become financially and legally dependent on the central government. As their originally concurrent sovereignty slips away, the states approach a political relationship by which they would become mere administrative subdivisions of the central government. The swelling of its activities cements the central government's strength, while within its structure Congress sinks in power as the courts, becoming manned by liberals formed by the same ideology that has earlier penetrated the bureaus, tend to act as handmaidens of the pre-Caesarean executive and the intrenched bureaucracy.

The decline of the intermediary institutions brings a weakening of constitutional government and the rule of law. In an atmosphere of continuous emergency, of unceasingly proclaimed military and economic crisis, the conduct of government is handled, more and more, through the decrees of the executive and the great administrative agencies of the bureaucratic apparatus. This shift had become plain enough a good many years ago, and I summarized it as follows in 1941:

Congress, with occasional petty rebellions, sank lower and lower as sovereignty shifted from the parliament toward the bureaus and agencies. One after another, the executive bureaus took into their hands the attributes and functions of sovereignty; the bureaus became the de facto "lawmakers." By 1940 it was plain that Congress no longer possessed even the war-making power, the crux of sovereignty. The constitutional provision could not stand against the structural changes in modern society and in the nature of modern war: the decisions about war and peace had left the control of the parliament. Time after time this last fact was flung publicly in the face of Congress—by the holdup of the *Bremen,* the freezing of foreign balances in accordance with policies never submitted to Congress, the dispatch of confidential personal emissaries in the place of regular diplomatic officials, the release of military supplies and secrets to belligerent powers, outstandingly by the executive trade of destroyers for naval bases and by the provisions of the "lend-lease" plan (and by all that these two acts implied). The parliament had so far lost even its confidence that it did not dare protest.[2]

Comparable processes, both ideological and structural, have been going on in nearly every technologically advanced nation and in many that are less advanced. "The shift from parliament to the bureaus occurs on a world scale. . . . The rules, regulations, laws, decrees have more and more issued from an interconnected group of administrative boards, commissions, bureaus—or whatever other name may be used for comparable agencies. Sovereignty becomes, de facto and then de jure also, localized in these boards and bureaus. They become the publicly recognized and accepted lawmaking bodies of the new society."[3] The degree of the shift, the extent to which the full logic of the implicit pattern is carried out in fact, differs in the different nations, but not the direction and general form. An extreme degree has

2. James Burnham, *The Managerial Revolution* (New York: John Day Company, 1941), pp. 256–7.
3. James Burnham, *ibid.,* pp. 147–8.

been reached in the totalitarian structures of the Soviet Union and Empire, somewhat less in Nazi Germany and fascist Italy; but the pattern is also discernible in the structural tendencies within 20th-century Britain and France, as well as the United States.

These tendencies—democratist, plebiscitary, bureaucratic, centralist, Caesarean—are the political phase of the general historical transformation of our era that in 1940 I named "the managerial revolution." Economically the managerial revolution is a shift from entrepreneurial private capitalism to large-scale mass industry organized into gigantic and anonymous management-controlled public corporations, state enterprises, or "mixed" combinations of these two forms. Sociologically, the managerial revolution is a shift in the composition of the élite, from "private owners skilled in the manipulation of financial profits or losses on the market, and of the old sort of parliamentary politician [to] those whom I call 'managers'—the production executives and organizers of the industrial process, officials trained in the manipulation of the great labor organizations, and the administrators, bureau chiefs and commissars developed in the executive branch of the unlimited modern state machines."[4]

Within the emergent managerial society the typical political form links a huge, pervasive governmental bureaucracy with a Caesarism-tending political leadership sanctioned by mass plebiscites. This combination, supported by a bureaucratized military and police apparatus, operates primarily through administrative decree while using an assembly as recording device and sounding board.

2

On a national scale, then, Congress has been dropping in relative power along a descending curve of sixty years' duration, with the

4. James Burnham, *The Machiavellians* (New York: John Day Company, 1943), p. 232.

rate of fall markedly increased since 1933. On a world scale the fall of the American Congress seems to be correlated with a more general historical transformation toward political and social forms within which the representative assembly—the major political organism of post-Renaissance western civilization—does not have a primary political function. To date, of course, the American Congress, though fallen, is not dead. But its own history as well as the apparent trends of our age pose the question: Can Congress survive?

The question means: Can Congress survive as an autonomous, active political entity with some measure of real power, not merely as a rubber stamp, a name and a ritual, or an echo of powers lodged elsewhere. There is no reason to believe that in the predictable future there is any likelihood of the formal and literal abolition of Congress. As we have already noted, Augustus did not abolish the Roman Senate nor Hitler the German Reichstag nor Perón the Argentine Congress; and though the Bolsheviks dropped the Duma of the old regime they substituted an assembly of their own. In fact, bureaucratic democratism, whether or not fully Caesarean in form, finds a plebiscitary assembly to be an indispensable instrument of its managerial rule.

To resume, in a few words, the system of the Imperial government as it was instituted by Augustus and maintained by those princes who understood their own interest and that of the people, it may be defined as an absolute monarchy disguised by the forms of a commonwealth. The masters of the Roman world surrounded their throne with darkness, concealed their irresistible strength, and humbly professed themselves the accountable ministers of the Senate, whose supreme decrees they dictated and obeyed.[5]

5. Edward Gibbon, *Decline and Fall of the Roman Empire* (Chicago & New York: Belford, Clarke & Co., 1845), p. 83.

To ask whether Congress can survive is, in turn, equivalent to the question: Can constitutional government, can *liberty,* survive in the United States? This equation between Congress and liberty may at first seem paradoxical. Undoubtedly Congress has sometimes acted, in recent as well as in more distant times, in ways that have served to undermine both law and liberty, and it has done so both in consort with and in opposition to the other branches of the government. In Reconstruction days, after the Civil War, Congress overrode resistances from both Court and Presidency to strike some heavy blows against the liberty of the citizens. More frequently Congress has softened the foundations of constitutional government through the indirect consequences of its measures: by fostering statism and centralization, squandering public funds, curbing or coddling the states, ducking responsibilities, yielding to executive usurpations, eroding the personal independence of the citizens. Moreover, it cannot be argued that there is a permanent or necessary connection between representative assemblies and liberty. Constitutional government and liberty have existed under political structures that did not include a representative assembly of the post-Renaissance kind.

The tie in this century and this nation between the survival of Congress and liberty is not abstract and formal but historical and specific. Within the United States today Congress is in existing fact the prime intermediary institution, the chief political organ of the people as distinguished from the masses, the one body to which the citizenry can now appeal for redress not merely from individual despotic acts (with respect to which the courts are still relevant and sometimes efficacious) but from large-scale despotic innovations, trends and principles. The role of Congress among the nation's intermediary institutions has become more than ever critical with the continuing decline in the power of the states—a decline for which, ironically enough, Congress carries a full share of responsibility, along with the President, the Court and the Northern armies. Congress, having helped to beat down the states, found itself in an altered set of political relations within which it was compelled to take over the burden of the victim.

Among the political institutions of the American system it is Congress that now remains as the one major curb on the soaring executive and the unleashed bureaucracy. The judiciary, indeed, long ago recognized its impotence against the office of President:

> By the decision of the Court in State of Mississippi v. Johnson in 1867, the President was put beyond the reach of judicial direction in the exercise of any of his powers, whether constitutional or statutory, political or otherwise. An application for an injunction to forbid President Johnson to enforce the Reconstruction Acts, on the ground of their unconstitutionality, was answered by Attorney General Stanbery as follows: "It is not upon any peculiar immunity that the individual has who happens to be President; upon any idea that he cannot do wrong; upon any idea that there is any particular sanctity belonging to him as an individual, as is the case with one who has royal blood in his veins; but it is on account of the office that he holds that I say the President of the United States is above the process of any court or the jurisdiction of any court to bring him to account as President. . . ." Speaking by Chief Justice Chase, the Court agreed: "The impropriety of such interference will be clearly seen upon consideration of its possible consequences. . . . If the President refuse obedience, it is needless to observe that the court is without power to enforce its process."[6]

True enough, the congressional curb on the executive has been potential, for the most part, in recent years. It has seldom been directly and wisely applied. But a political curb, even if it remains latent and potential, can be remarkably effective. After the failure in

6. *The Constitution of the United States,* pp. 499–500.

the affair of Andrew Johnson, the impeachment of a President is exceedingly improbable; but it is not impossible, and no President can ever forget the possibility, which sets a tacitly understood limit to the amount that a President can stretch the Constitution in a single pull. Congress has been unwilling to abolish any of the important newer agencies, bureaus or programs of the executive branch; but by reasserting the power of the purse it still might do so, and this the bureaucracy must keep, however scornfully and reluctantly, in mind. So long as Congressmen continue to have personal immunity and the power to compel testimony, they can inform themselves and the citizens about the conduct of the bureaucracy, no matter how closely the executive guards the files. The people, and the groups by which the people carry out their organized activities, have ready access to Congress. Through Congress they still can, if they choose, exert their counter-pressures to bureaucratic usurpations. And so long as Congressmen are selected by decentralizing procedures that provide political channels for a diversity of interests, there will be opposition members who can, if they will, pull counter to the despotic drift of the executive-bureaucracy.

3

In earlier days, when the central government was only a minor element in the life of the nation, and when within the central government the office of President was so narrow as to seem secondary and almost contemptible to a foreigner like James Bryce,[7] the problem of liberty, of lawful and constitutional government, was presented in a different frame of specific relations. Today the issues are both more acute and much simplified. The gigantic managerial state, intertwined with all facets of the national life, has burst beyond all bounds that were traditionally assigned to government—beyond,

---

7. *Cf.* James Bryce, *The American Commonwealth* (1888), *passim.*

even, the bounds of the most total tyrannies of other times.[8] Necessarily, the active, daily direction of the managerial state is in the hands of the executive, his principal officers and the higher echelons of the permanent bureaucratic apparatus. Their fingers are on the throttle. Liberty's problem in our day is to keep someone else, someone independent of their control and designs, at their side to restrain them somehow, to be ready to reach for the brake when the signals show red or the tracks plunge downhill.

Caesarism, like other forms of bureaucratic despotism, cannot be finally established unless the independent representative assembly is crushed, or abdicates. And if the assembly is crushed, then in the conditions of our time despotism is certain. For the United States, a small exercise of imagination should make this obvious.

Let us suppose that tomorrow Congress became a Nazi Reichstag or Supreme Soviet type of assembly: that is, a political appendage of the executive which, after a certain amount of verbal ritual, and without genuine debate, invariably and predictably approved the executive's proposals by a unanimous or close to unanimous vote. Now there are some persons in the United States, as elsewhere, and perhaps a good many, who believe that such a form of government would be preferable to the present American system: that it would be more effective, more suited to the problems of our age, more fitted to serve the interests of the masses, and more likely to meet the challenges from world rivals. There are many other persons who, though they do not believe in the superiority of such a form of government, nevertheless, by their espousal of policies derived from democratist ideology, are helping to bring it into being. However, there can be few persons who suppose that under such a government political liberty could be very secure. Full employment, welfare, security, military strength, perhaps: the fate of these is at least arguable. But not liberty. Under such a form of government, by the nature of the situation, the constitution and the law could only be

8. Except, perhaps, for the Incaic Empire.

what Caesar or the executive-managerial apparatus decided. If they were both wise and benevolent, then their government might be one of the good, or less evil, despotisms. But it would still be a despotism. And of course they would not remain benevolent for long: there is no benevolent way for despotisms to deal with the disagreements which, men being what they are, inevitably arise.

An "assembly dictatorship" is an idea much bruited by the current defenders of executive supremacy, and occasionally mentioned by some of the Fathers. In historical fact, an assembly dictatorship is an illusion of perspective, usually derived from a misreading of one period of the French Revolution. On technical grounds alone, a large assembly, in particular an assembly for which the membership is chosen by a decentralized non-plebiscitary procedure, is not capable of exercising a despotic dictatorship. Where an assembly exists as part of the political structure, a despotism can be established only if the assembly is abolished; or if an individual or small group resting on an independent political foundation gets control of the assembly and reduces it to a mere instrument. Thus, though the French National Convention took decisions in 1792 that many will judge abominable, its government was not that of a true despotism. This supervened only in 1793, when the leaders of the Jacobin club, winning control of the Paris Commune and operating through the Committee of Public Safety, established a dictatorship *over* the Convention. And the fullness of the despotism was not, in truth, reached until 1794, when a single man, Robespierre, leading a monolithic wing of the prevailing political tendency, wiped out Hébert, Danton and all other rivals, to become—as usually (though not quite invariably) happens—the supreme despot who in his proper person embodies the despotism.

With the fall of Robespierre on 9th Thermidor (July 27, 1794) the sovereignty of the Convention (and then of the Council) was briefly restored, so far as any clear sovereignty was exercised during those confused and half-anarchic months. But through the political series, Directory-Consulate-First Consul-Emperor, Bonaparte, basing himself first on the army and then, for the first time in modern history, on the masses filling the streets and speaking in a binary plebiscite, again established a dictatorship *over* the new assembly. In the one instance, the Jacobins operated from a beachhead within the assembly; in the other, Bonaparte, acting primarily from the outside, brought his gradually heightening pressures to bear on the assembly from an external command post. But in both cases the despotism expressed a focus of political force very different from the constellation of forces represented by the whole assembly, and triumphed only by reducing the assembly to impotence: that is, by the political destruction of the assembly.

The critics of France's Fourth Republic also spoke of "assembly dictatorship," but what they really meant was an "assembly paralysis"—as the dismal collapse of the Fourth Republic's assembly in 1958 sufficiently proved. More generally, it is paralysis, partial or entire, not despotism, that is the typical lesion in the pathology of the representative assembly. The paralysis of the assembly—real or alleged—in the face of a national emergency—real or alleged—is, in fact, the usual plea in a shift to despotism.

If the despotism is to be more than a temporary expedient, such as the American—like the Roman—constitutional tradition allows for, if the despotism is going to take hold as a new mode of government, then the assembly must be politically crushed. This seems to be true as a general law of political history; but whether or not true in general, the correlation is most manifest in our time.

In this century, all despotisms of all the many modern varieties have had to abolish the representative assembly, replace it or render it politically impotent, as part of the process of establishing despotic state power. Indeed, the destinies of liberty, constitutional government, and the representative assembly have become more ineluctably linked than in the past. In the past as in the present, despotism could not conquer without crushing the representative assembly (if such an assembly existed within the governmental system). But in the past it was sometimes possible to have constitutional government, and thus liberty, even though there was no representative assembly in any usual sense. The traditional "orders"—nobles, clergy, elders, communes—or a binding set of traditional beliefs operating through a network of traditional institutions, could provide the institutional check on the sovereign executive which we have seen to be the operational prerequisite for liberty and a law that is not identical with the sovereign's subjective will.

But the traditional orders have dissolved; and the traditional beliefs and institutions, though they have not altogether disappeared, are no longer cohesive and strong enough to serve as a counterpoise to the formidable sovereigns of the 20th century. Thus the representative assembly, which was always incompatible with sustained despotism,[9] is today inseparable from constitutional government, juridical defense and liberty. In theory there can be constitutional government and liberty without the presence of a representative assembly; in the past there have been such governments, and in the distant and much changed future there again may be. But for the present, such governments seem to be excluded.

The obvious definition of a monarchy seems to be that of a state in which a single person, by whatsoever name he may be distinguished, is entrusted with the execution of the laws, the management of the revenue, and the command of the army. But unless public liberty is protected by intrepid and vigilant guardians, the authority of so formidable a magistrate will soon degenerate into despotism. The influence of the clergy, in an age of superstition, might be usefully employed to assert the rights of mankind; but so intimate is the connection between the throne and the altar that the banner of the church has very seldom been seen on the side of the people. A mar-

9. Representative assemblies, can, of course, perform, and have performed, individually despotic acts; and can conduct themselves despotically for short periods of time.

tial nobility and stubborn commons, possessed of arms, tenacious of property, and collected into constitutional assemblies, form the only balance capable of preserving a free constitution against enterprises of an aspiring prince.[10]

With the clergy so much diminished in an age that is no longer one of "superstition" (Gibbon's term for "religious belief"), the nobility gone, and the commons no longer either independently possessed of arms or unduly tenacious of property, it is only the constitutional assembly, supported by what stubbornness the commons do retain, that today still stands as a major "balance capable of preserving a free constitution." And Gibbon, continuing his description of the steps by which Augustus completed the transition from the fading republic to the Caesarean despotism, summarized the basic act in the familiar political language of the 18th century that he shared with our Founding Fathers: "He destroyed the independence of the senate. The principles of a free constitution are irrecoverably lost, when the legislative power is nominated by the executive."

The essential link between the active survival of Congress and of political liberty is so often obscured or misconstrued that it is well to fix our attention on it repeatedly, from many logical perspectives. If Congress ceases to be an actively functioning political institution, then political liberty in the United States will soon come to an end. If Congress continues to have and to exercise a political function, then there will be at least a measure of political liberty—a workable minimum, and a chance of more. It is impossible to have the executive unchallengeably supreme over Congress and to reduce Congress to a mere channel between the executive and the masses—as Walter Lippmann seems to be proposing in *The Public Philosophy*,

10. Edward Gibbon, *op. cit.*, p. 76. Gibbon permits his usual anti-clericalism to denigrate the potential and frequently achieved role of the clergy in helping to support constitutional government and, thus, liberty.

and as many others today in substance propose—and at the same time to have political liberty. No one can deny the accuracy and the cogency of many of the adverse criticisms that have been made of Congress as an institution and of many individual Congressmen. But the hard relation remains: if liberty, then Congress; if no Congress, no liberty.

4

If we put the question in the form of a prediction concerning the future, and ask: Will Congress survive? we must reply that it is not probable on the evidence; possible, of course, but not probable. The trends, both national and world-wide, no longer episodic but holding over a number of decades, are against the survival of Congress (or of any other representative assembly in any major nation) as an active, independent political institution. Our only way to estimate the future is by examining the past and the present. Unless we find contrary factors of significant weight, we must expect observable trends to continue according to the curve that a past of sufficient duration has served to define. And the falling curve of the representative assembly since the start of the 20th century is unmistakably defined.

It may be, as some thoughtful observers as well as many demagogues have concluded, that representative assemblies are inherently unfit to be primary political institutions in a technological-mass age that is at the same time an age of wars and revolutions and H-bombs. Not only their inescapable defects as political institutions but even their characteristic virtues, it has been said, make the assemblies incapable of handling the problems which a contemporary government must try to handle. Certainly the assemblies, by their very nature, cannot be bureaucratized in the modern mode. Among the giant institutions into which society is currently for the most part arranged, the assemblies are undoubtedly anomalous, a breach in the pattern; and if all modern institutions have got to conform to the managerial-bureaucratic norms, then the assemblies are on an irreversible way out. If the assemblies cannot function effectively at the summit of modern states, then they will have to disappear, if for no other reason, because the nations that atavistically persist in retaining them will be wiped out by those that adapt their institutions more suitably to the contemporary imperatives. For the historians of the 21st century, if there still is history in the 21st century, the representative assembly may be studied as one among the many human institutions that have appeared, developed, expanded, flowered rather briefly—as the assembly did so impressively in the 19th century—sickened, declined and died.

This may, and even probably will, be the outcome if the trends continue unchanged. But it is nowhere decreed that men must submit to impersonal trends, however well established; and it is men who make history. Let us shift the question somewhat, and ask not, Will Congress survive? but, What are the conditions for its survival? If it is to survive, that is to say, what conditions must be fulfilled?

The first is a certain amount of luck—what Machiavelli called Fortune.

Fortune [he writes in *The Prince*] I do resemble to a rapid and impetuous River, which when swelled, and enraged, overwhelms the Plains, subverts the Trees, and the Houses, forces away the Earth from one place, and carries it to another, everybody fears, everybody shuns, but nobody knows how to resist it; Yet though it be thus furious sometimes, it does not follow but when it is quiet and calm, men may by banks, and fences, and other provisions correct it in such manner, that when it swells again, it may be carried off by some Canal, or the violence thereof rendered less licentious and destructive.

He adds in the *Discourses:*

> Yet this shall I assert again (and by the occurrences in all History there is nothing more true) that men may second their fortune, not resist it; and follow the order of her designs, but by no means defeat them: Nevertheless men are not wholly to abandon themselves, because they know not her end; for her ways being unknown and irregular, may possibly be at last for our good; so that we are always to hope the best, and that hope is to preserve us in whatever troubles or distresses we shall fall.[11]

If the impetuous, enraged River of Fortune swells during these next decades into the flood of a total nuclear war in which the deaths would rapidly mount into the tens or scores of millions, there is little doubt that Congress and the other representative assemblies of the West—and perhaps all civil government—would be overwhelmed and subverted. Political liberty would be on the casualty list of the first saturation attack and counterattack. So also if, without total nuclear war, the wave of world communism, joined with the exploding masses of Asia and spreading over the earth's surface, pushes the United States back within the narrow limits of a confined and desperate continental fortress. It is hardly conceivable that republican institutions and political liberty could endure for long in the exhausting atmosphere of a perpetual siege.

That Congress should survive thus presupposes, if not a favorable solution of the deepening world crisis, at least a development short of the worst that is now possible. The Congress of the United States is not going to survive if western civilization does not survive. We must then assume, as one of the conditions for the survival of Congress, the survival of western civilization in general, on something more than a bare subsistence level.

11. Niccolo Machiavelli, *The Prince,* Chap. 25; *Discourses on Livy,* Book II, Chap. 29.

If we now shift focus from this world-historical perspective to the actual working of Congress in the generation past, we may state a second and more specific condition that must be met if Congress is going to continue as an active primary element within the American governmental system. Congress must find a way to concentrate on essentials. If it is to continue to be a partner and peer within the central government, then its principal energies must go to deciding major issues of policy, not to the critique of details.

So long as the activities of the central government were relatively modest in amount and scope, it was possible for Congress to be fairly well acquainted with actual government operations, and to prescribe in some detail how, where and by whom the public funds, appropriated by law, were to be spent, just how the departments and offices were to be organized, just what the duties of officials were to be, and so on. This concern with detail made sufficient sense prior, let us say roughly, to the epoch when the annual budget crossed the billion-dollar mark: that is, prior to 1916.[12] Since then, and increasingly, as the technical complexity as well as the fields of government operations have multiplied, the continuing obsession with details has not only become futile but has diverted Congress from the major policy decisions that are the proper business of the sovereign legislature, if it is indeed sovereign. Congress has let major policy decisions go by default to the unchecked will of the executive and the bureaucracy. The twenty-pound, million-itemed budget that is dropped annually into Congress' lap perfectly symbolizes the paralyzing effect of too many details. Since that kind of budget cannot even be comprehended, it obviously cannot be effectively controlled.

Let us consider the problem through two or three examples. Congress as a collective body cannot possibly understand the detailed technical problems of setting up installations on the moon. Out of its own knowledge it cannot possibly tell what has to be

12. This was the first billion-dollar year, except for the 1862–65 Civil War years.

done or exactly how much it should cost. But after listening to what the qualified technical experts have to say on the matter, literate adults should be able to form reasonably qualified opinions on the desirability of a moon installation in terms of the nation's needs, security and resources; on the cost range, and the nation's ability to pay costs of that order; and on what sort of agency—military, civilian, international—ought to carry the project out, if it is attempted. These are issues of policy, which involve public values, attitudes, goals, sacrifices as well as certain factual data. Even if Congressmen are not, ideally, the best persons in the world to decide such questions, they, as members of the sovereign legislature, are the individuals so charged within a republican, representative governmental system. But when Congress squanders its time on fiscal and bureaucratic details, it is the executive which—by default if not by design—ends up making the policy decisions.

Or take the varied operations that are misleadingly grouped under the elastic term, "foreign aid." Congress cannot judge of its own knowledge whether a high dam in Afghanistan is a technically and sociologically sound enterprise; if it is, Congress cannot tell at all accurately what it ought to cost. But Congress can come to a reasoned, responsible judgment whether economic aid to underdeveloped neutralist countries is consonant with our own national needs, goals and capabilities; and if so, how much, granted other obligations, we can afford. It is not the current congressional procedure to confront these policy issues clearly, and then to give firm decisions concerning them. The result is that Congress keeps an illusory appearance of mastery in its own legislative house, but in reality loses control of the basic decisions. On this matter of aid to underdeveloped countries, as an instance, it is the executive and the bureaucracy administering the programs that have really decided the policy question. Congress dissipates its energies uncovering some picturesque extravagance here or graft there, and cutting out a few padded millions that had been tacked on to the budget just to allow for normal congressional whittling.

Similar examples can be taken from most fields in which the government operations are both extensive and technically complicated. Congress doesn't know how to build nuclear power plants, or what types are cheapest and most efficient. But Congress, if it so chooses, can make the decision whether they ought to be built by the government, by private industry or by some combination of both. Congress cannot staff the United nations Secretariat or check all the items in the United Nations budget. But Congress can, if it chooses, decide that membership in the United Nations no longer serves—or supremely serves—the interests of the United States, and can draw the direct fiscal consequences of such a decision. Congress is likely to make a fool of itself arguing what pictures should be shown as part of a United States exhibit at an international fair; but Congress can give a responsible decision about whether the United States government ought to participate in international fairs, and how much national effort, as measured by money, such participation is worth. It is difficult for Congress to be sure how the sciences can best be taught; but Congress can determine whether money for teaching them ought to be dispensed from the national purse.

So in general: the primary business[13] of the legislature in a democratic republic is to answer the big questions of policy. In our day these questions have become so encrusted with technical, administrative and bureaucratic detail that it takes a deliberate and sustained digging even to find out what they are. In this past generation of its political decline, Congress has not shown itself both able and willing to make and focus the necessary effort. But unless Congress redirects its energy toward the great and controlling decisions, it will inevitably become, like the Senate of imperial Rome, a legislature in form only.

---

13. Primary in political importance, that is, not always in allocation of time. In addition to basic issues of national policy, each member of an assembly chosen, like Congress, from local districts of the nation must of course concern himself with the special interests and problems of his own constituents.

A seemingly paradoxical corollary follows. Congress, in order to regain a due level within the governmental equilibrium and to be able to exert the control over the executive and bureaucracy which is an essential part of the legislative function, must give them more leeway. If the reins are kept too tight, the horse will get the bit in its teeth; they must normally be loose, if the curbing is to be effective. If Congress tries to watch each million, the billions will get away. It is the bureaucracy, which never sleeps, that conducts the active daily operations of the government. Under modern circumstances the bureaucracy will always be able to circumvent the detailed provisos of the legislature. The only way to control the chief officials of the colossal managerial-bureaucratic state is to give an unambiguous main policy directive, to define clear limits, to provide sufficient but not wasteful funds, and then to insist on strict public accountability for satisfactory performance. And it must be known in advance that accountability means quick and adequate sanctions, if the balance is negative: abolition of a project or a bureau that subverts the legislature's intent; action of an appropriate severity against derelict officials.

5

In order to concentrate a greater part of its collective energy on basic questions of policy, and to exercise its oversight of administration rather by clarity of purpose and strict accountability than by elaborate rules and prior prescription, Congress would have to accept some procedural changes: in the way it conducts its affairs, writes its laws, and divides its corporate time. No changes in method and procedure will mean very much of themselves, however, apart from the attitude and purposes of the individual members of Congress. In an earlier chapter we had occasion to remark that the fall of Congress in this century has been the result as much of an abdication on the part of Congressmen as of aggression from the rivals and enemies of Congress. Congress will not survive unless the members of Congress, or a sufficient portion of them, have the will to survive. For Congress to survive politically means that it shall be prepared to say *Yes* or *No*, on its own finding and responsibility, in answer to the questions of major policy; and this it cannot do unless the individual members of Congress have the courage to speak, to say *No* even against the tidal pressures from the executive, the bureaucracy, and the opinion-molders so often allied in our day with executive and bureaucracy, even against the threat that the semi-Caesarean executive will rouse his masses for reprisal at the polls—or in the streets.

Political courage is a quality very different from and much rarer than physical courage. I recall a steaming Washington afternoon not long ago when I listened to the easily flowing talk of two elderly ex-members of Congress, one of the Senate and the other of the House, as they reminisced about the years of the New Deal, which both had undeviatingly served. "Joe Robinson [Democratic leader and White House spokesman in the Senate] would tell us," the ex-Senator said as his ironic eyes followed a nearby tennis match, "this is the bill the chief sent over this morning, and he wants it passed this week. Of course there was hardly a one of those New Deal bills I ever believed in in my heart—I was brought up for States' Rights and a man standing on his own two feet—but the minute I'd get the nod after the session got going, there I'd be asking for recognition and waving my arms while I poured it on about we've got to stand by our great leader, and he's shown us what the country needs, and in this great emergency we can't sit here idly quibbling. . . . And I wasn't the only one, by a long shot, who didn't believe a word he was saying. And why were we doing it? There's just one answer, and that's because each of us figured Roosevelt had the votes, and could get the voters to do what he wanted in our own state just like in all the rest of the country, once he turned on that voice and grin, and started flaying the money-changers. We figured if we didn't go along with him, we'd be out in the cold after the next election."

Political courage is not the same, of course, as political foolhardiness. It would be absurd to suggest that the members of a representative assembly can or should make a general practice of "defying" their constituents: if they did, they would soon (assuming uncoerced elections) cease being members. It will therefore be impossible for the members of Congress to display the independence, courage and responsibility without which the fall of Congress will go on to political extinction, unless they have the people's support.

Congressmen are not likely to get that support unless the citizens become more generally aware of what is happening and what is at stake: aware that in this generation the American political system has shifted a good part of the way toward a fundamental change; that by this shift the relative power of Congress has been drastically weakened; that the completion of the shift would bring an end to the role of Congress—of the representative assembly—as an effectual "coordinate branch" of the government; that the political death of Congress would mean plebiscitary despotism for the United States in place of constitutional government, and thus the end of political liberty.

This knowledge, though simple enough in summary, is not so easy to come by, because it is obscured by the semantic mist spread so widely in our day by liberal-democratist ideology. In any case, the knowledge, without an implementing conviction, is of no practical import. More citizens may come to realize, as many of them already realize, that Congress is on its way out, that this means a constitutional revolution in the American political system, and that in the new order there is not likely to be much of what has traditionally been called political liberty. But their realization of the trend and its direction does not guarantee that they will oppose it. They may still cling to the mass ideals and the egalitarian statist goals of the democratist ideology. Though the loss of Congress and the end of our traditional political system with its traditional kind of political liberty may seem regrettable, there are many who feel these a price worth paying for the welfare state's seductive promise of social security, full employment and peace.

To keep their political liberty, Americans must keep and cherish their Congress. They will keep neither unless they want liberty more than any other political value. In easy times we can get lots of the things we want without sacrificing this for the sake of that, the cake for the bread; but these are hard times, and in hard times men must choose. The choice of liberty, made for us at the nation's beginning by the Founding Fathers, is now up for review on the national as on the world arena. Is it really true that men can learn the value of liberty only by losing it?

INDEX